THE
POETICS OF THE
NEW AMERICAN POETRY

THE
POETICS
OF THE NEW
AMERICAN POETRY

Edited by
Donald Allen & Warren Tallman

Grove Press

New York

Published by Grove Press
a division of Wheatland Corporation
841 Broadway
New York, N.Y. 10003

ISBN: 0-394-17801-7
ISBN: 0-8021-5113-2 (pbk.)
Library of Congress Catalog Card Number: 73-6222

Manufactured in the United States of America
This book is printed on acid-free paper.
First Evergreen Edition 1973

10 9 8 7 6 5

ACKNOWLEDGMENTS

Robin Blaser "The Fire" from *Pacific Nation* #2, copyright © 1968 by Robin Blaser and reprinted with his permission.

Hart Crane "General Aims and Theories," "A Letter to Harriet Monroe," and "A Letter to Otto H. Kahn" from *The Complete Poems and Selected Letters and Prose of Hart Crane*, copyright © 1933, 1958, 1966 by the Liveright Publishing Corporation and reprinted with their permission.

Robert Creeley "A Note on Ezra Pound," "Louis Zukofsky: *All: The Collected Short Poems, 1923-1958*," "Introduction to *The New Writing in the USA*," and "I'm Given to Write Poems" from *A Quick Graph: Collected Notes and Essays*, copyright © 1970 by Robert Creeley. Reprinted with the permission of Mr. Creeley and the Four Seasons Foundation. "Linda Wagner: An Interview with Robert Creeley" from *Minnesota Review*, copyright © 1965 and *Contexts of Poetry: Interviews 1961–1971*, copyright © 1973. Reprinted with the permission of Mr. Creeley and Four Seasons Foundation.

H.D. "Epitaph" from *Selected Poems of H.D.*, copyright © 1957 by Norman Holmes Pearson. Reprinted by permission of Professor Pearson.

Edward Dorn "What I See in *The Maximus Poems*" from *Kulchur* #4, 1961. Copyright © 1961 by Edward Dorn and reprinted with his permission.

Robert Duncan "From a Notebook" from *Black Mountain Review* #5, copyright © 1955, "Notes on Poetics Regarding Olson's *Maximus*" from *Black Mountain Review* #6, copyright © 1956, "Ideas of the Meaning of

Of the Measure in which
Jerusalem is written

We who dwell on Earth can do nothing to ourselves; every thing is conducted by Spirits, no less than Digestion or Sleep. *I fear the best . . . in Jesus whom we . . .* When this Verse was first dictated to me, I consider'd a Monotonous Cadence, like that used by Milton & Shakespeare & all writers of English Blank Verse, derived from the modern bondage of Rhyming, to be a necessary and indispensible part of Verse. But I soon found that in the mouth of a true Orator such monotony was not only awkward, but as much a bondage as rhyme itself. I therefore have produced a variety in every line, both of cadences & number of syllables. Every word and every letter is studied and put into its fit place; the terrific numbers are reserved for the terrific parts, the mild & gentle for the mild & gentle parts, and the prosaic for inferior parts; all are necessary to each other. Poetry Fetter'd Fetters the Human Race. Nations are Destroy'd or Flourish in proportion as Their Poetry, Painting and Music are Destroy'd or Flourish! The Primeval State of Man was Wisdom, Art and Science.

WILLIAM BLAKE, 1804

Preface

Walt Whitman's 1856 letter to Ralph Waldo Emerson comes first both for its eloquence and as prophecy, a new poetry to emerge in the New World he saw opening up around him. We feel that the poets whose statements we include achieve spectacular fulfillments in our century of what Whitman was calling for in his. This isn't to suppose that their poetics stem directly from his since in a number of instances they obviously don't. But he is our great national poet because great national traits shine through and keep on shining. Even one of his more reluctant admirers, Ezra Pound, is only forging Whitman's large vision into a hammering point when he says, "Make It New." And whatever else the poets in this volume may or may not have in common all demonstrably are seeking a new or re-newed writing in hopes of a new or re-newed world. Thus it isn't surprising to discover one of Walt's more direct inheritors, Allen Ginsberg—who also shines—speaking for all concerned when he "woke up alive and excited" and decided poetry should be that way too.

We scarcely need more than mention that the "new" we have in view has to do with poetry written in the English language, specifically by Americans, and we hope no one will mind too much our adopting García Lorca and D. H. Lawrence into this company. They, after all, didn't hesitate to adopt both America and Whitman into their own searches for the new. Which we see coming into American poetry in two separate but closely related waves, the first gathering effective force circa 1912 and the second shortly after 1945. Although it isn't strictly accurate we find it convenient to name the first, Pound's generation, and the second, Charles Olson's, if only because, having written most inventively, explicitly, and widely, they best exemplify the concerns of their respective periods. We trust it will be evident we have chosen to look through the eyes of Olson's generation in selecting statements made by Pound's. That W. B. Yeats, T. S. Eliot, Wallace Stevens, Marianne Moore and e e cummings are not included isn't intended to deny their importance as poets, or even to indicate that they had no influence on Olson's generation. It's rather that they figure less decisively than those we include. Yeats is a magnificent poet but is perhaps nearer to some endpoint of a great British line than to the emergence of a new American poetry. And however ambiguously large Eliot looms up in our century he has seemed to most of the writers in this book to be casting back rather than moving forward, more urbane perhaps than urgent.

New has a way of having to struggle for footing in the world, and that this has been so for the writers in this volume can best be remembered by glancing briefly at three symptomatic anthologies. On publication in 1938 the first edition of Cleanth Brooks' and Robert Penn Warren's *Understanding Poetry* became a kind of instant bible for initiating a generation of university students into the art of reading poetry. Yet in retrospect it's clear that their handbook is an attempt to sensitize readers to traditional orders and that its effectiveness weakens markedly for readers interested in Pound, William Carlos Williams, Gertrude Stein, H. D., Lawrence, Hart Crane, and Louis Zukofsky. Which means that nearly 30 years after these poets had begun contriving effective ways and means to "resuscitate the dead art of poetry" the official arbiters of American literary intelligence were looking and listening—rather breathlessly—elsewhere. It's not therefore surprising, looking through the eyes of Olson's generation, that we have been able to discern little or no influence by Brooks, Warren, or the other professors, poets, and critics with whom they are associated: John Crowe Ransom, Allen Tate, Robert Frost, R. P. Blackmur, or, on the English side of the waters, I. A. Richards and William Empson. Tate is perhaps the one poet and theorist of this school that Olson's generation would most respect for his intelligent, consistent, and catholic defense of a classicism they happen not to prefer. The extent to which his views, and those of the others, have not taken hold is best indicated in Robert Duncan's brilliantly argumentative impromptu, "Ideas of the Meaning of Form."

That the blank places in *Understanding Poetry* stayed blank

well beyond 1939 begins to come clear in 1957 with the appear-
ance of yet another "official" anthology, *New Poets of England
and America,* edited by Donald Hall, Robert Pack, and Louis
Simpson with a preface by Robert Frost. Given the enormous
vogue for *Understanding Poetry* in university circles it's scarcely
surprising that most of the American poets in the Hall-Pack-
Simpson anthology are discussible in light of the distinctions
Brooks and Warren had established 18 years earlier. The surprise
comes in 1960 in the form of *The New American Poetry, 1945–
1960,* edited by Donald Allen, who somehow managed to conjure
44 poets into presence from some blue beyond the range of
"official" attention. And if the first edition of *Understanding
Poetry* had provided little help in the matter of reading Pound,
Williams, Stein, H. D., Lawrence, Crane, and Zukofsky, the third
edition, which appeared in 1960, keeps the record consistent by
providing no help whatever in the matter of reading Olson, Dun-
can, Ginsberg, Robert Creeley, Denise Levertov, Lawrence Ferlin-
ghetti, Frank O'Hara, Edward Dorn, Jack Spicer, Michael
McClure, Robin Blaser, Philip Whalen and Gary Snyder, to name
some of the poets the Allen anthology introduces. It must have
required a considerable effort of attention for the editors of *New
Poets of England and America* to look so completely past Olson's
generation. It's difficult to believe that their work was so desper-
ately fugitive as to have escaped notice entirely, more reasonable
to assume that the news they had to offer was still too new.

But nowadays all that literary schizophrenia is happily if not
past at least passing. Just as the poets of Pound's generation began
to be widely heard in America and abroad, belatedly, in the late
1940s, the poets of Olson's generation are now heard here and
abroad with that quickening of attention which occurs among the
lighthearted upon discovering something new under the sun. In
Canada, England, and Europe there has been an opening-wide of
many intelligent and sympathetic eyes. Yet even though many
statements in this book are now widely known they have remained
scattered through more volumes than readers can conveniently lay
hands on. We hope this collection will solve at least some of that
problem while bringing less well-known but equally important
statements to the attention of those concerned. Whitman said, "I
am with you you men and women of future generations," and we

hope above all that this volume as a whole presents convincing evidence of men and women in our century who are significantly with him as of the day he gathered his forces close and decided to "strike up for a new world."

Vancouver,   —WARREN TALLMAN
November 1972

Contents

THE
POETICS OF THE
NEW AMERICAN POETRY

Walt Whitman
to Ralph Waldo Emerson[1]

Here are thirty-two Poems, which I send you, dear Friend and Master, not having found how I could satisfy myself with sending any usual acknowledgment of your letter. The first edition, on which you mailed me that till now unanswered letter, was twelve poems—I printed a thousand copies, and they readily sold; these thirty-two Poems I stereotype, to print several thousand copies of. I much enjoy making poems. Other work I have set for myself to do, to meet people and The States face to face, to confront them with an American rude tongue; but the work of my life is making poems. I keep on till I make a hundred, and then several hundred—perhaps a thousand. The way is clear to me. A few years, and the average annual call for my Poems is ten or twenty thousand copies—more, quite likely. Why should I hurry or compromise? In poems or in speeches I say the word or two that has got to be said, adhere to the body, step with the countless common footsteps, and remind every man and woman of something.

Master, I am a man who has perfect faith. Master, we have not come through centuries, caste, heroisms, fables, to halt in this land today. Or I think it is to collect a ten-fold impetus that any halt is made. As nature, inexorable, onward, resistless, impassive amid the threats and screams of disputants, so America. Let all defer. Let all attend respectfully the leisure of These States, their politics,

[1] Whitman included this open letter to Emerson in the second edition of *Leaves of Grass* (1856).

3

poems, literature, manners, and their free-handed modes of training their own offspring. Their own comes, just matured, certain, numerous and capable enough, with egotistical tongues, with sinewed wrists, seizing openly what belongs to them. They resume Personality, too long left out of mind. Their shadows are projected in employments, in books, in the cities, in trade; their feet are on the flights of the steps of the Capitol; they dilate, a larger, brawnier, more candid, more democratic, lawless, positive native to The States, sweet-bodied, completer, dauntless, flowing, masterful, beard-faced, new race of men.

Swiftly, on limitless foundations, the United States too are founding a literature. It is all as well done, in my opinion, as could be practicable. Each element here is in condition. Every day I go among the people of Manhattan Island, Brooklyn, and other cities, and among the young men, to discover the spirit of them, and to refresh myself. These are to be attended to; I am myself more drawn here than to those authors, publishers, importations, reprints, and so forth. I pass coolly through those, understanding them perfectly well, and that they do the indispensable service, outside of men like me, which nothing else could do. In poems, the young men of The States shall be represented, for they out-rival the best of the rest of the earth.

The lists of ready-made literature which America inherits by the mighty inheritance of the English language—all the rich repertoire of traditions, poems, histories, metaphysics, plays, classics, translations, have made, and still continue, magnificent preparations for that other plainly signified literature, to be our own, to be electric, fresh, lusty, to express the full-sized body, male and female—to give the modern meanings of things, to grow up beautiful, lasting, commensurate with America, with all the passions of home, with the inimitable sympathies of having been boys and girls together, and of parents who were with our parents.

What else can happen [to?] The States, even in their own despite? That huge English flow, so sweet, so undeniable, has done incalculable good here, and is to be spoken of for its own sake with generous praise and with gratitude. Yet the price The States have had to lie under for the same has not been a small price. Payment prevails; a nation can never take the issues of the needs of other nations for nothing. America, grandest of lands in the theory of its politics, in popular reading, in hospitality, breadth, animal beauty, cities, ships, machines, money, credit, collapses quick as lightning at the repeated, admonishing, stern words, Where are any mental expressions from you, beyond what you have copied or stolen? Where the born throngs of poets, literats, orators, you promised? Will you but tag after other nations? They struggled long for their literature, painfully working their way, some with deficient languages, some with priest-craft, some in the endeavor just to live— yet achieved for their times, works, poems, perhaps the only solid consolation left to them through ages afterward of shame and decay. You are young, have the perfectest of dialects, a free press, a free government, the world forwarding its best to be with you. As justice has been strictly done to you, from this hour do strict justice to yourself. Strangle the singers who will not sing you loud and strong. Open the doors of The West. Call for new great masters to comprehend new arts, new perfections, new wants. Submit to the most robust bard till he remedy your barrenness. Then you will not need to adopt the heirs of others; you will have true heirs, begotten of yourself, blooded with your own blood.

With composure I see such propositions, seeing more and more every day of the answers that serve. Expressions do not yet serve, for sufficient reasons; but that is getting ready, beyond what the earth has hitherto known, to take home the expressions when they come, and to identify them with the populace of The States, which is the schooling cheaply procured by any outlay any number of years. Such schooling The States extract from the swarms of reprints, and from the current authors and editors. Such service and extract are done after enormous, reckless, free modes, characteristic of The States. Here are to be attained results never elsewhere thought possible; the modes are very grand too. The instincts of the American people are all perfect, and tend to make heroes. It is a rare thing in a man here to understand The States.

All current nourishments to literature serve. Of authors and editors I do not know how many there are in The States, but there are thousands, each one building his or her step to the stairs by which giants shall mount. Of the twenty-four modern mammoth two-double, three-double, and four-double cylinder presses now in the world, printing by steam, twenty-one of them are in These States. The twelve thousand large and small shops for dispensing books and newspapers—the same number of public libraries, any one of which has all the reading wanted to equip a man or woman for American reading—the three thousand different newspapers, the nutriment of the imperfect ones coming in just as usefully as any—the story papers, various, full of strong-flavored romances, widely circulated—the one-cent and two-cent journals—the political ones, no matter what side—the weeklies in the country—the sporting and pictorial papers—the monthly magazines, with plentiful imported feed—the sentimental novels, numberless copies of them—the low-priced flaring tales, adventures, biographies—all are prophetic; all waft rapidly on. I see that they swell wide, for reasons. I am not troubled at the movement of them, but greatly pleased. I see plying shuttles, the active ephemeral myriads of books also, faithfully weaving the garments of a generation of men, and a generation of women, they do not perceive or know. What a progress popular reading and writing has made in fifty years! What a progress fifty years hence! The time is at hand when inherent literature will be a main part of These States, as general and real as steam-power, iron, corn, beef, fish. First-rate American persons are to be supplied. Our perennial materials for fresh thoughts, histories, poems, music, orations, religions, recitations, amusements, will then not be disregarded, any more than our perennial fields, mines, rivers, seas. Certain things are established, and are immovable; in those things millions of years stand justified. The mothers and fathers of whom modern centuries have come, have not existed for nothing; they too had brains and hearts. Of course all literature, in all nations and years, will share marked attributes in common, as we all, of all ages, share the common human attributes. America is to be kept coarse and broad. What is to be done is to withdraw from precedents, and be directed to men and women—also to The States in their federalness; for the union of the parts of the body is not more necessary to their life than the union of These States is to their life.

A profound person can easily know more of the people than they know of themselves. Always waiting untold in the souls of the armies of common people, is stuff better than anything that can possibly appear in the leadership of the same. That gives final verdicts. In every department of These States, he who travels with a coterie, or with selected persons, or with imitators, or with infidels, or with the owners of slaves, or with that which is ashamed of the body of a man, or with that which is ashamed of the body of a woman, or with any thing less than the bravest and the openest, travels straight for the slopes of dissolution. The genius of all foreign literature is clipped and cut small, compared to our genius, and is essentially insulting to our usages, and to the organic compacts of These States. Old forms, old poems, majestic and proper in their own lands here in this land are exiles; the air here is very strong. Much that stands well and has a little enough place provided for it in the small scales of European kingdoms, empires, and the like, here stands haggard, dwarfed, ludicrous, or has no place little enough provided for it. Authorities, poems, models, laws, names, imported into America, are useful to America today to destroy them, and so move disencumbered to great works, great days.

Just so long, in our country or any country, as no revolutionists advance, and are backed by the people, sweeping off the swarms of routine representatives, officers in power, book-makers, teachers, ecclesiastics, politicians, just so long, I perceive, do they who are in power fairly represent that country, and remain of use, probably of very great use. To supersede them, when it is the pleasure of These States, full provision is made; and I say the time has arrived to use it with a strong hand. Here also the souls of the armies have not only overtaken the souls of the officers, but passed on, and left the souls of the officers behind out of sight many weeks' journey; and the souls of the armies now go en-masse without officers. Here also formulas, glosses, blanks, minutiæ, are choking the throats of the spokesmen to death. Those things most listened for, certainly those are the things least said. There is not a single History of the World. There is not one of America, or of the organic compacts of These States, or of Washington, or of Jefferson, nor of Language, nor any Dictionary of the English Language. There is no great author; every one has demeaned himself to some etiquette or some impotence. There is no manhood or lifepower in poems; there are shoats and geldings more like. Or literature will be dressed up, a fine gentleman, distasteful to our instincts, foreign to our soil. Its neck bends right and left wherever it goes. Its costumes and jewelry prove how little it knows Nature. Its flesh is soft; it shows less and less of the indefinable hard something that is Nature.

Where is any thing but the shaved Nature of synods and schools?
Where is a savage and luxuriant man? Where is an overseer? In
lives, in poems, in codes of law, in Congress, in tuitions, theatres,
conversations, argumentations, not a single head lifts itself clean
out, with proof that it is their master, and has subordinated them
to itself, and is ready to try their superiors. None believes in These
States, boldly illustrating them in himself. Not a man faces round
at the rest with terrible negative voice, refusing all terms to be
bought off from his own eye-sight, or from the soul that he is, or
from friendship, or from the body that he is, or from the soil and
sea. To creeds, literature, art, the army, the navy, the executive,
life is hardly proposed, but the sick and dying are proposed to cure
the sick and dying. The churches are one vast lie; the people do
not believe them, and they do not believe themselves; the priests
are continually telling what they know well enough is not so, and
keeping back what they know is so. The spectacle is a pitiful one. I
think there can never be again upon the festive earth more bad-
disordered persons deliberately taking seats, as of late in These
States, at the heads of the public tables—such corpses' eyes for
judges—such a rascal and thief in the Presidency.

Up to the present, as helps best, the people, like a lot of large
boys, have no determined tastes, are quite unaware of the grandeur
of themselves, and of their destiny, and of their immense strides—
accept with voracity whatever is presented them in novels, his-
tories, newspapers, poems, schools, lectures, every thing. Pretty
soon, through these and other means, their development makes the
fibre that is capable of itself, and will assume determined tastes.
The young men will be clear what they want, and will have it.
They will follow none except him whose spirit leads them in the
like spirit with themselves. Any such man will be welcome as the
flowers of May. Others will be put out without ceremony. How
much is there anyhow, to the young men of These States, in a
parcel of helpless dandies, who can neither fight, work, shoot, ride,
run, command—some of them devout, some quite insane, some
castrated—all second-hand, or third, fourth, or fifth hand—waited
upon by waiters, putting not this land first, but always other lands
first, talking of art, doing the most ridiculous things for fear of
being called ridiculous, smirking and skipping along, continually
taking off their hats—no one behaving, dressing, writing, talking,

loving, out of any natural and manly tastes of his own, but each one looking cautiously to see how the rest behave, dress, write, talk, love—pressing the noses of dead books upon themselves and upon their country—favoring no poets, philosophs, literats here, but dog-like danglers at the heels of the poets, philosophs, literats, of enemies' lands—favoring mental expressions, models of gentlemen and ladies, social habitudes in These States, to grow up in sneaking defiance of the popular substratums of The States? Of course they and the likes of them can never justify the strong poems of America. Of course no feed of theirs is to stop and be made welcome to muscle the bodies, male and female, for Manhattan Island, Brooklyn, Boston, Worcester, Hartford, Portland, Montreal, Detroit, Buffalo, Cleaveland, Milwaukee, St. Louis, Indianapolis, Chicago, Cincinnati, Iowa City, Philadelphia, Baltimore, Raleigh, Savannah, Charleston, Mobile, New Orleans, Galveston, Brownsville, San Francisco, Havana, and a thousand equal cities, present and to come. Of course what they and the likes of them have been used for, draws toward its close, after which they will all be discharged, and not one of them will ever be heard of any more.

America, having duly conceived, bears out of herself offspring of her own to do the workmanship wanted. To freedom, to strength, to poems, to personal greatness, it is never permitted to rest, not a generation or part of a generation. To be ripe beyond further increase is to prepare to die. The architects of These States laid their foundations, and passed to further spheres. What they laid is a work done; as much more remains. Now are needed other architects, whose duty is not less difficult, but perhaps more difficult. Each age forever needs architects. America is not finished, perhaps never will be; now America is a divine true sketch. There are Thirty-Two States sketched—the population thirty millions. In a few years there will be Fifty States. Again in a few years there will be A Hundred States, the population hundreds of millions, the freshest and freest of men. Of course such men stand to nothing less than the freshest and freest expression.

Poets here, literats here, are to rest on organic different bases from other countries; not a class set apart, circling only in the circle of themselves, modest and pretty, desperately scratching for rhymes, pallid with white paper, shut off, aware of the old pictures and traditions of the race, but unaware of the actual race around them—not breeding in and in among each other till they all have the scrofula. Lands of ensemble, bards of ensemble! Walking freely out from the old traditions, as our politics has walked out, American poets and literats recognize nothing behind them superior to what is present with them—recognize with joy the sturdy living forms of the men and women of These States, the divinity of sex, the perfect eligibility of the female with the male, all The States, liberty and equality, real articles, the different trades, mechanics, the young fellows of Manhattan Island, customs, instincts, slang, Wisconsin, Georgia, the noble Southern heart, the hot blood, the spirit that will be nothing less than master, the filibuster spirit, the Western man, native-born perceptions, the eye for forms, the perfect models of made things, the wild smack of freedom, California, money, electric-telegraphs, free-trade, iron and the iron mines—recognize without demur those splendid resistless black poems, the steam-ships of the sea-board states, and those other resistless splendid poems, the locomotives, followed through the interior states by trains of rail-road cars.

A word remains to be said, as of one ever present, not yet permitted to be acknowledged, discarded or made dumb by literature, and the results apparent. To the lack of an avowed, empowered, unabashed development of sex, (the only salvation for the same,) and to the fact of speakers and writers fraudulently assuming as always dead what every one knows to be always alive, is attributable the remarkable non-personality and indistinctness of modern productions in books, art, talk; also that in the scanned lives of men and women most of them appear to have been for some time past of the neuter gender; and also the stinging fact that in orthodox society today, if the dresses were changed, the men might easily pass for women and the women for men.

Infidelism usurps most with fœtid polite face; among the rest infidelism about sex. By silence or obedience the pens of savans, poets, historians, biographers, and the rest, have long connived at the filthy law, and books enslaved to it, that what makes the manhood of a man, that sex, womanhood, maternity, desires, lusty animations, organs, acts, are unmentionable and to be ashamed of, to be driven to skulk out of literature with whatever belongs to them. This filthy law has to be repealed—it stands in the way of

great reforms. Of women just as much as men, it is the interest
that there should not be infidelism about sex, but perfect faith.
Women in These States approach the day of that organic equality
with men, without which, I see, men cannot have organic equality
among themselves. This empty dish, gallantry, will then be filled
with something. This tepid wash, this diluted deferential love, as in
songs, fictions, and so forth, is enough to make a man vomit; as to
manly friendship, everywhere observed in The States, there is not
the first breath of it to be observed in print. I say that the body of a
man or woman, the main matter, is so far quite unexpressed in
poems; but that the body is to be expressed, and sex is. Of bards
for These States, if it come to a question, it is whether they shall
celebrate in poems the eternal decency of the amativeness of
Nature, the motherhood of all, or whether they shall be the bards
of the fashionable delusion of the inherent nastiness of sex, and of
the feeble and querulous modesty of deprivation. This is important
in poems, because the whole of the other expressions of a nation
are but flanges out of its great poems. To me, henceforth, that
theory of any thing, no matter what, stagnates in its vitals,
cowardly and rotten, while it cannot publicly accept, and publicly
name, with specific words, the things on which all existence, all
souls, all realization, all decency, all health, all that is worth being
here for, all of woman and of man, all beauty, all purity, all
sweetness, all friendship, all strength, all life, all immortality
depend. The courageous soul, for a year or two to come, may be
proved by faith in sex, and by disdaining concessions.

   To poets and literats—to every woman and man, today or any
day, the conditions of the present, needs, dangers, prejudices, and
the like, are the perfect conditions on which we are here, and the
conditions for wording the future with undissuadable words. These
States, receivers of the stamina of past ages and lands, initiate the
outlines of repayment a thousand fold. They fetch the American
great masters, waited for by old worlds and new, who accept evil
as well as good, ignorance as well as erudition, black as soon as
white, foreign-born materials as well as home-born, reject none,
force discrepancies into range, surround the whole, concentrate
them on present periods and places, show the application to each
and any one's body and soul, and show the true use of precedents.
Always America will be agitated and turbulent. This day it is

taking shape, not to be less so, but to be more so, stormily, capriciously, on native principles, with such vast proportions of parts! As for me, I love screaming, wrestling, boiling-hot days.

Of course, we shall have a national character, an identity. As it ought to be, and as soon as it ought to be, it will be. That, with much else, takes care of itself, is a result, and the cause of greater results. With Ohio, Illinois, Missouri, Oregon—with the states around the Mexican sea—with cheerfully welcomed immigrants from Europe, Asia, Africa—with Connecticut, Vermont, New Hampshire, Rhode Island—with all varied interests, facts, beliefs, parties, genesis—there is being fused a determined character, fit for the broadest use for the freewomen and freemen of The States, accomplished and to be accomplished, without any exception whatever—each indeed free, each idiomatic, as becomes live states and men, but each adhering to one enclosing general form of politics, manners, talk, personal style, as the plenteous varieties of the race adhere to one physical form. Such character is the brain and spine to all, including literature, including poems. Such character, strong, limber, just open-mouthed, American-blooded, full of pride, full of ease, of passionate friendliness, is to stand compact upon that vast basis of the supremacy of Individuality—that new moral American continent without which, I see, the physical continent remained incomplete, may-be a carcass, a bloat—that newer America, answering face to face with The States, with ever-satisfying and ever-unsurveyable seas and shores.

Those shores you found. I say you have led The States there— have led Me there. I say that none has ever done, or ever can do, a greater deed for The States, than your deed. Others may line out the lines, build cities, work mines, break up farms; it is yours to have been the original true Captain who put to sea, intuitive, positive, rendering the first report, to be told less by any report, and more by the mariners of a thousand bays, in each tack of their arriving and departing, many years after you.

Receive, dear Master, these statements and assurances through me, for all the young men, and for an earnest that we know none before you, but the best following you; and that we demand to take your name into our keeping, and that we understand what you have indicated, and find the same indicated in ourselves, and that we will stick to it and enlarge upon it through These States.

WALT WHITMAN

ERNEST FENOLLOSA

From *The Chinese Written Character As a Medium for Poetry*

[*This essay was practically finished by the late Ernest Fenollosa; I have done little more than remove a few repetitions and shape a few sentences.*

We have here not a bare philological discussion, but a study of the fundamentals of all aesthetics. In his search through unknown art Fenollosa, coming upon unknown motives and principles unrecognised in the West, was already led into many modes of thought since fruitful in "new" Western painting and poetry. He was a forerunner without knowing it and without being known as such.

He discerned principles of writing which he had scarcely time to put into practice. In Japan he restored, or greatly helped to restore, a respect for the native art. In America and Europe he cannot be looked upon as a mere searcher after exotics. His mind was constantly filled with parallels and comparisons between Eastern and Western art. To him the exotic was always a means of fructification. He looked to an American renaissance. The vitality of his outlook can be judged from the fact that although this essay was written some time before his death in 1908 I have not had to change the allusions to Western conditions. The later movements in art have corroborated his theories. Ezra Pound, 1918.]

. . . My subject is poetry, not language, yet the roots of poetry are in language. In the study of a language so alien in form to ours as is Chinese in its written character, it is necessary to inquire how

13

these universal elements of form which constitute poetics can derive appropriate nutriment.

In what sense can verse, written in terms of visible hieroglyphics, be reckoned true poetry? It might seem that poetry, which like music is a *time art,* weaving its unities out of successive impressions of sound, could with difficulty assimilate a verbal medium consisting largely of semi-pictorial appeals to the eye.

Contrast, for example, Gray's line:

The curfew tolls the knell of parting day

with the Chinese line:

| Moon | Rays | Like | Pure | Snow |

Unless the sound of the latter be given, what have they in common? It is not enough to adduce that each contains a certain body of prosaic meaning; for the question is, how can the Chinese line imply, *as form,* the very element that distinguishes poetry from prose?

On second glance, it is seen that the Chinese words, though visible, occur in just as necessary an order as the phonetic symbols of Gray. All that poetic form requires is a regular and flexible sequence, as plastic as thought itself. The characters may be seen and read, silently by the eye, one after the other:

Moon rays like pure snow.

Perhaps we do not always sufficiently consider that thought is successive, not through some accident or weakness of our subjective operations but because the operations of nature are successive. The tranferences of force from agent to object, which constitute natural phenomena, occupy time. Therefore, a reproduction of them in imagination requires the same temporal order.*

---

* Style, that is to say, limpidity, as opposed to rhetoric. E. P.

Suppose that we look out of a window and watch a man. Suddenly he turns his head and actively fixes his attention upon something. We look ourselves and see that his vision has been focused upon a horse. We saw, first, the man before he acted; second, while he acted; third, the object toward which his action was directed. In speech we split up the rapid continuity of this action and of its picture into its three essential parts or joints in the right order, and say:

Man sees horse.

It is clear that these three joints, or words, are only three phonetic symbols, which stand for the three terms of a natural process. But we could quite as easily denote these three stages of our thought by symbols equally arbitrary, *which had no basis in sound;* for example, by three Chinese characters:

Man   Sees   Horse

If we all knew *what division* of this mental horse-picture each of these signs stood for, we could communicate continuous thought to one another as easily by drawing them as by speaking words. We habitually employ the visible language of gesture in much this same manner.

But Chinese notation is something much more than arbitrary symbols. It is based upon a vivid shorthand picture of the operations of nature. In the algebraic figure and in the spoken word there is no natural connection between thing and sign: all depends upon sheer convention. But the Chinese method follows natural suggestion. First stands the man on his two legs. Second, his eye moves through space: a bold figure represented by running legs under an eye, a modified picture of an eye, a modified picture of running legs, but unforgettable once you have seen it. Third stands the horse on his four legs.

The thought-picture is not only called up by these signs as well as by words, but far more vividly and concretely. Legs belong to all three characters: they are *alive*. The group holds something of the quality of a continuous moving picture.

The untruth of a painting or a photograph is that, in spite of its concreteness, it drops the element of natural succession.

Contrast the Laocoön statue with Browning's lines:

> I sprang to the stirrup, and Joris, and he
>
> . . . . . .
>
> And into the midnight we galloped abreast.

One superiority of verbal poetry as an art rests in its getting back to the fundamental reality of *time*. Chinese poetry has the unique advantage of combining both elements. It speaks at once with the vividness of painting, and with the mobility of sounds. It is, in some sense, more objective than either, more dramatic. In reading Chinese we do not seem to be juggling mental counters, but to be watching *things* work out their own fate.

Leaving for a moment the form of the sentence, let us look more closely at this quality of vividness in the structure of detached Chinese words. The earlier forms of these characters were pictorial, and their hold upon the imagination is little shaken, even in later conventional modifications. It is not so well known, perhaps, that the great number of these ideographic roots carry in them a *verbal idea of action*. It might be thought that a picture is naturally the picture of a *thing*, and that therefore the root ideas of Chinese are what grammar calls nouns.

But examination shows that a large number of the primitive Chinese characters, even the so-called radicals, are shorthand pictures of actions or processes.

For example, the ideograph meaning "to speak" is a mouth with two words and a flame coming out of it. The sign meaning "to grow up with difficulty" is grass with a twisted root. But this concrete *verb* quality, both in nature and in the Chinese signs, becomes far more striking and poetic when we pass from such simple, original pictures to compounds. In this process of compounding, two things added together do not produce a third thing but suggest some fundamental relation between them. For example, the ideograph for a "messmate" is a man and a fire.

A true noun, an isolated thing, does not exist in nature. Things are only the terminal points, or rather the meeting points, of actions, cross-sections cut through actions, snapshots. Neither can a pure verb, an abstract motion, be possible in nature. The eye sees noun and verb as one: things in motion, motion in things, and so the Chinese conception tends to represent them.*

The sun underlying the bursting forth of plants=spring.

The sun sign tangled in the branches of the tree sign=east.

"Rice-field" plus "struggle"=male.

"Boat" plus "water"—boat-water, a ripple.

Let us return to the form of the sentence and see what power it adds to the verbal units from which it builds. I wonder how many people have asked themselves why the sentence form exists at all, why it seems so universally necessary *in all languages?* Why *must* all possess it, and what is the normal type of it? If it be so universal, it ought to correspond to some primary law of nature.

I fancy the professional grammarians have given but a lame response to this inquiry. Their definitions fall into two types: one, that a sentence expresses a "complete thought"; the other, that in it we bring about a union of subject and predicate.

The former has the advantage of trying for some natural objective standard, since it is evident that a thought can not be the test of its own completeness. But in nature there is *no* completeness. On the one hand, practical completeness may be expressed by a mere interjection, as "Hi! there!," or "Scat!," or even by shaking one's fist. No sentence is needed to make one's meaning more clear. On the other hand, no full sentence really completes a thought. The man who sees and the horse which is seen will not stand still. The man was planning a ride before he looked. The horse kicked when the man tried to catch him. The truth is that acts are successive, even continuous; one causes or passes into another. And though we may string never so many clauses into a single compound sentence, motion leaks everywhere, like electricity from an exposed wire. All processes in nature are interrelated; and thus there could be no complete sentence (according to this definition) save one which it would take all time to pronounce.

* Axe *striking* something; dog *attending* man=dogs him.

In the second definition of the sentence, as "uniting a subject and a predicate," the grammarian falls back on pure subjectivity. *We* do it all; it is a little private juggling between our right and left hands. The subject is that about which *I* am going to talk; the predicate is that which *I* am going to say about it. The sentence according to this definition is not an attribute of nature but an accident of man as a conversational animal.

If it were really so, then there could be no possible test of the truth of a sentence. Falsehood would be as specious as verity. Speech would carry no conviction.

Of course this view of the grammarians springs from the discredited, or rather the useless, logic of the Middle Ages. According to this logic, thought deals with abstractions, concepts drawn out of things by a sifting process. These logicians never inquired how the "qualities" which they pulled out of things came to be there. The truth of all their little checker-board juggling depended upon the natural order by which these powers or properties or qualities were folded in concrete things, yet they despised the "thing" as a mere "particular," or pawn. It was as if Botany should reason from the leaf-patterns woven into our table-cloths. Valid scientific thought consists in following as closely as may be the actual and entangled lines of forces as they pulse through things. Thought deals with no bloodless concepts but watches *things move* under its microscope.

The sentence form was forced upon primitive men by nature itself. It was not we who made it; it was a reflection of the temporal order in causation. All truth has to be expressed in sentences because all truth is the *transference of power*. The type of sentence in nature is a flash of lightning. It passes between two terms, a cloud and the earth. No unit of natural process can be less than this. All natural processes are, in their units, as much as this. Light, heat, gravity, chemical affinity, human will, have this in common, that they redistribute force. Their unit of process can be represented as:

term	transference	term
from	of	to
which	force	which

If we regard this transference as the conscious or unconscious act
of an agent we can translate the diagram into:

agent   act   object

In this the act is the very substance of the fact denoted. The agent
and the object are only limiting terms.

It seems to me that the normal and typical sentence in English
as well as in Chinese expresses just this unit of natural process. It
consists of three necessary words: the first denoting the agent or
subject from which the act starts, the second embodying the very
stroke of the act, the third pointing to the object, the receiver of
the impact. Thus:

Farmer   pounds   rice

The form of the Chinese transitive sentence, and of the English
(omitting particles), exactly corresponds to this universal form of
action in nature. This brings language close to *things,* and in its
strong reliance upon verbs it erects all speech into a kind of
dramatic poetry.

A different sentence order is frequent in inflected languages like
Latin, German or Japanese. This is because they are inflected, i.e.
they have little tags and word-endings, or labels, to show which is
the agent, the object, etc. In uninflected languages, like English and
Chinese, there is nothing but the order of the words to distinguish
their functions. And this order would be no sufficient indication,
were it not the *natural order*—that is, the order of cause and
effect.

It is true that there are, in language, intransitive and passive
forms, sentences built out of the verb "to be," and, finally, nega-
tive forms. To grammarians and logicians these have seemed more
primitive than the transitive, or at least exceptions to the transitive.
I had long suspected that these apparently exceptional forms had
grown from the transitive or worn away from it by alteration, or
modification. This view is confirmed by Chinese examples, wherein
it is still possible to watch the transformation going on.

The intransitive form derives from the transitive by dropping a
generalised, customary, reflexive or cognate object: "He runs (a
race)." "The sky reddens (itself)." "We breathe (air)." Thus we

get weak and incomplete sentences which suspend the picture and lead us to think of some verbs as denoting states rather than acts. Outside grammar the word "state" would hardly be recognised as scientific. Who can doubt that when we say "The wall shines," we mean that it actively reflects light to our eye?

The beauty of Chinese verbs is that they are all transitive or intransitive at pleasure. There is no such thing as a naturally intransitive verb. The passive form is evidently a correlative sentence, which turns about and makes the object into a subject. That the object is not in itself passive, but contributes some positive force of its own to the action, is in harmony both with scientific law and with ordinary experience. The English passive voice with "is" seemed at first an obstacle to this hypothesis, but one suspected that the true form was a generalised transitive verb meaning something like "receive," which had degenerated into an auxiliary. It was a delight to find this the case in Chinese.

In nature there are no negations, no possible transfers of negative force. The presence of negative sentences in language would seem to corroborate the logicians' view that assertion is an arbitrary subjective act. *We* can assert a negation, though nature can not. But here again science comes to our aid against the logician: all apparently negative or disruptive movements bring into play other positive forces. It requires great effort to annihilate. Therefore we should suspect that, if we could follow back the history of all negative particles, we should find that they also are sprung from transitive verbs. It is too late to demonstrate such derivations in the Aryan languages, the clue has been lost; but in Chinese we can still watch positive verbal conceptions passing over into so-called negatives. Thus in Chinese the sign meaning "to be lost in the forest" relates to a state of non-existence. English "not"=the Sanskrit *na,* which may come from the root *na,* to be lost, to perish.

Lastly comes the infinitive which substitutes for a specific colored verb the universal copula "is," followed by a noun or an adjective. We do not say a tree "greens itself," but "the tree is green"; not that monkeys "bring forth live young," but that "the monkey is a mammal." This is an ultimate weakness of language. It has come from generalising all intransitive words into one. As "live," "see," "walk," "breathe," are generalised into states by dropping their objects, so these weak verbs are in turn reduced to the abstractest state of all, namely bare existence.

There is in reality no such verb as a pure copula, no such original conception: our very word *exist* means "to stand forth," to show oneself by a definite act. "Is" comes from the Aryan root *as,* to breathe. "Be" is from *bhu,* to grow.

In Chinese the chief verb for "is" not only means actively "to have," but shows by its derivation that it expresses something even more concrete, namely "to snatch from the moon with the hand."

 Here the baldest symbol of prosaic analysis is trans-

formed by magic into a splendid flash of concrete poetry.

I shall not have entered vainly into this long analysis of the sentence if I have succeeded in showing how poetical is the Chinese form and how close to nature. In translating Chinese, verse especially, we must hold as closely as possible to the concrete force of the original, eschewing adjectives, nouns and intransitive forms wherever we can, and seeking instead strong and individual verbs.

Lastly we notice that the likeness of form between Chinese and English sentences renders translation from one to the other exceptionally easy. The genius of the two is much the same. Frequently it is possible by omitting English particles to make a literal word-for-word translation which will be not only intelligible in English, but even the strongest and most poetical English. Here, however, one must follow closely what is said, not merely what is abstractly meant.

Let us go back from the Chinese sentence to the individual written word. How are such words to be classified? Are some of them nouns by nature, some verbs and some adjectives? Are there pronouns and prepositions and conjunctions in Chinese as in good Christian languages?

One is led to suspect from an analysis of the Aryan languages that such differences are not natural, and that they have been unfortunately invented by grammarians to confuse the simple poetic outlook on life. All nations have written their strongest and most vivid literature before they invented a grammar. Moreover, all Aryan etymology points back to roots which are the equivalents of simple Sanskrit verbs, such as we find tabulated at the back of our Skeat. Nature herself has no grammar.* Fancy picking up a man and telling him that he is a noun, a dead thing rather than a bundle of functions! A "part of speech" is only *what it does*. Frequently our lines of cleavage fail, one part of speech acts for another. They *act for* one another because they were originally one and the same.

Few of us realise that in our own language these very differences once grew up in living articulation; that they still retain life. It is only when the difficulty of placing some odd term arises, or when we are forced to translate into some very different language, that we attain for a moment the inner heat of thought, a heat which melts down the parts of speech to recast them at will.

One of the most interesting facts about the Chinese language is that in it we can see, not only the forms of sentences, but literally the parts of speech growing up, budding forth one from another. Like nature, the Chinese words are alive and plastic, because *thing* and *action* are not formally separated. The Chinese language naturally knows no grammar. It is only lately that foreigners, European and Japanese, have begun to torture this vital speech by forcing it to fit the bed of their definitions. We import into our reading of Chinese all the weakness of our own formalisms. This is especially sad in poetry, because the one necessity, even in our own poetry, is to keep words as flexible as possible, as full of the sap of nature.

Let us go further with our example. In English we call "to shine" a *verb in the infinitive,* because it gives the abstract meaning of the verb without conditions. If we want a corresponding adjective we take a different word, "bright." If we need a noun we say "luminosity," which is abstract, being derived from an adjective. To get a tolerably concrete noun, we have to leave behind the verb

---

* Even Latin, living Latin, had not the network of rules they foist upon unfortunate school-children. These are borrowed sometimes from Greek grammarians, even as I have seen English grammars borrowing oblique cases from Latin grammars. Sometimes they sprang from the grammatising or categorising passion of pedants. Living Latin had only the feel of the cases: the ablative and dative emotion. E.P.

and adjective roots, and light upon a thing arbitrarily cut off from its power of action, say "the sun" or "the moon." Of course there is nothing in nature so cut off, and therefore this nounising is itself an abstraction. Even if we did have a common word underlying at once the verb "shine," the adjective "bright" and the noun "sun," we should probably call it an "infinitive of the infinitive." According to our ideas, it should be something extremely abstract, too intangible for use.*

The Chinese have one word, *ming* or *mei*. Its ideograph is the sign of the sun together with the sign of the moon. It serves as verb, noun, adjective. Thus you write literally, "the sun and moon of the cup" for "the cup's brightness." Placed as a verb, you write "the cup sun-and-moons," actually "cup sun-and-moon," or in a weakened thought, "is like sun," i.e. shines. "Sun-and-moon cup" is naturally a bright cup. There is no possible confusion of the real meaning, though a stupid scholar may spend a week trying to decide what "part of speech" he should use in translating a very simple and direct thought from Chinese to English.

The fact is that almost every written Chinese word is properly just such an underlying word, and yet it is *not* abstract. It is not exclusive of parts of speech, but comprehensive; not something which is neither a noun, verb, nor adjective, but something which is all of them at once and at all times. Usage may incline the full meaning now a little more to one side, now to another, according to the point of view, but through all cases the poet is free to deal with it richly and concretely, as does nature.

In the derivation of nouns from verbs, the Chinese language is forestalled by the Aryan. Almost all the Sanskrit roots, which seem to underlie European languages, are primitive verbs, which express characteristic actions of visible nature. The verb must be the primary fact of nature, since motion and change are all that we can recognise in her. In the primitive transitive sentence, such as "Farmer pounds rice," the agent and the object are nouns only in so far as they limit a unit of action. "Farmer" and "rice" are mere hard terms which define the extremes of the pounding. But in

---

* A good writer would use "shine" (i.e., to shine), "shining," and "the shine" or "sheen," possibly thinking of the German *"schöne"* and *"Schönheit"*; but this does not invalidate Professor Fenollosa's contention. E.P.

themselves, apart from this sentence-function, they are naturally verbs. The farmer is one who tills the ground, and the rice is a plant which grows in a special way. This is indicated in the Chinese characters. And this probably exemplifies the ordinary derivation of nouns from verbs. In all languages, Chinese included, a noun is originally "that which does something," that which performs the verbal action. Thus the moon comes from the root *ma,* and means, "the measurer." The sun means that which begets.

The derivation of adjectives from the verb need hardly be exemplified. Even with us, today, we can still watch participles passing over into adjectives. In Japanese the adjective is frankly part of the inflection of the verb, a special mood, so that every verb is also an adjective. This brings us close to nature, because everywhere the quality is only a power of action regarded as having an abstract inherence. Green is only a certain rapidity of vibration, hardness a degree of tenseness in cohering. In Chinese the adjective always retains a substratum of verbal meaning. We should try to render this in translation, not be content with some bloodless adjectival abstraction plus "is."

Still more interesting are the Chinese "prepositions"—they are often post-positions. Prepositions are so important, so pivotal in European speech only because we have weakly yielded up the force of our intransitive verbs. We have to add small supernumerary words to bring back the original power. We still say "I see a horse," but with the weak verb "look" we have to add the directive particle "at" before we can restore the natural transitiveness.*

Prepositions represent a few simple ways in which incomplete verbs complete themselves. Pointing toward nouns as a limit, they bring force to bear upon them. That is to say, they are naturally verbs, of generalised or condensed use. In Aryan languages it is often difficult to trace the verbal origins of simple prepositions. Only in *"off"* do we see a fragment of the thought "to throw off." In Chinese the preposition is frankly a verb, specially used in a generalised sense. These verbs are often used in their special verbal

* This is a bad example: we can say 'I look a fool." "Look," transitive, now means resemble. The main contention is, however, correct. We tend to abandon specific words like *resemble* and substitute, for them, vague verbs with prepositional directors, or riders. E.P.

sense, and it greatly weakens an English translation if they are systematically rendered by colorless prepositions.

Thus in Chinese, by=to cause; to=to fall toward; in=to remain, to dwell; from=to follow; and so on.

Conjunctions are similarly derivative; they usually serve to mediate actions between verbs, and therefore they are necessarily themselves actions. Thus in Chinese, because=to use; and=to be included under one; another form of "and"=to be parallel; or=to partake; if=to let one do, to permit. The same is true of a host of other particles, no longer traceable in the Aryan tongues.

Pronouns appear a thorn in our evolution theory, since they have been taken as unanalysable expressions of personality. In Chinese, even they yield up their striking secrets of verbal metaphor. They are a constant source of weakness if colorlessly translated. Take, for example, the five forms of "I." There is the sign of a "spear in the hand"=a very emphatic I; five and a mouth=a weak and defensive I, holding off a crowd by speaking; to conceal=a selfish and private I; self (the cocoon sign) and a mouth=an egoistic I, one who takes pleasure in his own speaking; the self presented is used only when one is speaking to one's self.

I trust that this digression concerning parts of speech may have justified itself. It proves, first, the enormous interest of the Chinese language in throwing light upon our forgotten mental processes, and thus furnishes a new chapter in the philosophy of language. Secondly, it is indispensable for understanding the poetical raw material which the Chinese language affords. Poetry differs from prose in the concrete colors of its diction. It is not enough for it to furnish a meaning to philosophers. It must appeal to emotions with the charm of direct impression, flashing through regions where the intellect can only grope.* Poetry must render what is said, not what is merely meant. Abstract meaning gives little vividness, and fullness of imagination gives all. Chinese poetry demands that we abandon our narrow grammatical categories, that we follow the original text with a wealth of concrete verbs.

But this is only the beginning of the matter. So far we have exhibited the Chinese characters and the Chinese sentence chiefly

* Cf. principle of Primary apparition, "Spirit of Romance." E.P.

as vivid shorthand pictures of actions and processes in nature. These embody true poetry as far as they go. Such actions are *seen,* but Chinese would be a poor language, and Chinese poetry but a narrow art, could they not go on to represent also what is unseen. The best poetry deals not only with natural images but with lofty thoughts, spiritual suggestions and obscure relations. The greater part of natural truth is hidden in processes too minute for vision and in harmonies too large, in vibrations, cohesions and in affinities. The Chinese compass these also, and with great power and beauty.

You will ask, how could the Chinese have built up a great intellectual fabric from mere picture writing? To the ordinary Western mind, which believes that thought is concerned with logical categories and which rather condemns the faculty of direct imagination, this feat seems quite impossible. Yet the Chinese language with its peculiar materials has passed over from the seen to the unseen by exactly the same process which all ancient races employed. This process is metaphor, the use of material images to suggest immaterial relations.*

The whole delicate substance of speech is built upon substrata of metaphor. Abstract terms, pressed by etymology, reveal their ancient roots still embedded in direct action. But the primitive metaphors do not spring from arbitrary *subjective* processes. They are possible only because they follow objective lines of relations in nature herself. Relations are more real and more important than the things which they relate. The forces which produce the branch-angles of an oak lay potent in the acorn. Similar lines of resistance, half-curbing the out-pressing vitalities, govern the branching of rivers and of nations. Thus a nerve, a wire, a roadway, and a clearing-house are only varying channels which communication forces for itself. This is more than analogy, it is identity of structure. Nature furnishes her own clues. Had the world not been full of homologies, sympathies, and identities, thought would have been starved and language chained to the obvious. There would have been no bridge whereby to cross from the minor truth of the seen to the major truth of the unseen. Not more than a few hundred roots out of our large vocabularies could have dealt

* Compare Aristotle's *Poetics:* "Swift perception of relations, hallmark of genius." E.P.

directly with physical processes. These we can fairly well identify in primitive Sanskrit. They are, almost without exception, vivid verbs. The wealth of European speech grew, following slowly the intricate maze of nature's suggestions and affinities. Metaphor was piled upon metaphor in quasi-geological strata.

Metaphor, the revealer of nature, is the very substance of poetry. The known interprets the obscure, the universe is alive with myth. The beauty and freedom of the observed world furnish a model, and life is pregnant with art. It is a mistake to suppose, with some philosophers of aesthetics, that art and poetry aim to deal with the general and the abstract. This misconception has been foisted upon us by mediaeval logic. Art and poetry deal with the concrete of nature, not with rows of separate "particulars," for such rows do not exist. Poetry is finer than prose because it gives us more concrete truth in the same compass of words. Metaphor, its chief device, is at once the substance of nature and of language. Poetry only does consciously* what the primitive races did unconsciously. The chief work of literary men in dealing with language, and of poets especially, lies in feeling back along the ancient lines of advance.† He must do this so that he may keep his words enriched by all their subtle undertones of meaning. The original metaphors stand as a kind of luminous background, giving color and vitality, forcing them closer to the concreteness of natural processes. Shakespeare everywhere teems with examples. For these reasons poetry was the earliest of the world arts; poetry, language and the care of myth grew up together.

I have alleged all this because it enables me to show clearly why I believe that the Chinese written language has not only absorbed the poetic substance of nature and built with it a second work of metaphor, but has, through its very pictorial visibility, been able to retain its original creative poetry with far more vigor and vividness than any phonetic tongue. Let us first see how near it is to the

* *Vide* also an article on "Vorticism" in the *Fortnightly Review* for September 1914. "The language of exploration" now in my "Gaudier-Brzeska." E.P.

† I would submit in all humility that this applies in the rendering of ancient texts. The poet, in dealing with his own time, must also see to it that language does not petrify on his hands. He must prepare for new advances along the lines of true metaphor, that is interpretative metaphor, or image, as diametrically opposed to untrue, or ornamental, metaphor. E.P.

heart of nature in its metaphors. We can watch it passing from the seen to the unseen, as we saw it passing from verb to pronoun. It retains the primitive sap, it is not cut and dried like a walking-stick. We have been told that these people are cold, practical, mechanical, literal, and without a trace of imaginative genius. That is nonsense.

Our ancestors built the accumulations of metaphor into structures of language and into systems of thought. Languages today are thin and cold because we think less and less into them. We are forced, for the sake of quickness and sharpness, to file down each word to its narrowest edge of meaning. Nature would seem to have become less like a paradise and more and more like a factory. We are content to accept the vulgar misuse of the moment.

A late stage of decay is arrested and embalmed in the dictionary.

Only scholars and poets feel painfully back along the thread of our etymologies and piece together our diction, as best they may, from forgotten fragments. This anaemia of modern speech is only too well encouraged by the feeble cohesive force of our phonetic symbols. There is little or nothing in a phonetic word to exhibit the embryonic stages of its growth. It does not bear its metaphor on its face. We forget that personality once meant, not the soul, but the soul's mask. This is the sort of thing one can not possibly forget in using the Chinese symbols.

In this Chinese shows its advantage. Its etymology is constantly visible. It retains the creative impulse and process, visible and at work. After thousands of years the lines of metaphoric advance are still shown, and in many cases actually retained in the meaning. Thus a word, instead of growing gradually poorer and poorer as with us, becomes richer and still more rich from age to age, almost consciously luminous. Its uses in national philosophy and history, in biography and in poetry, throw about it a nimbus of meanings. These centre about the graphic symbol. The memory can hold them and use them. The very soil of Chinese life seems entangled in the roots of its speech. The manifold illustrations which crowd its annals of personal experience, the lines of tendency which converge upon a tragic climax, moral character as the very core of the principle—all these are flashed at once on the mind as reinforcing values with accumulation of meaning which a phonetic language can hardly hope to attain. Their ideographs are like blood-stained battle-flags to an old campaigner. With us, the poet is the only one for whom the accumulated treasures of the race-words are real and active. Poetic language is always vibrant with fold on fold of overtones and with natural affinities, but in Chinese the visibility of the metaphor tends to raise this quality to its intensest power.

I have mentioned the tyranny of mediaeval logic. According to this European logic thought is a kind of brickyard. It is baked into little hard units or concepts. These are piled in rows according to size and then labeled with words for future use. This use consists in picking out a few bricks, each by its convenient label, and sticking them together into a sort of wall called a sentence by the use either of white mortar for the positive copula "is," or of black mortar for the negative copula "is not." In this way we produce such admirable propositions as "A ring-tailed baboon is not a constitutional assembly."

Let us consider a row of cherry trees. From each of these in turn we proceed to take an "abstract," as the phrase is, a certain common lump of qualities which we may express together by the name cherry or cherry-ness. Next we place in a second table several such characteristic concepts: cherry, rose, sunset, iron-rust, flamingo. From these we abstract some further common quality, dilutation or mediocrity, and label it "red" or "redness." It is evident that this process of abstraction may be carried on indefinitely and with all sorts of material. We may go on for ever building pyramids of attenuated concept until we reach the apex "being."

But we have done enough to illustrate the characteristic process. At the base of the pyramid lie *things,* but stunned, as it were. They can never know themselves for things until they pass up and down among the layers of the pyramids. The way of passing up and down the pyramid may be exemplified as follows: We take a concept of lower attenuation, such as "cherry"; we see that it is contained under one higher, such as "redness." Then we are permitted to say in sentence form, "Cherryness is contained under redness," or for short, "(The) cherry is red." If, on the other hand, we do not find our chosen subject under a given predicate we use the black copula and say, for example, "(The) cherry is not liquid."

From this point we might go to the theory of the syllogism, but we refrain. It is enough to note that the practised logician finds it convenient to store his mind with long lists of nouns and adjectives, for these are naturally the names of classes. Most text-books on language begin with such lists. The study of verbs is meagre, for in such a system there is only one real working verb, to wit, the quasi-verb "is." All other verbs can be transformed into participles and gerunds. For example, "to run" practically becomes a case of "running." Instead of thinking directly, "The man runs," our logician makes two subjective equations, namely: The individual in question is contained under the class "man"; and the class "man" is contained under the class of "runing things."

The sheer loss and weakness of this method are apparent and flagrant. Even in its own sphere it can not think half of what it wants to think. It has no way of bringing together any two concepts which do not happen to stand one under the other and in the same pyramid.

It is impossible to represent change in this system or any kind of growth.

This is probably why the conception of evolution came so late in Europe. *It could not make way until it was prepared to destroy the inveterate logic of classification.*

Far worse than this, such logic can not deal with any kind of interaction or with any multiplicity of function. According to it, the function of my muscles is as isolated from the function of my nerves, as from an earthquake in the moon. For it the poor neglected things at the bases of the pyramids are only so many particulars or pawns.

Science fought till she got at the things.

All her work has been done from the base of the pyramids, not from the apex. She has discovered how functions cohere in things. She expresses her results in grouped sentences which embody no nouns or adjectives but verbs of special character. The true formula for thought is: The cherry tree is all that is does. Its correlated verbs compose it. At bottom these verbs are transitive. Such verbs may be almost infinite in number.

In diction and in grammatical form science is utterly opposed to logic. Primitive men who created language agreed with science and

not with logic. Logic has abused the language which they left to
her mercy.

Poetry agrees with science and not with logic.

The moment we use the copula, the moment we express subjec-
tive inclusions, poetry evaporates. The more concretely and vividly
we express the interactions of things the better the poetry. We need
in poetry thousands of active words, each doing its utmost to show
forth the motive and vital forces. We can not exhibit the wealth of
nature by mere summation, by the piling of sentences. Poetic
thought works by suggestion, crowding maximum meaning into the
single phrase pregnant, charged, and luminous from within.

In Chinese character each word accumulated this sort of energy
in itself.

Should we pass formally to the study of Chinese poetry, we
should warn ourselves against logicianised pitfalls. We should be
ware of modern narrow utilitarian meanings ascribed to the words
in commercial dictionaries. We should try to preserve the meta-
phoric overtones. We should be ware of English grammar, its hard
parts of speech, and its lazy satisfaction with nouns and adjectives.
We should seek and at least bear in mind the verbal undertone of
each noun. We should avoid "is" and bring in a wealth of
neglected English verbs. Most of the existing translations violate
all of these rules.

The development of the normal transitive sentence rests upon
the fact that one action in nature promotes another; thus the agent
and the object are secretly verbs. For example, our sentence,
"Reading promotes writing," would be expressed in Chinese by
three full verbs. Such a form is the equivalent of three expanded
clauses and can be drawn out into adjectival, participial, infinitive,
relative or conditional members. One of many possible examples
is, "If one reads it teaches him how to write." Another is, "One
who reads becomes one who writes." But in the first condensed
form a Chinese would write, "Read promote write." The domi-
nance of the verb and its power to obliterate all other parts of
speech give us the model of terse fine style.

I have seldom seen our rhetoricians dwell on the fact that the
great strength of our language lies in its splendid array of transitive
verbs, drawn both from Anglo-Saxon and from Latin sources.

These give us the most individual characterisations of force. Their power lies in their recognition of nature as a vast storehouse of forces. We do not say in English that things seem, or appear, or eventuate, or even that they are; but that they *do*. Will is the foundation of our speech.* We catch the Demi-urge in the act. I had to discover for myself why Shakespeare's English was so immeasurably superior to all others. I found that it was his persistent, natural, and magnificent use of hundreds of transitive verbs. Rarely will you find an "is" in his sentences. "Is" weakly lends itself to the uses of our rhythm, in the unaccented syllables; yet he sternly discards it. A study of Shakespeare's verbs should underlie all exercises in style.

We find in poetical Chinese a wealth of transitive verbs, in some way greater even than in the English of Shakespeare. This springs from their power of combining several pictorial elements in a single character. We have in English no verb for what two things, say the sun and moon, both do together. Prefixes and affixes merely direct and qualify. In Chinese the verb can be more minutely qualified. We find a hundred variants clustering about a single idea. Thus "to sail a boat for purposes of pleasure" would be an entirely different verb from "to sail for purposes of commerce." Dozens of Chinese verbs express various shades of grieving, yet in English translations they are usually reduced to one mediocrity. Many of them can be expressed only by periphrasis, but what right has the translator to neglect the overtones? There are subtle shadings. We should strain our resources in English.

It is true that the pictorial clue of many Chinese ideographs can not now be traced, and even Chinese lexicographers admit that combinations frequently contribute only a phonetic value. But I find it incredible that any such minute subdivision of the idea could have ever existed alone as abstract sound without the concrete character. It contradicts the law of evolution. Complex ideas arise only gradually, as the power of holding them together arises. The paucity of Chinese sound could not so hold them. Neither is it conceivable that the whole list was made at once, as commercial codes of cipher are compiled. Foreign words sometimes recalled Chinese ideograms associated with vaguely similar

* Compare Dante's definition of "rectitudo" as the direction of the will.

sound? Therefore we must believe that the phonetic theory is in large part unsound? The metaphor once existed in many cases where we can not now trace it. Many of our own etymologies have been lost. It is futile to take the ignorance of the Han dynasty for omniscience.* It is not true, as Legge said, that the original picture characters could never have gone far in building up abstract thought. This is a vital mistake. We have seen that our own languages have all sprung from a few hundred vivid phonetic verbs by figurative derivation. A fabric more vast could have been built up in Chinese by metaphorical composition. No attenuated idea exists which it might not have reached more vividly and more permanently than we could have been expected to reach with phonetic roots. Such a pictorial method, whether the Chinese exemplified it or not, would be the ideal language of the world.

Still, is it not enough to show that Chinese poetry gets back near to the processes of nature by means of its vivid figure, its wealth of such figures? If we attempt to follow it in English we must use words highly charged, words whose vital suggestion shall interplay as nature interplays. Sentences must be like the mingling of the fringes of feathered banners, or as the colors of many flowers blended into the single sheen of a meadow.

The poet can never see too much or feel too much. His metaphors are only ways of getting rid of the dead white plaster of the copula. He resolves its indifference into a thousand tints of verb.

---

* Professor Fenollosa is borne out by chance evidence. Gaudier-Brzeska sat in my room before he went off to war. He was able to read the Chinese radicals and many compound signs almost at pleasure. He was used to consider all life and nature in the terms of planes and of bounding lines. Nevertheless he had spent only a fortnight in the museum studying the Chinese characters. He was amazed at the stupidity of lexicographers who could not, for all their learning, discern the pictorial values which were to him perfectly obvious and apparent. A few weeks later Edmond Dulac, who is of a totally different tradition, sat here, giving an impromptu panegyric on the elements of Chinese art, on the units of composition, drawn from the written characters. He did not use Professor Fenollosa's own words—he said "bamboo" instead of "rice." He said the essence of the bamboo is in a certain way it grows; they have this in their sign for bamboo, all designs of bamboo proceed from it. Then he went on rather to disparage vorticism, on the grounds that it could not hope to do for the Occident, in one lifetime, what had required centuries of development in China. E.P.

His figures flood things with jets of various light, like the sudden up-blaze of fountains. The prehistoric poets who created language discovered the whole harmonious framework of nature, they sang out her processes in their hymns. And this diffused poetry which they created, Shakespeare has condensed into a more tangible substance. Thus in all poetry a word is like a sun, with its corona and chromosphere; words crowd upon words, and enwrap each other in their luminous envelopes until sentences become clear, continuous light-bands.

Now we are in condition to appreciate the full splendor of certain lines of Chinese verse. Poetry surpasses prose especially in that the poet selects for juxtaposition those words whose overtones blend into a delicate and lucid harmony. All arts follow the same law; refined harmony lies in the delicate balance of overtones. In music the whole possibility and theory of harmony are based on the overtones. In this sense poetry seems a more difficult art.

How shall we determine the metaphorical overtones of neighbouring words? We can avoid flagrant breaches like mixed metaphor. We can find the concord or harmonising at its intensest, as in Romeo's speech over the dead Juliet.

Here also the Chinese ideography has its advantage, in even a simple line; for example, "The sun rises in the east."

The overtones vibrate against the eye. The wealth of composition in characters makes possible a choice of words in which a single dominant overtone colors every plane of meaning. That is perhaps the most conspicuous quality of Chinese poetry. Let us examine our line.

日　　　昇　　　東

Sun　　　Rises (in the) East

The sun, the shining, on one side, on the other the sign of the east, which is the sun entangled in the branches of a tree. And in the middle sign, the verb "rise," we have further homology; the sun is above the horizon, but beyond that the single upright line is like the growing trunk-line of the tree sign. This is but a beginning, but it points a way to the method, and to the method of intelligent reading.

TERMINAL NOTE. E.P., 1935. Whatever a few of us learned from Fenollosa twenty years ago, the whole Occident is still in crass ignorance of the Chinese art of verbal sonority. I now doubt if it was inferior to the Greek. Our poets being slovenly, ignorant of music, and earless, it is useless to blame professors for squalor.

EZRA POUND

A Retrospect*

There has been so much scribbling about a new fashion in poetry, that I may perhaps be pardoned this brief recapitulation and restrospect.

In the spring or early summer of 1912, "H.D.," Richard Aldington and myself decided that we were agreed upon the three principles following:

1. Direct treatment of the "thing" whether subjective or objective.

2. To use absolutely no word that does not contribute to the presentation.

3. As regarding rhythm: to compose in the sequence of the musical phrase, not in sequence of a metronome.

Upon many points of taste and of predilection we differed, but agreeing upon these three positions we thought we had as much right to a group name, at least as much right, as a number of French "schools" proclaimed by Mr. Flint in the August number of Harold Monro's magazine for 1911.

This school has since been "joined" or "followed" by numerous people who, whatever their merits, do not show any signs of agreeing with the second specification. Indeed *vers libre* has become as prolix and as verbose as any of the flaccid varieties that preceded it. It has brought faults of its own. The actual language and phrasing is often as bad as that of our elders without even the

* A group of early essays and notes which appeared under this title in *Pavannes and Divisions* (1918). "A Few Don'ts" was first printed in *Poetry*, I, 6 (March, 1913).

excuse that the words are shovelled in to fill a metric pattern or to complete the noise of a rhyme-sound. Whether or no the phrases followed by the followers are musical must be left to the reader's decision. At times I can find a marked metre in *"vers libres,"* as stale and hackneyed as any pseudo-Swinburnian, at times the writers seem to follow no musical structure whatever. But it is, on the whole, good that the field should be ploughed. Perhaps a few good poems have come from the new method, and if so it is justified.

Criticism is not a circumscription or a set of prohibitions. It provides fixed points of departure. It may startle a dull reader into alertness. That little of it which is good is mostly in stray phrases; or if it be an older artist helping a younger it is in great measure but rules of thumb, cautions gained by experience.

I set together a few phrases on practical working about the time the first remarks on imagisme were published. The first use of the word "Imagiste" was in my note to T. E. Hulme's five poems, printed at the end of my "Ripostes" in the autumn of 1912. I reprint my cautions from *Poetry* for March, 1913.

A FEW DON'TS

An "Image" is that which presents an intellectual and emotional complex in an instant of time. I use the term "complex" rather in the technical sense employed by the newer psychologists, such as Hart, though we might not agree absolutely in our application.

It is the presentation of such a "complex" instantaneously which gives that sense of sudden liberation; that sense of freedom from time limits and space limits; that sense of sudden growth, which we experience in the presence of the greatest works of art.

It is better to present one Image in a lifetime than to produce voluminous works.

All this, however, some may consider open to debate. The immediate necessity is to tabulate A LIST OF DON'TS for those beginning to write verses. I can not put all of them into Mosaic negative.

To begin with, consider the three propositions (demanding direct treatment, economy of words, and the sequence of the musical phrase), not as dogma—never consider anything as dogma—but as the result of long contemplation, which, even if it is some one else's contemplation, may be worth consideration.

Pay no attention to the criticism of men who have never themselves written a notable work. Consider the discrepancies between the actual writing of the Greek poets and dramatists, and the theories of the Graeco-Roman grammarians, concocted to explain their metres.

LANGUAGE

Use no superfluous word, no adjective which does not reveal something.

Don't use such an expression as "dim lands *of peace.*" It dulls the image. It mixes an abstraction with the concrete. It comes from the writer's not realizing that the natural object is always the *adequate* symbol.

Go in fear of abstractions. Do not retell in mediocre verse what has already been done in good prose. Don't think any intelligent person is going to be deceived when you try to shirk all the difficulties of the unspeakably difficult art of good prose by chopping your composition into line lengths.

What the expert is tired of today the public will be tired of tomorrow.

Don't imagine that the art of poetry is any simpler than the art of music, or that you can please the expert before you have spent at least as much effort on the art of verse as the average piano teacher spends on the art of music.

Be influenced by as many great artists as you can, but have the decency either to acknowledge the debt outright, or to try to conceal it.

Don't allow "influence" to mean merely that you mop up the particular decorative vocabulary of some one or two poets whom you happen to admire. A Turkish war correspondent was recently caught red-handed babbling in his despatches of "dove-grey" hills, or else it was "pearl-pale," I can not remember.

Use either no ornament or good ornament.

RHYTHM AND RHYME

Let the candidate fill his mind with the finest cadences he can discover, preferably in a foreign language,* so that the meaning of the words may be less likely to divert his attention from the movement; e.g. Saxon charms, Hebridean Folk Songs, the verse of Dante, and the lyrics of Shakespeare—if he can dissociate the vocabulary from the cadence. Let him dissect the lyrics of Goethe coldly into their component sound values, syllables long and short, stressed and unstressed, into vowels and consonants.

It is not necessary that a poem should rely on its music, but if it does rely on its music that music must be such as will delight the expert.

Let the neophyte know assonance and alliteration, rhyme immediate and delayed, simple and polyphonic, as a musician would expect to know harmony and counterpoint and all the minutiae of his craft. No time is too great to give to these matters or to any one of them, even if the artist seldom have need of them.

Don't imagine that a thing will "go" in verse just because it's too dull to go in prose.

Don't be "viewy"—leave that to the writers of pretty little philosophic essays. Don't be descriptive; remember that the painter can describe a landscape much better than you can, and that he has to know a deal more about it.

When Shakespeare talks of the "Dawn in russet mantle clad" he presents something which the painter does not present. There is in this line of his nothing that one can call description; he presents.

Consider the way of the scientists rather than the way of an advertising agent for a new soap.

The scientist does not expect to be acclaimed as a great scientist until he has *discovered* something. He begins by learning what has been discovered already. He goes from that point onward. He does not bank on being a charming fellow personally. He does not expect his friends to applaud the results of his freshman class work. Freshmen in poetry are unfortunately not confined to a definite and recognizable class room. They are "all over the shop." Is it any wonder "the public is indifferent to poetry"?

* This is for rhythm, his vocabulary must of course be found in his native tongue.

Don't chop your stuff into separate *iambs*. Don't make each line stop dead at the end, and then begin every next line with a heave. Let the beginning of the next line catch the rise of the rhythm wave, unless you want a definite longish pause.

In short, behave as a musician, a good musician, when dealing with that phase of your art which has exact parallels in music. The same laws govern, and you are bound by no others.

Naturally, your rhythmic structure should not destroy the shape of your words, or their natural sound, or their meaning. It is improbable that, at the start, you will be able to get a rhythm-structure strong enough to affect them very much, though you may fall a victim to all sorts of false stopping due to line ends and cæsurae.

The Musician can rely on pitch and the volume of the orchestra. You can not. The term harmony is misapplied in poetry; it refers to simultaneous sounds of different pitch. There is, however, in the best verse a sort of residue of sound which remains in the ear of the hearer and acts more or less as an organ-base.

A rhyme must have in it some slight element of surprise if it is to give pleasure; it need not be bizarre or curious, but it must be well used if used at all.

Vide further Vildrac and Duhamel's notes on rhyme in *"Technique Poétique."*

That part of your poetry which strikes upon the imaginative *eye* of the reader will lose nothing by translation into a foreign tongue; that which appeals to the ear can reach only those who take it in the original.

Consider the definiteness of Dante's presentation, as compared with Milton's rhetoric. Read as much of Wordsworth as does not seem too unutterably dull.

If you want the gist of the matter go to Sappho, Catullus, Villon, Heine when he is in the vein, Gautier when he is not too frigid; or, if you have not the tongues, seek out the leisurely Chaucer. Good prose will do you no harm, and there is good discipline to be had by trying to write it.

Translation is likewise good training, if you find that your original matter "wobbles" when you try to rewrite it. The meaning of the poem to be translated can not "wobble."

If you are using a symmetrical form, don't put in what you want to say and then fill up the remaining vacuums with slush.

Don't mess up the perception of one sense by trying to define it in terms of another. This is usually only the result of being too lazy to find the exact word. To this clause there are possibly exceptions.

The first three simple prescriptions will throw out nine-tenths of all the bad poetry now accepted as standard and classic; and will prevent you from many a crime of production.

". . . *Mais d'abord il faut être un poète,*" as MM. Duhamel and Vildrac have said at the end of their little book, *Notes sur la Technique Poétique.*

Since March 1913, Ford Madox Hueffer has pointed out that Wordsworth was so intent on the ordinary or plain word that he never thought of hunting for *le mot juste.*

John Butler Yeats has handled or man-handled Wordsworth and the Victorians, and his criticism, contained in letters to his son, is now printed and available.

I do not like writing *about* art, my first, at least I think it was my first essay on the subject, was a protest against it.

PROLEGOMENA *

Time was when the poet lay in a green field with his head against a tree and played his diversion on a ha'penny whistle, and Caesar's predecessors conquered the earth, and the predecessors of golden Crassus embezzled, and fashions had their say, and let him alone. And presumably he was fairly content in this circumstance, for I have small doubt that the occasional passerby, being attracted by curiosity to know why any one should lie under a tree and blow diversion on a ha'penny whistle, came and conversed with him, and that among these passers-by there was on occasion a person of charm or a young lady who had not read *Man and Superman;* and looking back upon this naive state of affairs we call it the age of gold.

Metastasio, and he should know if any one, assures us that this

* *Poetry and Drama* (then the *Poetry Review,* edited by Harold Monro), Feb. 1912.

age endures—even though the modern poet is expected to holloa his verses down a speaking tube to the editors of cheap magazines—S. S. McClure, or some one of that sort—even though hordes of authors meet in dreariness and drink healths to the "Copyright Bill"; even though these things be, the age of gold pertains. Imperceivably, if you like, but pertains. You meet unkempt Amyclas in a Soho restaurant and chant together of dead and forgotten things—it is a manner of speech among poets to chant of dead, half-forgotten things, there seems no special harm in it; it has always been done—and it's rather better to be a clerk in the Post Office than to look after a lot of stinking, verminous sheep—and at another hour of the day one substitutes the drawing-room for the restaurant and tea is probably more palatable than mead and mare's milk, and little cakes than honey. And in this fashion one survives the resignation of Mr. Balfour, and the iniquities of the American customs-house, *e quel bufera infernal,* the periodical press. And then in the middle of it, there being apparently no other person at once capable and available one is stopped and asked to explain oneself.

I begin on the chord thus querulous, for I would much rather lie on what is left of Catullus' parlour floor and speculate the azure beneath it and the hills off to Salo and Riva with their forgotten gods moving unhindered amongst them, than discuss any processes and theories of art whatsoever. I would rather play tennis. I shall not argue.

CREDO

Rhythm.—I believe in an "absolute rhythm," a rhythm, that is, in poetry which corresponds exactly to the emotion or shade of emotion to be expressed. A man's rhythm must be interpretative, it will be, therefore, in the end, his own, uncounterfeiting, uncounterfeitable.

Symbols.—I believe that the proper and perfect symbol is the natural object, that if a man use "symbols" he must so use them that their symbolic function does not obtrude; so that *a* sense, and the poetic quality of the passage, is not lost to those who do not understand the symbol as such, to whom, for instance, a hawk is a hawk.

Technique.—I believe in technique as the test of a man's sincerity; in law when it is ascertainable; in the trampling down of every convention that impedes or obscures the determination of the law, or the precise rendering of the impulse.

Form.—I think there is a "fluid" as well as a "solid" content, that some poems may have form as a tree has form, some as water poured into a vase. That most symmetrical forms have certain uses. That a vast number of subjects cannot be precisely, and therefore not properly rendered in symmetrical forms.

"Thinking that alone worthy wherein the whole art is employed."* I think the artist should master all known forms and systems of metric, and I have with some persistence set about doing this, searching particularly into those periods wherein the systems came to birth or attained their maturity. It has been complained, with some justice, that I dump my note-books on the public. I think that only after a long struggle will poetry attain such a degree of development, or, if you will, modernity, that it will vitally concern people who are accustomed, in prose, to Henry James and Anatole France, in music to Debussy. I am constantly contending that it took two centuries of Provence and one of Tuscany to develop the media of Dante's masterwork, that it took the latinists of the Renaissance, and the Pleiade, and his own age of painted speech to prepare Shakespeare his tools. It is tremendously important that great poetry be written, it makes no jot of difference who writes it. The experimental demonstrations of one man may save the time of many—hence my furore over Arnaut Daniel—if a man's experiments try out one new rime, or dispense conclusively with one iota of currently accepted nonsense, he is merely playing fair with his colleagues' when he chalks up his result.

No man ever writes very much poetry that "matters." In bulk, that is, no one produces much that is final, and when a man is not doing this highest thing, this saying the thing once for all and perfectly; when he is not matching Ποικιλόθρον', ἀθάνατ' Ἀφρόδιτα, or "Hist—said Kate the Queen," he had much better be making the sorts of experiment which may be of use to him in his later work, or to his successors.

* Dante, *De Volgari Eloquio.*

"The lyf so short, the craft so long to lerne." It is a foolish thing for a man to begin his work on a too narrow foundation, it is a disgraceful thing for a man's work not to show steady growth and increasing fineness from first to last.

As for "adaptations"; one finds that all the old masters of painting recommend to their pupils that they begin by copying masterwork, and proceed to their own composition.

As for "Every man his own poet," the more every man knows about poetry the better. I believe in every one writing poetry who wants to; most do. I believe in every man knowing enough of music to play "God bless our home" on the harmonium, but I do not believe in every man giving concerts and printing his sin.

The mastery of any art is the work of a lifetime. I should not discriminate between the "amateur" and the "professional." Or rather I should discriminate quite often in favour of the amateur, but I should discriminate between the amateur and the expert. It is certain that the present chaos will endure until the Art of poetry has been preached down the amateur gullet, until there is such a general understanding of the fact that poetry is an art and not a pastime; such a knowledge of technique; of technique of surface and technique of content, that the amateurs will cease to try to drown out the masters.

If a certain thing was said once for all in Atlantis or Arcadia, in 450 before Christ or in 1290 after, it is not for us moderns to go saying it over, or to go obscuring the memory of the dead by saying the same thing with less skill and less conviction.

My pawing over the ancients and semi-ancients has been one struggle to find out what has been done, once for all, better than it can ever be done again, and to find out what remains for us to do, and plenty does remain, for if we still feel the same emotions as those which launched the thousand ships, it is quite certain that we come on these feelings differently, through different nuances, by different intellectual gradations. Each age has its own abounding. gifts yet only some ages transmute them into matter of duration. No good poetry is ever written in a manner twenty years old, for to write in such a manner shows conclusively that the writer thinks from books, convention and *cliché,* and not from life, yet a man feeling the divorce of life and his art may naturally try to resurrect a forgotten mode if he finds in that mode some leaven, or if he think he sees in it some element lacking in contemporary art which might unite that art again to its sustenance, life.

In the art of Daniel and Cavalcanti, I have seen that precision which I miss in the Victorians, that explicit rendering, be it of external nature, or of emotion. Their testimony is of the eyewitness, their symptoms are first hand.

As for the nineeenth century, with all respect to its achievements, I think we shall look back upon it as a rather blurry, messy sort of a period, a rather sentimentalistic, mannerish sort of a period. I say this without any self-righteousness, with no self-satisfaction.

As for there being a "movement" or my being of it, the conception of poetry as a "pure art" in the sense in which I use the term, revived with Swinburne. From the puritanical revolt to Swinburne, poetry had been merely the vehicle—yes, definitely, Arthur Symons' scruples and feelings about the word not withholding—the ox-cart and post-chaise for transmitting thoughts poetic or otherwise. And perhaps the "great Victorians," though it is doubtful, and assuredly the "nineties" continued the development of the art, confining their improvements, however, chiefly to sound and to refinements of manner.

Mr. Yeats has once and for all stripped English poetry of its perdamnable rhetoric. He has boiled away all that is not poetic—and a good deal that is. He has become a classic in his own lifetime and *nel mezzo del cammin*. He has made our poetic idiom a thing pliable, a speech without inversions.

Robert Bridges, Maurice Hewlett and Frederic Manning are* in their different ways seriously concerned with overhauling the metric, in testing the language and its adaptability to certain modes. Ford Hueffer is making some sort of experiments in modernity. The Provost of Oriel continues his translation of the *Divina Commedia*.

As to Twentieth century poetry, and the poetry which I expect to see written during the next decade or so, it will, I think, move against poppy-cock, it will be harder and saner, it will be what Mr. Hewlett calls "nearer the bone." It will be as much like granite as it can be, its force will lie in its truth, its interpretative power (of

* (Dec. 1911).

course, poetic force does always rest there); I mean it will not try to seem forcible by rhetorical din, and luxurious riot. We will have fewer painted adjectives impeding the shock and stroke of it. At least for myself, I want it so, austere, direct, free from emotional slither.

What is there now, in 1917, to be added?

RE VERS LIBRE

I think the desire for *vers libre* is due to the sense of quantity reasserting itself after years of starvation. But I doubt if we can take over, for English, the rules of quantity laid down for Greek and Latin, mostly by Latin grammarians.

I think one should write *vers libre* only when one "must," that is to say, only when the "thing" builds up a rhythm more beautiful than that of set metres, or more real, more a part of the emotion of the "thing," more germane, intimate, interpretative than the measure of regular accentual verse; a rhythm which discontents one with set iambic or set anapaestic.

Eliot has said the thing very well when he said, "No *vers* is *libre* for the man who wants to do a good job."

As a matter of detail, there is *vers libre* with accent heavily marked as a drum-beat (as par example my "Dance Figure"), and on the other hand I think I have gone as far as can profitably be gone in the other direction (and perhaps too far). I mean I do not think one can use to any advantage rhythms much more tenuous and imperceptible than some I have used. I think progress lies rather in an attempt to approximate classical quantitative metres (NOT to copy them) than in a carelessness regarding such things.*

I agree with John Yeats on the relation of beauty to certitude. I prefer satire, which is due to emotion, to any sham of emotion.

I have had to write, or at least I have written a good deal about art, sculpture, painting and poetry. I have seen what seemed to me the best of contemporary work reviled and obstructed. Can any one write prose of permanent or durable interest when he is merely saying for one year what nearly every one will say at the end of

* Let me date this statement 20 Aug. 1917.

three or four years? I have been battistrada for a sculptor, a
painter, a novelist, several poets. I wrote also of certain French
writers in *The New Age* in nineteen twelve or eleven.

I would much rather that people would look at Brzeska's sculp-
ture and Lewis's drawings, and that they would read Joyce, Jules
Romains, Eliot, than that they should read what I have said of
these men, or that I should be asked to republish argumentative
essays and reviews.

All that the critic can do for the reader or audience or spectator
is to focus his gaze or audition. Rightly or wrongly I think my
blasts and essays have done their work, and that more people are
now likely to go to the sources than are likely to read this book.

Jammes's "Existences" in *La Triomphe de la Vie* is available.
So are his early poems. I think we need a convenient anthology
rather than descriptive criticism. Carl Sandburg wrote me from
Chicago, "It's hell when poets can't afford to buy each other's
books." Half the people who care, only borrow. In America so few
people know each other that the difficulty lies more than half in
distribution. Perhaps one should make an anthology: Romains's
Un Etre en Marche and *Prières,* Vildrac's *Visite.* Retrospectively
the fine wrought work of Laforgue, the flashes of Rimbaud, the
hard-bit lines of Tristan Corbière, Tailhade's sketches in *Poèmes
Aristophanesques,* the *Litanies* of De Gourmont.

It is difficult at all times to write of the fine arts, it is almost
impossible unless one can accompany one's prose with many
reproductions. Still I would seize this chance or any chance to
reaffirm my belief in Wyndham Lewis's genius, both in his draw-
ings and his writings. And I would name an out of the way prose
book, the *Scenes and Portraits* of Frederic Manning, as well as
James Joyce's short stories and novel, *Dubliners* and the now well
known *Portrait of the Artist* as well as Lewis's *Tarr,* if, that is, I
may treat my strange reader as if he were a new friend come into
the room, intent on ransacking my bookshelf.

ONLY EMOTION ENDURES

"Only emotion endures." Surely it is better for me to name over
the few beautiful poems that still ring in my head than for me to

search my flat for back numbers of periodicals and rearrange all that I have said about friendly and hostile writers.

The first twelve lines of Padraic Colum's "Drover"; his "O Woman shapely as a swan, on your account I shall not die"; Joyce's "I hear an army"; the lines of Yeats that ring in my head and in the heads of all young men of my time who care for poetry: Braseal and the Fisherman, "The fire that stirs about her when she stirs"; the later lines of "The Scholars," the faces of the Magi; William Carlos Williams's "Postlude," Aldington's version of "Atthis," and H. D.'s waves like pine tops, and her verse in *Des Imagistes,* the first anthology; Hueffer's "How red your lips are" in his translation from Von der Vogelweide, his "Three Ten," the general effect of his "On Heaven"; his sense of the prose values or prose qualities in poetry; his ability to write poems that half-chant and are spoiled by a musician's additions; beyond these a poem by Alice Corbin, "One City Only," and another ending "But sliding water over a stone." These things have worn smooth in my head and I am not through with them, nor with Aldington's "In Via Sestina" nor his other poems in *Des Imagistes,* though people have told me their flaws. It may be that their content is too much embedded in me for me to look back at the words.

I am almost a different person when I come to take up the argument for Eliot's poems.

Arnold Dolmetsch

I have seen the God Pan and it was in this manner: I heard a bewildering and pervasive music moving from precision to precision within itself. Then I heard a different music, hollow and laughing. Then I looked up and saw two eyes like the eyes of a wood-creature peering at me over a brown tube of wood. Then someone said: Yes, once I was playing a fiddle in the forest and I walked into a wasps' nest.

Comparing these things with what I can read of the Earliest and best authenticated appearances of Pan, I can but conclude that they relate to similar occurrences. It is true that I found myself later in a room covered with pictures of what we now call ancient instruments, and that when I picked up the brown tube of wood I found that it had ivory rings upon it. And no proper reed has ivory rings on it, by nature. Also, they told me it was a "recorder," whatever that is.

Our only measure of truth is, however, our own perception of truth. The undeniable tradition of metamorphoses teaches us that things do not remain always the same. They become other things by swift and unanalysable process. It was only when men began to mistrust the myths and to tell nasty lies about the Gods for a moral purpose that these matters became hopelessly confused. Then some unpleasing Semite or Parsee or Syrian began to use myths for social propaganda, when the myth was degraded into an allegory or a fable, and that was the beginning of the end. And the Gods no longer walked in men's gardens. The first myths arose when a man walked sheer into "nonsense," that is to say, when some very vivid and undeniable adventure befell him, and he told someone else who called him a liar. Thereupon, after bitter experience, perceiving that no one could understand what he meant when he said that he "turned into a tree" he made a myth—a work of art that is—an impersonal or objective story woven out of his own emotion, as the nearest equation that he was capable of putting into words. That story, perhaps, then gave rise to a weaker copy of his emotion in others, until there arose a cult, a company of people who could understand each other's nonsense about the gods.

These things were afterwards incorporated for the condemnable "good of the State," and what was once a species of truth became only lies and propaganda. And they told horrid tales to little boys in order to make them be good; or to the ignorant populace in order to preserve the empire; and religion came to an end and civic science began to be studied. Plato said that artists ought to be kept out of the ideal republic, and the artists swore by their gods that nothing would drag them into it. That is the history of "civilization," or philology, or Kultur.

When any man is able, by a pattern of notes or by an arrangement of planes or colours, to throw us back into the age of truth, everyone who has been cast back into that age of truth for one instant gives honour to the spell which has worked, to the witchwork or the art-work, or to whatever you like to call it. I say, therefore, that I saw and heard the God Pan; shortly afterwards I saw and heard Mr. Dolmetsch. Mr. Dolmetsch was talking volubly, and he said, something very derogatory to music, which needs 240 (or some such number of) players, and can only be performed in one or two capitals. Pepys writes, that in the Fire of London, when the people were escaping by boat on the Thames, there was scarcely a boat in which you would not see them taking a pair of virginals as among their dearest possessions.

Older journalists tell me it is "cold mutton," that Mr. Dolmetsch was heard of fifteen years ago. This shows a tendency that I have before remarked in a civilization which rests upon journalism, and which has only a sporadic care for the arts. Everyone in London over forty "has heard of" Mr. Dolmetsch, his instruments, etc. The generation under thirty may have heard of him, but you cannot be sure of it. His topical interest is over. I have heard of Mr. Dolmetsch for fifteen years, because I am a crank and am interested in such matters. Mr. Dolmetsch has always been in France or America, or somewhere I wasn't when he was. Also, I have seen broken-down spinets in portentous and pretentious drawing-rooms. I have heard harpsichords played in Parisian concerts, and they sounded like the scratching of multitudinous hens, and I did not wonder that pianos had superseded them. Also, I have known good musicians and have favoured divers sorts of good music. And I have supposed that clavichords were things you might own if you were a millionaire; and that virginals went with citherns and citoles in the poems of the late D. G. Rossetti.

So I had two sets of adventures. First, I perceived a sound which is undoubtedly derived from the Gods, and then I found myself in a reconstructed century—in a century of music, back before Mozart or Purcell, listening to clear music, to tones clear as brown amber. And this music came indifferently out of the harpsichord or the clavichord or out of virginals or out of odd-shaped viols, or whatever they may be. There were two small girls playing upon them with an exquisite precision; with a precision quite

unlike anything I have ever heard from an orchestra. Then some-
one said in a tone of authority: "It is nonsense to teach people
scales. It is rubbish to make them play *this* (tum, tum, tum, tum
tum). They must begin to play music. Three years playing scales,
that is what they tell you. How can they ever be musicians?"

It reduces itself to about this. Once people played music. It was
gracious, exquisite music, and it was played on instruments which
gave out the players' exact mood and personality. "It is beautiful
even if you play it wrong." The clavichord has the beauty of three
or four lutes played together. It has more than that, but no matter.
You have your fingers always en rapport with the strings; it is not
one dab and then either another dab or else nothing, as with the
piano; the music is always lying on your own finger-tips.

This old music was not theatrical. You played it yourself as you
read a book of precision. A few people played it together. It was
not an interruption but a concentration.

Now, on the other hand, I remember a healthy concert pianist
complaining that you couldn't "really give" a big piano concert
unless you had the endurance of an ox; and that "women couldn't,
of course"; and that gradually the person with long hands was
being eliminated from the pianistic world, and that only people
with little, short fat fingers could come up to the technical require-
ments. Whether this is so or not, we have come to the pianola.
And one or two people are going in for sheer pianola. They cut
their rolls for the pianola itself, and make it play as if with two
dozen fingers when necessary. That is, perhaps, better art than
making a pianola imitate the music of two hands of five fingers
each. But still something is lacking.

Oriental music is under debate. We say we "can't hear it." Im-
pressionism has reduced us to such a dough-like state of receptivity
that we have ceased to like concentration. Or if it has not done this
it has at least set a fashion of passivity that has held since the
romantic movement. The old music was fit for the old instruments.
That was natural. It is proper to play piano music on pianos. But
in the end we find that nothing less than a full orchestra will satisfy
our modernity.

That is the whole flaw of impressionist or "emotional" music as
opposed to pattern music. It is like a drug; you must have more
drug, and more noise each time, or this effect, this impression

which works from the outside, in from the nerves and sensorium upon the self—is no use, its effect is constantly weaker and weaker. I do not mean that Bach is not emotional, but the early music starts with the mystery of pattern; if you like, with the vortex of pattern; with something which is, first of all, music, and which is capable of being, after that, many things. What I call emotional, or impressionist music, starts with being emotion or impression and then becomes only approximately music. It is, that is to say, something in the terms of something else. If it produces an effect, if, from sounding as music, it moves at all, it can only recede into the original emotion or impression. Programme music is merely a weaker, more flabby and descriptive sort of impressionist music, needing, perhaps, a guide and explanation.

Mr. Dolmetsch was, let us say, enamoured of ancient music. He found it misunderstood. He saw a beauty so great and so various that he stopped composing. He found that the beauty was untranslatable with modern instruments; he has repaired and has entirely remade "ancient instruments." The comfort is that he has done this not for a few rich faddists, as one had been led to suppose. He makes his virginals and clavichords for the price of a bad, of a very bad piano. You can have a virginal for £25 if you order it when he is making a dozen; and you can have a clavichord for a few pounds more, even if he is not making more than one.

My interest in these things is not topical. Mr. Dolmetsch was a topic some years ago, but you are not *au courant,* and you do not much care for music unless you know that a certain sort of very beautiful music is no longer impossible. It is not necessary to wait for a great legacy, or to inhabit a capital city in order to hear magical voices, in order to hear perfect music which does not depend upon your ability to approximate the pianola, or upon great physical strength. Of the clavichord, one can only say, very inexactly, that it is to the piano what the violin is to the bass viol.

As I believe that [Wyndham] Lewis and Picasso are capable of revitalizing the instinct of design so I believe that a return, an awakening to the possibilities, not necessarily of "Old" music, but of pattern music played upon ancient instruments, is, perhaps, able to make music again a part of life, not merely a part of theatricals. The musician, the performing musician as distinct from the composer, might again be an interesting person, an artist, not merely a sort of manual saltimbanque or a stage hypnotist. It is, perhaps, a question of whether you want music, or whether you want to see an obsessed personality trying to "dominate" an audience.

I have said little that can be called technical criticism. I have perhaps implied it. There is precision in the making of ancient instruments. Men still make passable violins; I do not see why the art of beautiful-keyed instruments need be regarded as utterly lost. There has been precision in Mr. Dolmetsch's study of ancient texts and notation; he has routed out many errors.* He has even, with certain help, unravelled the precision of ancient dancing. He has found a complete notation which might not interest us were it not that this very dancing forces one to a greater precision with the old music. One finds, for instance, that certain tunes called dance tunes must be played double the time at which they are modernly taken.

One art interprets the other. It would almost touch upon theatricals, which I am trying to avoid, if I should say that one steps into a past era when one sees all the other Dolmetsches dancing quaint, ancient steps of Sixteenth-Century dancing. One feels that the dance would go on even if there were no audience. That is where real drama begins, and where we leave what I have called, with odium, "theatricals." It is a dance, danced for the dance's sake, not a display. It is music that exists for the sake of being music, not for the sake of, as they say, producing an impression.

Of course there are other musicians working with this same ideal. I take Mr. Dolmetsch as perhaps a unique figure, as perhaps the one man who knows most definitely whither he is going, and why, and who has given most time to old music.

They tell me "everyone knows Dolmetsch who knows of old music, but not many people know of it." Is that sheer nonsense, or what is the fragment of truth or rumour upon which it is based? Why is it that the fine things always seem to go on in a corner? Is it a judgment on democracy? Is it that what has once been the pleasure of the many, of the pre-Cromwellian many,† has been

* *Vide* his *The Interpretation of the Music of the XVIIth and XVIIIth Centuries.*

† Mme. de Genlis notes the efforts of Charles II to restore the language of England after the Cromwellian squalor.

permanently swept out of life? Musical England? A wild man comes into my room and talks of piles of turquoises in a boat, a sort of shop-house-boat east of Cashmere. His talk is full of the colour of the Orient. Then I find he is living over an old-clothes shop in Bow. "And there they seem to play all sorts of instruments."

Is there a popular instinct for anything different from what my ex-landlord calls "the four-hour-touch"? Is it that the aristocracy, which ought to set the fashion, is too weakened and too unreal to perform the due functions of "aristocracy"? Is it that nature can, in fact, only produce a certain number of vortices? That the quattrocento shines out because the vortices of social power coincided with the vortices of creative intelligence? And that when these vortices do not coincide we have an age of "art in strange corners" and of great dullness among the quite rich? Is it that real democracy can only exist under feudal conditions, when no man fears to recognise creative skill in his neighbour?

[*1918*]

Medievalism (from "Cavalcanti"[1])

Safe may'st thou go my canzon whither thee pleaseth
Thou art so fair attired

Apart from the welcome given to or withheld from a fine performance, it seems to me that the vogue of Guido's canzone, *Donna mi Prega,* was due to causes not instantly apparent to the modern reader. I mean that it shows traces of a tone of thought no longer

[1] As published in *Make It New* (1934), but the essay as a whole must be dated 1910–1931. T.S.E.

considered dangerous, but that may have appeared about as sooth-
ing to the Florentine of A.D. 1290 as conversation about Tom
Paine, Marx, Lenin and Bucharin would to-day in a Methodist
bankers' board meeting in Memphis, Tenn.

The teaching of Aristotle had been banned in the University of
Paris in 1213. This prejudice had been worn down during the
century, but Guido shows, I think, no regard for anyone's preju-
dice. We may trace his ideas to Averroes, Avicenna; he does not
definitely proclaim any heresy, but he shows learnings toward not
only the proof by reason, but toward the proof by experiment. I do
not think that he swallowed Aquinas. It may be impossible to
prove that he had heard of Roger Bacon, but the whole canzone is
easier to understand if we suppose, or at least one finds, a con-
siderable interest in the speculation, that he had read Grosseteste
on the Generation of Light.

In all of which he shows himself much more "modern" than his
young friend Dante Alighieri, *qui était diablement dans les idées
reçues,* and whose shock is probably recorded in the passage of
Inferno X where he finds Guido's father and father-in-law paying
for their mental exertions. In general, one may conclude that the
conversation in the Cavalcanti-Uberti family was more stimulating
than that in Tuscan bourgeois and ecclesiastical circles of the
period.

My conclusions are based on the whole text of Guido, or at least
the serious part of the text, excluding rhymed letters, skits and
simple pastorals; the canzone by itself does not conclusively prove
my assertions.

II

The medieval Italian poets brought into poetry something which
had not been or not been in any so marked and developed degree
in the poetry of the troubadours. It is still more important for
anyone wishing to have well-balanced critical appreciation of
poetry in general to understand that this quality, or this assertion
of value, has not been in poetry *since;* and that the English "philo-
sophical" and other "philosophical" poets have not produced a
comparable *Ersatz.*

The Greek aesthetic would seem to consist wholly in plastic, or in plastic moving toward coitus, and limited by incest, which is the sole Greek taboo. This new thing in medieval work that concerns us has nothing to do with Christianity, which people both praise and blame for utterly irrelevant and unhistorical reasons. Erotic sentimentality we can find in Greek and Roman poets, and one may observe that the main trend of Provençal and Tuscan poets is not toward erotic sentimentality.

But they are not pagans, they are called pagans, and the troubadours are also accused of being Manichaeans, obviously because of a muddle somewhere. They are opposed to a form of stupidity not limited to Europe, that is, idiotic asceticism and a belief that the body is evil. This more or less masochistic and hell-breeding belief is always accompanied by bad and niggled sculpture (Angoulême or Bengal); Gandhi[2] to-day is incapable of making the dissociation that it is not the body but its diseases and infirmities which are evil. The same statement is true of mind: the infections of mind being no less hideous than those of physique. In fact, a man's toothache annoys himself, but a fool annoys the whole company. Even for epidemics, a few cranks may spread a wider malefaction than anything short of plague universal. This invention of hells for one's enemies, and mess, confusion in sculpture, is always symptomatic of supineness, bad hygiene, bad physique (possibly envy); even the diseases of mind, they do not try to cure as such, but devise hells to punish, not to heal, the individual sufferer.

Against these European Hindoos we find the "medieval clean line," as distinctive from medieval niggle. Byzantium gives us perhaps the best architecture, or at least the best inner structure, that we know, I mean for proportions, for ornament flat on the walls, and not bulging and bumping and indulging in bulbous excrescence. The lines for example of the Byzantine heritage in Sicily, from which the best "Romanesque," developing to St Hilaire in Poictiers; or if the term Romanesque has become too ambiguous through loose usage, let me say that there are medieval churches such as the cathedral at San Leo or San Zeno in Verona, and others of similar form which are simply the Byzantine minus riches. It is the bare wall that the Constantinopolitan would have had money enough to cover with gold mosaic.

[2] Possibly false attribution, i.e., in so far as it applied to Gandhi.

Perhaps out of a sand-swept country, the need of interior harmony. That is conjecture. Against this clean architecture, we find the niggly Angoulême, the architectural ornament of bigotry, superstition, and mess.

What is the difference between Provençe and Hellas? There is, let us grant, a line in Propertius about *ingenium nobis fecit*. But the subject is not greatly developed. I mean that Propertius remains mostly inside the classic world and the classic aesthetic, plastic to coitus. Plastic plus immediate satisfaction.

The whole break of Provençe with this world, and indeed the central theme of the troubadours, is the dogma that there is some proportion between the fine thing held in the mind, and the inferior thing ready for instant consumption.

Their freedom is not an attack on Christian prudery, because prudery is not a peculiarly Christian excrescence. There is plenty of prudery in Virgil, and also in Ovid, where rumour would less lead one to expect it.

I am labouring all this because I want to establish a disjunction as to the Tuscan aesthetic. The term metaphysic might be used if it were not so appallingly associated in people's minds with unsupportable conjecture and devastated terms of abstraction.

The Tuscan demands harmony in something more than the plastic. He declines to limit his aesthetic to the impact of light on the eye. It would be misleading to reduce his aesthetic to terms of music, or to distort the analysis of it by analogies to the art of sonority. Man shares plastic with the statue, sound does not require a human being to produce it. The bird, the phonograph, sing. Sound can be exteriorized as completely as plastic. There is the residue of perception, perception of something which requires a human being to produce it. Which even may require a certain individual to produce it. This really complicates the aesthetic. You deal with an interactive force: the *virtu* in short.

And dealing with it is not anti-life. It is not maiming, it is not curtailment. The senses at first seem to project for a few yards beyond the body. Effect of a decent climate where a man leaves his nerve-set open, or allows it to tune in to its ambience, rather than struggling, as a northern race has to for self-preservation, to guard the body from assaults of weather.

He declines, after a time, to limit reception to his solar plexus.

The whole thing has nothing to do with taboos and bigotries. It is more than the simple athleticism of the *mens sana in corpore sano*. The conception of the body as perfect instrument of the increasing intelligence pervades. The lack of this concept invalidates the whole of monastic thought. Dogmatic asceticism is obviously not essential to the perceptions of Guido's ballate.

Whether it is necessary to modernize or nordicize our terminology and call this "the aesthetic or interactive vasomotor magnetism in relation to the consciousness," I leave to the reader's own taste and sense of proportion. I am inclined to think that a habit of mind which insists upon, or even tends toward, such terminology somewhat takes the bloom off the peach.

Out of these fine perceptions, or subsequent to them, people say that the Quattrocento, or the sculpture of the Quattrocento, discovered "personality." All of which is perhaps rather vague. We might say: The best Egyptian sculpture is magnificent plastic; but its force comes from a non-plastic idea, i.e., the god is inside the statue.

I am not considering the merits of the matter, much less those merits as seen by a modern aesthetic purist. I am using historic method. The god is inside the stone, *vacuos exercet aera morsus*. The force is arrested, but there is never any question about its latency, about the force being the essential, and the rest "accidental" in the philosophic technical sense. The shape occurs.

There is hardly any debate about the Greek classical sculpture, to them it is the plastic that matters. In the case of the statue of the Etruscan Apollo at Villa Giulia (Rome) the "god is inside," but the psychology is merely that of an Hallowe'en pumpkin. It is a weak derivation of fear motive, strong in Mexican masks, but here reduced to the simple briskness of small boy amused at startling his grandma. This is a long way from Greek statues, in which "the face don't matter."

This sculpture with something inside, revives in the Quattrocento portrait bust. But the antecedents are in verbal manifestation.

Nobody can absorb the *poeti dei primi secoli* and then the paintings of the Uffizi without seeing the relation between them, Daniel, Ventadour, Guido, Sellaio, Botticelli, Ambrogio Praedis, Nic. del Cossa.

All these are clean, all without hell-obsession.

Certain virtues are established, and the neglect of them by later writers and artists is an impoverishment of their art. The stupidity of Rubens, the asinine nature of French court life from Henry IV to the end of it, the insistence on two dimensional treatment of life by certain modernists, do not constitute a progress. A dogma builds on vacuum, and is ultimately killed or modified by, or accommodated to knowledge, but values stay, and ignorant neglect of them answers no purpose.

Loss of values is due usually to lumping and to lack of dissociation. The disproved is thrown out, and the associated, or contemporarily established, goes temporarily with it.

"Durch Rafael ist das Madonnenideal Fleisch geworden," says Herr Springer, with perhaps an unintentional rhyme. Certainly the metamorphosis into carnal tissue becomes frequent and general somewhere about 1527. The people are corpus, corpuscular, but not in the strict sense "animate," it is no longer the body of air clothed in the body of fire; it no longer radiates, light no longer moves from the eye, there is a great deal of meat, shock absorbing, perhaps—at any rate absorbent. It has not even Greek marmoreal plastic to restrain it. The dinner scene is more frequently introduced, we have the characters in definite act of absorption; later they will be but stuffing for expensive upholsteries.

Long before that a change had begun in the poetry. The difference between Guido and Petrarch is not a mere difference in degree, it is a difference in kind.

There are certain things Petrarch does not know, cannot know. I am not postulating him as "to blame" for anything, or even finding analogy for his tone in post-Peruginian painting.

Leave all questions of any art save poetry. In that art the gulf between Petrarch's capacity and Guido's is the great gulf, not of degree, but of kind. In Guido the "figure," the strong metamorphic or "picturesque" expression is there with purpose to convey or to interpret a definite meaning. In Petrarch it is ornament, the prettiest ornament he could find, but not an irreplaceable ornament, or one that he couldn't have used just about as well somewhere else. In fact he very often does use it, and them, somewhere, and nearly everywhere, else, all over the place.

We appear to have lost the radiant world where one thought

cuts through another with clean edge, a world of moving energies
"mezzo oscuro rade," "risplende in sè perpetuale effecto," magne-
tisms that take form, that are seen, or that border the visible, the
matter of Dante's *paradiso,* the glass under water, the form that
seems a form seen in a mirror, these realities perceptible to the
sense, interacting, *"a lui si tiri"* untouched by the two maladies,
the Hebrew disease, the Hindoo disease, fanaticisms and excess
that produce Savonarola, asceticisms that produce fakirs, St Cle-
ment of Alexandria, with his prohibition of bathing by women.
The envy of dullards who, not having *"intelletto,"* blame the lack
of it on innocent muscles. For after asceticism, that is anti-flesh,
we get the asceticism that is anti-intelligence, that praises stupidity
as "simplicity," the cult of *naïveté.* To many people the term
"medieval" connotes only the two diseases. We must avoid these
unnecessary idea-clots. Between those diseases, existed the Medi-
terranean sanity. The *"section d'or,"* if that is what is meant, that
gave the churches like St Hilaire, San Zeno, the Duomo di
Modena, the clear lines and proportions. Not the pagan worship of
strength, nor the Greek perception of visual non-animate plastic, or
plastic in which the being animate was not the main and principal
quality, but this "harmony in the sentience" or harmony *of* the
sentient, where the thought has its demarcation, the substance its
virtu, where stupid men have not reduced all "energy" to un-
bounded undistinguished abstraction.

For the modern scientist energy has no borders, it is a shapeless
"mass" of force; even his capacity to differentiate it to a degree
never dreamed by the ancients has not led him to think of its shape
or even its loci. The rose that his magnet makes in the iron filings,
does not lead him to think of the force in botanic terms, or wish to
visualize that force as floral and extant (*ex stare*).

A medieval "natural philosopher" would find this modern world
full of enchantments, not only the light in the electric bulb, but the
thought of the current hidden in air and in wire would give him a
mind full of forms, *"Fuor di color"* or having their hyper-colours.
The medieval philosopher would probably have been unable to
think the electic world, and *not* think of it as a world of forms.
Perhaps algebra has queered our geometry. Even Bose with his
plant experiments seems intent on the plant's capacity to feel—not
on the plant idea, for the plant brain is obviously filled with, or is

one idea, an *idée fixe,* a persistent notion of pattern from which only cataclysm or a Burbank can shake it. Or possibly this will fall under the eye of a contemporary scientist of genius who will answer: But, damn you, that is exactly what we do feel; or under the eye of a painter who will answer: Confound you, you *ought* to find just that in my painting.

Treatise on Metre

I

I heard a fair lady sigh: "I wish someone would write a good treatise on prosody."

As she had been a famous actress of Ibsen, this was not simple dilettantism, but the sincere wish for something whereof the lack had been inconvenient. Apart from Dante's *De Vulgari Eloquio* I have encountered only one treatise on metric which has the slightest value. It is Italian and out of print, and has no sort of celebrity.

The confusion in the public mind has a very simple cause: the desire to get something for nothing or to learn an art without labour.

Fortunately or unfortunately, people CAN write stuff that passes for poetry, before they have studied music.

The question is extremely simple. Part of what a musician HAS to know is employed in writing with words; there are no special "laws" or "differences" in respect to *that part.* There is a great laxity or vagueness permitted the poet in regard to *pitch.* He may be as great a poet as Mr. Yeats and still think he doesn't know one note from another.

Mr. Yeats probably would distinguish between a *g* and a *b flat*, but he is happy to think that he doesn't, and he would certainly be incapable of whistling a simple melody in tune.

Nevertheless before writing a lyric he is apt to "get a chune* in his head."

He is very sensitive to a limited gamut of rhythms.

Rhythm is a form cut into TIME, as a design is determined SPACE.

A melody is a rhythm in which the pitch of each element is fixed by the composer.

(Pitch: the number of vibrations per second.)

I said to a brilliant composer** and pupil of Kodaly:

These people can't make a melody, they can't make a melody four bars long.

He roared in reply: Four bars, they can't make one TWO bars long!

Music is so badly taught that I don't suggest every intending poet should bury himself in a conservatory. The *Laurencie et Lavignac Encyclopédie de la Musique et Dictionnaire du Conservatoire*† has however an excellent section on Greek metric, better than one is likely to find in use in the Greek language department of your university.

In making a line of verse (and thence building the lines into passages) you have certain primal elements:

That is to say, you have the various "articulate sounds" of the language, of its alphabet, that is, and the various groups of letters in syllables.

These syllables have differing weights and durations

A. original weights and durations

* *ch*, Neo-Celtic for *t*   ** Tibor Serly   † Pub. Delagrave, Paris

B. weights and durations that seem naturally imposed on them
by the other syllable groups around them.

Those are the medium wherewith the poet cuts his design in
TIME.

If he hasn't a sense of time and of the different qualities of
sound, this design will be clumsy and uninteresting just as a bad
draughtsman's drawing will be without distinction.

The bad draughtsman is bad because he does not perceive space
and spatial relations, and cannot therefore deal with them.

The writer of bad verse is a bore because he does not perceive
time and time relations, and cannot therefore delimit them in an
interesting manner, by means of longer and shorter, heavier and
lighter syllables, and the varying qualities of sound inseparable
from the words of his speech.

He expects his faculty to descend from heaven? He expects to
train and control that faculty without the labour that even a
mediocre musician expends on qualifying to play fourth tin horn in
an orchestra, and the result is often, and quite justly, disesteemed
by serious members of his profession.

Symmetry or strophic forms naturally HAPPENED in lyric poetry
when a man was singing a long poem to a short melody which he
had to use over and over. There is no particular voodoo or sacro-
sanctity about symmetry. It is one of many devices, expedient some-
times, advantageous sometimes for certain effects.

It is hard to tell whether music has suffered more by being
taught than has verse-writing from having no teachers. Music in
the past century of shame and human degradation slumped in large
quantities down into a soggy mass of tone.

In general we may say that the deliquescence of instruction in
any art proceeds in this manner.

I.   A master invents a gadget, or procedure to perform a particular
function, or a limited set of functions.

Pupils adopt the gadget. Most of them use it less skilfully than

the master. The next genius may improve it, or he may cast it aside
for something more suited to his own aims.

II.   Then comes the paste-headed pedagogue or theorist and
proclaims the gadget a law, or rule.

III   Then a bureaucracy is endowed, and the pin-headed secre-
tariat attacks every new genius and every form of inventiveness for
not obeying the law, and for perceiving something the secretariat
does not.

The great savants ignore, quite often, the idiocies of the ruck of
the teaching profession. Friedrich Richter can proclaim that the
rules of counterpoint and harmony have nothing to do with
composition, Sauzay can throw up his hands and say that when
Bach composed he appears to have done so by a series of "proce-
dures" whereof the secret escapes us, the hard sense of the one,
and not altogether pathetic despair of the other have no appre-
ciable effect on the ten thousand calves led up for the yearly
stuffing.

Most arts attain their effects by using a fixed element and a
variable.
From the empiric angle: verse usually has some element roughly
fixed and some other that varies, but which element is to be fixed
and which vary, and to what degree, is the affair of the author.
Some poets have chosen the bump, as the boundary.
Some have chosen to mark out their course with repetition of
consonants; some with similar terminations of words. All this is a
matter of detail. You can make a purely empiric list of successful
manœuvres, you can compile a catalogue of your favourite poems.
But you cannot hand out a receipt for making a Mozartian melody
on the basis of take a crotchet, then a quaver, then a semi-quaver,
etc. . . .
You don't ask an art instructor to give you a recipe for making a
Leonardo da Vinci drawing.
Hence the extreme boredom caused by the usual professorial
documentation or the aspiring thesis on prosody.

The answer is:

LISTEN to the sound that it makes.

I I

The reader who has understood the first part of this chapter has no need of reading the second. Nothing is more boring than an account of errors one has not committed.

Rhythm is a form cut into time.

. . . . . .

The perception that the mind, either of an individual or a nation can decay, and give off all the displeasing vapours of decomposition has unfortunately gone into desuetude. Dante's hell was of those who had lost the increment of intelligence with the capital. Shakespeare, already refining the tough old Catholic concept, refers to ignorance merely as darkness.

From the time Thos. Jefferson jotted down an amateur's notes on what seemed to be the current practice of English versification, the general knowledge, especially among hacks, appears to have diminished to zero, and to have passed into infinite negative. I suppose the known maxima occurred in the *North American Review* during Col. Harvey's intumescence. During that era when the directing minds and characters in America had reached a cellarage only to be gazed at across the barriers of libel law, the said editorial bureau rebuked some alliterative verse on the grounds that a consonant had been repeated despite Tennyson's warning.

A parallel occurs in a recent professorial censure of Mr. Binyon's *Inferno*, the censor being, apparently, in utter ignorance of the nature of Italian syllabic verse, which is composed of various syllabic groups, and not merely strung along with a swat on syllables two, four, six, eight, ten of each line.

You would not expect to create a Mozartian melody or a Bach theme by the process of bumping alternate notes, or by merely alternating quavers and crotchets.

Great obfuscation spread from the failure to dissociate heavy accent and duration.

Other professors failed to comprehend the "regularity" of classic hexameter.

So called dactylic hexameter does NOT start from ONE type of verse.

There are, mathematically, sixty-four basic general forms of it; of which twenty or thirty were probably found to be of most general use, and several of which would probably have been stunts or rarities.

But this takes no count either of shifting caesura (pause at some point in the line), nor does it count any of the various shadings.

It ought to be clear that the variety starting FROM a colony of sixty-four different general rhythm shapes, or archetypes, will be vastly more compendious, will naturally accommodate a vastly greater amount of real speech, than will a set of variants starting from a single type of line, whether measured by duration or by the alternating heaviness of syllables,

> specifically:
> ti tum ti tum ti tum ti tum ti tum

from which every departure is treated as an exception.

The legal number of syllables in a classic hexameter varied from twelve to eighteen.

When the Greek dramatists developed or proceeded from anterior Greek prosody, they arrived at chorus forms which are to all extents "free," though a superstructure of nomenclature has been gummed on to them by analysers whom neither Aeschylus nor Euripides would ever have bothered to read.

These nomenclatures were probably invented by people who had never LISTENED to verse, and who probably wouldn't have been able to distinguish Dante's movement from Milton's had they heard it read out aloud.

I believe Shakespeare's "blank verse" runs from ten to seventeen syllables, but have no intention of trying to count it again, or make a census.

None of these professorial pint pots has anything to do with the question.

Homer did not start by thinking which of the sixty-four permitted formulae was to be used in his next verse.

THE STROPHE

The reason for strophic form has already been stated. The mediaeval tune, obviously, demanded an approximately even number of syllables in each strophe, but as the duration of the notes was not strictly marked, the tune itself was probably subject to variation within limits. These limits were in each case established by the auditive precision of the troubadour himself.

In Flaubert's phrase: *"Pige moi le type!"* Find me the guy that will set out with sixty-four general matrices for rhythm and having nothing to say, or more especially nothing germane or kindred to the original urge which created those matrices, and who will therewith utter eternal minstrelsy, or keep the reader awake.

As in the case of Prof. Wubb or whatever his name was, the ignorant of one generation set out to make laws, and gullible children next try to obey them.

III

The populace loved the man who said "Look into thine owne hearte and write" or approved Uc St. Circ, or whoever it was who recorded: "He made songs because he had a will to make songs and not because love moved him thereto. And nobody paid much attention to either him or his poetry."

All of which is an infinite remove from the superstition that poetry isn't an art, or that prosody isn't an art WITH LAWS.

But like the laws of any art they are not laws to be learnt by rule of thumb. *"La sculpture n'est pas pour les jeunes hommes,"* said Brancusi. Hokusai and Chaucer have borne similar witness.

Pretended treatises giving recipes for metric are as silly as would be a book giving you measurements for producing a masterpiece à la Botticelli.

Proportion, laws of proportion. Pier della Francesca having thought longer, knew more than painters who have not taken the trouble.

"La section d'or"* certainly helped master architects. But you learn painting by eye, not by algebra. Prosody and melody are attained by the listening ear, not by an index of nomenclatures, or by learning that such and such a foot is called spondee. Give your draughtsman sixty-four stencils of "Botticelli's most usual curves"? And he will make you a masterpiece?

Beyond which we will never recover the art of *writing to be sung* until we begin to pay some attention to the sequence, or scale, of vowels in the line, and of the vowels terminating the group of lines in a series.

* Traditions of architectural proportion.

D. H. LAWRENCE

Preface to the American Edition
of *New Poems*

―――――――――

It seems when we hear a skylark singing as if sound were running forward into the future, running so fast and utterly without consideration, straight on into futurity. And when we hear a nightingale, we hear the pause and the rich, piercing rhythm of recollection, the perfected past. The lark may sound sad, but with the lovely lapsing sadness that is almost a swoon of hope. The nightingale's triumph is a pæan, but a death-pæan.

So it is with poetry. Poetry is, as a rule, either the voice of the far future, exquisite and ethereal, or it is the voice of the past, rich, magnificent. When the Greeks heard the *Iliad* and the *Odyssey,* they heard their own past calling in their hearts, as men far inland sometimes hear the sea and fall weak with powerful, wonderful regret, nostalgia; or else their own future rippled its time-beats through their blood, as they followed the painful, glamorous progress of the Ithacan. This was Homer to the Greeks: their Past, splendid with battles won and death achieved, and their Future, the magic wandering of Ulysses through the unknown.

With us it is the same. Our birds sing on the horizons. They sing out of the blue, beyond us, or out of the quenched night. They sing at dawn and sunset. Only the poor, shrill, tame canaries whistle while we talk. The wild birds begin before we are awake, or as we drop into dimness, out of waking. Our poets sit by the gateways, some by the east, some by the west. As we arrive and as we go out our hearts surge with response. But whilst we are in the midst of life, we do not hear them.

The poetry of the beginning and the poetry of the end must have that exquisite finality, perfection which belongs to all that is far off. It is in the realm of all that is perfect. It is of the nature of all that is complete and consummate. This completeness, this consummateness, the finality and the perfection are conveyed in exquisite form: the perfect symmetry, the rhythm which returns upon itself like a dance where the hands link and loosen and link for the supreme moment of the end. Perfected bygone moments, perfected moments in the glimmering futurity, these are the treasured gemlike lyrics of Shelley and Keats.

But there is another kind of poetry: the poetry of that which is at hand: the immediate present. In the immediate present there is no perfection, no consummation, nothing finished. The strands are all flying, quivering, intermingling into the web, the waters are shaking the moon. There is no round, consummate moon on the face of running water, nor on the face of the unfinished tide. There are no gems of the living plasm. The living plasm vibrates unspeakably, it inhales the future, it exhales the past, it is the quick of both, and yet it is neither. There is no plasmic finality, nothing crystal, permanent. If we try to fix the living tissue, as the biologists fix it with formation, we have only a hardened bit of the past, the bygone life under our observation.

Life, the ever-present, knows no finality, no finished crystallisation. The perfect rose is only a running flame, emerging and flowing off, and never in any sense at rest, static, finished. Herein lies its transcendent loveliness. The whole tide of all life and all time suddenly heaves, and appears before us as an apparition, a revelation. We look at the very white quick of nascent creation. A water-lily heaves herself from the flood, looks around, gleams, and is gone. We have seen the incarnation, the quick of the ever-swirling flood. We have seen the invisible. We have seen, we have touched, we have partaken of the very substance of creative change, creative mutation. If you tell me about the lotus, tell me of nothing changeless or eternal. Tell me of the mystery of the inexhaustible, forever-unfolding creative spark. Tell me of the incarnate disclosure of the flux, mutation in blossom, laughter and decay perfectly open in their transit, nude in their movement before us.

Let me feel the mud and the heavens in my lotus. Let me feel the heavy, silting, sucking mud, the spinning of sky winds. Let me feel them both in purest contact, the nakedness of sucking weight, nakedly passing radiance. Give me nothing fixed, set, static. Don't give me the infinite or the eternal: nothing of infinity, nothing of eternity. Give me the still, white seething, the incandescence and the coldness of the incarnate moment: the moment, the quick of all change and haste and opposition: the moment, the immediate present, the Now. The immediate moment is not a drop of water running downstream. It is the source and issue, the bubbling up of the stream. Here, in this very instant moment, up bubbles the stream of time, out of the wells of futurity, flowing on to the oceans of the past. The source, the issue, the creative quick.

There is poetry of this immediate present, instant poetry, as well as poetry of the infinite past and the infinite future. The seething poetry of the incarnate Now is supreme, beyond even the everlasting gems of the before and after. In its quivering momentaneity it surpasses the crystalline, pearl-hard jewels, the poems of the eternities. Do not ask for the qualities of the unfading timeless gems. Ask for the whiteness which is the seethe of mud, ask for that incipient putrescence which is the skies falling, ask for the never-pausing, never-ceasing life itself. There must be mutation, swifter than iridescence, haste, not rest, come-and-go, not fixity, inconclusiveness, immediacy, the quality of life itself, without dénouement or close. There must be the rapid momentaneous association of things which meet and pass on the for ever incalculable journey of creation: everything left in its own rapid, fluid relationship with the rest of things.

This is the unrestful, ungraspable poetry of the sheer present, poetry whose very permanency lies in its wind-like transit. Whitman's is the best poetry of this kind. Without beginning and without end, without any base and pediment, it sweeps past for ever, like a wind that is forever in passage, and unchainable. Whitman truly looked before and after. But he did not sigh for what is not. The clue to all his utterance lies in the sheer appreciation of the instant moment, life surging itself into utterance at its very wellhead. Eternity is only an abstraction from the actual present. Infinity is only a great reservoir of recollection, or a reservoir of aspiration: man-made. The quivering nimble hour of the present, this is the quick of Time. This is the immanence. The quick of the universe is the *pulsating, carnal self,* mysterious and palpable. So it is always.

Because Whitman put this into his poetry, we fear him and respect him so profoundly. We should not fear him if he sang only of the "old unhappy far-off things," or of the "wings of the morning." It is because his heart beats with the urgent, insurgent Now, which is even upon us all, that we dread him. He is so near the quick.

From the foregoing it is obvious that the poetry of the instant present cannot have the same body or the same motion as the poetry of the before and after. It can never submit to the same conditions. It is never finished. There is no rhythm which returns upon itself, no serpent of eternity with its tail in its own mouth. There is no static perfection, none of that finality which we find so satisfying because we are so frightened.

Much has been written about free verse. But all that can be said, first and last, is that free verse is, or should be direct utterance from the instant, whole man. It is the soul and the mind and body surging at once, nothing left out. They speak all together. There is some confusion, some discord. But the confusion and the discord only belong to the reality, as noise belongs to the plunge of water. It is no use inventing fancy laws for free verse, no use drawing a melodic line which all the feet must toe. Free verse toes no melodic line, no matter what drill-sergeant. Whitman pruned away his clichés—perhaps his clichés of rhythm as well as of phrase. And this is about all we can do, deliberately, with free verse. We can get rid of the sterotyped movements and the old hackneyed associations of sound or sense. We can break down those artificial conduits and canals through which we do so love to force our utterance. We can break the stiff neck of habit. We can be in ourselves spontaneous and flexible as flame, we can see that utterance rushes out without artificial form or artificial smoothness. But we cannot positively prescribe any motion, any rhythm. All the laws we invent or discover—it amounts to pretty much the same—will fail to apply to free verse. They will only apply to some form of restricted, limited unfree verse.

All we can say is that free verse does *not* have the same nature as restricted verse. It is not of the nature of reminiscence. It is not the past which we treasure in its perfection between our hands.

Neither is it the crystal of the perfect future, into which we gaze. Its tide is neither the full, yearning flow of aspiration, nor the sweet, poignant ebb of remembrance and regret. The past and the future are the two great bournes of human emotion, the two great homes of the human days, the two eternities. They are both conclusive, final. Their beauty is the beauty of the goal, finished, perfected. Finished beauty and measured symmetry belong to the stable, unchanging eternities.

But in free verse we look for the insurgent naked throb of the instant moment. To break the lovely form of metrical verse, and to dish up the fragments as a new substance, called *vers libre,* this is what most of the free-versifiers accomplish. They do not know that free verse has its own *nature,* that it is neither star nor pearl, but instantaneous like plasm. It has no goal in either eternity. It has no finish. It has no satisfying stability, satisfying to those who like the immutable. None of this. It is the instant; the quick; the very jetting source of all will-be and has-been. The utterance is like a spasm, naked contact with all influences at once. It does not want to get anywhere. It just takes place.

For such utterance any externally applied law would be mere shackles and death. The law must come new each time from within. The bird is on the wing in the winds, flexible to every breath, a living spark in the storm, its very flickering depending upon its supreme mutability and power of change. Whence such a bird came: whither it goes: from what solid earth it rose up, and upon what solid earth it will close its wings and settle, this is not the question. This is a question of before and after. Now, *now,* the bird is on the wing in the winds.

Such is the rare new poetry. One realm we have never conquered: the pure present. One great mystery of time is terra incognita to us: the instant. The most superb mystery we have hardly recognized: the immediate, instant self. The quick of all time is the instant. The quick of all the universe, of all creation, is the incarnate, carnal self. Poetry gave us the clue: free verse: Whitman. Now we know.

The ideal—what is the ideal? A figment. An abstraction. A static abstraction, abstracted from life. It is a fragment of the before or the after. It is a crystallised aspiration, or a crystallised remembrance: crystallised, set, finished. It is a thing set apart, in the great storehouse of eternity, the storehouse of finished things.

We do not speak of things crystallised and set apart. We speak of the instant, the immediate self, the very plasm of the self. We speak also of free verse.

All this should have come as a preface to *Look! We Have Come Through!* But is it not better to publish a preface long after the book it belongs to has appeared? For then the reader will have had his fair chance with the book, alone.

Pangbourne, 1919

HART CRANE

General Aims and Theories

When I started writing "Faustus & Helen" it was my intention to embody in modern terms (words, symbols, metaphors) a contemporary approximation to an ancient human culture or mythology that seems to have been obscured rather than illumined with the frequency of poetic allusions made to it during the last century. The name of Helen, for instance, has become an all-too-easily employed crutch for evocation whenever a poet felt a stitch in his side. The real evocation of this (to me) very real and absolute conception of beauty seemed to consist in a reconstruction in these modern terms of the basic emotional attitude toward beauty that the Greeks had. And in so doing I found that I was really building a bridge between so-called classic experience and many divergent realities of our seething, confused cosmos of today, which has no formulated mythology yet for classic poetic reference or for religious exploitation.

So I found "Helen" sitting in a street car; the Dionysian revels of her court and her seduction were transferred to a Metropolitan roof garden with a jazz orchestra; and the *katharsis* of the fall of Troy I saw approximated in the recent World War. The importance of this scaffolding may easily be exaggerated, but it gave me a series of correspondences between two widely separated worlds on which to sound some major themes of human speculation—love, beauty, death, renascence. It was a kind of grafting process that I shall doubtless not be interested in repeating, but which is consistent with subsequent theories of mine on the relation of tradition to the contemporary creating imagination.

It is a terrific problem that faces the poet today—a world that is so in transition from a decayed culture toward a reorganization of human evaluations that there are few common terms, general denominators of speech that are solid enough or that ring with any vibration or spiritual conviction. The great mythologies of the past (including the Church) are deprived of enough façade to even launch good raillery against. Yet much of their traditions are operative still—in millions of chance combinations of related and unrelated detail, psychological reference, figures of speech, precepts, etc. These are all a part of our common experience and the terms, at least partially, of that very experience when it defines or extends itself.

The deliberate program, then, of a "break" with the past or tradition seems to me to be a sentimental fallacy. . . . The poet has a right to draw on whatever practical resources he finds in books or otherwise about him. He must tax his sensibility and his touchstone of experience for the proper selections of these themes and details, however—and that is where he either stands, or falls into useless archeology.

I put no particular value on the simple objective of "modernity." The element of the temporal location of an artist's creation is of very secondary importance; it can be left to the impressionist or historian just as well. It seems to me that a poet will accidentally define his time well enough simply by reacting honestly and to the full extent of his sensibilities to the states of passion, experience and rumination that fate forces on him, first hand. He must, of course, have a sufficiently universal basis of experience to make his imagination selective and valuable. His picture of the "period," then, will simply be a by-product of his curiosity and the relation of his experience to a postulated "eternity."

I am concerned with the future of America, but not because I think that America has any so-called par value as a state or as a group of people. . . . It is only because I feel persuaded that here are destined to be discovered certain as yet undefined spiritual quantities, perhaps a new hierarchy of faith not to be developed so completely elsewhere. And in this process I like to feel myself as a potential factor; certainly I must speak in its terms and what discoveries I may make are situated in its experience.

But to fool one's self that definitions are being reached by merely referring frequently to skyscrapers, radio antennae, steam whistles, or other surface phenomena of our time is merely to paint a photograph. I think that what is interesting and significant will emerge only under the conditions of our submission to, and examination and assimilation of the organic effects on us of these and other fundamental factors of our experience. It can certainly not be an organic expression otherwise. And the expression of such values may often be as well accomplished with the vocabulary and blank verse of the Elizabethans as with the calligraphic tricks and slang used so brilliantly at times by an impressionist like Cummings.

It may not be possible to say that there is, strictly speaking, any "absolute" experience. But it seems evident that certain aesthetic experience (and this may for a time engross the total faculties of the spectator) can be called absolute, inasmuch as it approximates a formally convincing statement of a conception or apprehension of life that gains our unquestioning assent, and under the conditions of which our imagination is unable to suggest a further detail consistent with the design of the aesthetic whole.

I have been called an "absolutist" in poetry, and if I am to welcome such a label it should be under the terms of the above definition. It is really only a *modus operandi,* however, and as such has been used organically before by at least a dozen poets such as Donne, Blake, Baudelaire, Rimbaud, etc. I may succeed in defining it better by contrasting it with the impressionistic method. The impressionist is interesting as far as he goes—but his goal has been reached when he has succeeded in projecting certain selected factual details into his reader's consciousness. He is really not interested in the *causes* (metaphysical) of his materials, their emotional derivations or their utmost spiritual consequences. A kind of retinal registration is enough, along with a certain psychological stimulation. And this is also true of your realist (of the Zola type), and to a certain extent of the classicist, like Horace, Ovid, Pope, etc.

Blake meant these differences when he wrote:

We are led to believe in a lie
When we see *with* not *through* the eye.

The impressionist creates only with the eye and for the readiest surface of the consciousness, at least relatively so. If the effect has been harmonious or even stimulating, he can stop there, relinquishing entirely to his audience the problematic synthesis of the details into terms of their own personal consciousness.

It is my hope to go *through* the combined materials of the poem, using our "real" world somewhat as a spring-board, and to give the poem *as a whole* an orbit or predetermined direction of its own. I would like to establish it as free from my own personality as from any chance evaluation on the reader's part. (This is, of course, an impossibility, but it is a characteristic worth mentioning.) Such a poem is at least a stab at a truth, and to such an extent may be differentiated from other kinds of poetry and called "absolute." Its evocation will not be toward decoration or amusement, but rather toward a state of consciousness, an "innocence" (Blake) or absolute beauty. In this condition there may be discoverable under new forms certain spiritual illuminations, shining with a morality essentialized from experience directly, and not from previous precepts or preconceptions. It is as though a poem gave the reader as he left it a single, new *word,* never before spoken and impossible to actually enunciate, but self-evident as an active principle in the reader's consciousness henceforward.

As to technical considerations: the motivation of the poem must be derived from the implicit emotional dynamics of the materials used, and the terms of expression employed are often selected less for their logical (literal) significance than for their associational meanings. Via this and their metaphorical inter-relationships, the entire construction of the poem is raised on the organic principle of a "logic of metaphor," which antedates our so-called pure logic, and which is the genetic basis of all speech, hence consciousness and thought-extension.

These dynamics often result, I'm told, in certain initial difficulties in understanding my poems. But on the other hand I find them at times the only means possible for expressing certain concepts in any forceful or direct way whatever. To cite two examples:—when, in "Voyages" (II), I speak of "adagios of islands," the reference is to the motion of a boat through islands clustered thickly, the rhythm of the motion, etc. And it seems a much more direct and creative statement than any more logical employment of words such as "coasting slowly through the islands," besides ushering in a whole world of music. Similarly in

"Faustus and Helen" (III), the speed and tense altitude of an aeroplane are much better suggested by the idea of "nimble blue plateaus"—*implying* the aeroplane and its speed against a contrast of stationary elevated earth. Although the statement is pseudo in relation to formal logic—it *is* completely logical in relation to the truth of the imagination, and there is expressed a concept of speed and space that could not be handled so well in other terms.

In manipulating the more imponderable phenomena of psychic motives, pure emotional crystallizations, etc. I have had to rely even more on these dynamics of inferential mention, and I am doubtless still very unconscious of having committed myself to what seems nothing but obscurities to some minds. A poem like "Possessions" really cannot be technically explained. It must rely (even to a large extent with myself) on its organic impact on the imagination to successfully imply its meaning. This seems to me to present an exceptionally difficult problem, however, considering the real clarity and consistent logic of many of the other poems.

I know that I run the risk of much criticism by defending such theories as I have, but as it is part of a poet's business to risk not only criticism—but folly—in the conquest of consciousness I can only say that I attach no intrinsic value to what means I use beyond their practical service in giving form to the living stuff of the imagination.

New conditions of life germinate new forms of spiritual articulation. And while I feel that my work includes a more consistent extension of traditional literary elements than many contemporary poets are capable of appraising, I realize that I am utilizing the gifts of the past as instruments principally; and that the voice of the present, if it is to be known, must be caught at the risk of speaking in idioms and circumlocutions sometimes shocking to the scholar and historians of logic. Language has built towers and bridges, but itself is inevitably as fluid as always.

[*1925*]

Hart Crane to Harriet Monroe

Your good nature and manifest interest in writing me about the obscurities apparent in my Melville poem certainly prompt a wish to clarify my intentions in that poem as much as possible. But I realize that my explanations will not be very convincing. For a paraphrase is generally a poor substitute for any organized conception that one has fancied he has put into the more essentialized form of the poem itself.

At any rate, and though I imagine us to have considerable differences of opinion regarding the relationship of poetic metaphor to ordinary logic (I judge this from the angle of approach you use toward portions of the poem), I hope my answers will not be taken as a defense of merely certain faulty lines. I am really much more interested in certain theories of metaphor and technique involved generally in poetics, than I am concerned in vindicating any particular perpetrations of my own.

My poem may well be elliptical and actually obscure in the ordering of its content, but in your criticism of this very possible deficiency you have stated your objections in terms that allow me, at least for the moment, the privilege of claiming your ideas and ideals as theoretically, at least, quite outside the issues of my own aspirations. To put it more plainly, as a poet I may very possibly be more interested in the so-called illogical impingements of the connotations of words on the consciousness (and their combinations and interplay in metaphor on this basis) than I am interested in the preservation of their logically rigid significations at the cost of limiting my subject matter and perceptions involved in the poem.

This may sound as though I merely fancied juggling words and images until I found something novel, or esoteric; but the process

is much more predetermined and objectified than that. The
nuances of feeling and observation in a poem may well call for
certain liberties which you claim the poet has no right to take. I
am simply making the claim that the poet does have that authority,
and that to deny it is to limit the scope of the medium so consider-
ably as to outlaw some of the richest genius of the past.

This argument over the dynamics of metaphor promises as
active a future as has been evinced in the past. Partaking so exten-
sively as it does of the issues involved in the propriety or non-
propriety of certain attitudes toward subject matter, etc., it enters
the critical distinctions usually made between "romantic" [and]
"classic" as an organic factor. It is a problem that would require
many pages to state adequately—merely from my own limited
standpoint on the issues. Even this limited statement may prove
onerous reading, and I hope you will pardon me if my own interest
in the matter carries me to the point of presumption.

Its paradox, of course, is that its apparent illogic operates so
logically in conjunction with its context in the poem as to establish
its claim to another logic, quite independent of the original defini-
tion of the word or phrase or image thus employed. It implies (this
inflection of language) a previous or unprepared receptivity to its
stimulus on the part of the reader. The reader's sensibility simply
responds by identifying this inflection of experience with some
event in his own history or perceptions—or rejects it altogether.
The logic of metaphor is so organically entrenched in pure sensibil-
ity that it can't be thoroughly traced or explained outside of
historical sciences, like philology and anthropology. This "pseudo-
statement," Richards calls it in an admirable essay touching our
contentions in last July's *Criterion,* demands completely other
faculties of recognition than the pure rationalistic associations
permit. Much fine poetry may be completely rationalistic in its use
of symbols, but there is much great poetry of another order which
will yield the reader very little when inspected under the limitation
of such arbitrary concerns as are manifested in your judgment of
the Melville poem, especially when you constitute such require-
ments of ordinary logical relationship between word and word as
irreducible.

I don't wish to enter here defense of the particular symbols
employed in my own poem, because, as I said, I may well have

failed to supply the necessary emotional connectives to the content featured. But I would like to counter a question or so of yours with a similar question. Here the poem is less dubious in quality than my own, and as far as the abstract pertinacity of question and its immediate consequences are concerned the point I'm arguing about can be better demonstrated. Both quotations are familiar to you, I'm sure.

You ask me how a *portent* can possibly be wound in a *shell.* Without attempting to answer this for the moment, I ask you how Blake could possibly say that "a *sigh* is a *sword* of an Angel King." You ask me how *compass, quadrant and sextant "contrive"* tides. I ask you how Eliot can possibly believe that "Every street *lamp* that I pass *beats* like a fatalistic *drum!"* Both of my metaphors may fall down completely. I'm not defending their actual value in themselves; but your criticism of them in each case was leveled at an illogicality of relationship between symbols, which similar fault you must have either overlooked in case you have ever admired the Blake and Eliot lines, or have there condoned them on account of some more ultimate convictions pressed on you by the impact of the poems in their entirety.

It all comes to the recognition that emotional dynamics are not to be confused with any absolute order of rationalized definitions; ergo, in poetry the *rationale* of metaphor belongs to another order of experience than science, and is not to be limited by a scientific and arbitrary code of relationships either in verbal inflections or concepts.

There are plenty of people who have never accumulated a sufficient series of reflections (and these of a rather special nature) to perceive the relation between a *drum* and a *street lamp*—*via* the *unmentioned* throbbing of the heart and nerves in a distraught man which *tacitly* creates the reason and "logic" of the Eliot metaphor. They will always have a perfect justification for ignoring those lines and to claim them obscure, excessive, etc., until by some experience of their own the words accumulate the necessary connotations to complete their connection. It is the same with the "patient etherized upon a table," isn't it? Surely that line must lack all eloquence to many people who, for instance, would delight in agreeing that the sky was like a dome of many-colored glass.

If one can count on some such bases in the reader now and

then, I don't see how the poet has any chance to ever get beyond the simplest conceptions of emotion and thought, of sensation and lyrical sequence. If the poet is to be held completely to the already evolved and exploited sequences of imagery and logic—what field of added consciousness and increased perceptions (the actual province of poetry, if not lullabyes) can be expected when one has to relatively return to the alphabet every breath or so? In the minds of people who have sensitively read, seen, and experienced a great deal, isn't there a terminology something like short-hand as compared to usual description and dialectics, which the artist ought to be right in trusting as a reasonable connective agent toward fresh concepts, more inclusive evaluations? The question is more important to me than it perhaps ought to be; but as long as poetry is written, an audience, however small, is implied, and there remains the question of an active or an inactive imagination as its characteristic.

It is of course understood that a street-lamp simply can't beat with a sound like a drum; but it often happens that images, themselves totally dissociated, when joined in the circuit of a particular emotion located with specific relation to both of them, conduce to great vividness and accuracy of statement in defining that emotion.

Not to rant on forever, I'll beg your indulgence and come at once to the explanations you requested on the Melville poem:

> The dice of drowned men's bones he saw bequeath
> An embassy.

Dice bequeath an embassy, in the first place, by being ground (in this connection only, of course) in little cubes from the bones of drowned men by the action of the sea, and are finally thrown up on the sand, having "numbers" but no identification. These being the bones of dead men who never completed their voyage, it seems legitimate to refer to them as the only surviving evidence of certain messages undelivered, mute evidence of certain things, experiences that the dead mariners might have had to deliver. Dice as a symbol of chance and circumstance is also implied.

> The calyx of death's bounty giving back, *etc*.

This calyx refers in a double ironic sense both to a cornucopia and the vortex made by a sinking vessel. As soon as the water has closed over a ship, this whirlpool sends up broken spars, wreckage, etc., which can be alluded to as livid *hieroglyphs,* making a *scattered chapter* so far as any complete record of the recent ship and her crew is concerned. In fact, about as much definite knowledge might come from all this as anyone might gain from the roar of his own veins, which is easily heard (haven't you ever done it?) by holding a shell close to one's ear.

Frosted eyes lift altars

Refers simply to a conviction that a man, not knowing perhaps a definite god yet being endowed with a reverence for deity—such a man naturally postulates a deity somehow, and the altar of that deity by the very *action* of the eyes *lifted* in searching.

> Compass, quadrant and sextant contrive
> No farther tides . . .

Hasn't it often occurred that instruments originally invented for record and computation have inadvertently so extended the concepts of the entity they were invented to measure (concepts of space, etc.) in the mind and imagination that employed them, that they may metaphorically be said to have extended the original boundaries of the entity measured? This little bit of "relativity" ought not to be discredited in poetry now that scientists are proceeding to measure the universe on principles of pure *ratio,* quite as metaphorical, so far as previous standards of scientific methods extended, as some of the axioms in Job.

I may have completely failed to provide any clear interpretation of these symbols in their context. And you will no doubt feel that I have rather heatedly explained them for anyone who professes no claims for their particular value. I hope, at any rate, that I have clarified them enough to suppress any suspicion that their obscurity derives from a lack of definite intentions in the subject-matter of the poem. The execution is another matter, and you must be accorded a superior judgment to mine in that regard.

[1926]

Hart Crane to Otto H. Kahn

Patterson, New York
September 12th 1927

Dear Mr. Kahn:

I am taking for granted your continued interest in the progress of *The Bridge,* in which I am still absorbed, and which has reached a stage where its general outline is clearly evident. The Dedication (recently published in *The Dial*) and Part I (now in *The American Caravan*) you have already seen, but as you may not have them presently at hand I am including them in a ms. of the whole, to date, which I am sending you under separate cover.

At the risk of complicating your appreciation of Part II ("Powhatan's Daughter"), I nevertheless feel impelled to mention a few of my deliberate intentions in this part of the poem, and to give some description of my general method of construction. Powhatan's daughter, or Pocahontas, is the mythological nature-symbol chosen to represent the physical body of the continent, or the soil. She here takes on much the same role as the traditional Hertha of ancient Teutonic mythology. The five sub-sections of Part II are mainly concerned with a gradual exploration of this "body" whose first possessor was the Indian. It seemed altogether ineffective from the poetic standpoint to approach this material from the purely chronological angle—beginning with, say, the landing of "The Mayflower," continuing with a résumé of the Revolution through the conquest of the West, etc. One can get that viewpoint in any history primer. What I am after is an assimilation of this experience, a more organic panorama, showing the continuous and living evidence of the past in the inmost vital substance of the present.

Consequently I jump from the monologue of Columbus in "Ave

Maria"—right across the four intervening centuries—into the harbor of 20th-century Manhattan. And from that point in time and place I begin to work backward through the pioneer period, always in terms of the present—finally to the very core of the nature-world of the Indian. What I am really handling, you see, is the Myth of America. Thousands of strands have had to be searched for, sorted and interwoven. In a sense I have had to do a great deal of pioneering myself. It has taken a great deal of energy—which has not been so difficult to summon as the necessary patience to wait, simply wait much of the time—until my instincts assured me that I had assembled my materials in proper order for a final welding into their natural form. For each section of the entire poem has presented its own unique problem of form, not alone in relation to the materials embodied within its separate confines, but also in relation to the other parts, *in series,* of the major design of the entire poem. Each is a separate canvas, as it were, yet none yields its entire significance when seen apart from the others. One might take the Sistine Chapel as an analogy. It might be better to read the following notes *after* rather than *before* your reading of the ms. They are not necessary for an understanding of the poem, but I think they may prove interesting to you as a commentary on my architectural method.

1. "The Harbor Dawn":

Here the movement of the verse is in considerable contrast to that of the "Ave Maria," with its sea-swell crescendo and the climacteric vision of Columbus. This legato, in which images blur as objects only half apprehended on the border of sleep and consciousness, makes an admirable transition between the intervening centuries.

The love-motif (in italics) carries along a symbolism of the life and ages of man (here the sowing of the seed) which is further developed in each of the subsequent sections of "Powhatan's Daughter," though it is never particularly stressed. In 2 ("Van Winkle") it is Childhood; in 3 it is Youth; in 4, Manhood; in 5 it is Age. This motif is interwoven and tends to be implicit in the imagery rather than anywhere stressed.

2. "Van Winkle":

The protagonist has left the room with its harbor sounds, and is walking to the subway. The rhythm is quickened; it is a transition

between sleep and the immanent tasks of the day. Space is filled
with the music of a hand organ and fresh sunlight, and one has the
impression of the whole continent—from Atlantic to Pacific—
freshly arisen and moving. The walk to the subway arouses remi-
niscences of childhood, also the "childhood" of the continental
conquest, viz., the conquistadores, Priscilla, Capt. John Smith, etc.
These parallelisms unite in the figure of Rip Van Winkle who
finally becomes identified with the protagonist, as you will notice,
and who really boards the subway with the reader. He becomes the
"guardian angel" of the journey into the past.

3. "The River":

The subway is simply a figurative, psychological "vehicle" for
transporting the reader to the Middle West. He lands on the rail-
road tracks in the company of several tramps in the twilight. The
extravagance of the first twenty-three lines of this section is an
intentional burlesque on the cultural confusion of the present—a
great conglomeration of noises analogous to the strident impres-
sion of a fast express rushing by. The rhythm is jazz.

Thenceforward the rhythm settles down to a steady pedestrian
gait, like that of wanderers plodding along. My tramps are psycho-
logical vehicles, also. Their wanderings as you will notice, carry
the reader into interior after interior, finally to the great River.
They are the left-overs of the pioneers in at least this respect—that
their wanderings carry the reader through an experience parallel to
that of Boone and others. I think [I] have caught some of the
essential spirit of the Great Valley here, and in the process have
approached the primal world of the Indian, which emerges with a
full orchestra in the succeeding dance.

5.[4] "The Dance":

Here one is on the pure mythical and smoky soil at last! Not
only do I describe the conflict between the two races in this
dance—I also become identified with the Indian and his world
before it is over, which is the only method possible of ever really
possessing the Indian and his world as a cultural factor. I think I
really succeed in getting under the skin of this glorious and dying
animal, in terms of expression, in symbols, which he himself would
comprehend. Pocahontas (the continent) is the common basis of
our meeting, she survives the extinction of the Indian, who finally,
after being assumed into the elements of nature (as he understood

them), persists only as a kind of "eye" in the sky, or as a star that hangs between day and night—"the twilight's dim perpetual throne."

6.[5] "Indiana":

I regret that this section is not completed as yet. It will be the monologue of an Indiana farmer; time, about 1860. He has failed in the gold-rush and is returned to till the soil. His monologue is a farewell to his son, who is leaving for a life on the sea. It is a lyrical summary of the period of conquest, and his wife, the mother who died on the way back from the gold-rush, is alluded to in a way which implies her succession to the nature-symbolism of Pocahontas. I have this section well-nigh done, but there is no use including [it] in the present ms. without the final words.

The next section, "Cutty Sark," is a phantasy on the period of the whalers and clipper ships. It also starts in the present and "progresses backwards." The form of the poem may seem erratic, but it is meant to present the hallucinations incident to rum-drinking in a South Street dive, as well as the lurch of a boat in heavy seas, etc. So I allow myself something of the same freedom which E. E. Cummings often uses.

"Cutty Sark" is built on the plan of a *fugue*. Two "voices"—that of the world of Time, and that of the world of Eternity—are interwoven in the action. The Atlantis theme (that of Eternity) is the transmuted voice of the nickel-slot pianola, and this voice alternates with that of the derelict sailor and the description of the action. The airy regatta of phantom clipper ships seen from Brooklyn Bridge on the way home is quite effective, I think. It was a pleasure to use historical names for these lovely ghosts. Music still haunts their names long after the wind has left their sails.

"Cape Hatteras," which follows, is unfinished. It will be a kind of ode to Whitman. I am working as much as possible on it now. It presents very formidable problems, as, indeed, all the sections have. I am really writing an epic of the modern consciousness, and indescribably complicated factors have to be resolved and blended. . . . I don't wish to tire you [with] too extended an analysis of my work, and so shall leave the other completed sections to explain themselves. In the ms., where the remaining incompleted sections occur, I am including a rough synopsis of their respective themes, however. The range of *The Bridge* has been called colossal by more than one critic who has seen the ms. And though I have found the subject to be vaster than I had at first realized, I am still highly confident of its final articulation into a continuous and eloquent span. Already there are evident signs of recognition: the following magazines have taken various sections:

"Dedication: To Brooklyn Bridge"	*The Dial*
"Ave Maria"	*The American Caravan*
"The Harbor Dawn"	*transition* (Paris)
"Van Winkle"	*"*
"The River"	*The Virginia Quarterly*
"The Dance"	*The Dial*
"Cutty Sark"	*Poetry* (Chicago)
"Three Songs"	*The Calendar* (London)
"The Tunnel"	*The Criterion* (London)

(I have been especially gratified by the reception accorded me by *The Criterion,* whose director, Mr. T. S. Eliot, is representative of the most exacting literary standards of our times.)

For some time past I have been seeking employment in New York, but without success so far. It's the usual problem of mechanical prejudices that I've already grown grey in trying to deal with. But all the more difficult now, since the only references I can give for the last two years are my own typewriter and a collection of poems. I am, as you will probably recall, at least avowedly—a perfectly good advertising writer. I am wondering if you would possibly give me some recommendation to the publicity department of The Metropolitan Opera Company, where I am certain of making myself useful. I was in New York two days last week, trying to secure employment as a waiter on one of the American lines. I found that I needed something like a diploma from Annapolis before hoping for an interview. A few years ago I registered with the Munson Line with reference to my qualifications for a particular position which every ship includes—that of "ship's writer," or "deck yeoman"; but I always found that such jobs were dispensed to acquaintances of the captain or to office workers, and that my references were never taken from the file. I am not particular what I do, however, so long as there is reasonable chance of my doing it well, and any recommendation you might care to offer in any practical direction whatever will be most welcome. My present worried state of mind practically forbids any progress on *The Bridge,* the chances for which are considerably better under even greatly limited time conditions.

I am still assured of a definite inheritance, previously mentioned in my first letter to you; and if you care to consider advancing me, say 800 or 1,000 dollars, on the same basis of insurance security as your previous assistance I should be glad to come into New York and talk it over. There is no monetary standard of evaluation for works of art, I know, but I cannot help feeling that a great poem may well be worth at least the expenditure necessary for merely the scenery and costumes of many a flashy and ephemeral play, or for a motor car. *The Aeneid* was not written in two years—nor in four, and in more than one sense I feel justified in comparing the historic and cultural scope of *The Bridge* to this great work. It is at least a symphony with an epic theme, and a work of considerable profundity and inspiration. Even with the torturing heat of my sojourn in Cuba I was able to work faster than before or since then, in America. The "foreign-ness" of my surroundings stimulated me to the realization of natively American materials and viewpoints in myself not hitherto suspected, and in one month I was able to do more work than I had done in the three previous years. If I could work in Mexico or Mallorca this winter I could have *The Bridge* finished by next spring. But that is a speculation which depends entirely on your interest.

Please pardon the inordinate length of this letter. I shall, of course, hope to hear from you regarding your impressions of the poem as it now stands. Along with the ms., I am enclosing three critical articles which may interest you somewhat.

FEDERICO GARCÍA LORCA

Theory and Function of the *Duende*[1]

Anyone travelling in that stretched bull-hide between the Júcar, the Guadalete, the Sil, or the Pisuerga rivers, would sooner or later hear the expression: "This has much *duende*." Manuel Torres, a great Andalusian artist, on one occasion said to a singer: "You have voice, you have style, but you will never be a success because you have no *duende*."

All through Andalusia, from the rock of Jaén to the shell of Cádiz, people constantly speak of the *duende,* and recognize it with unfailing instinct when it appears. The wonderful flamenco singer *El Lebrijano,* creator of the *Debla,*[2] said: "When I sing with *duende* nobody can equal me." The old gipsy dancer *La Malena* exclaimed once on hearing Brailowsky play Bach: "Olé! This has *duende*!," yet she was bored by Gluck, Brahms, and Darius Milhaud. And Manuel Torres, a man with more culture in his veins than anybody I have known, when listening to Falla playing his own "Nocturno del Generalife," made this splendid pronouncement: "All that has dark sounds has *duende*." And there is no greater truth.

These "dark sounds" are the mystery, the roots thrusting into the fertile loam known to all of us, ignored by all of us, but from which we get what is real in art. Torres here agrees with Goethe who defined the *duende* when he attributed to Paganini "a mysterious power that everyone feels but that no philosopher has explained."

[1] A lecture delivered by Lorca in Havana and Buenos Aires. Translated by J. L. Gili, who also supplied the notes.

[2] *Debla*, a variant of the Andalusian *cante jondo* (deep-song).

Thus the *duende* is a power and not a behaviour, it is a struggle and not a concept. I have heard an old guitarist master say: "The *duende* is not in the throat; the *duende* surges up from the soles of the feet." Which means that it is not a matter of ability, but of real live form; of blood; of ancient culture; of creative action.

This "mysterious power that everyone feels but that no philosopher has explained" is in fact the spirit of the earth. It is the same *duende* that gripped the heart of Nietzsche, who had been seeking its external forms on the Rialto Bridge or in the music of Bizet without ever finding it or being aware that the *duende* he pursued had jumped from the mysterious Greeks to the dancers of Cádiz or the broken Dionysiac cry of Silverio's *seguiriya*.[3]

I do not want anybody to confuse the *duende* with Luther's theological daemon of doubt, at whom with a Bacchic touch he flung an inkpot in Nuremberg; nor with the Catholic daemon, destructive and not very intelligent, who disguises himself as a bitch in order to enter convents.

No. The dark and quivering *duende* that I am talking about is a descendant of the merry daemon of Socrates, all marble and salt, who angrily scratched his master on the day he drank hemlock; a descendant also of Descartes' melancholy daemon, small as a green almond, who, tired of lines and circles, went out along the canals to hear the drunken sailors sing.

Every step that a man, or as Nietzsche would say an artist, takes towards the tower of his perfection is at the cost of the struggle he maintains with a *duende,* not with an angel, as has been said, and not with a muse. It is necessary to draw this fundamental distinction in order to arrive at the root of any work.

The angel guides and endows with gifts like St. Raphael, or defends and wards off like St. Michael, or warns like St. Gabriel.

The angel may dazzle, but he merely hovers over the head of man; he bestows his graces, and man quite effortlessly achieves his work, his sympathy, or his dance. The angel on the road to Damascus and the one who entered through the lattice of the little window at Assisi, or the one who followed the steps of Heinrich

---

[3] Refers to Silverio Franconetti, an Italian singer who in Andalusia cultivated the *cante jondo*. The *seguiriya* is a development of this.

Suso, is an angel that *commands,* and no one can resist his radiance because he moves his steel wings in the ambit of the elect.

The muse dictates and, occasionally, inspires. There is relatively little she can do, for she is by now distant and so weary—I have seen her twice—that I had to strengthen her with half a heart of marble. The muse-inspired poets hear voices without knowing where they come from; they come from the muse, who encourages them and sometimes swallows them up. Such was the case of Apollinaire, a great poet destroyed by the horrible muse with whom the magnificent and angelic Rousseau painted him. The muse arouses the intellect, and brings colonnaded landscapes and a false taste of laurel. Very often intellect is poetry's enemy because it is too much given to imitation, because it lifts the poet to a throne of sharp edges and makes him oblivious of the fact that he may suddenly be devoured by ants, or a great arsenic lobster may fall on his head. Against all this the muses who appear in monocles or among the faintly warm lacquer-roses of a little salon are powerless.

Angel and muse come from without; the angel gives radiance, the muse gives precepts (Hesiod learned from them). Gold leaf or fold of tunics, the poet receives his norms in his coppice of laurels. On the other hand, the *duende* has to be roused in the very cells of the blood.

We must repel the angel, and kick out the muse, and lose our fear of the violet fragrance irradiating from eighteenth-century poetry, and of the great telescope in whose lenses sleeps the confining, ailing muse.

The real struggle is with the *duende*.

One knows how to seek God, whether it be by the rough ways of the hermit or by the subtlety of the mystic; with a tower like St. Theresa's, or with the three pathways of St. John of the Cross. And even if we have to exclaim with Isaiah's voice: "Truly thou art the hidden God," ultimately God sends his first thorns of fire to whoever seeks him.

To help us seek the *duende* there is neither map nor discipline. All one knows is that it burns the blood like powdered glass, that it exhausts, that it rejects all the sweet geometry one has learned, that it breaks with all styles, that it compels Goya, master of greys, silvers, and of those pinks in the best English paintings, to paint with his knees and with his fists horrible bitumen blacks; or that it leaves Mossen Cinto Verdaguer[4] naked in the cold air of the Pyrenees; or that it takes Jorge Manrique[5] to wait for death in the wilderness of Ocaña; or that it dresses the delicate body of Rimbaud in an acrobat's green suit; or that it puts the eyes of a dead fish on Count Lautréamont in the early morning Boulevard.

The great artists of Southern Spain, gipsy or flamenco, whether they sing or dance or play, know that no real emotion is possible unless there is *duende.* They may even deceive an audience by giving the impression of possessing *duende,* in the same manner as one is deceived every day by writers, painters, or literary fashions without *duende;* but if one looks closely and is not misled by being inattentive, the fraud will soon be discovered and the *duende*-artifice put to flight.

On one occasion, the Andalusian flamenco singer Pastora Pavón, *La Niña de los Peines* (The Girl with the Combs), a sombre Hispanic genius with an imagination matching that of Goya or Rafael *El Gallo,*[6] was singing in a small tavern at Cádiz. She sang with her voice of shadow, with her voice of liquid metal, with her moss-covered voice, and with her voice entangled in her long hair. She would soak her voice in *manzanilla,* or lose it in dark and distant thickets. Yet she failed completely; it was all to no purpose. The audience remained silent.

Among the audience was Ignacio Espeleta, handsome as a Roman tortoise, who was once asked: "How is it that you never work?", and with a smile worthy of Argantonio, he replied: "Why should I work if I come from Cádiz?"

Also present was Eloísa, the fiery aristocratic whore of Seville, direct descendant of Soledad Vargas, who in the year 1930 refused to marry a Rothschild because he was not her equal in blood. There were also the Floridas, believed by many to be butchers,

---

[4] Jacint Verdaguer, Catalan poet, a leading figure of the Catalan Renaixença, or literary renaissance of the nineteenth century. Wrote lyric poetry and two great epic poems, *L'Atlàntida* and *Canigó,* hence the Pyrenean reference in the present context.

[5] Fifteenth-century Spanish poet, famous for his *Coplas* on the death of his father.

[6] A famous bullfighter.

while in reality they were ancient priests still sacrificing bulls to Geryon; and in a corner sat that imposing breeder of bulls Don Pablo Murube, looking like a Cretan mask. Pastora Pavón finished singing in the midst of silence. Only a little man, one of those emasculated dancers who suddenly spring up from behind bottles of white brandy, said sarcastically in a very low voice: "Viva Paris!", as if to say: "Here we do not care for ability, technique, or mastery. Here we care for something else."

At that moment *La Niña de los Peines* got up like a woman possessed, broken as a medieval mourner, drank without pause a large glass of *cazalla,* a fire-water brandy, and sat down to sing without voice, breathless, without subtlety, her throat burning, but . . . with *duende.* She succeeded in getting rid of the scaffolding of the song, to make way for a furious and fiery *duende,* companion of sand-laden winds, that made those who were listening tear their clothes rhythmically, like Caribbean Negroes clustered before the image of St. Barbara.

La Niña de los Peines had to tear her voice, because she knew that she was being listened to by an *élite* not asking for forms but for the marrow of forms, for music exalted into purest essence. She had to impoverish her skills and aids; that is, she had to drive away her muse and remain alone so that the *duende* might come and join in a hand-to-hand fight. And how she sang! Now she was in earnest, her voice was a jet of blood, admirable because of its pain and its sincerity, and it opened like a ten-fingered hand in the nailed but tempestuous feet of a Christ by Juan de Juni.

The appearance of the *duende* always presupposes a radical change of all forms based on old structures. It gives a sensation of freshness wholly unknown, having the quality of a newly created rose, of miracle, and produces in the end an almost religious enthusiasm.

In all Arabic music, dance, or song, the appearance of the *duende* is greeted with vociferous shouts of "Alá! Alá!", "God! God!" which are not far from the *olé* of bullfighting. And in the singing of Southern Spain, the presence of the *duende* is followed by shouts of "Viva Dios!", a profound, human, and tender cry of communion with God through the five senses, by virtue of the *duende* which stirs the voice and body of the dancer, a real and poetical abstraction from this world, as pure as that obtained through seven gardens by the rare seventeenth-century poet Pedro Soto de Rojas,[7] or by St. John Climacus[8] on his trembling ladder of lament.

It follows that when this abstraction is reached, its effects are felt by everyone; by the initiated, who have seen how style can conquer poor matter, and by the ignorant in an indefinable but authentic emotion. A few years ago, in a dancing contest at Jerez de la Frontera, an old woman of eighty carried off the prize against beautiful women and girls with waists like water, merely by raising her arms, throwing back her head, and stamping her foot on the platform; in that gathering of muses and angels, beauties of shape and beauties of smile, the moribund *duende,* dragging her wings of rusty knives along the ground, was bound to win and did in fact win.

All the Arts are capable of possessing *duende,* but naturally the field is widest in music, in dance, and in spoken poetry, because they require a living body as interpreter—they are forms that arise and die ceaselessly, and are defined by an exact present.

Often the composer's *duende* passes to the interpreter. It is also worth noting that even if the composer or poet is false, the interpreter's *duende* can create a new marvel bearing little resemblance to the original work. Such was the case of the *duende*-possessed Eleonora Duse, who unearthed failures in order to turn them into successes, by virtue of what she put into them; or of Paganini, who, according to Goethe, could produce profound melodies out of quite commonplace music; or of a delightful girl in Puerto de Santa María whom I once saw sing and dance that frightful Italian song *O Mari!,* with such rhythm, such pauses, and such meaning that she transformed the cheap Italian song into a firm snake of solid gold. In every instance it was indeed a case of the interpreter re-creating the original work: living blood and artistic genius were put into bodies void of expression.

All the Arts, and all countries too, are capable of *duende,* angel, or muse. While Germany has, with some exceptions, a muse, and Italy has permanently an angel, Spain is always moved by the

[7] Lorca makes reference here to Soto de Rojas' book *Paraíso cerrado para muchos, jardines abiertos para todos,* evocative of the gardens of Granada.

[8] St. John Climacus, sixth-century ascetic, author of the *Scala Spiritualis* or "Spiritual Ladder."

duende, being a country of ancient music and dance, where the
duende squeezes lemons of daybreak, as well as being a nation of
death, a nation open to death.

In every country death has finality. It arrives and the blinds are
drawn. Not in Spain. In Spain they are lifted. Many Spaniards live
between walls until the day they die, when they are taken out to
the sun. A dead person in Spain is more alive when dead than is
the case anywhere else—his profile cuts like the edge of a barber's
razor. The jest about death and the silent contemplation of it is
familiar to Spaniards. From Quevedo's "Dream of the skulls" to
the "Putrescent bishop" of Valdés Leal, and from the Marbella of
the seventeenth century, who died in childbirth on the highway,
saying:

> La sangre de mis entrañas
> cubriendo el caballa está.
> Las patas de tu caballo
> echan fuego de alquitrán . . .[9]

to the recent youth of Salamanca, killed by a bull, who exclaimed:

> Amigos, que yo me muero;
> amigos, yo estoy muy malo.
> Tres pañuelos tengo dentro
> y este que meto son cuatro . . .[10]

there is a fence of saltpetre flowers, over which rises a people
contemplating death, a people who at their most austere are
inspired by the verses of Jeremiah, or at their most lyrical by
fragrant cypresses. But also a country where what matters most
has the ultimate metallic quality of death.

The knife and the cart-wheel, the razor and the prickly beards of
shepherds, the bare moon, the fly, damp cupboards, rubble, reli-
gious images covered with lacework, quick-lime, and the wound-
ing outline of eaves and watch-towers, in Spain all these have
minute grass-blades of death, as well as allusions and voices
perceptible to the alert mind, exciting our memory with the inert

[9] The blood from my womb now covers the horse. The hooves of your horse
spark tarry fire . . .

[10] Friends, I am dying; friends, I am in a bad way. Three handkerchiefs I
have inside, and now this is the fourth . . .

air of our own passing. The link of Spanish art with the soil is not entirely fortuitous, it is an art abounding in thistles and tangible stones; the lamentation of Pleberio or the dances of the master Josef María de Valdivielso are not isolated examples; it is no accident that from all European balladry this Spanish love-song stands out:

> «Si tú eres mi linda amiga,
> ¿cómo no me miras, di?»
> «Ojos con que te miraba
> a la sombra se los di.»
> «Si tú eres mi linda amiga,
> ¿cómo no me besas, di?»
> «Labios con que te besaba
> a la tierra se los di.»
> «Si tú eres mi linda amiga,
> ¿cómo no me abrazas, di?»
> «Brazos con que te abrazaba,
> de gusanos los cubrí.»[11]

Neither is it unexpected to find this song among the earliest Spanish lyric poetry:

> Dentro del vergel
> moriré,
> dentro del rosal
> matar me han.
> Yo me iba, mi madre,
> las rosas coger,
> hallara la muerte
> dentro del vergel.
> Yo me iba, mi madre,
> las rosas cortar,
> hallara la muerte

[11] "If you are my sweetheart, why won't you look at me, pray?"
"Eyes I had to look at thee, to the shadow I gave them."
"If you are my sweetheart, why won't you kiss me, pray?"
"Lips I had to kiss thee, to the earth I gave them."
"If you are my sweetheart, why won't you embrace me, pray?"
"Arms I had to embrace thee, with worms I covered them."

dentro del rosal.
Dentro del vergel
moriré,
dentro del rosal
matar me han.[12]

The moon-frozen heads which Zurbarán painted, the butter-yellow and the lightning yellow of El Greco, the prose of Fr Sigüenza, the whole of Goya's work, the apse of the church at El Escorial, all our polychrome sculpture, the crypt of the ducal house of Osuna, "Death with the guitar" in the chapel of the Benaventes at Medina de Rioseco, all these are the cultured counterpart of the pilgrimages to St Andrés de Teixido, where the dead have a place in the procession; of the dirges sung by the women of Asturias by lantern-light on the November night; of the dance of the Sibyl in the cathedrals of Majorca and Toledo; of the obscure *In recort* from Tortosa; and of the innumerable Good Friday ceremonies which, together with the most civilized spectacle of bullfighting, constitute the popular triumph of death in Spain. Of all the countries in the world, only Mexico can match Spain in this.

As soon as the muse is aware of death, she shuts her door, or raises a plinth, or parades an urn, or writes an epitaph with waxen hand. And she immediately tears her wreath in a silence that wavers between two breezes. Beneath the truncated arch of the ode, she binds with a mournful touch the precise flowers that the Italians painted in the fifteenth century, and summons the dependable cockerel of Lucretius to frighten away unsuspected shadows.

When the angel is aware of death, he slowly circles round, and weaves with icy tears and narcissi the elegy we have seen trembling in the hands of Keats, or Villasandino, or Herrera, or Bécquer, or Juan Ramón Jiménez. But, what a flutter if the angel feels a spider, however minute, on his tender rosy feet!

The *duende,* on the other hand, does not appear if it sees no possibility of death, if it does not know that it will haunt death's

[12] In the garden I shall die, in the rose-bush I shall be killed. I was going, dear mother, to pick some roses, I found death in the garden. I was going, dear mother, to cut some roses, I found death in the rose-bush. In the garden I shall die, in the rose-bush I shall be killed.

house, if it is not certain that it can move those branches we all carry, which neither enjoy nor ever will enjoy any solace.

In idea, in sound, or in gesture, the *duende* likes a straight fight with the creator on the edge of the well. While angel and muse are content with violin or measured rhythm, the *duende* wounds, and in the healing of this wound which never closes is the prodigious, the original in the work of man.

The magical quality of a poem consists in its being always possessed by the *duende*, so that whoever beholds it is baptized with dark water. Because with *duende* it is easier to love and to understand, and also one is *certain* to be loved and understood; and this struggle for expression and for the communication of expression reaches at times, in poetry, the character of a fight to the death.

Let us remember the case of the very flamenca- and *duende*-possessed St. Theresa, flamenca nor for having stopped a fierce bull with three magnificent passes, which she did; not for having boasted of her good looks in front of Fr. Juan de la Miseria, nor for having slapped the Papal Nuncio, but for being one of the few creatures whose *duende* (not whose angel, for the angel never attacks) transfixed her with a dart, wishing her dead for having stolen its last secret—the delicate bridge uniting the five senses with that core made living flesh, living cloud, living sea, of Love freed from Time.

She was a brave vanquisher of the *duende*, in contrast with Philip of Austria, who, hankering after the muse and the angel of Theology, found himself imprisoned by the *duende* of bleak fervours in that edifice of El Escorial, where geometry borders on dream, and where the *duende* wears a muse's mask for the eternal punishment of the great king.

We have said that the *duende* likes the edge of things, the wound, and that it is drawn to where forms fuse themselves in a longing greater than their visible expressions.

In Spain (as in the East, where dance is a religious expression) the *duende* has a boundless field in the bodies of the girl dancers of Cádiz, praised by Martial, in the breasts of singers, praised by Juvenal, and in the whole liturgy of bullfighting, a true religious drama where, as in the Mass, there is adoration and a God is sacrificed.

It is as though the whole *duende* of the classical world converged into this perfect spectacle, symbol of the culture and great sensibility of a people who have discovered man's finest anger, his finest melancholy, and his finest grief. Neither in Spanish dancing nor in bullfighting does anybody have any enjoyment; the *duende* takes care to make one suffer through the drama, in living forms, and prepares the steps for an escape from the surrounding reality.

The *duende* works on the body of a dancer like a breeze on the sand. With magic powers it transforms a girl into a paralytic of the moon, or fills with adolescent blushes an old broken man begging round the taverns, or conveys in tresses of long hair the scent of a harbour at night, and at every moment it works the arms into movements which have generated the dances of all times.

But, it is worth emphasizing, the *duende* can never repeat itself, as the shapes of the sea do not repeat themselves in the storm.

It is in bullfighting that the *duende* attains its most impressive character, because, on the one hand, it has to fight with death, which may bring destruction, and on the other, with geometry, the fundamental basic measure of the spectacle.

The bull has its orbit, the bullfighter his, and between orbit and orbit there exists a point of danger where lies the apex of the terrible game.

It is possible to have muse with the *muleta*[13] and angel with the *banderillas*,[14] and be considered a good bullfighter; but in the work with the cape when the bull is still free of wounds, and again at the final killing, the help of the *duende* is required to hit the nail of artistic truth.

The bullfighter scaring the spectators by his temerity is not bull-fighting, he is on the absurd plane of one playing with his life, which anyone can do; on the other hand, the bullfighter who is bitten by the *duende* gives a lesson of Pythagorian music, and we forget that he is constantly throwing his heart at the horns.

Lagartijo with his Roman *duende,* Joselito with his Jewish *duende,* Belmonte with his baroque *duende,* and Cagancho with his gipsy *duende,* from the twilight of the bull-ring they show

13 *Muleta:* scarlet cloth folded and doubled over a tapered wooden stick with a sharp steel point.

14 *Banderillas:* thin stick with harpoon-like steel point, adorned with coloured paper or flags, and placed in pairs in the withers of the bull to provoke a charge.

poets, painters, and musicians, the four great pathways of Spanish tradition.

Spain is the only country where death is a natural spectacle, where death blows long fanfares at the arrival of each spring, and its art is always governed by a shrewd *duende* which has given it its distinctive character and its inventive quality.

The *duende* that for the first time in sculpture fills the cheeks of the master Mateo of Compostela's saints with red blood, is the same that makes St. John of the Cross moan, or burns naked nymphs in the religious sonnets of Lope de Vega.

The *duende* that raised the tower of Sahagún or worked warm bricks in Calatayud or Teruel, is the same *duende* that breaks the clouds of El Greco and sends Quevedo's bailiffs rolling with a kick, and kindles Goya's visions.

When it rains, it brings out a *duende*-possessed Velázquez, secretly, behind the greys of his monarchs; in the snow it brings out Herrera[15] naked to prove that coldness does not kill; when the *duende* burns, it· draws Berruguete into its blaze, and makes him discover a new dimension in sculpture.

The muse of Góngora and the angel of Garcilaso have to relinquish the laurel wreath when the *duende* of St. John of the Cross appears, when

> El ciervo vulnerado
> por el otero asoma.[16]

The muse of Gonzalo de Berceo and the angel of the Archpriest of Hita draw aside to let Jorge Manrique pass when he comes to the gates of Belmonte castle mortally wounded. The muse of Gregorio Hernández and the angel of José de Mora have to withdraw to allow the *duende* to pass, weeping Mena's tears of blood. Similarly, the melancholy muse of Catalonia, and the rain-drenched angel of Galicia, have to look with loving wonder at the *duende* of Castille, so remote from the warm bread and the placid cow grazing outside a compass of wind-swept skies and dry earth.

The *duende* of Quevedo and the *duende* of Cervantes, the one with phosphorescent green anemones, and the other with anem-

[15] Juan de Herrera, architect of El Escorial.

[16] The wounded deer over the hill appears.

ones of plaster of Ruidera, crown the altar-piece of the *duende* in Spain.

It is clear that each art has a *duende* of a different kind and form, but they all join their roots at a point where the "dark sounds" of Manuel Torres emerge, ultimate matter, uncontrollable and quivering common foundation of wood, of sound, of canvas, and of words.

"Dark sounds" behind which we discover in tender intimacy volcanoes, ants, gentle breezes, and the Milky Way clasping the great night to her waist.

Ladies and gentlemen: I have raised three arches and with clumsy hand I have placed in them the muse, the angel, and the *duende*.

The muse remains quiet; she can assume the closely pleated tunic, or the staring cow's eyes of Pompeii, or the large nose with four faces which her friend Picasso gave her. The angel may stir in the tresses painted by Antonello of Messina, or in Lippi's tunic or in the violin of Masolino and of Rousseau.

The *duende*—where is the *duende*? Through the empty arch comes an air of the mind that blows insistently over the heads of the dead, in search of new landscapes and unsuspected accents; an air smelling of a child's saliva, of pounded grass, and medusal veil announcing the constant baptism of newly created things.

[*1933*]

Narration: Lecture 2

I have said and anybody can say anybody might say that knowledge is what you know. Knowledge is what you know and there is nothing more difficult to say than that that knowledge is what you know.

Let's make our flour meal and meat in Georgia.

Is that prose or poetry and why.

Let's make our flour meal and meat in Georgia.

This is a sign I read as we rode on a train from Atlanta to Birmingham and I wondered then and am still wondering is it poetry or is it prose let's make our flour meal and meat in Georgia, it might be poetry and it might be prose and of course there is a reason why a reason why it might be poetry and a reason why it might be prose.

Does let's make our flour meal and meat in Georgia move in various ways and very well and has that to do really to do with narrative in poetry, has it really to do with narrative at all and is it more important in poetry that a thing should move in various kinds of ways than it is in prose supposing both of them to be narrative. I think about these things a great deal these days because things anything any one can see does move move about and just move in various kinds of ways and sometimes I wonder if that makes poetry and sometimes I wonder if that makes prose and now I wonder is there any such thing as poetry is there any such thing as prose or is it just that now anything moves about in various ways it sometimes stays still but a great deal it does move about in various ways. Since what you know is what you know do you or do you not know this.

There are now several questions is there anything that is not narrative and what is narrative what has narrative gotten to be now. When one used to think of narrative one meant a telling of what is happening in successive moments of its happening the quality of telling depending upon the conviction of the one telling that there was a distinct succession in happening, that one thing happened after something else and since that happening in succession was a profound conviction in every one then really there was no difference whether any one began in the beginning or the middle or the ending because since narrative was a progressive telling of things that were progressively happening it really did not make any difference where you were at what moment you were in your happening since the important part of telling anything was the conviction that anything that everything was progressively happening. But now we have changed all that we really have. We really now do not really know that anything is progressively happening and as knowledge is what you know and as now we do not know that anything is progressively happening where are we then in narrative writing and what has this to do with poetry and with prose if it has that is to say if poetry and prose have anything to do with anything and anything has anything to do with narrative that is the telling of what is happening.

I know what poetry and prose has been and I have been telling this thing telling what poetry and prose has been and when I told it I said it in this way. This is what I said about what poetry and prose has been.

Does telling anything as it is being needed being telling now by any one does it mean cutting loose from anything, no because there is nothing to cut loose from. Remember this that is do not remember but know this when there is no more to tell about what prose and poetry has been.

It is funny that Americans that an American who has always believed that they were the people knowing everything about repression are really the ones who have naturally been moving in the direction that there is nothing to cut loose from.

So to begin to tell what I did tell because I knew it then very very well what prose and poetry has been.

I said prose concerned itself with the internal balance of sentences which are things that exist in and for themselves and are not complete as anything because anything existing in and for itself does not have to have completion, if it exists in and for itself there is no relation of it to it and therefore there is no element of completion, it is a thing that exists by internal balancing that is what a sentence is and since that is what a sentence is or rather what a sentence was perhaps now there is no longer any need for a sentence to be existing perhaps not, in any case certainly that is what a sentence has been a thing that by internal balancing made itself what it was. I further have said and do say that a succession of these sentences were used in paragraphing and that these sentences existing in that way and being included by a paragraphing ending made not by their balancing but by the need of progression made a paragraph that had an emotional meaning while the sentence itself had none. This is what I said the sentence and the paragraph had been has been and now let me say it again.

Let me say again what the sentence and the paragraph has been and what has been its relation to narrative that is the telling of anything.

Narrative has been the telling of anything because there has been always has been a feeling that something followed another thing that there was succession in happening.

In a kind of a way what has made the Old Testament such permanently good reading is that really in a way in the Old Testament writing there really was not any such thing there was not really any succession of anything and really in the Old Testament there is really no sentence existing and no paragraphing, think about this thing, think if you have not really been knowing this thing and then let us go on telling about what paragraphs and sentences have been what prose and poetry has been. So then in the Old Testament writing there is really no actual conclusion that anything is progressing that one thing is succeeding another thing, that anything in that sense in the sense of succeeding happening is a narrative of anything, but most writing is based on this thing most writing has been a real narrative writing a telling of the story of anything in the way that thing has been happening and now everything is not that thing there is at present not a sense of anything being successively happening, moving is in every direction beginning and ending is not really exciting, anything is anything, anything is happening and anybody can know anything at any time that anything is happening and so really and truly is there any sentence and any paragraphing is there prose and poetry as the same thing or different things is there now any narrative of any successive thing.

I always remember during the war being so interested in one thing in seeing the American soldiers standing, standing and doing nothing standing for a long time not even talking but just standing and being watched by the whole French population and their feeling the feeling of the whole population that the American soldier standing there and doing nothing impressed them as the American soldier as no soldier could impress by doing anything. It is a much more impressive thing to any one to see any one standing, that is not in action than acting or doing anything doing anything being a successive thing, standing not being a successive thing but being something existing. That is then the difference between narrative as it has been and narrative as it is now. And this has come to be a natural thing in a perfectly natural way that the narrative of to-day is not a narrative of succession as all the writing for a good many hundreds of years has been.

And so to begin again with what I have said that poetry and prose has been that sentences and paragraphs have been that narrative has been.

I said then that sentences as they have for centuries been written were a balancing a complete inner balance of something that stated something as being existing and that a paragraph was a succession of these sentences that going on and then stopping made the emotional content of something having a beginning and middle and ending. Sentences are contained within themselves and anything really contained within itself has no beginning or middle or ending, any one can know this thing by knowing anything at any moment of their living, in short by knowing anything. How do you know anything, well you know anything as complete knowledge as having it completely in you at the actual moment that you have it. That is what knowledge is, and essentially therefore knowledge is not succession but an immediate existing. All these things then are as they are and we come back to what poetry is what prose is and the reason why and what it all has to do with narrative and whether any narrative is existing now and how and why.

Knowledge then is what you know at the time at any time that you really know anything. And in knowing anything you know it as you know it, you know it at the time that you are knowing it and in that way the way of knowing it knowing has not succession there may be continuous states of knowing anything but at no time of knowing is there anything but knowing that thing the thing you know, know carefully what you do know and of course anybody can know that this is so. And once more I say the Old Testament is the thing that has the way of knowing anything as knowing anything and not feeling or thinking about anything succeeding anything. Knowing is knowing anything at the knowing the thing when that thing is what you know. The Old Testament has always been so. So there we are and in a curious way we now and in this day at this time have come again to have this as our own, that there is no succession, there is moving in any and any various direction and that being a thing existing knowing is what you know at the moment anything is being as knowing. The exciting thing about all this is that as it is new it is old and as it is old it is new, but now really we have come to be in our way which is an entirely different way from the way the Old Testament had its way we have come to be that knowledge is what you know when you know and as you know there is no succession of what you know since you do know what you know. Any one really any one can really know that this is so.

To come back again to what prose was and what poetry was and what it is if it is going to be prose and poetry again. Perhaps it is not going to be prose and poetry again. Nothing really changes everything is as it was but perhaps it is not going to be prose and poetry again perhaps it is not poetry and prose now in spite of anything and everything being always having been what it was.

So to begin again about what prose and poetry has been.

Prose has been a thing made of sentences and paragraphs, the sentences saying a thing and then one after the other the sentences making a paragraph the thing by reason of it succeeding one sentence succeeding another one come finally to giving a beginning and ending and a middle to anything in other words having it that a paragraph has come to give a thing the emotion that anything having a beginning and a middle and an ending can give to anything. Think of narrative from this thing, a narrative can give emotion because an emotion is dependent upon succession upon a

thing having a beginning and a middle and an ending. That is why
every one used to like sequels and some still do anybody still may
but actually in modern writing sequels have no meaning do you
begin to see now why I say that sentences and paragraphs need not
necessarily go on existing. Do you begin to see what I mean by
saying this thing.

So then prose has been for a long time has been made of sen-
tences and paragraphs, sentences which within themselves carry no
emotion because a thing balanced within itself does not give out
nor have within any emotion but sentences existing within them-
selves by the balance that holds them when they are in succession
one after the other and make a paragraph have the emotion that
any succession can give to anything. A sentence has not really any
beginning or middle or ending because each part is its part as its
part and so the whole exists within by the balance within but the
paragraph exists not by a balance within but by a succession.
Anybody really anybody can realize this thing and realizing this
thing can realize that narrative up to the present time has been not
a succession of paragraphing but a continuing of paragraphing, a
quite entirely different thing.

Let me explain again.

A sentence is inside itself by its internal balancing, think how a
sentence is made by its parts of speech and you will see that it is
not dependent upon a beginning a middle and an ending but by
each part needing its own place to make its own balancing, and
because of this in a sentence there is no emotion, a sentence does
not give off emotion. But one sentence coming after another
sentence makes a succession and the succession if it has a begin-
ning a middle and an ending as a paragraph has does form create
and limit an emotion.

So now we really do know what sentences and paragraphs are
and they have to do everything in narrative writing the way nar-
rative has been written. Because as narrative has mostly been
written it is dependent upon things succeeding upon a thing having
a beginning and a middle and an ending.

Now these are two things do not forget that they are not one
thing. Succeeding one thing succeeding another thing is succeeding
and having a beginning a middle and an ending is entirely another
thing.

When I first began writing really just began writing, I was tremendously impressed by anything by everything having a beginning a middle and an ending. I think one naturally is impressed by anything having a beginning a middle and an ending when one is beginning writing and that is a natural thing because when one is emerging from adolescence, which is really when one first begins writing one feels that one would not have been one emerging from adolescence if there had not been a beginning and a middle and an ending to anything. So paragraphing is a thing then any one is enjoying and sentences are less fascinating, but then gradually well if you are an American gradually you find that really it is not necessary not really necessary that anything that everything has a beginning and a middle and an ending and so you struggling with anything as anything has begun and begun and began does not really mean that thing does not really mean beginning or begun.

I found myself at this time quite naturally using the present participle, in The Making of Americans I could not free myself from the present participle because dimly I felt that I had to know what I knew and I knew that the beginning and middle and ending was not where I began.

So then that was the way prose was written and that was narrative writing as I say practically with everything the average English reading person was reading or writing with the exception of the Old Testament yes with the exception of the Old Testament which was not English writing, it was the writing of another kind of living, it was the writing whose beginning and middle and ending was really not existing was a writing where events in succession were not existing, where events one succeeding another event was not at all exciting no not at all exciting.

So now we know how narrative prose was and is written and now let us begin to think about how poetry was written and had that too any sense of succession of one thing succeeding another thing as the thing really producing emotion really holding the attention.

Yes I must have you have to hold it as I have to have you have it that gradually as English literature came more and more to be written it came always more and more to have it that it needed to have emotion in it the emotion that only could come from everything having something that came before and after that thing. In the earlier poetry in English writing it was there of course it was always there but they could feel something without feeling that thing that anything could only be anything if it was succeeding some other thing, and finally then English writing was entirely that thing, in its poetry as well as in its narrative writing that one thing came after another thing and that not anything existing aroused any one to feeling but that a thing having beginning and middle and ending made every one have the emotion they had about anything. Did this make poetry as well as prose then. Yes it did.

The fact that anything was existing was moving around by itself in any way it wanted to move did not arouse any emotion it was only anything succeeding any other thing anything having middle and beginning and ending could and did and would arouse emotion.

A great deal perhaps all of my writing of The Making of Americans was an effort to escape from this thing to escape from inevitably feeling that anything that everthing had meaning as beginning and middle and ending.

And it was right and quite a natural thing that the book I wrote in which I was escaping from the inevitable narrative of anything of everything succeeding something of needing to be succeeding that is following anything of anything of everything consisting that is the emotional and the actual value of anything counting in anything having beginning and middle and ending it was natural that the book I wrote in which I was escaping from all this inevitably in narrative writing I should have called The Making of Americans. I did not call it this for that reason but I called it this and this is what is happening, American writing has been an escaping not an escaping but an existing without the necessary feeling of one thing succeeding another thing of anything having a beginning and a middle and an ending.

And now all this has everything to do with poetry and prose and whether now whether there really is now any such thing.

Poetry and prose. I came to the conclusion that poetry was a calling an intensive calling upon the name of anything and that prose was not the using the name of anything as a thing in itself but the creating of sentences that were self-existing and following one after the other made of anything a continuous thing which is paragraphing and so a narrative that is a narrative of anything.

That is what a narrative is of course one thing following any other thing.

If poetry is the calling upon a name until that name comes to be anything if one goes on calling on that name more and more calling upon that name as poetry does then poetry does make of that calling upon a name a narrative it is a narrative of calling upon that name. That is what poetry has been and as it has been that thing as it has been a calling upon a name instead of a succession of internal balancing as prose has been then naturally at the time all the time the long time after the Elizabethans poetry and prose has not been the same thing no not been at all the same thing. Before the end of the Elizabethans and then in the eighteenth century when the inner balancing of sentences really invaded poetry and poetry was less the calling upon a name of anything than it was an inner balancing of anything, Pope is an excellent example it is hard telling really about the eighteenth century whether there is any really any internal feeling that makes poetry poetry and a different thing from prose.

But during the nineteenth century there was no doubt no doubt about it. Prose was the sentence and paragraphing and the use not of nouns but of parts of speech that made their use that use and poetry was the calling upon names the really calling upon names. There has always been this real difference between prose and poetry, that prose is dependent upon the sentence and then upon the paragraph and poetry upon the calling upon names. There have been some centuries never forget that a century is always more or less about one hundred years, but always there has been this difference and now well now is there this difference is there this difference and if not why not.

Very well then.

It is certain that there has been this thing prose and poetry and narrative which is roughly a telling of anything where anything happens after any other thing.

In the beginning there really was no difference between poetry and prose in the beginning of writing in the beginning of talking in the beginning of hearing anything or about anything. How could there be how could there have been since the name of anything was then as important as anything as anything that could be said about anything. Once more I tell you that the Old Testament did this thing there was not really any difference between prose and poetry then, they told what they were and they felt what they saw and they knew how they knew and everything they had to say came as it had to come to do what it had to do.

Really can you say that there was any difference between prose and poetry then. No not at all. Not then.

And then slowly they came to know that what they knew might mean something different from what they had known it was when they knew simply knew what it was. And so they began telling about it then how one thing meant something then and how something else meant something else then and in poetry they tried to say what they knew as they knew it and then more and more then they simply tried to name it and that made poetry then, anything made poetry then and they told anything and as they told anything they felt it as a telling of anything and so it meant more and more that they called it by its name as they knew it and that more and more made poetry then.

At the same time as I say they began to feel what they said when they said anything when they knew anything and this made them then think about how they said anything how they knew anything and in telling this thing telling how they knew anything how they said anything prose began, and so then there was prose and poetry. Before that there had been only one thing, the one thing any one knew as they knew anything.

Prose and poetry then went on and more and more as it went on prose was more and more telling and by sentences balancing and then by paragraphing prose was more and more telling how anything happened if any one had anything to say about what happened how anything was known if any one had anything to say about how anything was known, and poetry poetry tried to remain with knowing anything and knowing its name, gradually it came to really not knowing but really only knowing its name and that is at last what poetry became.

And now.

Well and now, now that we have been realizing that anything having a beginning and middle and ending is not what is making anything anything, and now that everything is so completely moving the name of anything is not really anything to interest any one about anything, now it is coming that once again nobody can be certain that narrative is existing that poetry and prose have different meanings.

Let's make our flour meal and meat in Georgia.

Well believe it or not it is very difficult to know whether that is prose or poetry and does it really make any difference if you do or do not know. This.

And so things moving perhaps perhaps moving in any direction, names being not existing because anybody can know what any body else is talking about without any name being mentioning, without any belief in any name being existing, I have just been trying to write the history of some one if his name had not been the name he had and I have called it Four In America and it is very interesting. You can slowly change any one by their name changing to any other name, and so slowly just knowing the name of anything and so making any one remember about such a thing the thing whose name its name anybody has happened to be mentioning cannot really very much interest any one, not really very much, and so perhaps narrative and poetry and prose have all come where they do not have to be considered as being there. Perhaps not I very much really very much think perhaps not, and that may make one thing or anything or everything say itself in a different way yes in a different way, who shall say, and all this now and always later we will come to say, perhaps yes, perhaps no, no and yes are still nice words, yes I guess I still will believe that I will.

You will perhaps say no and yes perhaps yes.

[*1935*]

WILLIAM CARLOS WILLIAMS

Edgar Allan Poe

———————

Poe was not "a fault of nature," "a find for French eyes," ripe but unaccountable, as through our woollyheadedness we've sought to designate him, but a genius intimately shaped by his locality and time. It is to save our faces that we've given him a crazy reputation, a writer from whose classic accuracies we have not known how else to escape.

The false emphasis was helped by his Parisian vogue and tonal influence on Baudelaire, but the French mind was deeper hit than that. Poe's work strikes by its scrupulous originality, *not* "originality" in the bastard sense, but in its legitimate sense of solidity which goes back to the ground, a conviction that he *can* judge within himself. These things the French were *ready* to perceive and quick to use to their advantage: a new point from which to re-adjust the trigonometric measurements of literary form.

It is the New World, or to leave that for the better term, it is a *new locality* that is in Poe assertive; it is America, the first great burst through to expression of a re-awakened genius of *place*.

Poe gives the sense for the first time in America, that literature is *serious,* not a matter of courtesy but of truth. (See *Maria Lucretia Davidson*).

The aspect of his critical statements as a whole, from their hundred American titles to the inmost structure of his sentences, is that of a single gesture, not avoiding the trivial, to sweep all worthless chaff aside. It is a movement, first and last to clear the GROUND.

There is a flavor of provincialism that IS provincialism in the plainness of his reasoning upon elementary grammatical, syntactical and prosodic grounds which awakened Lowell's derision. But insistence upon primary distinctions, that seems coldly academic, was in this case no more than evidence of a strong impulse to begin at the beginning. Poe was unsophisticated, when contrasted with the puerile sophistications of a Lowell. It is a *beginning* he has in mind, a juvenescent *local* literature. By this he avoids the clownish turn of trying to join, contrary to every reasonable impulsion, a literature (the English) with which he had no actual connection and which might be presumed, long since, to have passed that beginning which to the *new* condition was requisite.

But Mr. Lowell's comment had to be answered:

> Here comes Poe with his Raven, like Barnaby Rudge—
> Three fifths of him genius, and two fifths sheer fudge;
> Who talks like a book of iambs and pentameters
> In a way to make all men of common sense damn meters
> Who has written some things far the best of their kind;
> But somehow the heart seems squeezed out by the mind.

It brings a technical retort from Poe upon the grounds that, "We may observe here that *profound* ignorance on any particular topic is always sure to manifest itself by some allusion to 'common sense' as an all-sufficient instructor." Then he tears L.'s versification to pieces, adding, "Mr. L. should not have meddled with the anapestic rhythm: it is exceedingly awkward in the hands of one who knows nothing about it and who *will* persist in fancying that he can write it by ear." But, previously, he had nailed the matter in a different vein. Lowell "could not do a better thing than to take the advice of those who mean him well, and leave prose, with satiric verse, to those who are better able to manage them; while he contents himself with that class of poetry for which, and for which alone, he seems to have an especial vocation—the poetry of *sentiment*." But Poe might have added finally, in his own defense, what he says elsewhere, concerning the accusation in L.'s last two lines: "The *highest* order of the imaginative intellect is always preëminently mathematical—"

The whole passage is noteworthy not only for the brilliance of such a statement as that, but also because of its use of the provincial "we" (*Mr. Griswold and the Poets*): "That we are not a poetical people has been asserted so often and so roundly, both at home and abroad that the slander, through mere dint of repetition, has come to be received as truth. Yet nothing can be farther removed from it. The mistake is but a portion, or corollary, of the old dogma, that the calculating faculties are at war with the ideal; while, in fact, it may be demonstrated that the two divisions of mental power are never to be found in perfection apart. The highest order of the imaginative intellect is always preëminently mathematical; and the converse."

"The idiosyncrasy of our political position has stimulated into early action whatever practical talent we possessed. Even in our national infancy we evinced a degree of utilitarian ability which put to shame the mature skill of our forefathers. While yet in leading strings we proved ourselves adepts in all the arts and sciences which promoted the *comfort* of the animal man. But the arena of exertion, and of consequent distinction, into which our first and most obvious wants impelled us, has been regarded as the field of our deliberate choice. Our necessities have been taken for our propensities. Having been forced to make railroads, it has been deemed impossible that we should make verse. Because it suited us to construct an engine in the first instance, it has been denied that we could compose an epic in the second. Because we are not all Homers in the beginning, it has been somewhat rashly taken for granted that we shall be all Jeremy Benthams to the end."

"But this is purest insanity ... ."

In the critical note upon *Francis Marryat,* the distinction between "nationality in letters," which Poe carefully slights, and the preëminent importance, in letters as in all other branches of imaginative creation, of the *local,* which is his constant focus of attention, is to be noted.

Poe was NOT, it must be repeated, a Macabre genius, *essentially* lost upon the grotesque and the arabesque. If we have appraised him a morass of "lolling lilies," *that* is surface only.

The local causes shaping Poe's genius were two in character: the necessity for a fresh beginning, backed by a native vigor of extraordinary proportions,—with the corollary, that all "colonial imitation" must be swept aside. This was the conscious force which rose in Poe as innumerable timeless insights resulting, by his genius, in firm statements on the character of form, profusely illustrated by his practices; and, *second* the immediate effect of the locality upon the first, upon his nascent impulses, upon his original thrusts; tormenting the depths into a surface of bizarre designs by which he's known and which are *not at all* the major point in question.

Yet BOTH influences were determined by the locality, which, in the usual fashion, finds its mind swayed by the results of its stupidity rather than by a self-interest bred of greater wisdom. As with all else in America, the value of Poe's genius TO OURSELVES must be *uncovered* from our droppings, or at least uncovered from the "protection" which it must have raised about itself to have survived in any form among us—where everything is quickly trampled.

Poe "saw the end"; unhappily he saw his own despair at the same time, yet he continued to attack, with amazing genius seeking to discover, and discovering, points of firmness by which to STAND and grasp, against the slipping way they had of holding on in his locality. Either the New World must be mine as I will have it, or it is a worthless bog. There can be no concession. His attack was *from the center out.* Either I exist or I do not exist and no amount of pap which I happen to be lapping can dull me to the loss. It was a doctrine, anti-American. Here everything was makeshift, everything was colossal, in profusion. The frightened hogs or scared birds feeding on the corn— It left, in 1840, the same mood as ever dominant among us. Take what you can get. What you lack, copy. It was a population puffed with braggadocio, whom Poe so beautifully summarizes in many of his prose tales. To such men, all of them, the most terrible experience in the world is to be shown up. This Poe did, in his criticisms, with venomous accuracy. It was a gesture to BE CLEAN. It was a wish to HAVE the world or leave it. It was the truest instinct in America demanding to be satisfied, and an end to makeshifts, self deceptions and grotesque excuses. And yet the grotesque inappropriateness of the life about him forced itself in among his words.

One is forced on the conception of the New World as a woman. Poe was a new De Soto. The rest might be content with little things, not he.

"Rather the ice than their way."

His attack upon the difficulty which faced him was brilliantly conceived, faultlessly maintained and successful. The best term is perhaps: immaculate.

What he wanted was connected with no particular place; there-fore it *must* be where he *was*.

"We have at length arrived at that epoch when our literature may and must stand on its own merits, or fall through its own defects. We have snapped asunder the leading-strings of our British Grandmama, and, better still, we have survived the first hours of our novel freedom,—the first licentious hours of hobble-dehoy braggadocio and swagger. *At last,* then, we are in a condi-tion to be criticized—even more, to be neglected; . . ."

What Poe says gains power by his not diminishing his force for the slightness of the object; it is a sense of an inevitable, impartial tide. "We have *no* design to be bitter. We notice this book at all, only because it is an unusually large one of its kind, because it is lying here upon our table, and because, whether justly or unjustly, whether for good reason or for none, it has attracted some portion of the attention of the public." There is no softening for the department of names, old or new, but a sense of the evidence examined, as it lies on the page, by a faultless mechanism which he brings from the rear of his head for the trial.

Lowell, Bryant, etc., concerned poetry with literature, Poe con-cerned it with the soul; hence their differing conceptions of the use of language. With Poe, words were not hung by usage with associa-tions, the pleasing wraiths of former masteries, this is the senti-mental trap-door to beginnings. With Poe words were figures; an old language truly, but one from which he carried over only the most elemental qualities to his new purpose; which was, to find a way to tell his soul. Sometimes he used words so playfully his sentences seem to fly away from sense, the destructive! with the conserving abandon, foreshadowed, of a Gertrude Stein. The particles of language must be clear as sand. (See *Diddling.*)

This was an impossible conception for the gluey imagination of his day. Constantly he labored to detach SOMETHING from the inchoate mass—That's it:

His concern, the apex of his immaculate attack, was to detach a "method" from the smear of common usage—it is the work of nine tenths of his criticism. He struck to lay low the *"niaiseries"* of form and content with which his world abounded. It was a machine-gun fire; even in the slaughter of banality he rises to a merciless distinction. (See *Rufus Dawes.*) He sought by stress upon construction to hold the loose-strung mass off even at the cost of an icy coldness of appearance; it was the first need of his time, an escape from the formless mass he hated. It is the very sense of a beginning, as *it is the impulse which drove him to the character of all his tales;* to get from sentiment to form, a backstroke from the swarming "population."

He has a habit, borrowed perhaps from algebra, of balancing his sentences in the middle, or of reversing them in the later clauses, a sense of play, as with objects, or numerals which he *has* in the original, disassociated, that is, from other literary habit; separate words which he feels and turns about as if he fitted them to his design with *some* sense of their individual quality: "those who belong properly to books, and to whom books, perhaps, do not quite so properly belong."

The strong sense of a beginning in Poe is in *no one* else before him. What he says, being thoroughly local in origin, has some chance of being universal in application, a thing they never dared conceive. Made to fit a *place* it will have that actual quality of *things* anti-metaphysical—

About Poe there is—

No supernatural mystery—

No extraordinary eccentricty of fate—

He is American, understandable by a simple exercise of reason; a light in the morass—which *must* appear eerie, even to himself, by force of terrific contrast, an isolation that would naturally lead to drunkenness and death, logically and simply—by despair, as the very final evidence of a too fine seriousness and devotion.

It is natural that the French (foreigners, unacquainted with American conditions) should be attracted by the SURFACE of his genius and copy the wrong thing, (but the expressive thing), the strange, the bizarre (the recoil) without sensing the actuality, of which that is the complement,—and we get for Poe a REPUTATION for eccentric genius, maimed, the curious, the sick—at least the unexplainable crop-up, unrelated to his ground—which has become his inheritance.

. . . .

"The fiery serpent that bit the children of Israel when they wandered through the wilderness was possibly the guinea worm, which enters the body as a water flea, develops, and ultimately, lies coiled under the skin, from one to six feet in length. It formerly was coaxed out by winding it on a stick little by little each day. Then the zoologist found that it seeks water in which to lay its eggs, and will naively crawl out if the affected leg or arm is simply submerged in water for a few hours.

"The mysterious is so simple when revealed by science!"

.   .   .   .

On him is FOUNDED A LITERATURE—typical; an anger to sweep out the unoriginal, that became ill-tempered, a monomaniacal driving to destroy, to annihilate the copied, the slavish, the FALSE literature about him: this is the major impulse in his notes— darkening as he goes, losing the battle, as he feels himself going under—he emerges as the ghoulish, the driven back. It is the crudeness with which he was attacked in his own person, scoffed at—

He declares, maintains himself, pre-supposes himself and IS first rate. FIRST!—madly, valiantly battling for the right to BE FIRST— to hold up his ORIGINALITY—

"If a man—if an Orphicist—or SEER—or whatever else he may choose to call himself, while the rest of the world calls him an ass—if this gentleman have an idea which he does not understand himself, the best thing he can do is to say nothing about it; . . . but if he have any idea which is actually intelligible to himself, and if he sincerely wishes to render it intelligible to others, we then hold it as indisputable that he should employ those forms of speech which are the best adapted to further his object. He should speak to the people in that people's ordinary tongue. He should arrange words such as are habitually employed for the preliminary and introductory ideas to be conveyed—he should arrange them in collocations such as those in which we are accustomed to see those words arranged." "Meantime we earnestly ask if *bread-and-butter* be the vast IDEA in question—if *bread-and-butter* be any portion of this vast IDEA? for we have often observed that when a SEER has to speak of even so usual a thing as bread-and-butter, he can never be induced to mention it outright . . ."

The language of his essays is a remarkable HISTORY of the locality he springs from. There is no aroma to his words, rather a luminosity, that comes of a disassociation from anything else than thought and ideals; a coldly nebulous, side to side juxtaposition of the words as the ideas—It seems to fall back continuously to a bare surface exhausted by having reached no perch in tradition. Seldom a long or sensuous sentence, but with frequent reduplication upon itself as if holding itself up by itself.

Thought, thought, mass—and the sense of SOMETHING over the heads of the composite particles of the logic, the insignificance of the details, WHICH HE DID ACTUALLY achieve. A "childlike," simple, deductive reasoning IS his criticism—a sense of BEGINNING —of originality that presupposes an intrinsic WORTH in the reasoner—a sense of *stripped,* being clothed, nevertheless.

Unwilling to concede the necessity for any prop to his logical constructions, save the locality upon which originality is rested, he is the diametric opposite of Longfellow—to say the least. But Longfellow was the apotheosis of all that had preceded him in America, to this extent, that he brought over the *most* from "the other side." In *"Longfellow and Other Plagiarists,"* Poe looses himself to the full upon them. But what had they done? No more surely than five hundred architects are constantly practicing. Longfellow did it without genius, perhaps, but he did no more and no less than to bring the tower of the Seville Cathedral to Madison Square.

This is the expression of a "good" spirit. It is the desire to have "culture" for America by "finding" it, full blown—somewhere. But we had wandered too far, suffered too many losses for that. Such a conception could be no more than a pathetic reminiscence. It had NOTHING of the New World in it. Yet, it was bred of the wish to bring to the locality what it lacked.

What it lacked, really, was to be cultivated. So they build an unrelated copy upon it; this, as a sign of intelligence,—vigor. That is, to bring out its qualities, they cover them. Culture is still the effect of cultivation, to work with a thing until it be rare; as a golden dome among the mustard fields. It implies a solidity capable of cultivation. Its effects are marble blocks that lie perfectly fitted and aligned to express by isolate distinction the rising lusts which threw them off, regulated, in moving through the mass of impedimenta which is the world.

This is culture; in mastering them, to burst through the peculiarities of an environment. It is NOT culture to *oppress* a novel environment with the stale, if symmetrical, castoffs of another battle. They are nearly right when they say: Destroy the museums! But that is only the reflection, after all, of minds that fear to be slavish. Poe could look at France, Spain, Greece, and NOT be impelled to copy. He could do this BECAUSE he had the sense within him of a locality of his own, capable of cultivation.

Poe's use of the tags of other cultures than his own manages to be novel, interesting, useful, *unaffected,* since it succeeds in giving the impression of being not in the least dragged in by rule or pretence but of a fresh purpose such as I have indicated. There is nothing offensively "learned" there, nothing contemptuous, even in the witty tricks with bogus Latin which he plays on his illiterate public, which by *its* power, in turn, *permits* him an originality, *allows him,* even when he is satiric, an authenticity—since he is not seeking to destroy but to assert, candidly, and to defend *his own.*

He was the first to realize that the hard, sardonic, truculent mass of the New World, hot, angry—was, in fact, not a thing to paint over, to smear, to destroy—for it WOULD not be destroyed, it was too powerful,—it smiled! That it is NOT a thing to be slighted by men. Difficult, its very difficulty was their strength. It was in the generous bulk of its animal crudity that their every fineness would be found safely imbedded.

Poe conceived the possibility, the sullen, volcanic inevitability of the *place.* He was willing to go down and wrestle with its conditions, using every tool France, England, Greece could give him,—but to use them to original purpose.

This is his anger against Longfellow.

The difficulty is in holding the mind down to the point of seeing the *beginning* difference between Poe and the rest. One cannot expect to see as wide a gap between him and the others as exists between the Greek and the Chinese. It is only in the conception of a *possibility* that he is most distinguished. His greatness is in that he turned his back and faced inland, to originality, with the identical gesture of a Boone.

And for *that* reason he is unrecognized. Americans have never recognized themselves. How can they? It is impossible until someone invent the ORIGINAL terms. As long as we are content to be called by somebody else's terms, we are incapable of being anything but our own dupes.

Thus Poe must suffer by his originality. Invent that which is new, even if it be made of pine from your own yard, and there's none to know what you have done. It is because there's no *name*. This is the cause of Poe's lack of recognition. He was American. He was the astounding, inconceivable growth of his locality. Gape at him they did, and he at them in amazement. Afterward with mutual hatred; he in disgust, they in mistrust. It is only that which is under your nose which seems inexplicable.

Here Poe emerges—in no sense the bizarre, isolate writer, the curious literary figure. On the contrary, in him American literature is anchored, in him alone, on solid ground.

In all he says there is a sense of him *surrounded* by his time, tearing at it, ever with more rancor, but always at battle, taking hold.

But Poe—differing from pioneers in other literatures, the great beginners—due to the nature of the people, *had first to lift his head through* a successful banality. This was a double impost But he did it, NOT by despising, ignoring, slighting the work that preceded him but by attacking it. "Among all the pioneers of American literature, whether prose or poetical, there is *not one* (Note: In his own estimate even, he begins.) whose productions have not been much overrated by his countrymen."

"But originality, as it is one of the highest, is also one of the rarest of merits. In America it is especially, and very remarkably, rare—this through causes sufficiently well understood."

He abhorred the "excessively opportune."—Of course, he says, to write of the Indians, the forests, the great natural beauty of the New World will be attractive and make a hit—so he counsels writers to AVOID it, for reasons crystal clear and well chosen. (See *Fenimore Cooper*.) His whole insistence has been upon method, in opposition to a nameless rapture over nature. He admired Claude Lorraine. Instead of to hog-fill the copied style with a gross rural sap, he wanted a lean style, rapid as a hunter and with an aim as sure. One way, in the New World, men must go. Bust gut or acute wit. Find the ground, on your feet or on your belly. It is a fight. He counsels writers to *borrow nothing* from the scene, but to put all the weight of effort into the WRITING. Put aside the GRAND scene and get to work to express yourself. Method, punctuation, grammar—

The local condition of literature FORCED Poe's hand. It is necessary to understand this if his names are to be grasped. By avoiding, of necessity, the fat country itself for its expression; to originate a style that does spring from the local conditions, not of trees and mountains, but of the "soul"—here starved, stricken by loss of liberty, ready to die—he is *forced in certain directions for his subjects.*

But this left him in difficulties. When he had narrowed himself down to a choice of method and subject, when all the meaningless lump of the lush landscape and all that that implies had been swept away, THEN, and only then will he begin to search for a subject. A voluntary lopping off of a NATURAL landscape, forced him into a field which he must have *searched* for, a field of cold logic, of invention, to which his work must still present a natural *appearance*: into his imaginative prose.

His criticism paves the way for what *must* be his prose—illustrating his favorite theory that the theory *includes the practice.*

No better means of transit from the criticism to the tales could be imagined than his discussion of the merits and demerits of Hawthorne as a proseist. He expresses his delight and surprise at finding Hawthorne's work of such excellence, but then he finds a fault:

"He has the purest style, the finest taste, the most available scholarship, the most delicate humor, the most touching pathos, the most radiant imagination, the most consummate ingenuity, and with these varied good qualities he has done well as a mystic. But is there any one of these qualities which would prevent his doing doubly as well in a career of honest, upright, sensible, prehensible, and comprehensible things? Let him mend his pen, get a bottle of visible ink, come out from the Old Manse, cut Mr. Alcott, hang (if possible) the Editor of *The Dial,* and throw out of the window to the pigs all his odd numbers of *The North American Review.*"

Hawthorne has no repugnance for handling what Poe purposely avoids, the contamination of the UNFORMED LUMP, the *"monstrum, horrendum, informe, ingens, cui lumen ademptum."* And it is precisely here that lies Hawthorne's lack of importance to our literature when he is compared with Poe; what Hawthorne *loses* by his willing closeness to the life of his locality in its vague humors; his lifelike copying of the New England melancholy; his reposeful closeness to the town pump—Poe *gains* by abhorring; flying to the ends of the earth for "original" material—

By such a simple, logical twist does Poe succeed in being the more American, heeding more the local necessities, the harder structural imperatives—by standing off to SEE instead of forcing himself too close. Whereas Hawthorne, in his tales, by doing what everyone else in France, England, Germany was doing *for his own milieu,* is no more than copying their *method* with another setting; does not ORIGINATE; has not a *beginning* literature at heart that must establish its own rules, own framework,—Poe has realized by adopting a more elevated mien.

This feeling in Poe's tales, that is, the hidden, under, unapparent part, gives him the firmness of INSIGHT into the conditions upon which our literature must rest, always the same, a local one, surely, but not of sentiment or mood, as not of trees and Indians, but of original fibre, the normal toughness which fragility of mood presupposes, if it will be expressive of anything— It is the expression of Poe's clearness of insight into the true difficulty, and his soundness of judgment.

.   .   .   .

To understand what Poe is driving at in his tales, one should read first NOT the popular, perfect—*Gold Bug, Murders in the Rue Morgue,* etc., which by their brilliancy detract from the observation of his deeper intent, but the less striking tales—in fact all, but especially those where his humor is less certain, his mood lighter, less tightly bound by the incident, where numerous illuminating *faults* are allowed to become expressive, *The Business Man, The Man That Was Used Up, Loss of Breath, BonBon, Diddling, The Angel of the Odd*—and others of his lesser Tales.

It should be noted how often certain things take place—how often there is death but not that only; it is the body broken apart, dismembered, as in *Loss of Breath*—

Then, as in *Hop Frog, The System of Dr. Tarr and Professor Fether* and the *Murders in the Rue Morgue*—the recurrent image of the ape. Is it his disgust with his immediate associates and his own fears, which cause this frequent use of the figure to create the emotion of extreme terror?—"Your majesty cannot conceive of the *effect* produced, at a masquerade, by eight chained orang-outangs, imagined to be real ones by the most of the company; and rushing in with savage cries, among the crowd of delicately and gorgeously habited men and women. The contrast is inimitable."

Note, in *Silence—a Fable:* "sorrow and weariness and disgust with mankind and a longing for solitude."

Many colloquial words could be detached from Poe's usage if it were worth while, to show how the language he practices varies from English, but such an exercise would be of little value—*hipped, crack,* etc.—it does not touch bottom.

The Tales continue the theories of the criticism, carrying out what they propose:

1. In choice of material, abstract. 2. In method, a logical construction that clips away, in great part, the "scenery" near at hand in order to let the real business of composition *show*. 3. A primitive awkwardness of diction, lack of polish, colloquialism that is, unexpectedly, especially in the dialogues, much in the vein of Mark Twain.

One feels that in the actual composition of his tales there must have been for him, as they embody it in fact, a fascination other than the topical one. The impulse that made him write them, that made him enjoy writing them—cannot have been the puerile one of amazement, but a deeper, logical enjoyment, in keeping with his own seriousness: it is that of PROVING even the most preposterous of his inventions plausible—that BY HIS METHOD he makes them WORK. They go: they *prove* him potent, they confirm his thought. And by the very extreme of their play, by so much the more do they hold up the actuality of that which he conceives.

If there ever had been another American to use his Greek, Sanscrit, Hebrew, Latin, French, German, Italian and Spanish—in the text—with anything like the unspoiled mastery of Poe, we should have known, long since, what it meant to have a literature of our own.

It is to have a *basis,* a local stanchion, by which to *bridge over* the gap between present learning and the classical; that asserts the continuity of the common virtues of style; that asserts their aristocratic origin, or their democratic origin, the same, as it has been pointed out recently, since an aristocracy is the flower of a locality and so the *full* expression of a democracy.

Of his method in the Tales, the significance and the secret is: authentic particles, a thousand of which spring to the mind for quotation, taken apart and reknit with a view to emphasize, enforce and make evident, the *method*. Their quality of skill in observation, their heat, local verity, being *overshadowed* only by the detached, the abstract, the cold philosophy of their joining together; a method springing so freshly from the local conditions which determine it, by their emphasis of firm crudity and lack of coordinated structure, as to be worthy of most painstaking study— The whole period, America 1840, could be rebuilt, psychologically (phrenologically) from Poe's "method."

.   .   .   .

It is especially in the poetry where "death looked gigantically down" that the horror of the formless resistance which opposed, maddened, destroyed him has forced its character into the air, the wind, the blessed galleries of paradise, above a morose, dead world, peopled by shadows and silence, and despair— It is the compelling force of his isolation.

The one earthly island he found where he might live in something akin to the state he imagined, the love of his wife, had to be single and inviolate. Failing of a more comprehensive passion, which might have possessed him had the place been of favorable omen, only in this narrow cell could he exist at all. Of this the poems are the full effect. He is known as a poet, yet there are but five poems, possibly three.

When she died, there was nothing left. In his despair he had nowhere to turn. It is the very apotheosis of the place and the time.

He died imploring from those about him a love he could not possess, since his own love, as his poems, had been so mingled in character with the iron revenge which completely surrounded him that it could not be repeated once its single object had been lost.

But here, in his poetry least of all, is there a mystery. It is but the accumulation of all that he has expressed, in the criticism, in the prose tales, but made as if so shaken with desire, that it has come off as a flame, destroying the very vial that contained it—and become, against his will almost it would seem,—himself.

It is not by a change in character but by its quickened motion that it has turned from mere heat into light—by its power of penetration that it has been brought to dwell upon love. By its acid power to break down truth that it has been *forced* upon love—

I mean that though in this his "method" has escaped him, yet his poems remain of the single stuff of his great "theory": to grasp the meaning, to understand, to reduce all things to method, to control, lifting himself to power—

And failing, truth turning to love, as if metamorphosed in his hands as he was about to grasp it—now the full horror of his isolation comes down—

In his prose he could still keep a firm hold, he still held the "arrangement" fast and stood above it, but in the poetry he was at the edge—there was nothing—

Here in poetry, where it is said "we approach the gods," Poe was caught, instead, in his time.

Now, defenseless, the place itself attacked him. Now the thinness of his coat, the terror of his isolation took hold.

Had he lived in a world where love throve, his poems might have grown differently. But living where he did, surrounded as he was by that world of unreality, a formless "population"—drifting and feeding—a huge terror possessed him.

His passion for the refrain is like an echo from a hollow. It is his own voice returning—

His imagery is of the desperate situation of his mind, thin as a flame to mount unsupported, successful for a moment in the love of—not so much his wife—but in the escape she filled for him with her frail person, herself afflicted as by "ghouls."

Disarmed, in his poetry the place itself comes through. This is the New World. It is this that it does, as if—

It is in this wraithlike quality of his poems, of his five poems, that Poe is most of the very ground, hard to find, as if we walked upon a cushion of light pressed thin beneath our feet, that insulates, satirises—while we lash ourselves up and down in a fury of impotence.

Poe stayed against the thin edge, driven to be heard by the

battering racket about him to a distant screaming—the pure essence of his locality.

The best poem is *To One in Paradise*.

[*1925*]

The Work of Gertrude Stein

Would I had seen a white bear!
(for how can I imagine it?)

Let it be granted that whatever is new in literature the germ of it will be found somewhere in the writings of other times; only the modern emphasis gives work a present distinction.

The necessity for this modern focus and the meaning of the changes involved are, however, another matter, the everlasting stumbling block to criticism. Here is a theme worth development in the case of Gertrude Stein—yet signally neglected.

Why in fact have we not heard more generally from American scholars upon the writings of Miss Stein? Is it lack of heart or ability or just that theirs is an enthusiasm which fades rapidly of its own nature before the risks of today?

> The verbs auxiliary we are concerned in here, con-
> tinued my father, are am; was; have; had; do; did;
> could; owe; make; made; suffer; shall; should; will;
> would; can; ought; used; or is wont . . . —or with these
> question added to them;—Is it? Was it? Will it be? . . .
> Or affirmatively . . . —Or chronologically . . . —Or
> hypothetically . . . —If it was? If it was not? What

would follow?—If the French beat the English? If the
Sun should go out of the Zodiac?

Now, by the right use and application of these, con-
tinued my father, in which a child's memory should be
exercised, there is no one idea can enter the brain how
barren soever, but a magazine of conceptions and conclu-
sions may be drawn forth from it.—Didst thou ever see a
white bear? cried my father, turning his head round to
Trim, who stood at the back of his chair.—No, an' please
your honour, replied the corporal.—But thou couldst dis-
course about one, Trim, said my father, in case of
need?—How is it possible, brother, quoth my Uncle
Toby, if the corporal never saw one?—'Tis the fact I
want, replied my father,—and the possibility of it as fol-
lows.

A white bear! Very well, Have I ever seen one? Might
I ever have seen one? Am I ever to see one? Ought I ever
to have seen one? Or can I ever see one?

Would I had seen a white bear! (for how can I imag-
ine it?)

If I should see a white bear, what should I say? If I
should never see a white bear, what then?

If I never have, can, must, or shall see a white bear
alive; have I ever seen the skin of one? Did I ever see one
painted?—described? Have I never dreamed of one?

Note how the words *alive, skin, painted, described, dreamed*
come into the design of these sentences. The feeling is of words
themselves, a curious immediate quality quite apart from their
meaning, much as in music different notes are dropped, so to
speak, into repeated chords one at a time, one after another—for
themselves alone. Compare this with the same effects common in
all that Stein does. See *Geography and Plays,* "They were both gay
there." To continue—

Did my father, mother, uncle, aunt, brothers or sisters,
ever see a white bear? What would they give? . . . How
would they behave? How would the white bear have be-
haved? Is he wild? Tame? Terrible? Rough? Smooth?

Note the play upon *rough* and *smooth* (though it is not certain that this was intended), *rough* seeming to apply to the bear's deportment, *smooth* to surface, presumably the bear's coat. In any case the effect is that of a comparison relating primarily not to any qualities of the bear himself but to the words rough and smooth. And so to finish—

> Is the white bear worth seeing?
> Is there any sin in it?
> Is it better than a black one?

In this manner ends Chapter 43 of *The Life and Opinions of Tristram Shandy*. The handling of the words and to some extent the imaginative quality of the sentence is a direct forerunner of that which Gertrude Stein has woven today into a synthesis of its own. It will be plain, in fact, on close attention, that Sterne exercises not only the play (or music) of sight, sense and sound contrast among the words themselves which Stein uses, but their grammatical play also—i.e. for, how, can I imagine it; did my . . . , what would, how would, compare Stein's "to have rivers; to halve rivers," etc. It would not be too much to say that Stein's development over a lifetime is anticipated completely with regard to subject matter, sense and grammar—in Sterne.

Starting from scratch we get, possibly, thatch; just as they have always done in poetry.

Then they would try to connect it up by something like—The mice scratch, beneath the thatch.

Miss Stein does away with all that. The free-versists on the contrary used nothing else. They saved—The mice, under the . . . ,

It is simply the skeleton, the "formal" parts of writing, those that make form, that she has to do with, apart from the "burden" which they carry. The skeleton, important to acknowledge where confusion of all knowledge of the "soft parts" reigns as at the present day in all intellectual fields.

Stein's theme is writing. But in such a way as to be writing envisioned as the first concern of the moment, dragging behind it a dead weight of logical burdens, among them a dead criticism which broken through might be a gap by which endless other enterprises of the understanding should issue—for refreshment.

It is a revolution of some proportions that is contemplated, the exact nature of which may be no more than sketched here but whose basis is humanity in a relationship with literature hitherto little contemplated.

And at the same time it is a general attack on the scholastic viewpoint, that medieval remnant with whose effects from generation to generation literature has been infested to its lasting detriment. It is a break-away from that paralyzing vulgarity of logic for which the habits of science and philosophy coming over into literature (where they do not belong) are to blame.

It is this logicality as a basis for literary action which in Stein's case, for better or worse, has been wholly transcended.

She explains her own development in connection with *Tender Buttons* (1914). "It was my first conscious struggle with the problem of correlating sight, sound and sense, and eliminating rhythm;—now I am trying grammar and eliminating sight and sound" (*transition* No. 14, fall, 1928).

Having taken the words to her choice, to emphasize further what she has in mind she has completely unlinked them (in her most recent work) from their former relationships in the sentence. This was absolutely essential and unescapable. Each under the new arrangement has a quality of its own, but not conjoined to carry the burden science, philosophy and every higgledy-piggledy figment of law and order have been laying upon them in the past. They are like a crowd at Coney Island, let us say, seen from an airplane.

Whatever the value of Miss Stein's work may turn out finally to be, she has at least accomplished her purpose of getting down on paper this much that is decipherable. She has placed writing on a plane where it may deal unhampered with its own affairs, unburdened with scientific and philosophic lumber.

For after all, science and philosophy are today, in their effect upon the mind, little more than fetishes of unspeakable abhorrence. And it is through a subversion of the art of writing that their grip upon us has assumed its steel-like temper.

What are philosophers, scientists, religionists, they that have filled up literature with their pap? Writers, of a kind. Stein simply erases their stories, turns them off and does without them, their logic (founded merely on the limits of the perceptions) which is supposed to transcend the words, along with them. Stein denies it. The words, in writing, she discloses, transcend everything.

Movement (for which in a petty way logic is taken), the so-called search for truth and beauty, is for us the effect of a break-down of the attention. But movement must not be confused with what we attach to it but, for the rescuing of the intelligence, must always be considered aimless, without progress.

This is the essence of all knowledge.

Bach might be an illustration of movement not suborned by a freight of purposed design, loaded upon it as in almost all later musical works; statement unmusical and unnecessary, Stein's "They lived very gay then" has much of the same quality of movement to be found in Bach—the composition of the words determining not the logic, not the "story," not the theme even, but the movement itself. As it happens, "They were both gay there" is as good as some of Bach's shorter figures.

Music could easily have a statement attached to each note in the manner of words, so that C natural might mean the sun, etc., and completely dull treatises be played—and even sciences finally expounded in tunes.

Either, we have been taught to think, the mind moves in a logical sequence to a definite end which is its goal, or it will embrace movement without goal other than movement itself for an end and hail "transition" only as supreme.

Take your choice, both resorts are an improper description of the mind in fullest play.

If the attention could envision the whole of writing, let us say, at one time, moving over it in swift and accurate pursuit of the modern imperative at the instant when it is most to the fore, something of what actually takes place under an optimum of intelligence could be observed. It is an alertness not to let go of a possibility of movement in our fearful bedazzlement with some concrete and fixed present. The goal is to keep a beleaguered line of understanding which has movement from breaking down and becoming a hole into which we sink decoratively to rest.

The goal has nothing to do with the silly function which logic, natural or otherwise, enforces. Yet it is a goal. It moves as the sense wearies, remains fresh, living. One is concerned with it as with anything pursued and not with the rush of air or the guts of the horse one is riding—save to a very minor degree.

Writing, like everything else, is much a question of refreshed interest. It is directed, not idly, but as most often happens (though not necessarily so) toward that point not to be predetermined where movement is blocked (by the end of logic perhaps). It is about these parts, if I am not mistaken, that Gertrude Stein will be found.

There remains to be explained the bewildering volume of what Miss Stein has written, the quantity of her work, its very apparent repetitiousness, its iteration, what I prefer to call its extension, the final clue to her meaning.

It is, of course, a progression (not a progress) beginning, conveniently, with "Melanctha" from *Three Lives,* and coming up to today.

How in a democracy, such as the United States, can writing which has to compete with excellence elsewhere and in other times remain in the field and be at once objective (true to fact), intellectually searching, subtle and instinct with powerful additions to our lives? It is impossible, without invention of some sort, for the very good reason that observation about us engenders the very opposite of what we seek: triviality, crassness and intellectual bankruptcy. And yet what we do see can in no way be excluded. Satire and flight are two possibilities but Miss Stein has chosen otherwise.

But if one remain in a place and reject satire, what then? To be democratic, local (in the sense of being attached with integrity to actual experience) Stein, or any other artist, must for subtlety ascend to a plane of almost abstract design to keep alive. To writing, then, as an art in itself. Yet what actually impinges on the senses must be rendered as it appears, by use of which, only, and under which, untouched, the significance has to be disclosed. It is one of the major problems of the artist.

"Melanctha" is a thrilling clinical record of the life of a colored woman in the present-day United States, told with directness and truth. It is without question one of the best bits of characterization produced in America. It is universally admired. This is where Stein began. But for Stein to tell a story of that sort, even with the utmost genius was not enough under the conditions in which we live, since by the very nature of its composition such a story does violence to the larger scene which would be portrayed.

True, a certain way of delineating the scene is to take an individual like Melanctha and draw her carefully. But this is what happens. The more carefully the drawing is made, the greater the genius involved and the greater the interest that attaches, therefore, to the character as an individual, the more exceptional that character becomes in the mind of the reader and the less typical of the scene.

It was no use for Stein to go on with *Three Lives*. There that phase of the work had to end. See *Useful Knowledge,* the parts on the U.S.A.

Stein's pages have become like the United States viewed from an airplane—the same senseless repetitions, the endless multiplications of toneless words, with these she had to work.

No use for Stein to fly to Paris and forget it. The thing, the United States, the unmitigated stupidity, the drab tediousness of the democracy, the overwhelming number of the offensively ignorant, the dull nerve—is there in the artist's mind and cannot be escaped by taking a ship. She must resolve it if she can, if she is to be.

That must be the artist's articulation with existence.

Truly, the world is full of emotion—more or less—but it is caught in bewilderment to a far more important degree. And the purpose of art, so far as it has any, is not at least to copy that, but lies in the resolution of difficulties to its own comprehensive organization of materials. And by so doing, in this case, rather than by copying, it takes its place as most human.

To deal with Melanctha, with characters of whomever it may be, the modern Dickens, is not therefore human. To write like that is not in the artist, to be human at all, since nothing is resolved, nothing is done to resolve the bewilderment which makes of emotion an inanity: That, is to overlook the gross instigation and with all subtlety to examine the object minutely for "the truth"— which if there is anything more commonly practiced or more stupid, I have yet to come upon it.

To be most useful to humanity, or to anything else for that matter, an art, writing, must stay art, not seeking to be science, philosophy, history, the humanities, or anything else it has been made to carry in the past. It is this enforcement which underlies Gertrude Stein's extension and progression to date.

[*1931*]

Introduction to *The Wedge*

The war is the first and only thing in the world today.

The arts generally are not, nor is this writing a diversion from that for relief, a turning away. It *is* the war or part of it, merely a different sector of the field.

Critics of rather better than average standing have said in recent years that after socialism has been achieved it's likely there will be no further use for poetry, that it will disappear. This comes from nothing else than a faulty definition of poetry—and the arts generally. I don't hear anyone say that mathematics is likely to be outmoded, to disappear shortly. Then why poetry?

It is an error attributable to the Freudian concept of the thing, that the arts are a resort from frustration, a misconception still entertained in many minds.

They speak as though action itself in all its phases were not compatible with frustration. All action the same. But Richard Coeur de Lion wrote at least one of the finest lyrics of his day. Take Don Juan for instance. Who isn't frustrated and does not prove it by his actions—if you want to say so? But through art the psychologically maimed may become the most distinguished man of his age. Take Freud for instance.

The making of poetry is no more an evidence of frustration than is the work of Henry Kaiser or of Timoshenko. It's the war, the driving forward of desire to a complex end. And when that shall have been achieved, mathematics and the arts will turn else-where—beyond the atom if necessary for their reward and let's all be frustrated together.

A man isn't a block that remains stationary though the psychologists treat him so—and most take an insane pride in believing it. Consistency! He varies; Hamlet today, Caesar tomorrow; here, there, somewhere—if he is to retain his sanity, and why not?

The arts have a *complex* relation to society. The poet isn't a fixed phenomenon, no more is his work. *That* might be a note on current affairs, a diagnosis, a plan for procedure, a retrospect—all in its own peculiarly enduring form. There need be nothing limited or frustrated about that. It may be a throw-off from the most violent and successful action or run parallel to it, a saga. It may be the picking out of an essential detail for memory, something to be set aside for further study, a sort of shorthand of emotional significances for later reference.

Let the metaphysical take care of itself, the arts have nothing to do with it. They will concern themselves with it if they please, among other things. To make two bald statements: There's nothing sentimental about a machine, and: A poem is a small (or large) machine made of words. When I say there's nothing sentimental about a poem I mean that there can be no part, as in any other machine, that is redundant.

Prose may carry a load of ill-defined matter like a ship. But poetry is the machine which drives it, pruned to a perfect economy. As in all machines its movement is intrinsic, undulant, a physical more than a literary character. In a poem this movement is distinguished in each case by the character of the speech from which it arises.

Therefore, each speech having its own character, the poetry it engenders will be peculiar to that speech also in its own intrinsic form. The effect is beauty, what in a single object resolves our complex feelings of propriety. One doesn't seek beauty. All that an artist or a Sperry can do is to drive toward his purpose, in the nature of his materials; not to take gold where Babbitt metal is called for; to make: make clear the complexity of his perceptions in the medium given to him by inheritance, chance, accident or whatever it may be to work with according to his talents and the will that drives them. Don't talk about frustration fathering the arts. The bastardization of words is too widespread for that today.

My own interest in the arts has been extracurricular. Up from the gutter, so to speak. Of necessity. Each age and place to its own. But in the U.S. the necessity for recognizing this intrinsic character has been largely ignored by the various English Departments of the academies.

When a man makes a poem, makes it, mind you, he takes words as he finds them interrelated about him and composes them—without distortion which would mar their exact significances—into an intense expression of his perceptions and ardors that they may constitute a revelation in the speech that he uses. It isn't what he *says* that counts as a work of art, it's what he makes, with such intensity of perception that it lives with an intrinsic movement of its own to verify its authenticity. Your attention is called now and then to some beautiful line or sonnet-sequence because of what is said there. So be it. To me all sonnets say the same thing of no importance. What does it matter what the line "says"?

There is no poetry of distinction without formal invention, for it is in the intimate form that works of art achieve their exact meaning, in which they most resemble the machine, to give language its highest dignity, its illumination in the evironment to which it is native. Such war, as the arts live and breathe by, is continuous.

It may be that my interests as expressed here are pre-art. If so I look for a development along these lines and will be satisfied with nothing else.

[*1944*]

William Carlos Williams
to Robert Creeley

March 3, 1950

Dear Creeley:

My own (moral) program can be chiefly stated. I send it for what it may be worth to you: To write badly is an offence to the state since the government can never be more than the government of the words.

If the language is distorted crime flourishes. It is well that in the unobstructed arts (because they can at favorable times escape the perversions which flourish elsewhere) a means is at least presented to the mind where a man can go on living.

For there is in each age a specific criterion which is the objective for the artist in that age. Not to attack that objective is morally reprehensible—as evil as it is awkward to excuse.

Bad art is then that which does not serve in the continual service of cleansing the language of all fixations upon dead, stinking dead, usages of the past. Sanitation and hygiene or sanitation that we may have hygienic writing.

W. C. W.

H. D.

EPITAPH

So I may say,
"I died of living,
having lived one hour";

so they may say,
"she died soliciting
illicit fervour";

so you may say,
"Greek flower; Greek ecstasy
reclaims forever

one who died
following
intricate song's lost measure."

LOUIS ZUKOFSKY

A Statement for Poetry

———————————

Any definition of poetry is difficult because the implications of poetry are complex—and that despite the natural, physical simplicity of its best examples. Thus poetry may be defined as an order of words that as movement and tone (rhythm and pitch) approaches in varying degrees the wordless art of music as a kind of mathematical limit. Poetry is derived obviously from everyday existence (real or ideal).

Whoever makes it may very well consider a poem as a design or construction. A contemporary American poet says: "A poem is a small (or large) machine made of words." The British mathematician George Hardy has envied poetry its fineness of immediate logic. A scientist may envy its bottomless perception of relations which, for all its intricacies, keeps a world of things tangible and whole. Perhaps poetry is what Hideki Yukawa is looking for when, with reference to his latest theory of particles that possess not only charge and mass but also dimensions in space, he says: "This problem of infinity is a disease that must be cured. I am very eager to be healthy."

"Poetry is something more philosophic and of graver import than history." (Aristole, *Poetics* 9.) True or not this statement recalls that poetry has contributed intense records to history. The rhythmic or intoned utterance that punctuates the movement of a body in a dance or ritual, aware of dead things as alive, as it fights animals and earth; Homer's heavenly singer who gave pleasure at a feast in a society accomplished in husbandry and craft, whose group beliefs *saw* the Muses presiding over the harmony that moved the words; the dry passages of Lucretius forced by his measures to sing despite their regard for abstract patterns of thought, beginnings of atomic speculation: the stages of culture are concretely delineated in these three examples.

Poetry has always been considered more literary than music, though so-called pure music may be literary in a communicative sense. The parts of a fugue, Bach said, should behave like reasonable men in an orderly discussion. But music does not depend mainly on the human voice, as poetry does, for rendition. And it is possible in imagination to divorce speech of all graphic elements, to let it become a movement of sounds. It is this musical horizon of poetry (which incidentally poems perhaps never reach) that permits anybody who does not know Greek to listen and get something out of the poetry of Homer: to "tune in" to the human tradition, to its voice which has developed among the sounds of natural things, and thus escape the confines of a time and place, as one hardly ever escapes them in studying Homer's grammar. In this sense poetry is international.

The foregoing definition of poetry has been, for the most part, cultural in its bearings. But what specifically is good poetry? It is precise information on existence out of which it grows, and information of its own existence, that is, the movement (and tone) of words. Rhythm, pulse, keeping time with existence, is the distinction of its technique. This integrates any human emotion, any discourse, into an order of words that exists as another created thing in the world, to affect it and be judged by it. Condensed speech is most of the method of poetry (as distinguished from the essentially discursive art of prose). The rest is ease, pause, grace. If read properly, good poetry does not argue its attitudes or beliefs; it exists independently of the reader's preferences for one kind of "subject" or another. Its conviction is in its mastery or technique. The length of a poem has nothing to do with its merits as composition in which each sound of a word is weighed, though obviously it is possible to have more of a good thing—a wider range of things felt, known, and conveyed.

The oldest recorded poems go back to the Egyptian *Chapters of Coming Forth by Day,* some of whose hieroglyphs were old by 3000 B.C. The human tradition that survives the esoteric significance of these poems remains, as in these lines praising the sun:

Millions of years have passed, we cannot count their number,
Millions of years shall come. You are above the years.

It is quite safe to say that the *means* and *objects* of poetry (cf.
Aristotle's *Poetics*) have been constant, that is, recognizably hu-
man, since ca. 3000 B.C.

I. The Means of Poetry: *Words*—consisting of *syllables,* in turn
made up of *phones* that are denoted by *letters* that were once
graphic symbols or pictures. Words grow out of affects of
   A. Sight, touch, taste, smell
   B. Hearing
   C. Thought with respect to other words, the interplay of con-
       cepts.

II. The Objects of Poetry: *Poems*—rhythmic compositions of
words whose components are
   A. Image
   B. Sound
   C. Interplay of Concepts (judgments of other words either ab-
       stract or sensible, or both at once).

Some peoms make use of—i.e. resolve—all three components.
Most poems use only A and B. Poems that use B and C are less
frequent, though C is a poetic device (invention) at least as old as
Homer's puns on the name of Odysseus: "the man of all odds,"
"how odd I see you Od-ysseus." (cf. also the earlier, homophonic
devices of syllabaries.)

A. *Image*. Composed groups of words used as symbols for things
and states of sight, touch, taste and smell present an image. For
example: Homer's "a dark purple wave made an arch over them
like a mountain cave"; the image of Hades evoked by the eleventh
book of *The Odyssey;* or the landscape and journey which is all of
The Odyssey—the homecoming of Odysseus.

> cf. Weight, grandeur, and energy in writing are very
> largely produced, dear pupil, by the use of "images."
> (That at least is what some people call the actual mental
> pictures.) For the term Imagination is applied in general
> to an idea which enters the mind from any source and en-

genders speech, but the word has now come to be used of passages where, inspired by strong emotion, you seem to see what you describe and bring it vividly before the eyes of your audience. That imagination means one thing in oratory and another in poetry you will yourself detect, and also that the object of poetry is to enthral, of prose writing to present ideas clearly, though both indeed aim at this latter and at excited feeling.

[Longinus (213–273), *On the Sublime* XV, 2.]

B. *Sound.* Besides the imitation in words of natural sound (the sound of the sea in Homer, the sound of birds in "Bare ruined choirs where late the sweet birds sang"), the component of sound in poetry, as conveyed by rendition, comprises sound that is

1. Spoken (e.g. "and we'll talk with them too,
   Who loses and who wins, who's in,
   who's out,"—*King Lear*)
2. Declaimed (e.g., Milton's *Paradise Lost*)
3. Intoned or Chanted (e.g. words used in a liturgical monotone)
4. Sung (to a melody, i.e. a musical phrase or idea. Some of the best examples in English are Campion's poems, Shakespeare's songs—which have been set to music by Purcell, Johnson, Arne—and Burns' songs written to folk tunes.)

C. *Interplay of Concepts.* This component effects compositions in which words involve other words in common or contrasting logical implications, and to this end it employs sound, and sometimes image, as an accessory. The elements of grammar and rhetorical balance (v.s., Shakespeare's "who's *in,* who's *out*") contribute to this type of poetry. (Examples: most of Donne's poems, Andrew Marvell's "The Definition of Love," George Herbert's "Heaven," Lord Rochester's "Ode to Nothing," Fitzgerald's translation of *Rubaiyat,* Eliot's "The Hollow Men.")

From the preceding analysis of the components of poems it is clear that their forms are achieved as a dynamics of speech and sound, that is, as a resolution of their interacting rhythms—with no loss of value to any word at the expense of the movement. In actual practice, this dynamics works out standards of measure—or metres. The good poems of the past have developed the "science" of prosody in the same way that the effective use of words has developed the logic of grammar. But poetry, though it has its constants, is made in every age.

Prosody analyses poems according to line lengths and groups of lines or verses as vehicles of rhythm, varieties of poetic feet or units of rhythm (analogous to a measure in music) *and* their variants (e.g., unexpected inversions of accent, unexpected "extra" syllables), rhymes *and* their variants (e.g. consonance, assonance, perfect rhyme—i.e. the same sound rhymes with itself, etc.), rhyming patterns, stanzas or strophes, fixed forms and free verse. No verse is "free," however, if its rhythms inevitably carry the words in contexts that do not falsify the function of words as speech probing the possibilities and attractions of existence. This being the practice of poetry, prosody as such is of secondary interest to the poet. He looks, so to speak, into his ear as he does at the same time into his heart and intellect. His ear is sincere, if his words convey his awareness of the range of differences and subtleties of duration. He does not measure with handbook, and is not a pendulum. He may find it right to count syllables, or their relative lengths and stresses, or to be sensitive to all these metrical factors. As a matter of fact, the good poets do all these things. But they do not impose their count on what is said or made—as may be judged from the impact of their poems.

Symmetry occurs in all the arts as they develop. It is usually present in some form in most good poetry. The stanza was perhaps invented in an attempt to fit a tune to more words than it had notes: the words were grouped into stanzas permitting the tune to be repeated. But existence does not foster this technique in all times indiscriminately. The least unit of a poem must support the stanza; it should never be inflicted on the least unit. As Sidney wrote in his *Apology* (1595): "One may be a poet without versing, and a versifier without poetry."

The best way to find out about poetry is to read the poems. That way the reader becomes something of a poet himself: not because he "contributes" to the poetry, but because he finds himself subject of its energy.

[1950]

CHARLES OLSON

Projective Verse

_____

(projectile   (percussive   (prospective
                    _vs._
                The NON-Projective

_(or what a French critic calls "closed" verse, that verse
which print bred and which is pretty much what we have
had, in English & American, and have still got, despite
the work of Pound & Williams:_

_it led Keats, already a hundred years ago, to see it
(Wordsworth's, Milton's) in the light of "the Egotistical
Sublime"; and it persists, at this latter day, as what you
might call the private-soul-at-any-public-wall)_

Verse now, 1950, if it is to go ahead, if it is to be of _essential_
use, must, I take it, catch up and put into itself certain laws and
possibilities of the breath, of the breathing of the man who writes
as well as of his listenings. (The revolution of the ear, 1910, the
trochee's heave, asks it of the younger poets.)

I want to do two things: first, try to show what projective or
OPEN verse is, what it involves, in its act of composition, how, in
distinction from the non-projective, it is accomplished; and II,
suggest a few ideas about what stance toward reality brings such
verse into being, what that stance does, both to the poet and to his
reader. (The stance involves, for example, a change beyond, and
larger than, the technical, and may, the way things look, lead to

147

new poetics and to new concepts from which some sort of drama, say, or of epic, perhaps, may emerge.)

I

First, some simplicities that a man learns, if he works in OPEN, or what can also be called COMPOSITION BY FIELD, as opposed to inherited line, stanza, over-all form, what is the "old" base of the non-projective.

(1) the *kinetics* of the thing. A poem is energy transferred from where the poet got it (he will have some several causations), by way of the poem itself to, all the way over to, the reader. Okay. Then the poem itself must, at all points, be a high energy-construct and, at all points, an energy-discharge. So: how is the poet to accomplish same energy, how is he, what is the process by which a poet gets in, at all points energy at least the equivalent of the energy which propelled him in the first place, yet an energy which is peculiar to verse alone and which will be, obviously, also different from the energy which the reader, because he is a third term, will take away?

This is the problem which any poet who departs from closed form is specially confronted by. And it involves a whole series of new recognitions. From the moment he ventures into FIELD COMPOSITION—puts himself in the open—he can go by no track other than the one the poem under hand declares, for itself. Thus he has to behave, and be, instant by instant, aware of some several forces just now beginning to be examined. (It is much more, for example, this push, than simply such a one as Pound put, so wisely, to get us started: "the musical phrase," go by it, boys, rather than by, the metronome.)

(2) is the *principle,* the law which presides conspicuously over such composition, and, when obeyed, is the reason why a projective poem can come into being. It is this: FORM IS NEVER MORE THAN AN EXTENSION OF CONTENT. (Or so it got phrased by one, R. Creeley, and it makes absolute sense to me, with this possible corollary, that right form, in any given poem, is the only and exclusively possible extension of content under hand.) There it is, brothers, sitting there, for USE.

Now (3) the *process* of the thing, how the principle can be made so to shape the energies that the form is accomplished. And I think it can be boiled down to one statement (first pounded into my head by Edward Dahlberg): ONE PERCEPTION MUST IMMEDI- ATELY AND DIRECTLY LEAD TO A FURTHER PERCEPTION. It means exactly what it says, is a matter of, at *all* points (even, I should say, of our management of daily reality as of the daily work) get on with it, keep moving, keep in, speed, the nerves, their speed, the perceptions, theirs, the acts, the split second acts, the whole business, keep it moving as fast as you can, citizen. And if you also set up as a poet, USE USE USE the process at all points, in any given poem always, always one perception must must must MOVE, IN- STANTER, ON ANOTHER!

So there we are, fast, there's the dogma. And its excuse, its usableness, in practice. Which gets us, it ought to get us, inside the machinery, now, 1950, of how projective verse is made.

If I hammer, if I recall in, and keep calling in, the breath, the breathing as distinguished from the hearing, it is for cause, it is to insist upon a part that breath plays in verse which has not (due, I think, to the smothering of the power of the line by too set a concept of foot) has not been sufficiently observed or practiced, but which has to be if verse is to advance to its proper force and place in the day, now, and ahead. I take it that PROJECTIVE VERSE teaches, is, this lesson, that that verse will only do in which a poet manages to register both the acquisitions of his ear *and* the pres- sures of his breath.

Let's start from the smallest particle of all, the syllable. It is the king and pin of versification, what rules and holds together the lines, the larger forms, of a poem. I would suggest that verse here and in England dropped this secret from the late Elizabethans to Ezra Pound, lost it, in the sweetness of meter and rime, in a honey- head. (The syllable is one way to distinguish the original success of blank verse, and its falling off, with Milton.)

It is by their syllables that words juxtapose in beauty, by these particles of sound as clearly as by the sense of the words which they compose. In any given instance, because there is a choice of words, the choice, if a man is in there, will be, spontaneously, the obedience of his ear to the syllables. The fineness, and the practice, lie here, at the minimum and source of speech.

O western wynd, when wilt thou blow
And the small rain down shall rain
O Christ that my love were in my arms
And I in my bed again

It would do no harm, as an act of correction to both prose and verse as now written, if both rime and meter, and, in the quantity words, both sense and sound, were less in the forefront of the mind than the syllable, if the syllable, that fine creature, were more allowed to lead the harmony on. With this warning, to those who would try: to step back here to this place of the elements and minims of language, is to engage speech where it is least careless— and least logical. Listening for the syllables must be so constant and so scrupulous, the exaction must be so complete, that the assurance of the ear is purchased at the highest—40 hours a day— price. For from the root out, from all over the place, the syllable comes, the figures of, the dance:

"Is" comes from the Aryan root, *as,* to breathe. The En-glish "not" equals the Sanscrit *na,* which may come from the root *na,* to be lost, to perish. "Be" is from *bhu,* to grow.

I say the syllable, king, and that it is spontaneous, this way: the ear, the ear which has collected, which has listened, the ear, which is so close to the mind that it is the mind's, that it has the mind's speed . . .

it is close, another way: the mind is brother to this sister and is, because it is so close, is the drying force, the incest, the sharp-ener . . .

it is from the union of the mind and the ear that the syllable is born.

But the syllable is only the first child of the incest of verse (always, that Egyptian thing, it produces twins!). The other child is the LINE. And together, these two, the syllable *and* the line, they make a poem, they make that thing, the—what shall we call it, the Boss of all, the "Single Intelligence." And the line comes (I swear it) from the breath, from the breathing of the man who writes, at the moment that he writes, and thus is, it is here that, the daily work, the WORK, gets in, for only he, the man who writes, can declare, at every moment, the line its metric and its ending—where its breathing, shall come to, termination.

The trouble with most work, to my taking, since the breaking away from traditional lines and stanzas, and from such wholes as, say, Chaucer's *Troilus* or S's *Lear,* is: contemporary workers go lazy RIGHT HERE WHERE THE LINE IS BORN.

Let me put it baldly. The two halves are:

the HEAD, by way of the EAR, to the SYLLABLE
the HEART, by way of the BREATH, to the LINE

And the joker? that it is in the 1st half of the proposition that, in composing, one lets-it-rip; and that it is in the 2nd half, surprise, it is the LINE that's the baby that gets, as the poem is getting made, the attention, the control, that it is right here, in the line, that the shaping takes place, each moment of the going.

I am dogmatic, that the head shows in the syllable. The dance of the intellect is there, among them, prose or verse. Consider the best minds you know in this here business: where does the head show, is it not, precise, here, in the swift currents of the syllable? can't you tell a brain when you see what it does, just there? It is true, what the master says he picked up from Confusion: all the thots men are capable of can be entered on the back of a postage stamp. So, is it not the PLAY of a mind we are after, is not that that shows whether a mind is there at all?

And the threshing floor for the dance? Is it anything but the LINE? And when the line has, is, a deadness, it is not a heart which has gone lazy, is it not, suddenly, slow things, similes, say, adjectives, or such, that we are bored by?

For there is a whole flock of rhetorical devices which have now to be brought under a new bead, now that we sight with the line. Simile is only one bird who comes down, too easily. The descriptive functions generally have to be watched, every second, in projective verse, because of their easiness, and thus their drain on the energy which composition by field allows into a poem. *Any* slackness takes off attention, that crucial thing, from the job in hand, from the *push* of the line under hand at the moment, under the reader's eye, in his moment. Observation of any kind is, like argument in prose, properly previous to the act of the poem, and, if allowed in, must be so juxtaposed, apposed, set in, that it does not, for an instant, sap the going energy of the content toward its form.

It comes to this, this whole aspect of the newer problems. (We now enter, actually, the large area of the whole poem, into the FIELD, if you like, where all the syllables and all the lines must be managed in their relations to each other.) It is a matter, finally, of OBJECTS, what they are, what they are inside a poem, how they got there, and, once there, how they are to be used. This is something I want to get to in another way in Part II, but, for the moment, let me indicate this, that every element in an open poem (the syllable, the line, as well as the image, the sound, the sense) must be taken up as participants in the kinetic of the poem just as solidly as we are accustomed to take what we call the objects of reality; and that these elements are to be seen as creating the tensions of a poem just as totally as do those other objects create what we know as the world.

The objects which occur at every given moment of composition (of recognition, we can call it) are, can be, must be treated exactly as they do occur therein and not by any ideas or preconceptions from outside the poem, must be handled as a series of objects in field in such a way that a series of tensions (which they also are) are made to *hold,* and to hold exactly inside the content and the context of the poem which has forced itself, through the poet and them, into being.

Because breath allows *all* the speech-force of language back in (speech is the "solid" of verse, is the secret of a poem's energy), because, now, a poem has, by speech, solidity, everything in it can now be treated as solids, objects, things; and, though insisting upon the absolute difference of the reality of verse from that other dispersed and distributed thing, yet each of these elements of a poem can be allowed to have the play of their separate energies and can be allowed, once the poem is well composed, to keep, as those other objects do, their proper confusions.

Which brings us up, immediately, bang, against tenses, in fact against syntax, in fact against grammar generally, that is, as we have inherited it. Do not tenses, must they not also be kicked around anew, in order that time, that other governing absolute may be kept, as must the space-tensions of a poem, immediate, contemporary to the acting-on-you of the poem? I would argue

that here, too, the LAW OF THE LINE, which projective verse
creates, must be hewn to, obeyed, and that the conventions which
logic has forced on syntax must be broken open as quietly as must
the too set feet of the old line. But an analysis of how far a new
poet can stretch the very conventions on which communication by
language rests, is too big for these notes, which are meant, I hope
it is obvious, merely to get things started.

Let me just throw in this. It is my impression that *all* parts of
speech suddenly, in composition by field, are fresh for both sound
and percussive use, spring up like unknown, unnamed vegetables
in the patch, when you work it, come spring. Now take Hart
Crane. What strikes me in him is the singleness of the push to the
nominative, his push along that one arc of freshness, the attempt
to get back to word as handle. (If logos is word as thought, what is
word as noun, as, pass me that, as Newman Shea used to ask, at
the galley table, put a jib on the blood, will ya.) But there is a loss
in Crane of what Fenollosa is so right about, in syntax, the sen-
tence as first act of nature, as lightning, as passage of force from
subject to object, quick, in the case, from Hart to me, in every
case, from me to you, the VERB, between two nouns. Does not
Hart miss the advantages, by such an isolated push, miss the point
of the whole front of syllable, line, field, and what happened to all
language, and to the poem, as a result?

I return you now to London, to beginnings, to the syllable, for
the pleasures of it, to intermit;

> If music be the food of love, play on,
> give me excess of it, that, surfeiting,
> the appetite may sicken, and so die.
> That strain again. It had a dying fall,
> o, it came over my ear like the sweet sound
> that breathes upon a bank of violets,
> stealing and giving odour.

What we have suffered from, is manuscript, press, the removal of
verse from its producer and its reproducer, the voice, a removal by
one, by two removes from its place of origin *and* its destination.
For the breath has a double meaning which latin had not yet
lost.

The irony is, from the machine has come one gain not yet

sufficiently observed or used, but which leads directly on toward projective verse and its consequences. It is the advantage of the typewriter that, due to its rigidity and its space precisions, it can, for a poet, indicate exactly the breath, the pauses, the suspensions even of syllables, the juxtapositions even of parts of phrases, which he intends. For the first time the poet has the stave and the bar a musician has had. For the first time he can, without the convention of rime and meter, record the listening he has done to his own speech and by that one act indicate how he would want any reader, silently or otherwise, to voice his work.

It is time we picked the fruits of the experiments of Cummings, Pound, Williams, each of whom has, after his way, already used the machine as a scoring to his composing, as a script to its vocalization. It is now only a matter of the recognition of the conventions of composition by field for us to bring into being an open verse as formal as the closed, with all its traditional advantages.

If a contemporary poet leaves a space as long as the phrase before it, he means that space to be held, by the breath, an equal length of time. If he suspends a word or syllable at the end of a line (this was most Cummings' addition) he means that time to pass that it takes the eye—that hair of time suspended—to pick up the next line. If he wishes a pause so light it hardly separates the words, yet does not want a comma—which is an interruption of the meaning rather than the sounding of the line—follow him when he uses a symbol the typewriter has ready to hand:

> What does not change / is the will to change

Observe him, when he takes advantage of the machine's multiple margins, to juxtapose:

> Sd he:
>> to dream takes no effort
>>> to think is easy
>>>> to act is more difficult
>>> but for a man to act after he has taken thought, this!
>> is the most difficult thing of all

Each of these lines is a progressing of both the meaning and the breathing forward, and then a backing up, without a progress or any kind of movement outside the unit of time local to the idea.

There is more to be said in order that this convention be recognized, especially in order that the revolution out of which it came may be so forwarded that work will get published to offset the reaction now afoot to return verse to inherited forms of cadence and rime. But what I want to emphasize here, by this emphasis on the typewriter as the personal and instantaneous recorder of the poets' work, is the already projective nature of verse as the sons of Pound and Williams are practicing it. Already they are composing as though verse was to have the reading its writing involved, as though not the eye but the ear was to be its measurer, as though the intervals of its composition could be so carefully put down as to be precisely the intervals of its registration. For the ear, which once had the burden of memory to quicken it (rime & regular cadence were its aids and have merely lived on in print after the oral necessities were ended) can now again, that the poet has his means, be the threshold of projective verse.

II

Which gets us to what I promised, the degree to which the projective involves a stance toward reality outside a poem as well as a new stance towards the reality of a poem itself. It is a matter of content, the content of Homer or of Euripides or of Seami as distinct from that which I might call the more "literary" masters. From the moment the projective purpose of the act of verse is recognized, the content does—it will—change. If the beginning and the end is breath, voice in its largest sense, then the material of verse shifts. It has to. It starts with the composer. The dimension of his line itself changes, not to speak of the change in his conceiving, of the matter he will turn to, of the scale in which he imagines that matter's use. I myself would pose the difference by a physical image. It is no accident that Pound and Williams both were involved variously in a movement which got called "objectivism." But that word was then used in some sort of a necessary quarrel, I take it, with "subjectivism." It is now too late to be bothered with the latter. It has excellently done itself to death, even though we are all caught in its dying. What seems to me a more valid formulation for present use is "objectism," a word to be taken to stand for the kind of relation of man to experience which a poet might state as the necessity of a line or a work to be as wood is, to be as clean as wood is as it issues from the hand of nature, to be as shaped as wood can be when a man has had his hand to it. Objectism is the getting rid of the lyrical interference of the individual as ego, of the "subject" and his soul, that peculiar presumption by which western man has interposed himself between what he is as a creature of nature (with certain instructions to carry out) and those other creations of nature which we may, with no derogation, call objects. For a man is himself an object, whatever he may take to be his advantages, the more likely to recognize himself as such the greater his advantages, particularly at that moment that he achieves an humilitas sufficient to make him of use.

It comes to this: the use of a man, by himself and thus by others, lies in how he conceives his relation to nature, that force to which he owes his somewhat small existence. If he sprawl, he shall find little to sing but himself, and shall sing, nature has such paradoxical ways, by way of artificial forms outside himself. But if he stays inside himself, if he is contained within his nature as he is participant in the larger force, he will be able to listen, and his hearing through himself will give him secrets objects share. And by an inverse law his shapes will make their own way. It is in this sense that the projective act, which is the artist's act in the larger field of objects, leads to dimensions larger than the man. For a man's problem, the moment he takes speech up in all its fullness, is to give his work his seriousness, a seriousness sufficient to cause the thing he makes to try to take its place alongside the things of nature. This is not easy. Nature works from reverence, even in her destructions (species go down with a crash). But breath is man's special qualification as animal. Sound is a dimension he has extended. Language is one of his proudest acts. And when a poet rests in these as they are in himself (in his physiology, if you like, but the life in him, for all that) then he, if he chooses to speak from these roots, works in that area where nature has given him size, projective size.

It is projective size that the play, *The Trojan Women,* possesses, for it is able to stand, is it not, as its people do, beside the Aegean—and neither Andromache or the sea suffer diminution. In a less "heroic" but equally "natural" dimension Seami causes the Fisherman and the Angel to stand clear in *Hagoromo*. And Homer, who is such an unexamined cliché that I do not think I need to press home in what scale Nausicaa's girls wash their clothes.

Such works, I should argue—and I use them simply because their equivalents are yet to be done—could not issue from men who conceived verse without the full relevance of human voice, without reference to where lines come from, in the individual who writes. Nor do I think it accident that, at this end point of the argument, I should use, for examples, two dramatists and an epic poet. For I would hazard the guess that, if projective verse is practiced long enough, is driven ahead hard enough along the course I think it dictates, verse again can carry much larger material than it has carried in our language since the Elizabethans. But it can't be jumped. We are only at its beginnings, and if I think that the *Cantos* make more "dramatic" sense than do the plays of Mr. Eliot, it is not because I think they have solved the problem but because the methodology of the verse in them points a way by which, one day, the problem of larger content and of larger forms may be solved. Eliot is, in fact, a proof of a present danger, of "too easy" a going on the practice of verse as it has been, rather than as it must be, practiced. There is no question, for example, that Eliot's line, from "Prufrock" on down, has speech-force, is "dramatic," is, in fact, one of the most notable lines since Dryden. I suppose it stemmed immediately to him from Browning, as did so many of Pound's early things. In any case Eliot's line has obvious relations backward to the Elizabethans, especially to the soliloquy. Yet O. M. Eliot is *not* projective. It could even be argued (and I say this carefully, as I have said all things about the non-projective, having considered how each of us must save himself after his own fashion and how much, for that matter, each of us owes to the non-projective, and will continue to owe, as both go alongside each other) but it could be argued that it is because Eliot has stayed inside the non-projective that he fails as a dramatist—that his root is the mind alone, and a scholastic mind at that (no high *intelletto* despite his apparent clarities)—and that, in his listenings he has stayed there where the ear and the mind are, has only gone from his fine ear outward rather than, as I say a projective poet will, down through the workings of his own throat to that place where breath comes from, where breath has its beginnings, where drama has to come from, where, the coincidence is, all act springs.

[*1950*]

Letter to Elaine Feinstein

May, 1959

Dear E. B. Feinstein,

Your questions catch me athwart any new sense I might have of a "poetics." The best previous throw I made on it was in *Poetry NY* some years ago on Projective Open or Field verse versus Closed, with much on the *line* and the *syllable*.

The basic idea anyway for me is that one, that form is never any more than an extension of content—a non-literary sense, certainly. I believe in Truth! (Wahrheit) My sense is that beauty (Schönheit) better stay in the thingitself: das Ding—Ja!—macht ring (the attack, I suppose, on the "completed thought," or, the Idea, yes? Thus the syntax question: what is the sentence?

The only advantage of speech rhythms (to take your 2nd question 1st) is illiteracy: the non-literary, exactly in Dante's sense of the value of the vernacular over grammar—that speech as a communicator is prior to the individual and is picked up as soon as and with ma's milk . . . he said nurse's tit. In other words, speech rhythm only as anyone of us has it, if we come on from the line of force as piped in as well as from piping we very much have done up to this moment—if we have, from, that "common" not grammatical source. The "source" question is damned interesting today—as Shelley saw, like Dante, that, if it comes in, that way,

primary, from Ma there is then a double line of chromosomic
giving (A) the inherent speech (thought, power) the "species,"
that is; and (B) the etymological: this is where I find "foreign"
languages so wild, especially the Indo-European line with the
advantage now that we have Hittite to back up to. I couldn't stress
enough on this speech rhythm question the pay-off in *traction* that
a non-literate, non-commercial and non-historical constant daily
experience of tracking *any* word, practically, one finds oneself
using, back along its line of force to Anglo-Saxon, Latin, Greek,
and out to Sanskrit, or now, if someone wld do it, some "dic-
tionary" of roots which wld include Hittite at least.

I'll give in a minute the connection of this to form if capturable
in the poem, that is, the usual "poetics" biz, but excuse me if I
hammer shortly the immense help archaeology, and some specific
linguistic scholarship—actually, from my experience mainly of
such completely different "grammars" as North American Indians
present, in the present syntax hangup: like Hopi. But also Tro-
briand space-Time premises. And a couple of North California
tongues, like Yani. But it is the archaeology *behind* our own
history proper, Hittite, for the above reason, but now that Canaan-
ite is known (Ugaritic) and Sumerian, and the direct connection of
the Celts to the Aryans and so to the Achaean-Trojan forbears
which has *slowed* and opened the speech language thing as we got
it, now, in our hands, to make it do more form than how form got
set by Sappho & Homer, and hasn't changed much since.

I am talking from a new "double axis": the replacement of the
Classical-representational by the *primitive-abstract* ((if this all
sounds bloody German, excuse the weather, it's from the east
today, and wet)). I mean of course not at all primitive in that
stupid use of it as opposed to civilized. One means it now as
"primary," as how one finds anything, pick it up as one does
new—fresh/first. Thus one is equal across history forward and
back, and it's all levy, as present is, but sd that way, one states
. . . a different space-time. Content, in other words, is also
shifted—at least from humanism, as we've had it since the Indo-
Europeans got their fid in there (circum 1500 BC) ((Note: I'm for
'em on the muse level, and agin 'em on the content, or "Psyche"
side.

Which gets me to yr 1st question—"the use of the Image." "the

Image" (wow, that you capitalize it makes *sense:* it is *all* we had
(post-circum *The Two Noble Kinsmen*), as we had a sterile
grammar (an insufficient "sentence") we had analogy only:
images, no matter how learned or how simple: even Burns say,
allowing etc and including Frost! Comparison. Thus representation
was never off the dead-spot of description. Nothing was *happening*
as of the poem itself—ding and zing or something. It was referen-
tial to reality. And that a p. poor crawling actuarial "real"—good
enough to keep banks and insurance companies, plus mediocre
governments etc. But not Poetry's *Truth* like my friends from the
American Underground cry and spit in the face of "Time."

The Image also has to be taken by a double: that is, if you
bisect a parabola you get an enantiomorph (The Hopi say what
goes on over there isn't happening here therefore it isn't the same:
pure "localism" of space-time, but such localism can now be
called: what you find out for yrself (*'istorin*) keeps all accompany-
ing circumstance.

The basic trio wld seem to be: topos/typos/tropos, 3 in 1. The
"blow" hits here, and me, "bent" as born and of sd one's own
decisions for better or worse (allowing clearly, by Jesus Christ,
that you do love or go down)
if this sounds "mystical" I plead so. Wahrheit: I find the con-
temporary substitution of society for the cosmos captive and
deathly.

Image, therefore, is vector. It carries the trinity via the double to
the single form which one makes oneself able, if so, to issue from
the "content" (multiplicity: originally, and repetitively, chaos—
Tiamat: wot the Hindo-Europeans knocked out by giving the Old
Man (Juice himself) all the lightning.

The Double, then (the "home"/heartland/of the post-Mesopo-
tamians AND the post-Hindo Eees:

At the moment it comes out   the Muse ("world"
                                  the Psyche (the "life"

You wld know already I'm buggy on say the Proper Noun, so
much so I wld take it Pun is Rime, all from tope/type/trope, that
built in is the connection, in each of us, to Cosmos, and if one
taps, via psyche, plus a "true" adherence of Muse, one does reveal
"Form"

in other words the "right" (wahr-) proper noun, however apparently idiosyncratic, if "tested" by one's own experience (out plus in) ought to yield along this phylo-line (as the speech thing, above) because—*decently* what one oneself can know, as well as what the word *means*—ontogenetic.

The other part is certainly "landscape"—the other part of the double of Image to "noun." By Landscape I mean what "narrative"; scene; event; climax; crisis; hero; development; posture; all that *meant*—all the substantive of what we call literary. To animate the scene today: wow: You say "orientate me." Yessir. Place it!

again

I drag it back: Place (topos, plus one's own bent plus what one *can* know, makes it possible to name.

O.K. I'm running out of appetite. Let this swirl—a bit like Crab Nebula—do for now. And please come back on me if you are interested. *Yrs*

CHARLES OLSON
[*1959*]

Human Universe

There are laws, that is to say, the human universe is as discoverable as that other. And as definable.

The trouble has been, that a man stays so astonished he can triumph over his own incoherence, he settles for that, crows over it, and goes at a day again happy he at least makes a little sense. Or, if he says anything to another, he thinks it is enough—the struggle does involve such labor and some terror—to wrap it in a little mystery: ah, the way is hard but this is what you find if you go it.

The need now is a cooler one, a discrimination, and then, a shout. Der Weg stirbt, sd one. And was right, was he not? Then the question is : was ist der Weg?

I

The difficulty of discovery (in the close world which the human is because it is ourselves and nothing outside us, like the other) is, that definition is as much a part of the act as is sensation itself, in this sense, that life *is* preoccupation with itself, that conjecture about it is as much of it as its coming at us, its going on. In other words, we are ourselves both the instrument of discovery and the instrument of definition.

Which is of course, why language is a prime of the matter and why, if we are to see some of the laws afresh, it is necessary to examine, first, the present condition of the language—and I mean language exactly in its double sense of discrimination (logos) and of shout (tongue).

We have lived long in a generalizing time, at least since 450 B.C. And it has had its effects on the best of men, on the best of things. Logos, or discourse, for example, has, in that time, so worked its abstractions into our concept and use of language that language's other function, speech, seems so in need of restoration that several of us got back to hieroglyphs or to ideograms to right the balance. (The distinction here is between language as the act of the instant and language as the act of thought about the instant.)

But one can't any longer stop there, if one ever could. For the habits of thought are the habits of action, and here, too, particularism has to be fought for anew. In fact, by the very law of the identity of definition and discovery, who can extricate language from action? (Though it is one of the first false faces of the law which I shall want to try to strike away, it is quite understandable—in the light of its identity—that the Greeks went on to declare all speculation as enclosed in the "UNIVERSE of discourse." It is their word, and the refuge of all metaphysicians since—as though language, too, was an absolute, instead of (as even man is) instrument, and not to be extended, however much the urge, to cover what each, man and language, is in the hands of: what we share, and which is enough, of power and of beauty, not to need an exaggeration of words, especially that spreading one, "universe." For discourse is hardly such, or at least only arbitrarily a universe. In any case, so extended (logos given so much more of its part than live speech), discourse has arrogated to itself a good deal of experience which needed to stay put—needs now to be returned to the only two universes which count, the two phenomenal ones, the two a man has need to bear on because they bear so on him: that of himself, as organism, and that of his environment, the earth and planets.

We stay unaware how two means of discourse the Greeks appear to have invented hugely intermit our participation in our experience, and so prevent discovery. They are what followed from Socrates' readiness to generalize, his willingness (from his own bias) to make a "universe" out of discourse instead of letting it rest in its most serviceable place. (It is not sufficiently observed that logos, and the reason necessary to it, are only a stage which a man must master and not what they are taken to be, final discipline. Beyond them is direct perception and the contraries which dispose of argument. The harmony of the universe, and I include man, is not logical, or better, is post-logical, as is the order of any created thing.) With Aristotle, the two great means appear: logic and classification. And it is they that have so fastened themselves on habits of thought that action is interfered with, absolutely interfered with, I should say.

Nor can I let the third of the great Greeks, Plato, go free—he who had more of a sort of latitude and style my tribe of men are apt to indulge him for. His world of Ideas, of forms as extricable from content, is as much and as dangerous an issue as are logic and classification, and they need to be seen as such if we are to get on to some alternative to the whole Greek system. Plato may be a honey-head, as Melville called him, but he is precisely that— treacherous to all ants, and where, increasingly, my contemporaries die, or drown the best of themselves. Idealisms of any sort, like logic and like classification, intervene at just the moment they become more than the means they are, are allowed to become ways as end instead of ways *to* end, END, which is never more than this instant, than you on this instant, than you, figuring it out, and acting, so. If there is any absolute, it is never more than this one, you, this instant, in action.

Which ought to get us on. What makes most acts—of living and of writing—unsatisfactory, is that the person and/or the writer satisfy themselves that they can only make a form (what they say or do, or a story, a poem, whatever) by selecting from the full content some face of it, or plane, some part. And at just this point, by just this act, they fall back on the dodges of discourse, and immediately, they lose me, I am no longer engaged, this is not what I know is the going-on (and of which going-on I, as well as they, want some illumination, and so, some pleasure). It comes out a demonstration, a separating out, an act of classification, and so, a stopping, and all that I know is, it is not there, it has turned false. For any of us, at any instant, are juxtaposed to any experience, even an overwhelming single one, on several more planes than the arbitrary and discursive which we inherit can declare.

It is not the Greeks I blame. What it comes to is ourselves, that we do not find ways to hew to experience as it is, in our definition and expression of it, in other words, find ways to stay in the human universe, and not be led to partition reality at any point, in any way. For this is just what we do do, this is the real issue of what has been, and the process, as it now asserts itself, can be exposed. It is the function, *comparison,* or, its bigger name, *symbology.* These are the false faces, too much seen, which hide and keep from us the active intellectual states, metaphor and performance. All that comparison ever does is set up a series of reference points: to compare is to take one thing and try to understand it by marking its similarities to or differences from another thing. Right here is the trouble, that each thing is not so much like or different from another thing (these likenesses and differences are apparent) but that such an analysis only accomplishes a *description,* does not come to grips with what really matters: that a thing, any thing, impinges on us by a more important fact, its self-existence, without reference to any other thing, in short, the very character of it which calls our attention to it, which wants us to know more about it, its particularity. This is what we are confronted by, not the thing's "class," any hierarchy, of quality or quantity, but the thing itself, and its *relevance* to ourselves who are the experience of it (whatever it may mean to someone else, or whatever other relations it may have).

There must be a means of expression for this, a way which is

not divisive as all the tag ends and upendings of the Greek way
are. There must be a way which bears *in* instead of away, which
meets head on what goes on each split second, a way which does
not—in order to define—prevent, deter, distract, and so cease the
act of, discovering.

I have been living for some time amongst a people who are
more or less directly the descendants of a culture and civilization
which was a contrary of that which we have known and of which
we are the natural children. The marked thing about them is, that
it is only love and flesh which seems to carry any sign of their
antecedence, that all the rest which was once a greatness different
from our own has gone down before the poundings of our way.
And, now, except as their bodies jostle in a bus, or as they disclose
the depth and tenacity of love among each other inside a family,
they are poor failures of the modern world, incompetent even to
arrange that, in the month of June, when the rains have not come
far enough forward to fill the wells, they have water to wash in or
to drink. They have lost the capacity of their predecessors to do
anything in common. But they do one thing no modern knows the
secret of, however he is still by nature possessed of it: they wear
their flesh with that difference which the understanding that it is
common leads to. When I am rocked by the roads against any of
them—kids, women, men—their flesh is most gentle, is granted,
touch is in no sense anything but the natural law of flesh, there is
none of that pull-away which, in the States, causes a man for all
the years of his life the deepest sort of questioning of the rights of
himself to the wild reachings of his own organism. The admission
these people give me and one another is direct, and the individual
who peers out from that flesh is precisely himself, is a curious
wandering animal like me—it is so very beautiful how animal
human eyes are when the flesh is not worn so close it chokes, how
human and individuated the look comes out of a human eye when
the house of it is not exaggerated.

This is not easy to save from subjectivism, to state so that you
understand that this is not an observation but a first law to a
restoration of the human house. For what is marked about these
Lermeros with whom I live (by contrast, for example, to the
people of the city nearby) is that, here, the big-eared, small-eyed
creatures stay as the minority they must always have been before

garages made them valuable and allowed them out of their holes to proliferate and overrun the earth. Nothing is accident, and man, no less than nature, does nothing without plan or the discipline to make plan fact. And if it is true that we now live in fear of our own house, and can easily trace the reason for it, it is also true that we can trace reasons why those who do not or did not so live found out how to do other than we.

My assumption is, that these contemporary Maya are what they are because once there was a concept at work which kept attention so poised that (1) men were able to stay so interested in the expression and gesture of all creatures, including at least three planets in addition to the human face, eyes and hands, that they invented a system of written record, now called hieroglyphs, which, on its very face, is verse, the signs were so clearly and densely chosen that, cut in stone, they retain the power of the objects of which they are the images; (2) to mass stone with sufficient proportion to decorate a near hill and turn it into a fire-tower or an observatory or one post of an enclosure in which people, favored by its shadows, might swap camotes for sandals; and (3) to fire clay into pots porous enough to sieve and thus cool water, strong enough to stew iguana and fish, and handsome enough to put ceremony where it also belongs, in the most elementary human acts. And when a people are so disposed, it should come as no surprise that, long before any of these accomplishments, the same people did an improvement on nature—the domestication of maize—which remains one of the world's wonders, even to a nation of Burbanks, and that long after all their accomplishments, they still carry their bodies with some of the savor and the flavor that the bodies of the Americans are as missing in as is their irrigated lettuce and their green-picked refrigerator-ripened fruit. For the truth is, that the management of external nature so that none of its virtu is lost, in vegetables or in art, is as much a delicate juggling of her content as is the same juggling by any one of us of our own. And when men are not such jugglers, are not able to manage a means of expression the equal of their own or nature's intricacy, the flesh does choke. The notion of fun comes to displace work as what we are here for. Spectatorism crowds out participation as the condition of culture. And bonuses and prizes are the rewards of labor contrived by the monopolies of business and government to protect themselves from the advancement in position of able men or that old assertion of an inventive man, his own shop. All individual energy and ingenuity is bought off—at a suggestion box or the cinema. Passivity conquers all. Even war and peace die (to be displaced by world government?) and man reverts to only two of his components, inertia and gas.

It is easy to phrase, too easy, and we have had enough of bright description. To say that in America the goods are as the fruits, and the people as the goods, all glistening but tasteless, accomplishes nothing in itself, for the overwhelming fact is, that the rest of the world wants nothing but to be the same. Value is perishing from the earth because no one cares to fight down to it beneath the glowing surfaces so attractive to all. Der Weg stirbt.

II

Can one restate man in any way to repossess him of his dynamic? I don't know. But for myself a first answer lies in his systemic particulars. The trouble with the inherited formulations which have helped to destroy him (the notion of himself as the center of phenomenon by fiat or of god as the center and man as god's chief reflection) is that both set aside nature as an unadmitted or suppressed third party, a sort of Holy Ghost which was allowed in once to touch men's tongues and then, because the fire was too great, was immediately banished to some sort of half place in between god and the devil—who actually, of course, thereby became the most powerful agent of all. The result, we have been the witnesses of: discovering this discarded thing nature, science has run away with everything. Tapping her power, fingering her like a child, giving her again her place, but without somehow, remembering what truth there was in man's centering the use of anything, god, devil, or holy ghost, in himself, science has upset all balance and blown value, man's peculiar responsibility, to the winds.

If unselectedness is man's original condition (such is more accurate a word than that lovely riding thing, chaos, which sounds like what it is, the most huge generalization of all, obviously making it necessary for man to invent a bearded giant to shape it for him) but if likewise, selectiveness is just as orginally the

impulse by which he proceeds to do something about the un-
selectedness, then one is forced, is one not, to look for some
instrumentation in man's given which makes selection possible.
And it has gone so far, that is, science has, as to wonder if the
fingertips, are not very knowing knots in their own rights, little
brains (little photo-electric cells, I think they now call the skin)
which, immediately, in responding to external stimuli, make deci-
sions! It is a remarkable and usable idea. For it is man's first cause
of wonder how rapid he is in his taking in of what he does ex-
perience.

But when you have said that, have you not done one of two
things, either forever damned yourself by making "soul" mechani-
cal (it has long been the soul which has softly stood as a word to
cover man as a selecting internal reality posed dangerously in the
midst of those externals which the word chaos generously covers
like Williams' paint) or you have possibly committed a greater
crime. You have allowed that external reality is more than merely
the substance which man takes in. By making the threshold of
reception so important and by putting the instrumentation of selec-
tion so far out from its traditional place (the greatest humanist of
them all opened a sonnet, "Poor soul, the centre of my sinful
earth"), you have gone so far as to imply that the skin itself, the
meeting edge of man and external reality, is where all that matters
does happen, that man and external reality are so involved with
one another that, for man's purposes, they had better be taken as
one.

It is some such crime by which I am willing to hazard a guess at
a way to restore to man some of his lost relevance. For this
metaphor of the senses—of the literal speed of light by which a
man absorbs, instant on instant, all that phenomenon presents to
him—is a fair image as well, my experience tells me, of the ways
of his inner energy, of the ways of those other things which are
usually, for some reason, separated from the external pick-ups—
his dreams, for example, his thoughts (to speak as the prede-
cessors spoke), his desires, sins, hopes, fears, faiths, loves. I am
not able to satisfy myself that these so-called inner things are so
separable from the objects, persons, events which are the content
of them and by which man represents or re-enacts them despite the
suck of symbol which has increased and increased since the great

Greeks first promoted the idea of a transcendent world of forms. What I do see is that each man, does make his own special selection from the phenomenal field and it is true that we begin to speak of personality, however I remain unaware that this particular act of individuation is peculiar to man, observable as it is in individuals of other species of nature's making (it behooves man now not to separate himself too jauntily from any of nature's creatures).

Even if one does follow personality up, does take the problem further in to those areas of function which may seem more peculiarly human (at least are more peculiarly the concern of a humanist), I equally cannot satisfy myself of the gain in thinking that the process by which man transposes phenomena to his use is any more extricable from reception than reception itself is from the world. What happens at the skin is more like than different from what happens within. The process of image (to be more exact about transposition than the "soul" allows or than the analysts do with their tricky "symbol-maker") cannot be understood by separation from the stuff it works on. Here again, as throughout experience, the law remains, form is not isolated from content. The error of all other metaphysic is descriptive, is the profound error that Heisenberg had the intelligence to admit in his principle that a thing can be measured in its mass only by arbitrarily assuming a stopping of its motion, or in its motion only by neglecting, for the moment of the measuring, its mass. And either way, you are failing to get what you are after—so far as a human being goes, his life. There is only one thing you can do about kinetic, re-enact it. Which is why the man said, he who possesses rhythm possesses the universe. And why art is the only twin life has—its only valid metaphysic. Art does not seek to describe but to enact. And if man is once more to possess intent in his life, and to take up the responsibility implicit in his life, he has to comprehend his own process as intact, from outside, by way of his skin, in, and by his own powers of conversion, out again.

For there is this other part of the motion which we call life to be examined anew, that thing we overlove, man's action, that tremendous discharge of force which we overlove when we love it for its own sake but which (when it is good) is the equal of all intake plus all transposing. It deserves this word, that it is the equal of its cause only when it proceeds unbroken from the threshold of a man through him and back out again, without loss of quality, to the external world from which it came, whether that external world take the shape of another human being or of the several human beings hidden by the generalization "society" or of things themselves. In other words, the proposition here is that man at his peril breaks the full circuit of object, image, action at any point. The meeting edge of man and the world is also his cutting edge. If man is active, it is exactly here where experience comes in that it is delivered back, and if he stays fresh at the coming in he will be fresh at his going out. If he does not, all that he does inside his house is stale, more and more stale as he is less and less acute at the door. And his door is where he is responsible to more than himself. Man does influence external reality, and it can be stated without recourse to the stupidities of mysticism (which appears to love a mystery as much outside as it does in). If man chooses to treat external reality any differently than as part of his own process, in other words as anything other than relevant to his own inner life, then he will (being such a froward thing, and bound to use his energy willy-nilly, nature is so subtle) use it otherwise. He will use it just exactly as he has used it now for too long, for arbitrary and willful purposes which, in their effects, not only change the face of nature but actually arrest and divert her force until man turns it even against herself, he is so powerful, this little thing. But what little willful modern man will not recognize is, that when he turns it against her he turns it against himself, held in the hand of nature as man forever is, to his use of himself if he choose, to his disuse, as he has.

What gets me is, how man refuses to acknowledge the consequences of his disposing of himself at his own entrance—as though a kiss were a cheap thing, as though he were. He will give a Rimbaud a lot of lip and no service at all, as though Rimbaud were a sport of nature and not a proof. Or a people different from himself—they will be the subject of historians' studies or of tourists' curiosity, and be let go at that, no matter how much they may disclose values he and his kind, you would think, could make use of. I have found, for example, that the hieroglyphs of the Maya disclose a placement of themselves toward nature of enormous contradiction to ourselves, and yet I am not aware that any of the

possible usages of this difference have been allowed to seep out
into present society. All that is done is what a Toynbee does,
diminish the energy once here expended into the sieve phonetic
words have become to be offered like one of nature's pastes that
we call jewels to be hung as a decoration of knowledge upon some
Christian and therefore eternal and holy neck. It is unbearable
what knowledge of the past has been allowed to become, what
function of human memory has been dribbled out to in the hands
of these learned monsters whom people are led to think "know."
They know nothing in not knowing how to reify what they do
know. What is worse, they do not know how to pass over to us the
energy implicit in any high work of the past because they pur-
posely destroy that energy as dangerous to the states for which
they work—which it is, for any concrete thing is a danger to
rhetoricians and politicians, as dangerous as a hard coin is to a
banker. And the more I live the more I am tempted to think that
the ultimate reason why man departs from nature and thus departs
from his own chance is that he is part of a herd which wants to do
the very thing which nature disallows—that energy can be lost.
When I look at the filth and lumber which man is led by, I see
man's greatest achievement in this childish accomplishment—that
he damn well can, and does, destroy destroy destroy energy every
day. It is too much. It is too much to waste time on, this idiot who
spills his fluids like some truculent and fingerless chamaco here-
abouts who wastes water at the pump when birds are dying all over
the country in this hottest of the months and women come in
droves in the morning begging for even a tasa of the precious stuff
to be poured in the amphoras they swing on their hips as they
swing their babies. Man has made himself an ugliness and a bore.

It was better to be a bird, as these Maya seem to have been,
they kept moving their heads so nervously to stay alive, to keep
alerted to what they were surrounded by, to watch it even for the
snake they took it to be or that larger bird they had to be in awe
of, the zopilote who fed on them when they were dead or whom
they looked at of a morning in a great black heap like locusts
tearing up a deer that had broken his wind or leg in the night. Or
even Venus they watched, as though they were a grackle them-
selves and could attack her vertically in her house full of holes like
a flute through which, they thought, when she had the upper hand

she spread down on them, on an east wind, disease and those blows on their skin they call granitos. When she was new, when she buzzed the morning sky, they hid in their houses for fear of her, Shoosh Ek, for fear of her bite, the Wasp she was, the way she could throw them down like that electrical stick which, last year, pinched one of these fishermen on his cheek, in all the gulf hit him as he sat in the prow of his cayuco with a line out for dogfish of a day and laid him out dead, with no more mark burned on him than that little tooth of a kiss his wife was given as cause when they brought him out over the beach as he might have hauled in a well-paying shark.

Or to be a man and a woman as Sun was, the way he had to put up with Moon, from start to finish the way she was, the way she behaved, and he up against it because he did have the advantage of her, he moved more rapidly. In the beginning he was only young and full of himself, and she, well, she was a girl living with her grandfather doing what a girl was supposed to be doing, making cloth. Even then he had the advantage of her, he hunted, instead, and because he could hunt he could become a humming-bird, which he did, just to get closer to her, this loveliness he thought she was and wanted to taste. Only the trouble was, he had to act out his mask, and while he was coming closer, one tobacco flower to another toward the house, her grandfather brought him down with a clay shot from a blow gun. And sun fell, right into moon's arms, who took him to her room to mother him, for she was all ready to be a wife, a man's second mother as a wife is in these parts where birds are so often stoned and need to be brought back to consciousness and, if they have their wings intact, may fly away again. As sun was. Only he could also talk, and persuaded moon to elope with him in a canoe. But there you are: there is always danger. Grandfather gets rain to throw his fire at them and though sun converts to turtle and is tough enough to escape alive, moon, putting on a crab shell, is not sufficiently protected and is killed.

Which is only part of it, that part of it which is outside and seems to have all of the drama. But only seems. For dragonflies collect moon's flesh and moon's blood in thirteen hollow logs, the sort of log sun had scooped his helpless runaway boat out of, thinking he had made it, had moon finally for his own. Foolish sun. For now here he is back again, after thirteen days, digging out the thirteen logs, and finding that twelve of them contain nothing but all the insects and all the snakes which fly and crawl about the earth of man and pester people in a hot climate so that a lot die off before they are well begun and most are ready, at any instant, for a sickness or a swelling, and the best thing to do is to lie quiet, wait for the poison to pass. For there is log 13, and it reveals moon restored to life, only moon is missing that part which makes woman woman, and deer alone, only deer can give her what he does give her so that she and sun can do what man and woman have the pleasure to do as one respite from the constant hammering.

But you see, nothing lasts. Sun has an older brother, who comes to live with sun and moon, and sun has reason to suspect that something is going on between moon and the big star, for this brother is the third one of the sky, the devilish or waspish one who is so often with moon. By a trick, sun discovers them, and moon, dispirited, sitting off by herself on the river bank, is persuaded by the bird zopilote to go off with him to the house of the king of the vultures himself. And though a vulture is not, obviously, as handsome a thing as the sun, do not be fooled into thinking that this bird which can darken the sky as well as feed on dead things until they are only bones for the sun to whiten, has not his attractions, had not his attractions to moon, especially the king of them all. She took him, made him the third of her men, and was his wife.

But sun was not done with her, with his want of her, and he turned to that creature which empowered her, the deer, for aid. He borrowed a skin, and hiding under it—knowing as hot sun does the habits of vultures—he pretends to be a carcass. The first vulture comes in, landing awkwardly a distance off, hobbles his nervous way nearer until, as he is about to pick apart what he thinks is a small deer, sun leaps on his back and rides off to where moon is. He triumphantly seizes her, only to find that she is somewhat reluctant to return.

At which stage, for reasons of cause or not, sun and moon go up into the sky to assume forever their planetary duties. But sun finds there is one last thing he must do to the moon before human beings are satisfied with her. He must knock out one of her eyes, they complain she is so bright and that they cannot sleep, the night is so much the same as his day, and his day is too much anyhow, and a little of the sweetness of the night they must have. So he does, he puts out her eye, and lets human beings have what they want. But when he does more, when, occasionally, he eclipses her entirely, some say it is only a sign that the two of them continue to fight, presumably because sun cannot forget moon's promiscuity, though others say that moon is forever erratic, is very much of a liar, is always telling sun about the way people of the earth are as much misbehavers as she, get drunk, do the things she does, in fact, the old ones say, moon is as difficult to understand as any bitch is.

O, they were hot for the world they lived in, these Maya, hot to get it down the way it was—the way it is, my fellow citizens.

[1951]

The Resistance

---

for Jean Riboud

This is eternity. This now. This foreshortened span.

Men will recognize it more easily (& dwell in it so) when we regain what the species lost, how long ago: nature's original intention with the organism, that it live 130 years. Or so Bogomolets' researches into the nature of connective tissue seem to prove. True or not, with or without aid from his own biosis, man has no alternative: his mortal years are his enemy. He accepts this new position. It is the root act.

There are other aids. Time, for example, has been cut down to size, though I do not think that those who have come to the knowledge of now came here from that powerful abstraction space-time, no matter how its corrections of time reinforce the position.

Man came here by an intolerable way. When man is reduced to

so much fat for soap, superphosphate for soil, fillings and shoes for sale, he has, to begin again, one answer, one point of resistance only to such fragmentation, one organized ground, a ground he comes to by a way the precise contrary of the cross, of spirit in the old sense, in old mouths. It is his own physiology he is forced to arrive at. And the way—the way of the beast, of man and the Beast.

It is his body that is his answer, his body intact and fought for, the absolute of his organism in its simplest terms, this structure evolved by nature, repeated in each act of birth, the animal man; the house he is, this house that moves, breathes, acts, this house where his life is, where he dwells against the enemy, against the beast.

Or the fraud. This organism now our citadel never was cathedral, draughty tenement of soul, was what it is: ground, stone, wall, cannon, tower. In this intricate structure are we based, now more certainly than ever (besieged, overthrown), for its power is bone muscle nerve blood brain   a man, its fragile mortal force its old eternity, resistance.

                                                                    [*1953*]

Equal, That Is, to the Real Itself

Two years before Melville was born John Keats, walking home from the mummers' play at Christmas 1817, and afterwards, he'd had to listen to Coleridge again, thought to himself all that irritable reaching after fact and reason, it won't do. I don't believe in it. I do better to stay in the condition of things. No matter what it amounts to, mystery confusion doubt, it has a power, it is what I mean by *Negative Capability*.

Keats, without setting out to, had put across the century the inch of steel to wreck Hegel, if anything could. Within five years, two geometers, Bolyai and Lobatschewsky, weren't any longer satisfied with Euclid's picture of the world, and they each made a new one, independently of each other, and remarkably alike. It took thirty-one years (Melville's age when he wrote *Moby-Dick*) for the German mathematician Riemann to define the real as men since have exploited it: he distinguished two kinds of manifold, the discrete (which would be the old system, and it includes discourse, language as it had been since Socrates) and, what he took to be more true, the continuous.

Melville, not knowing any of this but in it even more as an American, down to his hips in things, was a first practicer (Rimbaud was born the year Riemann made his inaugural lecture, 1854) of the new equation, quantity as intensive.

The idea on which this book* is based, naturalism, is useless to cope with Melville, either as a life lived in such a time or as an art, the first art of space to arise from the redefinition of the real, and in that respect free, for the first time since Homer, of the rigidities of the discrete. Naturalism was already outmoded by the events above, whether one takes it as an 18th or 19th century idea. Mr. Stern, alas, takes it every way, including the unhappy thought that Melville can be put at the head of a literary use which includes Twain, Dreiser, Hemingway, and Faulkner!

It is the error on matter sitting in naturalism which gives it its appeal, that by it one can avoid the real, which is what is left out, at what cost all over the place Mr. Stern is only one of the fools of. He writes, in summary of what he takes it Melville did prove:

> that the naturalistic perception in the years of the modern
> could and must take from woe not only materialism but
> also the humanism and the deep morality of social ideal-
> ism, which are the true beginnings of wisdom.

The true beginnings of nothing but the Supermarket—the exact death quantity does offer, if it is numbers, and extension, and the appetite of matter, especially in human beings.

The change the 19th century did bring about is being squandered by the 20th, in ignorance and abuse of its truth. Melville was

* *The Fine Hammered Steel of Herman Melville*, by Milton R. Stern (Urbana: University of Illinois Press, 1957).

a part of the change, and I can do nothing, in the face of this book, but try to show how, in the terms of that change. He put it altogether accurately himself, in a single sentence of a letter to Hawthorne, written when he was writing *Moby-Dick* (1851): "By visible truth we mean the apprehension of the absolute condition of present things."

All things did come in again, in the 19th century. An idea shook loose, and energy and motion became as important a structure of things as that they are plural, and, by matter, mass. It was even shown that in the infinitely small the older concepts of space ceased to be valid at all. Quantity—the measurable and numerable—was suddenly as shafted in, to any thing, as it was also, as had been obvious, the striking character of the external world, that all things do extend out. Nothing was now inert fact, all things were there for feeling, to promote it, and be felt; and man, in the midst of it, knowing well how he was folded in, as well as how suddenly and strikingly he could extend himself, spring or, without even moving, go, to far, the farthest—he was suddenly possessed or repossessed of a character of being, a thing among things, which I shall call his physicality. It made a re-entry of or to the universe. Reality was without interruption, and we are still in the business of finding out how all action, and thought, have to be refounded.

Taking it in towards writing, the discrete, for example, wasn't any longer a good enough base for discourse: classification was exposed as mere taxonomy; and logic (and the sentence as poised on it, a completed thought, instead of what it has become, an exchange of force) was as loose and inaccurate a system as the body and soul had been, divided from each other and rattling, sticks in a stiff box.

Something like this are the terms of the real and of action Melville was an early inheritor of, and he is either held this way or he is missed entirely. With one thing more: the measurement question. What did happen to measure when the rigidities dissolved? When Newton's Scholium turned out to be the fulling-mill Melville sensed it was, via Bacon, whom he called that watchmaker brain? What is measure when the universe flips and no part is discrete from another part except by the flow of creation itself, in and out, intensive where it seemed before qualitative, and the extensive exactly the widest, which we also have the powers to include? Rhythm, suddenly, which had been so long the captive of meter, no matter how good (Shakespeare, say, in our own tongue, or Chaucer), was a pumping of the real so constant art had to invent measure anew.

Watching Melville in a lifetime trying to make prose do what his body and his soul as a heap, and his mind on top of them a tangle (this is also a way of putting a man's physicality), trying to get a measure of language to move himself into a book and over to another man's experience, is a study makes more sense now, in the midst of 20th century art, painting and music as well as narrative and verse, than it could have, previously. It wasn't image, it wasn't anything he lacked. Possibly it was only any reason he might be confident he was right, taking it all so differently as he did, from those around him, at least those known to him. Or say it as my friend Landreau does, who swings, with *The Confidence-Man:* "Melville seems entitled to 'disillusion itself,' and given his personal bitter life, possibly because of that vision, in the scene, society, he had to live it in."

Who still knows what's called for, from physicality, how far it does cover and reveal? No one has yet tried to say how Melville does manage to give the flukes of the whale immediacy as such. It is easier to isolate his skill over technology than to investigate the topological both in his soul and in his writing, but it is my experience that only some such sense of form as the topological includes, able to discriminate and get in between the vague *types* of form morphology offers and the *ideal* structures of geometry proper, explains Melville's unique ability to reveal the very large (such a thing as his whale, or himself on whiteness, or Ahab's monomania) by the small.

The new world of atomism offered a metrical means as well as a topos different from the discrete. Congruence, which there, in mathematicians' hands, lifted everything forward after Lobatschewsky (via Cayley especially, another contemporary of Melville, and Felix Klein) makes much sense, as no other meter does, to account for Melville's prose. Congruence was spatial intuition to Kant, and if I am right that Melville did possess its powers, he had them by his birth, from his time of the world, locally America. As it developed in his century, congruence, which had been the measure of the space a solid fills in two of its positions, became a point-by-point mapping power of such flexibility that anything which stays the same, no matter where it goes and into whatever varying conditions (it can suffer deformation), it can be followed, and, if it is art, led, including, what is so important to prose, such physical quantities as velocity, force and field strength.

Melville's prose does things which its rhetoric would seem to contradict. He manages almost any time he wants to, for example, to endow a more general space than other writers, than anyone except Homer I find. The delivery of Tashtego from the whale's head, say. The point is also the overall "space" of *Moby-Dick*. That space, and those of which it is made up, have the properties of projective space (otherwise they should all come out more familiar, and round, because they would stay Euclidean), and I conclude that Melville could not have achieved what amounts to elliptical and hyperbolic spaces (he makes things stand out at once transparent and homogeneous) if he were not using transformations which we have not understood and which only congruence makes possible. (The lack of it, in his verse, as negativism in his life, such as Keats knew, is one of the ways of putting how far Melville *didn't* go.)

His ideas also. In spite of the vocabulary of his time, much more is to be read out of him, I suspect, than any of us have allowed. In the rest of the letter to Hawthorne from which I have quoted, he goes on to discuss the effects of the absolute of present things on self, and being, and God and his insistence there, to get God in the street, looks to me like the first rate breakthrough of man's thought which was called for at 1851: the necessary secularization of His part in the world of things. (It doesn't diminish it, that it was probably the only time in a lifetime in which Melville did manage to throw off the Semitic notion of transcendence.)

Or take him just where so much academicism has wasted its time on classic American literature, and Mr. Stern does again: the place of allegory and symbol in Melville and his contemporaries. As the Master said to me in the dream, of rhythm is image/of image is knowing/of knowing there is/a construct. It is rather quantum physics than relativity which will supply a proper evidence here, as against naturalism, of what Melville was grabbing on to when he declared it was *visible* truth he was after. For example, that light is not only a wave but a corpuscle. Or that the electron is not only a corpuscle but a wave. Melville couldn't abuse object as symbol does by depreciating it in favor of subject. Or let image lose its relational force by transferring its occurrence as allegory does. He was already aware of the complementarity of each of two pairs of how we know and present the real—image & object, and action & subject—both of which have paid off so decisively since. At this end I am thinking of such recent American painting as Pollock's, and Kline's, and some recent American narrative and verse; and at his end, his whale itself for example, what an unfolding thing it is as it sits there written 100 years off, implicit intrinsic and incident to itself.

Melville was not tempted, as Whitman was, and Emerson and Thoreau differently, to inflate the physical: take the model for the house, the house for the model, death is the open road, the soul or body is a boat, etc. Melville equally couldn't spiritualize it, as Hawthorne tried, using such sets as the mirror image, M. de Miroir, etc., and Melville himself in *The Bell Tower,* but not in *The Encantadas,* or *Bartleby,* and how explain the way the remark "The negro" does hold off and free in *Benito* Cereno? Melville wouldn't have known it to say it this way, but he was essentially incapable of either allegory or symbol for the best of congruent reason: mirror and model are each figures in Euclidean space, and they are *not* congruent. They require a discontinuous jump.

Finally, to take the possibilities here suggested, at their fullest— the actual character and structure of the real itself. I pick up on calm, or passivity, Melville's words, and about which he knew something, having served as a boatsteerer himself, on at least his third voyage on a whaler in the Pacific. He says somewhere a harpoon can only be thrown accurately from such repose as he also likened the White Whale to, as it finally approached, a mighty mildness of repose in swiftness is his phrase. Likewise, in handling Ahab's monomania, he sets up a different sort of a possible man, one of a company which he calls the hustings of the Divine Inert.

I am able to stress the several aspects of Melville's thought on this because, note, in each case the feeling or necessity of the inert, or of passivity as a position of rest, is joined to the most instant and powerful actions Melville can invent: the whale itself's swiftness, Ahab's inordinate will, and the harpooneer's ability to strike to kill from calm only. *The inertial structure of the world is a real thing which not only exerts effects upon matter but in turn suffers such effects.*

I don't know a more relevant single fact to the experience of *Moby-Dick* and its writer than this. Unless it is the prior and lesser but more characteristic Riemannian observation, that the metrical structure of the world is so intimately connected to the inertial structure that the metrical field (art is measure) will of necessity become flexible (what we are finding out these days in painting writing and music) the moment the inertial field itself is flexible.

Which it is, Einstein established, by the phenomena of gravitation, and the dependence of the field of inertia on matter. I take care to be inclusive, to enforce the point made at the start, that matter offers perils wider than man if he doesn't do what still today seems the hardest thing for him to do, outside of some art and science: to believe that things, and present ones, are the absolute conditions; but that they are so because the structures of the real are flexible, quanta do dissolve into vibrations, all does flow, and yet is there, to be made permanent, if the means are equal.

[*1958*]

Proprioception

———

Physiology: the surface (senses—the 'skin': of 'Human Universe') the body itself—proper —one's own 'corpus': PROPRIOCEPTION the cavity of the body, in which the organs are slung: the viscera, or inter-

oceptive, the old 'psychology' of feeling,
the heart; of desire, the liver; of sympathy,
the 'bowels'; of courage—kidney etc—
gall. (Stasis—or as in Chaucer only,
spoofed)

Today: movement, at any cost. Kinesthesia: beat
(nik) the sense whose end organs lie in
the muscles, tendons, joints, and are
stimulated by bodily tensions (—or relax-
ations of same). Violence: knives/
anything, to get the body in.

To which   the data of depth sensibility/the 'body'
PROPRIOCEPTION: of us as object which spontaneously
or of its own order produces experiences
of 'depth' Viz

SENSIBILITY WITHIN THE ORGANISM
BY MOVEMENT OF ITS OWN TISSUES

'Psychology': the surface: consciousness as ego and thus
no flow because the 'senses' of same are
all that sd contact area is valuable for, to
THE WORKING report in to central. Inspection, followed
'OUT' OF hard on heels by, judgment (judicium,
'PROJECTION' dotha: cry, if you must/ all feeling may
flow, is all which can count, at sd point.
Direction outward is sorrow, or joy. Or
participation: active social life, like, for
no other reason than that—social life. In
the present. Wash the ego out, in its own
'bath' (os)

The 'cavity'/cave: probably the 'Uncon-
scious'? That is, the interior empty place
filled with 'organs'? for 'functions'?

The advantage is to 'place' the thing, in-
stead of it wallowing around sort of out-

THE 'PLACE'
OF THE
'UNCONSCIOUS'

side, in the universe, like, when the
experience of it is interoceptive: it is inside
us/ & at the same time does not feel
literally identical with our own physical or
mortal self (the part that can die). In this
sense likewise the heart, etc, the small
intestine etc, are or can be felt as—and
literally they can be—transferred. Or sub-
stituted for. Etc. The organs.—Probably
also why the old psychology was chiefly
visceral: neither dream, nor the uncon-
scious, was then known as such. Or allow-
ably inside, like.

'ACTION'—OR, AGAIN, 'MOVEMENT'

This 'demonstration' then leads to the
same third, or corpus, thing or 'place,'
the

>*proprious*-ception
>'one's own'-ception

the 'body' itself as, by movement of its
own tissues, giving the data of, depth.
Here, then wld be what is left out? Or

the soul is
proprioceptive

what is physiologically even the 'hard'
(solid, palpable), that one's life is
informed from and by one's own literal
body—as well, that is, as the whole inner
mechanism, which keeps us so damn
busy (like eating, sleeping, urinating,
dying there, by deterioration of sd
'functions' of sd 'organs')—that this
mid-thing between, which is what gets
'buried,' like, the flesh? bones, muscles,
ligaments, etc., what one uses, literally
to get about etc

that this is 'central,' that is—in this
½ of the picture—what they call the

SOUL, the intermediary, the intervening thing, the interruptor, the resistor. The self.

The gain: to have a third term, so that *movement* or *action* is 'home.' Neither the Unconscious nor Projection (here used to remove the false opposition of 'Conscious'; 'consciousness' is self) have a home unless the DEPTH implicit in physical being—built-in space-time specifics, and moving (by movement of 'its own')—is asserted, or found-out as such. Thus the advantage of the value 'proprioception.' As such.

its own   The 'soul' then is equally 'physical.' Is
perception   the self. Is such, 'corpus.' Or—to levy the gain psychology from 1900, or 1885, did supply until it didn't (date ? 1948?) —the three terms wld be:

surface (senses) projection
cavity (organs—here read 'archtypes')
unconscious the body itself—
consciousness: implicit accuracy, from
its own energy as a state of implicit
motion.

Identity,   therefore (the universe is one) is supplied; and the abstract-primitive character of the real (asserted) is 'placed': projection is discrimination (of the object from the subject) and the unconscious is the universe flowing-in, inside.

ROBERT DUNCAN

From a Notebook

―――――――――

This series of notes serves to explore a style and temperament in which the Romantic spirit is revived. Back it goes to recent readings again of George MacDonald's *Lilith,* to earlier pleasures and thrills in Coleridge and Poe. But thruout I am conscious of the debt to Wallace Stevens—that there is a route back to the Romantic in Stevens. Then, I discovered, having finally purchased *New Directions* 14 in order to study the Zukofsky, Charles Henri Ford's "Anthology of Prose Poetry." Mallarmé's "Penultimate" and Poe's "Shadow" are all of the vein along which I am working again. This is of course the radical disagreement that Olson has with me. In a sense he is so keen upon the *virtu* of reality that he rejects my "wisdom" not as it might seem at first glance because "wisdom" is a vice; but because my wisdom is not real wisdom. He suspects, and rightly, that I indulge myself in pretentious fictions. I, however, at this point take enuf delight in the available glamor that I do not stop to trouble the cheapness of such stuff. I mean that it is, for a man of rigor, an inexpensive irony to play with puns on pretending and pretension. I like rigor and even clarity as a quality of a work—that is, as I like muddle and floaty vagaries. It is the intensity of the conception that moves me. This intensity may be that it is all of a fervent marshmallow dandy lion fluff. In cloudy art I admire boldness, big lumps of it as in Marie Laurencin. And certainly I like intensely evasive art—like Corbett's big white canvas where the area is blushing with a rosyness that one sees without distinguishing.

The persistent idea in these notes that form is Form, a spirit in itself, we owe to the Romantics. To Mallarmé the area of the page is a void of meaning upon which, into which, in which, the poem appears. This is very different from later expressionism with its emphasis on the poem as a psychological event. And certainly it differs from the "classical" concept of thought articulated as perfectly as possible.

I am willing to pursue this art in search of itself, because for the time I have shaken off the insistent hounds of the critical posse. I have returned to the privacy of my craft and find that if I am my own judge I will allow the full play. As far as I can go gives me life again on the page.

Then a sense of perspective frees me also—that I am indeed to die, as you are to die, makes life all mine to live. The privacy is absolute and real: none of you, nor your counsels, will stand by me in my dying. And before the fact of the solitude which is my actually being alive—"the goods of the intellect" are clear indeed. What is vanity, what I wld not be caught dead doing . . . just as vivid. I have not time to solicit the good opinion of those who feel chummy: I have no time for the possibilities of success. Each fulfillment precludes it.

And a sense of perspective again—that making history, even writing a great poem, is out of the way. I don't want it. When I turn to my own vein, I see it is all very questionable—but the full joy of dancing there is enough. When I took mescaline I discoverd that I did not care—something suddenly happy and grandiose did not care: and it occurred to me that I might turn with a gladness to private meaningless pleasures, to profundities because they were depths, to ecstasies because they were heights—mere dimensions. Having all the importance of Arp's stone in a field.

These essays for the shape and current of them. Not yet extravagant; not yet care-free so that all cares could exfoliate into an orchestration. But even shame, and, of course, the fact that one does marvellously but not very well at writing.

The discovery of Pound, Stein, James Joyce, Eugene Jolas, Kafka—and then surrealists—when I was eighteen meant what Robert Browning and then Lawrence had meant earlier: that in an art everything was possible, nothing circumscribed the flowering of being into its particular forms. This too is on my mind, and these romantic notes are as much in homage to my eternal heroes, to the beauties, individual and bold, of the *Cantos,* or *Useful Knowledge,* or *Finnegans Wake,* or of a night language, as they are an homage to the charming Romantic flavor of Helen Adam's ballads and scrapbooks.

[*1954*]

Notes on Poetics Regarding Olson's *Maximus*

The mind, Ferrini,
is as much of a labor
as to lift an arm
flawlessly—Letter 5

No more difficult than walking, this leisurely and exact talking; if "leisure" be seen as an "increment of association" (which term I get out of Pound): no effort as great as the million-year gain incorporated by the child in his upright simple complexity (controi and coordination) of walking.

In American poetry the striding syllables show an aesthetic based on energies:

> Bulkeley, Hunt, Willard, Hosmer, Meriam, Flint,
> possessed the land which rendered to their toil
> hay, corn, roots, hemp, flax, apples, wool and wood.
> —Emerson, "Hamatraya"

John Dewey in *Art as Experience* points to the difference "between the art product (statue, painting or whatever), and the *work* of art." Again, he writes: "Order, rhythm and balance simply means that energies significant for experience are acting at their best." I point to Emerson or to Dewey to show that in American philosophy there are foreshadowings or forelightings of *Maximus*. In this aesthetic, conception cannot be abstracted from doing; beauty is related to the beauty of an archer hitting the mark. Referrd to its source in the act, the intellect actually manifest as energy, as presence is doing, is the measure of our *arêté* (as vision, claritas, light, illumination, was the measure of Medieval *arêté*).

Pose the visual spirit of Italian 14th century painting. And then the muscular spirit of American 20th century painting. In *Maximus,* Olson points to Marsden Hartley: "to get that rock in paint"—a getting, a taking grasp, a hand that is the eye. "But what he did with that bald jaw of stone." "Did with" not "saw in." And here Olson comes to the hand—Hartley's hand, Jake's hand: "a man's hands, / as his eyes."

American 20th century painting: the difference between energy referrd to (seen) as in the Vorticist and Futurist work—particularly Wyndham Lewis and Boccioni—and

energy

embodied in the painting (felt), which is now muscular as well as visual, contain as well as apparent: the work of Hofmann, Pollock, Kline—and most importantly (for this is the work that has given me my clues) in San Francisco of Still, Corbett, Bischoff (in his nonobjective period), Hassel Smith, Diebenkorn, Abend, Roeber, Lili Fenichel, Jacobus, Jess, Brockway, Sonia Getchtoff . . .

I I

Starting with the image, and so with Ezra Pound (but I mean this as beyond imagism—the vision he makes clear in the Cavalcanti piece) embodied in the language, a speech in which the eye works, and moving by means of the embodying in the language of the "act" toward the act—in taking hold. "I grasp what you mean." Hence, the *Cantos* are central, as active; and the *Wasteland* or *Four Quartets,* beside the point, as dramatic.

Pound circa 1928 in *How to Read* lists three "kinds of poetry." It is in the description of the third mode, *logopoeia,* that I find suggestions of what I am talking about. Indicating the first two for the purposes of my task here: *melopoeia* (summd up by Dante in *De Vulgari Eloquentia*) represents the gain of hearing, the physiological mastery ear-wise in the poem. By Dante's time a comprehensive explication could be made—the chips were down. (Edith Sitwell's notes on tone bear the relation to Dante's that the delights of antiquarian lore bear to the original necessity.) The sound now coheres (and so, sound is "sound"; the quality of a thing earliest is told by its "ringing true").

phanopoeia ("a casting of images upon the visual imagination"—why does Pound make it remote this way, almost passive, a Wraith of Plato in his neo-Platonic sourcer?) was initiated in Dante's gaining sight of the "psychological" universe and moves toward some point of summing up beyond the *Imagist Manifesto.* The chips are not down; but we have the responsibility of seeing. The discipline of the eye, clarity, is acknowledged measure. A poet who cant hear and who cant in addition see is now obviously deficient (tho they exist & thrive all about us, and greatest poets, like Milton and Joyce, have "lost sight" of the target). It is in point here to remind any reader who may be partisan to my argument that I am sketching out "a" way of poetry, not "the" way of poetry; and that terms—"responsibility," "gain," "deficiency"—are all terms along the way.

The hand is intimate to the measurings of the eye. Michael McClure in an early poem refers to the hand: "Opposable, . . . in the way, . . . dumb" and again, "this eye my thumb." A rule of thumb. McClure refers to the role of the hand in perception; the hand & eye estimate, and we feel what we see.

Metrics as it is still incoherent depends on accent. The consciousness, not yet having the "feel" of it, must have the boldest tum-te-tum to proceed by. For the inexpert there must be reference to a "ruler" in time. Hence the convention. Metrics, as it coheres, is actual—the sense of language in terms of weights and durations (by which we cohere in moving). This is a dance in whose measured steps time emerges, as space emerges from the dance of the body. The ear is intimate to muscular equilibrium. The line endures. It "feels right."

logopoeia—"the dance of the intellect among words," Pound writes. He describes this new mode (outside of this reference to the "dance") in terms of *placement and displacement;* as if he were attempting to convey or define the dance *as it is seen* (a series of photographd positions of the body playing upon one's visual expectations). "It is the latest come, and perhaps most tricky and undependable mode." Of course, tricky and undependable to the eye (seen as an aesthetics of arrangements); as we find it difficult to translate our image in the mirror (the body seen) into the language of movement. It may now be suggested that one may lose sight of the target in order to gain insight of the target. The eye retrained in the dark?

The significance of the mode lies for Pound in the meaning level. "It employs words not only for their direct meaning, but it takes count in a special way of habits of usage, of the context we *expect* to find with the word, its usual concomitants, of its known acceptances, and of ironical play." Its manifestation is verbal.

THE RISK: to suggest that the conquest of babble by the ear—to distinguish and organize, to make significant, to relate as experience, to name—is the origin of speech and emotion. Speech at this level articulates internal sensations. "The inner voice." The recurrence of vowels and consonants, the tonal structure, is related to heart and alimentary tract in its rhythmic organization; it is expressive. It is "moving"—melopoeia is the passionate system of the poem. The conquest of passion by the eye, *phanopoeia* is at once and in the same a physiological gain, a focusing, and a gain in meanings. To "see" is to re-form all speech. Significances are shift-ings and transformings possible in the relationship of eye and brain. The reality of what is witnessd disciplines the speech, and it is only by poetry, by the making-up of the real through language (I mean by poetry here all made-up things—language thus is as a man makes his way as well as as a man makes his speech, draw-ings, objects, governments, story) that one can witness. Meanings and functions are intimately related, if not merely different aspects of the same event. Now: Mr. Pound's *logopoeia* seems to be not only a verbal manifestation but a physiological manifestation. Ambiguities, word-play, ironies, disassociations appear as we watch the meanings; but it is the action of the language, the muscu-lar correlation of the now differentiated parts of the poem, that so expresses itself. The point: just as the ear and eye have been incorporated in the act of making in language, the locomotor muscular-nervous system is being calld into the adventure. The disciplines of the ear and the eye are primary—soundings and focusings—in order to be prepared in this work. The disciplines of movement, of those potentialities of the language analogous to the acts of "muscle control and use" are the task at hand.

/ I owe as much to Louis Zukofsky's work on Shakespeare as I owe to *Maximus*. Many of my ideas here spring from "Bottom's Dream" which appeard in *New Directions 14,* from subsequent talks with Zukofsky and from his manuscripts as yet unpublishd from which for an all too brief session he read to me. If the reader would understand what might be implied in "To see is to re-form all speech," he would do well to read "Bottom's Dream," and to follow Zukofsky's work as it may at last find the light of day. [Since the writing of this essay in 1955, published in 1956, Louis Zukofsky's *Bottom: On Shakespeare* has, of course, been published by the Ark Press in 1963; and remains for me a major work in our poetic heritage.—R.D., 1973.]

RECAPITULATION. The coming into life of the child: first, that the breath-blood circulation be gaind, an interjection! the levels of the passions and inspiration in phrases; second, that focus be gaind, a substantive, the level of vision; and third, the complex of muscular gains that are included in taking hold and balancing, verbs, but more, the movement of the language, the level of the ear, the hand, and the foot. All these incorporated in measure.

III

how to dance
sitting down
                    —"Tyrian Businesses"

There is reference everywhere in *Maximus* to the exercise of poetry. "By ear, he sd." This is the beginning point (as the discrimination of speech). But, if the muscular realization of language is the latest mode of poetry, the beginning point was muscular too, localized in the discharge of energy expressd in the gaining, first, breath, and then, tongue. The gift of spirit and of tongues.

Joyce after addressing his energies to clarity (*Portrait of the Artist*), goes on to the conquest of locomotor writing (*Ulysses*) which remains, like the *Cantos,* Marianne Moore's or William Carlos Williams' works, a masterpiece of this mode. If we are seriously involved, we must go to school to these.

Finnegans Wake returns (turns back) to the beginnings, not only in reference (intestinal alimentary mythic meaning levels) but in mimesis, as a thing done (the alimentary babbling speech; the gobbling, the breaking down into). Here meanings are being churnd up, digested back into the original chaos of noises, decomposed.

Certainly the masterpiece of a psychoanalytical period. In *logopoeia* meanings then may be puddled as in Joyce, or they can be playd as in H.D.'s *War Trilogy* by a sleight-of-mind. The one poses uniquely the proposition of letting go, back to the visceral process.

Olson insists upon the active. Homo maximus wrests his life from the underworld as the Gloucester fisherman wrests his from the sea.

> the underpart is, though stemmed, uncertain
> is, as sex is, as moneys are, facts
> to be dealt with as the sea is . . .

> be played by, said he coldly,
> the ear.

We are perhaps as deraild by the excitements of Freudian psychology as the Middle Ages were by the excitements of Aristotelian logic—with psychoanalysts as counterparts of scholastics, with infantology replacing angelology, and the phantasmagoria of metapsychology in place of the phantasmagoria of metaphysics.

> There are so many, children
> who want to go back, who want to lie down
> in Tiamat.
> You can tell them this: the land-spout's
> put all the diapers
> up in trees.

Not a digression: but to indicate that the "taking hold" of the *Maximus* poems is pitted against "letting go," is a conquest of Tiamat. The emergence from vitality of faculties. Joyce retreats from his faculties to his mere vitalities.

/ But the conversion of passions, the "use" of internal organs is not simply a turning back; it is parallel here again to the development of the individual. He discovers his "self"; that is, he achieves tone or *arêté* [backbone]—on the most common level, he is toilet traind, he governs his emotions, he withholds or releases tears at will, etc. Seen in this light, *Finnegan* represents not a "letting go" as I first saw it, but an integrating process: the will to let go or to use or to retain is achieved. Joyce is no longer prey of his emotions but preys upon his emotions. Seen thus, graspd thus, felt thus, Joyce sets his faculties at work upon his vitalities. What is in point is that he "lives off nature" and thus provides a contrary that might make clear the moral structure of *Maximus*. "ya, selva oscura." Joyce plays with his self. Olson, addressing himself to *homo maximus,* outraged by "those who use words cheap, who use us cheap," cries "that you should not be played with."

Against Tiamat:

> The carpenter is much on my mind:
> I think he was the first Maximus.
>
> Anyway, he was the first to make things,
> not just live off nature . . .
>
> for example, necessities the practice of the self,
> that matter, that wood.

Maximus is a *makar*; is then Olson, or his measure. Now I may be understood perhaps in saying that "The Songs of Maximus" (Letter 4) ring true, are clearly seen, take hold, measure up.

> No eyes or ears left
> to do their own doings

is a protest that rises from the, is rooted in, keen sense of what eye and ear need be. Sights and soundings, "the attention, and / the care."

It is enough. Enough surely. The reader can put it all together: the "by ear," "be played by . . . / the ear," "she looks / as the best of my people look / in one direction," "the hands he'd purposely allowed to freeze to the oars," "eyed (with a like eye)," "look right straight down into yr pages," "polis is / eyes," "that those who are sharp haven't got that way / by pushing their limits," "his eyes / as a gull's are," "by gift ? bah by love of self? try it by god? ask / the bean sandwich," "As hands are put to the eyes' commands," "a man's hands, / as his eyes, / can get sores)," "(each finger) their own lives' acts," "to have a heart,"

> And I feel that way,
> that the likeness is to nature's
> not to these tempestuous
> events.

The major address of the poem is to what the act need be—to

> facility
> resulting from life of activity in accordance with

On the level of reference, the gain from Whitman's address to his cosmic body to Olson's address to "The waist of a lion/for a man to move properly" is immense.

[*1956*]

Ideas of the Meaning of Form

Phases of meaning in the soul may be like phases of the moon, and, though rationalists may contend against the imagination, all men may be one, for they have their source out of the same earth, mothered in one ocean and fathered in the light and heat of one sun that is not tranquil but rages between its energy that is a disorder seeking higher intensities and its fate or dream of perfection that is an order where all light, heat, being, movement, meaning and form, are consumed toward the cold. The which men have imagined in the laws of thermodynamics.

But if our life is mixed, as the suspicion comes from the Gnostics and from Blake, and rays of many stars that are suns of all kinds, Aie! if we are so many fathered, or if, as theosophists have feared, we were many mothered in the various chemistries of the planets, still let the war be done and the adultery rage on, for my soul is sick with fear and contention whenever I remember the claim of mind against mind and some ass praises me because a line rimes who would despise me if he knew the meanings, and I am aroused myself toward thoughts of vengeance and triumph. Thus, I say, "Let the light rays mix," and, against the Gnostics, who would free the sparks of spirit from what is the matter, and against the positivists and semanticists who would free the matter from its inspirational chaos, I am glad that there is night and day, Heaven and Hell, love and wrath, sanity and ecstasie, together in a little place. Having taken thought upon death, I would be infected by what is.

> she said, Sir, it is a most beautiful fragrance,
> as of all flowering things together;

Thus, H.D., fifteen years ago, in *The Flowering of the Rod:* "But Kasper knew the seal of the jar was unbroken." And William Carlos Williams in the close of "Asphodel":

> Asphodel
>   has no odor
>   save to the imagination
> but it too
>   celebrates the light.
>   It is late
> But an odor
>   as from our wedding
>   has revived for me
> and begun again to penetrate
>   into all crevices
>   of my world.

The end of masterpieces . . . the beginning of testimony. Having their mastery obedient to the play of forms that makes a path between what is in the language and what is in their lives. In this light that has something to do with all flowering things together, a free association of living things then—for my longing moves beyond governments to a co-operation; that may have seeds of being in free verse or free thought, or in that other free association where Freud led men to re-member their lives, admitting into the light of the acknowledged and then of meaning what had been sins and guilts, heresies, shames and wounds;

that may have to do with following the sentence along a line of feeling until the law becomes a melody, and the imagination, going where it will—to the stars! may return to penetrate, a most beautiful fragrance, into all the crevices of our world:

in this light I attempt to describe what I most abhor, what most seems to exclude or mistake the exuberance of my soul.

CONVENTION, CONFORMITIES,
AND REGULATED METERS

Form to the mind obsessed by convention, is significant in so far
as it shows control. What has nor rime nor reason is a bogie that
must be dismissed from the horizons of the mind. It is a matter of
rules and conformities, taste, rationalization and sense. Beyond, as
beyond in the newly crowded Paris or London of the Age of
Reason, lies the stink of shit and pestilence. Wherever the feeling
of control is lost, the feeling of form is lost. The reality of the
world and men's habits must be constricted to a realm—a court or
a salon or a rationale—excluding whatever is feared. It is a magic
that still survives in Christian Science and the New Criticism, a
magic that removes the reasonable thing from its swarming back-
ground of unreason—unmentionable areas where all the facts that
reason cannot regulate are excluded and appear as error, savage
tribes, superstitions and anarchical mobs, passions, madnesses,
enthusiasms and bad manners. Metaphor must be fumigated or
avoided (thought of as displaying the author's fancy or wit) to rid
the mind of the poetic, where metaphor had led dangerously
toward Paracelsus' universe of psychic correspondences, toward a
life where men and things were beginning to mix and cross
boundaries of knowledge. Poets, who once had dreams and epiph-
anies, now admit only to devices and ornaments. Love, that had
been a passion, had best be a sentiment or a sensible affection.
Rational piety and respect for God stood strong against divine
inspiration and demonic possession. The struggle was to have ideas
and not to let ideas have one. Taste, reason, rationality rule, and
rule must be absolute and enlightened, because beyond lies the
chiaroscuro in which forces co-operate and sympathies and aver-
sions mingle. The glamor of this magic haunts all reasonable men
today, surrounding them with, and then protecting them from, the
shadows cast by the enlightenment, the darkness of possibilities
that control cannot manage, the world of thought and feeling in
which we may participate but not dominate, where we are used by
things even as we use them.

This frame of mind still holds a dominant place today. In liter-
ary circles—(literary societies were an expression of this pro-

phylactic genius against experience)—there are so many mentors of wit and taste, of what ought to be, "hoping with glory to trip up the Laureate's feet," whose meters must perform according to rules of iamb and spondee, these phantasms of the convention triumphing over the possible disorder or music that threatens in the contamination of actual stresses in the language.

So, one Miss Drew (selected by me at random from a library recommended-currents shelf to represent up-to-date academic opinion about form in poetry) defining the art of the poet: "A metrical scheme is itself simply a mechanical framework, a convention, within which and against which, the poet orders his individual poetic movement," reacts throughout against any thought that there might be, as Carlyle was not afraid to think, a music in the heart of things that the poet sought. What Carlyle saw was that the key to that music lay in the melody (which we must take it Miss Drew has never heard) of the language itself, where "all speech, even the commonest speech, has something of song in it: not a parish in the world but has its parish-accent;—the rhythm or *tune* to which the people there *sing* what they have to say." But Carlyle in those lectures in 1840 was concerned with the return of the heroic spirit. Miss Drew is a latter-day believer in men cut down to the proper size, a mistress of that critical demon that Pound in his *Cantos* calls Pusillanimity.

Contrast the voice and spirit of Carlyle, where imagination appears as an intuition of the real: "All deep things are Song. It seems somehow the very central essence of us, Song; as if all the rest were but wrappages and hulls! The primal element of us; of us, and of all things. The Greek fabled Sphere-Harmonies: it was the feeling they had of the inner structure of Nature; that the soul of all her voices and utterances was perfect music. Poetry, therefore, we call *musical Thought*. The Poet is he who *thinks* in that manner. At bottom, it turns still on power of intellect; it is a man's sincerity and depth of vision that makes him a Poet. See deep enough, and you see musically; the heart of Nature *being* everywhere music, if you can only reach it." Against which the voice and spirit of Miss Drew: "The convention sets up a pattern of recurrent sound effects which is pleasant to the ear. It is an element in a larger movement, his rhythm. Rhythm means flow, and flow is determined by meaning more than meter, by feeling more than feet. It represents the freedom the poet can use within his own self-imposed necessity. It is the personal voice speaking through the formal convention."

What we see in the contrast is, in scope of imagination, style, intellect, unfair perhaps. Carlyle is so obviously a mind troubled by genius; Miss Drew is so obviously a mind troubled only by, as she calls it, "a self-imposed necessity." But the genius of convention, that was brilliant in the 17th and 18th centuries, in our own is liable to come out small or trivial. Carlyle's thought opens a vista toward what our own inspired science of linguistics has made part of our responsibility, if we are concerned with the nature of things. Carlyle's thought going toward the inner structure of Nature had intuitions of the inner structure of language. The science of Sapir and Whorf has its origins in the thought of *The Hero As Poet*. Just as, exemplified in Miss Drew, one of the stands of the conventional, of all reasonable men, is against the heroic.

"Pound's cult of *Imagism*," Miss Drew goes on, "demanded no rhythmical stress at all, only a clear visual image in lines alleged to be in the pattern of the musical phrase. When read aloud, these patterns couldn't possibly be distinguished from prose. The result was a flood of poems such as William Carlos Williams' 'Red Wheelbarrow,' which proves perhaps only that words can't take the place of paint."

It is of the essence of the rationalist persuasion that we be protected, by the magic of what reasonable men agree is right, against unreasonable or upsetting information. Here, in order to follow Miss Drew's intelligence, we must be ignorant of (aggressively oppose the facts) or innocent of (passively evade the facts) history (what Imagism actually was), poetics (what Pound actually did say about tone and duration, stress and phrase), gestalt (what a pattern actually is in time, and how poetry and music have common characteristics by reason of that extension), linguistics (what the actual patterns of vowel and consonant, stress and pitch, are in the language); and, finally, we must be determined to read "The Red Wheelbarrow" to fit Miss Drew's determination that "these patterns couldn't possibly be distinguished from prose."

The base evil of Miss Drew's mind is that it must depend upon our taking its authority. Her evocation throughout of "mechanical framework," "orders his movement," "determined," "imposed," "alleged" and then "ought" and "ought not," "couldn't possibly," "can't" is the verbal effluvia of a mind holding its own ("self-imposed necessity") against experience. For were we to question her authority in light of the poem, we would find that there is some difference in movement between the poem she seems to have read that went as follows: "So much depends upon a red wheel barrow glazed with rain water beside the white chickens" and the actual poem. But it is part of her conviction that the appearance on the page of a line is a matter of convention, must indicate either following or disobeying what men have agreed on. Any other meaning, that the line might be a notation of how it is to be read, is intolerable.

So she must overlook or deny the lines as meaningful notation, where syllabic measures of variable number alternate with lines of two syllables to form a dance immediate to the eye as a rhythmic pattern:

> four syllables (two one-syllable words + one two-syllable word)
> one two-syllable word
> three syllables (three one-syllable words)
> one two-syllable word
> three syllables (three one-syllable words)
> one two-syllable word
> four syllables (one two-syllable word + two one-syllable words)
> one two-syllable word.

She must overlook, fail to hear, or deny the existence of riming vowels in "glazed" and "rain", "beside" and "white" that give a balanced emphasis to the measure in the close; much less an ear for the complex or subtle relations that syncopate the opening lines between "so much" and "barrow," "depends" and "red wheel," "a" and "upon."

At every level her mind was excited to resist against Williams's *so much depends*. Her goal in criticism was not to explore the meaning and form of the poem but to stand against it; to remain independent of red wheelbarrow, vowels and consonants, count of syllables and interchange of stresses, juncture, phrase.

"Whether this kind of thing pleases," she decides firmly, "must be a matter of personal taste, but it should not be called *verse,* since that word means that the rhythm *turns* and repeats itself; just as *prose* means that it runs straight on."

But criticism like this is a monster of poor sort. Though I am unread in contemporary verse of the conventional persuasion outside of the work of Marianne Moore, T.S. Eliot, and Robert Lowell, I realize that beyond these there is marshalled an imposing company of arbiters and camp followers, lady commandos of quatrains right! and myrmidons of the metaphysical stanza, holding the line against any occurrence of, much less the doctrines of, poetic genius or romantic imagination, handing out prizes (booby and otherwise) to balance the accounts and bolster standards. Schoolmarms and professors of literature affronted by the bardic presumptions of Dame Edith Sitwell.

Were our songs of the universe and our visions of that great Love who once appeared to Dante holding his smoking heart in his hand, were our feelings and thoughts that had flowed out of whatever originality they might have had into their origins in phrases of a melody, were our dreams and our architectures to come home at last, members of no more than a classroom education?

Convention, anyway, in these circles of literary critics and school masters is a proper mode, and seldom rises to any height above the general conventionality, having its roots (like the unconventionality of "beats") in what other men think. But in the vitality of poets, of Marianne Moore or of Robert Lowell, some personal necessity rather than social opportunity gives substance and meaning to their conventional verse. The rigorously counted syllables, the certainty of end rimes, the conformation of stanzas arise along lines, not of a self-imposed necessity but of a psychic need.

Stanza must conform to stanza in the work of Marianne Moore wherever the charge of emotion is carried, because awareness at all depends upon a character structure that proves itself in awareness. "Tell me the truth, / especially when it is / unpleasant," she says in *Light Is Speech;* and there is the sense of facing the facts, of "Test me, I will resist." Power over things, which is the keynote of the aesthetic of the Man of Reason, is at least related to the power to survive things that inspires Marianne Moore's art. It is not subtlety of movement and interrelation but the challenge of obstacles and particulars that informs her dance. "No more fanatical adjuster," she remarks in lines that keep their own "constant of the plumbline, of the tilted hat / than Escudero." Her metaphor is never a device but a meaningful disclosure. She is not conventional then by social class or by prejudice, but by nature. But to be conventional by nature leaves her personal and vulnerable, erecting around herself an armored modesty, that can show also an irritable sense of possible violation. In her strength and in her weakness she shows her likeness to this constellation I have been drawing of the genius of defensive Reason.

Robert Lowell, too, is not merely conventional as a matter of what men approve but holds his line and establishes his rime at the edge of disaster. His precisions arise not from a love of the melos, the particles that contribute to the melody, but from a mistrust throughout of free movements. When in *Life Studies* his line grows irregular, it conforms to the movement straining for balance that a drunk knows. Betrayal is immanent:

> In the ebb-
> light of morning, we stuck
> the duck
> -'s web-
> foot, like a candle, in a quart of gin we'd killed.

The notation of these lines is as accurate as in William Carlos Williams, and the art as admirable. But the concept of the verse is not free, but fearful. Where in the later poetry of Williams the end juncture makes possible a hovering uncertainy in which more may be gathered into the fulfillment of the form, in the *Life Studies* of Lowell the juncture appears as a void in measure that is some counterpart of the void in content. How / we feel / can this / foot / get across to / that / line. There.

In *O To Be a Dragon* Marianne Moore sees in *Combat Cultural* terms which relate directly to the rise in the 17th and 18th centuries of the Reasonable Convention confronted by intolerable threat:

> I recall a documentary
> of Cossacks: a visual fugue, a mist

> of swords that seemed to sever
> heads from bodies—feet stepping through
> harp-strings in a scherzo.

As, perhaps another conventional soul, Charles Bell, writing in *Diogenes* 19, speaks of "the transformations of Renaissance and Baroque" that filled architecture of churches "with voluptuous riot," bringing religion into a vertigo, "the dramatic contrasts of assertive ego of later religious music, of Gabrielli and Bach." And we recall that the rationalist aesthetic was an heroic effort to find balance against this admission of vertigo, against the swirl of a vastly increased vision of what man might be.

"However," Marianne Moore pauses, and begins her next stanza:

> the quadrille of Old Russia for me:
> with aimlessly drooping handkerchief
> snapped like the crack of a whip;

The tension, the reality of the verse, depends upon its being sufficiently haunted by the thought of its energy as a violence and the thought of its form as repose for the poet to take her stance. But the "aimlessly drooping handkerchief / snapped like the crack of a whip" is an image of the unnecessary conventionality of Marianne Moore's later work where recognition and admiration have disarmed her of the struggle that gave reality to her vigorous lines. Challenged, she may be aroused to display her backbone, to bristle her armatures. But window shopping among the ads of the *New Yorker,* it is not to the aepyornis or rock challenged by time that the figure refers but to the qivies with winning ways.

In her career Marianne Moore began, in certain poems like "An Octopus" or "In the Days of Prismatic Color," with some promise of a free verse, where movement of language had the vigor of a feeling and thought that was not self-conscious. Here the number of lines in the stanza can vary with the immediate sense of movement, and the actual kept feeling of the tempo gives measure rather than the systematic repeated count of syllables or the emphasis of rimes at the end of lines. It is the uneasy definition of what is "sophistication" and what are "the initial great truths" that is one proposition of the poem; it is "the days of Adam and Eve," of "complexity . . . committed to darkness," of smoke, modified color, even murkiness, on the one hand; and "when Adam was alone," where color keeps its place in "the blue-red-yellow band / of incandescence" on the other. These poems imagine terms of a nature where things may mingle still, though the soul is troubled and the mind already resolved to outlast unsureness.

But in the work in which she found what was typical or original, the metaphor is that of animal or hero who survives by resistence of his spine (backbone) and his spiney armature (protective character structure). Conventionality breeds personality. She conforms to her own society. Individuality, yes, but dependent thruout upon rules and orders even as it insists upon its individuality. Her splendid achievement is to excite our admiration of her performance, her risky equilibriums, and her resistence to deeper thought and feeling where personality is lost. Her skill and her craft are unexcelled. But they depend upon increased self-consciousness, and they divert then the attention of the poet and our attention in reading from the question they beg of the avoidance of emotions too common to be personalized.

In the resolution of "In the Days of Prismatic Color" we note the conditions were already potential where truth is identified with what resists but not with the experience that is resisted: "The wave may go over it if it likes," she says, where "it" is Truth and the wave is experience. "Know that it will be there when it says, 'I shall be there when the wave has gone by.' " She evokes in her most famous poetry, with its images of rigorists and armored animals, a heroism of the isolated remnant, a constantly reiterated picture of her own personality as determined in a "little-winged, magnificently speedy running-bird" poetry, increasingly specialized. These poems were practices meant to insure habitual virtues. Vision and flight of the imagination were sacrificed to survival in terms of personal signature.

In pieces like "Hometown Piece for Messrs. Alston and Reese, Enough," and "In the Public Garden," she sacrifices character to the possibilities of what America loves in public personality. What had been a display of boney determination and admirable protective structure becomes now a projection of loveable peculiarity, a profession of charming helplessness. In her career she has performed a range that once in history had its hopeful beginnings in

Dryden, then its heroic dimensions in the rage of Pope and Swift, and at last, its social occasions in our own day when "a British poet," as Auden writes in the Introduction to his 1956 *Book of Modern American Verse,* "can take writings more for granted and so write with a lack of strain and over-seriousness." We remember, for it applies here too, the "aimlessly drooping handkerchief" of *Combat Cultural* in this professional lack of over-seriousness, which is the secret superior possibility for Auden.

The vital phase of Rational Genius came as it met straight on the threat of an overwhelming expansion in consciousness that followed the breakthrough in the Renaissance on all levels. The inspiration of Reason was to close off consciousness in an area that was civilized, European, superior in race, practical and Christian (or at least rational in religion). The neo-Platonism and Hermeticism that had begun with Gemisthus Plethon, Ficino, and Pico della Mirandola and appeared in the Rosicrucianism of the early 17th century carried men's religious thought across barriers of right belief, church and civilization, into realms of imaginative synthesis. The agreement of reasonable men was to quarantine the fever of thought. Rationalism erected a taboo of social shame that still lasts against the story of the soul, against the dream and inner life of men the world over, that might be read were the prejudices of what's right and what's civilized lost. Only in the fairy-tales and lore of the common people or in the ritual and lore of cults whose members incurred the cost in their thought of their being outcast and shamed did the great imagination survive. Church-goer or atheist, the rational man was immune to revelation.

Ideas of race, of nation and progress, held and still in many circles hold against the recognition that mankind is involved in one life. Respectable critics and versifiers have been as shocked by the "Buddhism" of Allen Ginsberg or Kerouac as they are by the "sex." When the wall broke, and where it broke, orthodoxy or atheism was swept aside, and men began again to read inner meaning and experience in the arts of all places and times, the message of the soul in African masks, in Aeschylus or in Lady Murasaki, even as they read it in the lore of Catholic saints and Protestant mystics, letting the light from Asia come into their souls to wed and mingle with the light from Rome. It was against this flood of information that threatened once men began to explore the world that the genius of Reason was evoked. Against the imagination then.

The plagues and panics that swept men in their physical existence after 1492 had their counterparts in the plaguing contacts with fellow civilizations in America, Africa and Asia, and the panic that swept Christendom as time before Christendom and space beyond Christendom began to be real and men found their psychic resistences invaded. Up swirled minds and emotions, sciences and art, in a convulsive imagination. There were fearful architectures, gestures, efforts to hold what was not understood and might not be tolerable—in one swirling rhythm. So, in Milton's thundering syntax, the heaped-up effort at architecture, majesty and vastness, takes over the drama from even Satan, and leaves Adam and Eve impoverished in their identity and as overwhelmed as they are disobedient. How Eve is dwindled in conception from the vital conception of Lady Macbeth or Cleopatra.

There is then a lovely release in the Restoration. The beauty of what the Age of Enlightenment meant we can hear still in the "Ode on the Death of Henry Purcell," where Dryden and John Blow build their musical monument to the genius of art over chaos. Angels sing where demons had lurked in chaos. Had it held, had the lights and shadows played as they do in Watteau's pastoral charades, had all of humanity come in under the charm of the rational imagination, masked and playing in a masque, Eskimos and Congo warriors in costumes of the Commedia del'Arte, might it have been like that? a lovely surety gathering its strength in chaos and uncertainty, to banish care? But the art was based on care. Convention, as long as it was heroic, something greater and finer than what we mean today by conventional verse and conventional manners, held its own and needed care, could take nothing for granted. Those shepherds and milkmaids were what could stand against any thought of those who actually herded the sheep or milked. In a painting by Longhi, Venetian revellers give dimension that is real to a rhinoceros, an animal nature momentarily held in its place.

The crisis of the Enlightenment was the crisis that Keats saw recapitulated in Coleridge's collapse from the inspiration of "The Ancient Mariner" and "Cristobel" to the psychic despair, the rationalist obsession, of later years. "The Ancient Mariner" had evoked the revelation of the soul in terms of world exploration; "Cristobel" had evoked the revelation of the soul in the terms of psychic threat that came from sexual lore condemned by Christendom.

"Negative Capability," Keats wrote in a letter, December 21st, 1817: "that is, when a man is capable of being in uncertainties, mysteries, doubts, without any irritable reaching after fact and reason—Coleridge, for instance, would let go-by a fine isolated verisimilitude caught from the Penetralium of mystery, from being incapable of remaining content with half-knowledge."

Science, too, in Newton, sought fact and reason, some order that did not verge upon uncertainty. Whitehead in *Adventures in Ideas* notes that "Literature preserves the wisdom of the human race; but in this way it enfeebles the emphasis of first-hand intuition." It is against some first-hand intuition that men strove to render wisdom sensible and the immediate experience passing, haunted by some premonition of the uncertainty principle in physical measurements that our own science must face, of the uncertainty of self-knowledge in terms of our psychology and physiology, of the uncertainty of our role in life raised by information of evolution. A psyche that is not all to be lightened! a universe that is not all to be ours!

Fact and reason are creations of man's genius to secure a point of view protected against a vision of life where information and intelligence invade us, where what we know shapes us and we become creatures, not rulers, of what is. Where, more, we are part of the creative process, not its goal. It was against such intolerable realizations that these men took thought. The rationalist gardener's art is his control over nature, and beauty is conceived as the imposed order visible in the pruned hedge-row and the ultimate tree compelled into geometric globe of pyramid that gives certainty of effect.

The poet's art was one of control over the common speech, forcing natural metaphor from all hint of meaningful experience or intuition of the universe and maintaining it as a form of speech, and disciplining syntax and line away from the energies of the language itself into balanced phrases, regular meters and heroic couplets. —As too, in military arts, manoeuvres and disciplines occupy the conscious mind. Men are drilled in order that there be an authority, removing them from immediate concern in the acts of killing and destruction involved. A Frederick the Great may be on the edge of knowing that his wars are devastations, not drills. But to such modern triumphs of the conventional mind as Roosevelt or Eisenhower decisions are matters of reason and plan. Disease, death, terror and the ruin of cities are not experienced but dealt with, where rational theory wages its war. The question of the use of disease as a weapon has already been decided by reasonable men who developed the diseases to use and who appointed the military power to use them. Wrathful inspiration (divine or demonic) will not move our rulers to war, nor will some romantic drive to power or suicidal imagination: it is convention, what reasonable men agree upon, that will decide all. War, too, becomes rational.

The game of tennis and the minuet both subject the Yahoo of the animal man to the manners and rules of a court and give authority to that trained horse (and house-broken, too, I hope) of the rational faculty that is a Houyhnhnm. But this Yahoo and this Houyhnhnm is one man divided against himself, phantasy of the Enlightenment in his formal wig performing his ritual dance towards the riddance of Yahoos who know nothing of tennis or minuet. I think of those wigs that marked men of fashion and wit from the uneducated and impoverished mob, the conventional wig and the unconventional cap alike perched on the universally lousy scalp.

But my point here is that the minuet, the game of tennis, the heroic couplet, the concept of form as the imposing of rules and establishing of regularities, the theories of civilization, race, and progress, the performances in sciences and arts to rationalize the universe, to secure balance and class—all these are a tribal magic against a real threat of up-set and things not keeping their place.

The tonal scale of Mozart, where, even among the given notes on the piano, scales are established, so that certain notes are heard as discordant in relation to other notes, threatening to harmony, is a scale imagined to hold its own against threat. A change in mode, in what was permitted, once threatened demonic disorder. Now, unconventional usages threatened loss of reason or insurrection. It is an architecture built up of symmetries, for the mind feels even visual departures from the norm will bring vertigo and collapse. There must be regular sequences and a repetition of stanzas, because thought must not wander, possibility must contain the reassurance of an end to possibilities.

Even in that beginning that I pictured as a kind of health realized by this creation of "Reason" after the whirling orders of the early seventeenth century, there is an uneasy strain. Dryden in his Preface to *All for Love* needs the reassurance of "a subject which has been treated by the greatest wits of our nation" and "their example has given me the confidence to try myself." Then there must be—why?—"the middle course," "motive," "the excellency of moral," "all reasonable men have long since concluded"—these are the terms of the conventional art at its youthful beginning. The tenor throughout is prophylactic. *"Since our passions are, or ought to be, within our power,"* Dryden proposes. In all fields, in poetry as in government or religion, the goal is system or reason, motive or morality, some set of rules and standards that will bring the troubling plenitude of experience "within our power." As long as the battle is for real, where so much depends upon control of self or of environment, there is pathos and even terror in the reasonable man, for there is so much in man's nature and experiences that would never be within his authority.

Frost is right in his sense that the meters and rimes of regulation verse have a counterpart in the rules, marked areas of the court (establishing bounds and out-of bounds), and net of the tennis game. ("I would as soon write free verse as play tennis with the net down.") But, for those who see life as something other than a tennis game, without bounds, and who seek in their sciences and arts to come into that life, into an imagination of that life, the thought comes that the counterpart of free verse may be free thought and free movement. The explorer displays the meaning of physical excellence in a way different from that displayed by the tennis player.

Linnaeus, who, as Ernst Cassirer describes him in *The Philosophy of the Enlightenment,* "selected arbitrarily certain qualities and features according to which he tries to group the plant world," removing his specimens from the field in which they had their living significance, has a counterpart in anthologists of our day who strive to rise above schools and movements, to remove poetry from any reference to its environment and living associations, and to present what suits their taste—orders that display their acumen and avoid any reference to what is. The stamp or flower collection, the tasteful anthology, the values, weights, standards—all these are justly subject, if we are concerned not with what "all reasonable men have long since concluded" is good, but with what is actually happening, to the criticism science had to make in time of Linnaeus. As given by Cassirer: "He thinks he can give us a picture of the sequence, organization, and structure of this world on the basis of this procedure of mere arrangement, of analytical classification. Such a picture is possible only by a reversal of his procedure. We must apply the principle of connection rather than that of analytical differentiation; instead of assigning living creatures to sharply distinguished species, we must study them in relation to their kinship, their transition from one type to another, their evolution and transformations. For these are the things which constitute life as we find it in nature."

So, a Cecil Hemley wishes that a Donald Allen's anthology had shown better taste, and would group the "best" of Allen's anthology with poets who never in their lives or thoughts were connected with Olson or Creeley or myself or Denise Levertov. Cecil Hemley reflects that he does not have a "taste" for the work of Robert Creeley. Since he has no other conceivable route to knowledge of that work, taste must suffice. But I can have no recourse to taste. The work of Denise Levertov or Robert Creeley or Larry Eigner belongs not to my appreciations but to my immediate concerns in living. That I might "like" or "dislike" a poem of Zukofsky's or Charles Olson's means nothing where I turn to their work as evidence of the real. Movement and association here are not arbitrary, but arise as an inner need. I can no more rest with my impressions of *Maximus* than I can indulge my impressions at any vital point: I must study thru, deepen my experience, search out the challenge and salvation of the work.

What form is to the conventional mind is just what can be imposed, the rest is thought of as lacking in form. Taste can be imposed, but love and knowledge are conditions that life imposes upon us if we would come into her melodies. It is taste that holds out against feeling, originality that tries to hold out against origins. For taste is all original, all individual arbitration. Dryden's "reasonable men" who "have long since concluded" are a bogie of his own invention (though they may be devoutly believed in at Oxford or Harvard today) and lead at last to the howling dismay and scorn of Pope, Swift and Gibbon who must hold out everywhere against rampant Stupidity, Madness, and Superstition in the universe of man's psychic life. In the "Ode on the Death of Henry Purcell" the illusion is fresh, and the conflicts of conscience and intellect have not yet appeared, or, perhaps, are subsumed in the honest fact that the work is a tomb or memorial to its own genius.

How strangely Shakespeare's voice in Prospero's contrasts with Dryden's in that period when charm (a device, yes, but a reality of the psyche, no) is replaced by wit:

> Now my Charmes are all ore-throwne,
> And what strength I have's mine owne.

contrasted with Dryden's "their example has given me the confidence to try myself." Shakespeare who imagined something of that Negative Capability that Keats defines must rest not upon example but upon prayer, having his art by a grace that was not the grace Dryden knew of men's manners, but a mystery.

> Now I want
> Spirits to enforce; Art to inchant,
> And my ending is despaire

The Enlightenment was to correct even the spelling in its effort to postpone the knowledge.

Towards an Open Universe

─────────────

I was born January 7, 1919, in the hour before dawn, in the depth of winter at the end of a war. When I think of the hour, from their obscurity the tree at the window, the patterned curtain, the table and chair, the bowl of golden glass upon the chest of drawers are just emerging into view. Sleeping and waking fuse, things seen in an inner light mingle with things searched out by eyes that are still dim. Day "breaks," we say, and the light floods out over the land. The shining planets and the great stars, the galaxies beyond us, grow invisible in light of our sun.

The imagination of this cosmos is as immediate to me as the imagination of my household or my self, for I have taken my being in what I know of the sun and of the magnitude of the cosmos, as I have taken my being in what I know of domestic things. In the coda of the poem "Apprehensions," the "First Poem" calls upon the birth of life itself in the primal waters and may call upon my birth hour:

> It is the earth turning
> that lifts our shores from the dark
> into the cold light of morning,
> eastward turning,
>
> and that returns us from the sun's burning
> into passages of twilight and doubt,
> dim reveries and gawdy effects.
> The sun is the everlasting center of what we know,
> a steady radiance.
>
> The changes of light in which we dwell,
> colors among colors that come and go,
> are in the earth's turning.

Angels of light! raptures of early morning!
your figures gather what they look like
out of what cells once knew of dawn,
first stages of love that in the water thrived.

So we think of sperm
as spark-fluid, many-millioned,
in light of the occult egg striking
doctrine.

Twined angels of dark,
hornd master-reminders of from-where!
your snake- or animal-red eyes
store the fire's glare.

O flames! O reservoirs![1]

In the very beginnings of life, in the source of our cadences, with the first pulse of the blood in the egg then, the changes of night and day must have been there. So that in the configuration of the living, hidden in the exchanging orders of the chromosome sequences from which we have our nature, the first nature, child of deep waters and of night and day, sleeping and waking, remains.

We are, all the many expressions of living matter, grandchildren of Gaia, Earth, and Uranus, the Heavens. Late born, for the moon and ocean came before. The sea was our first mother and the sun our father, so our sciences picture the chemistry of the living as beginning in the alembic of the primal sea quickened by rays of the sun and even, beyond, by radiations of the cosmos at large. Tide-flow under the sun and moon of the sea, systole and diastole of the heart, these rhythms lie deep in our experience and when we let them take over our speech there is a monotonous rapture of persistent regular stresses and waves of lines breaking rhyme after rhyme. There have been poets for whom this rise and fall, the mothering swell and ebb, was all. Amoebic intelligences, dwelling in the memorial of tidal voice, they arouse in our awake minds a spell, so that we let our awareness go in the urgent wave of the

---

[1] The lines from "Apprehensions" (© 1962 *Evergreen Review*) are reprinted with the permission of New Directions from *Roots and Branches* by Robert Duncan.

verse. The rhyming lines and the repeating meters persuade us. To evoke night and day or the ancient hypnosis of the sea is to evoke our powerful longing to fall back into periodic structure, into the inertia of uncomplicated matter. Each of us, hungry with life, rises from the cast of seed, having just this unique identity or experience created in the dance of chromosomes, and having in that identity a time; each lives and falls back at last into the chemistry of death.

Our consciousness, and the poem as a supreme effort of consciousness, comes in a dancing organization between personal and cosmic identity. What gnosis of the ancients transcends in mystery the notion Schrödinger brings us of an aperiodic structure in *What Is Life?*: ". . . the more and more complicated organic molecule in which every atom, and every group of atoms, plays an individual role, not entirely equivalent to that of others."[2] *"Living matter evades the decay to equilibrium,"* Schrödinger titles a section of his essay of 1944. "When is a piece of matter said to be alive?" he asks, and answers: "When it goes on 'doing something,' moving, exchanging material with its environment."

What interests me here is that this picture of an intricately articulated structure, a form that maintains a disequilibrium or lifetime—whatever it means to the biophysicist—to the poet means that life is by its nature orderly and that the poem might follow the primary processes of thought and feeling, the immediate impulse of psychic life. As I start here, first with night and day, then with a genesis of life, and would go forward to the genesis and nature of consciousness, my mind balks at the complication. It is not that we are far afield from the poem. Each poet seeks to commune with creation, with the divine world; that is to say, he seeks the most *real* form in language. But this most real is something we apprehend; the poem, the creation of the poem, is itself our primary experience of it.

We work toward the Truth of things. Keats's ecstatic "Beauty is truth, truth beauty" rises from the sureness of poetic intuition or of recognition, our instant knowing of fitness as we work in the poem, where the descriptive or analytic mind would falter. Here the true is beautiful as an arrow flies from its bow with exact aim. Dirac in

[2] *What Is Life?* (Cambridge, Eng.: Cambridge University Press, 1944, 1956), p. 60.

"The Physicist's Picture of Nature" tells us: "It is more important to have beauty in one's equations than to have them fit experiment."[3] What is at issue here is that the truth does not lie outside the art. For the experimenter it is more important to have beauty in one's experiments than to have them fit mathematics.

The most real, the truth, the beauty of the poem is a configuration, but also a happening in language, that leads back into or on towards the beauty of the universe itself. I am but part of the whole of what I am, and wherever I seek to understand I fail what I know. In the poem "Atlantis" I had this sense of the fabulous as an intuition of the real:

> The long shadow thrown from this single ob-
> struction to its own light!
> Thought flies out from the old scars of the sea
> as if to land. Flocks that are longings
> come in to shake over the deep water.
>
> It's prodigies held in time's amber
> old destructions
> and the theme of revival the heart asks for.
> The past and future are
> full of disasters, splendors
> shaken to earth, seas rising to overshadow
> shores and roaring in.[4]

Beauty strikes us and may be fearful, as there is great beauty in each step as Oedipus seeks the heart of tragedy, his moment of truth, as he tears out his eyes, and sees at last. But this is a heroic and dramatic gesture and may obscure what I would get at. For in our common human suffering, in loss and longing, an intuition of poetic truth may arise. In the poem "A Storm of White" I spoke from my grief, let grief have its voice, in the loss of a cat, a beloved person of my household. He had died of pneumonia within a few weeks of our moving to a house on the coast north of San Francisco.

[3] *Scientific American* (May 1963), p. 47.

[4] From Robert Duncan, *The Opening of the Field* (New York: New Directions, 1960). © 1960 by Robert Duncan.

A STORM OF WHITE [5]

neither
sky nor earth, without horizon, it's
a-
nother tossing, continually in-
breaking

boundary of white
        foaming in gull-white weather
luminous in dull white,   and trees
        ghosts of blackness or verdure
that here are
        dark whites in storm.

White white white   like
        a boundary in death advancing
that is our life,   that's love,
        line upon line
breaking in radiance, so soft- so dim-
        ly glaring, dominating.

"What it would mean to us if
        he died," a friend writes of one she loves
and that she feels she'll
        outlive those about her.

        The line of outliving
        in this storm   bounding
obscurity from obscurity,   the foaming
        —as if half the universe
(neither sky nor earth, with
        horizon)   were forever

breaking into being another half,
        obscurity   flaring into a surf
upon an answering obscurity.

[5] From Robert Duncan, *The Opening of the Field* (New York: New Directions, 1960). © 1960 by Robert Duncan.

> O dear gray cat that died in this cold,
> you were born on my chest
>   six years ago.

> The sea of ghosts dances. It does not
>   send your little shadow to us.
> I do not understand this
> empty place in our happiness.

> Another friend writes in a poem
> (received today, March 25th 58)

>   "Death also
> can still propose the old labors."

It is not that poetry imitates but that poetry enacts in its order the order of first things, as just here in this consciousness, they may exist, and the poet desires to penetrate the seeming of style and subject matter to that most real where there is no form that is not content, no content that is not form. "A change of cadence," so the early Imagists realized, "means a new idea." But idea means something seen, a new image: here it is the Way, in which action, vision, and thought have their identity.

In the turn and return, the strophe and antistrophe, the prose and the versus of the choral mode, are remembered the alternations of night and day and the systole and diastole of the heart, and in the exchange of opposites, the indwelling of one in the other, dance and poetry emerge as ways of knowing. Heraclitus wrote the opposites or alternates large and imagined them as phases of a dynamic unity: "God is day, night, winter, summer, war, peace, satiety, hunger, and undergoes alteration in the way that fire, when it is mixed with spices is named according to the scent of each of them."

The Christian Hippolytus accuses Heraclitus of teaching "that the created world becomes maker and creator of itself." The Greek word for "created" being *poieitos* and for "creator" *poieiteis,* the created world is a poem and the creator a poet.

We begin to imagine a cosmos in which the poet and the poem are one in a moving process, not only here the given Creation and the Exodus or Fall, but also here the immanence of the Creator in

Creation. The most real is given and we have fallen away, but the most real is in the falling revealing itself in what is happening. Between the god *in* the story and the god *of* the story, the form, the realization of what is happening, stirs the poet. To answer that call, to become the poet, means to be aware of creation, creature, and creator coinherent in the one event. There is not only the immanence of God, His indwelling, but there is also the imminence of God, His impending occurrence. In the expectancy of the poem, grief and fear seem necessary to the revelation of Beauty.

Central to and defining the poetics I am trying to suggest here is the conviction that the order man may contrive or impose upon the things about him or upon his own language is trivial beside the divine order or natural order he may discover in them. To see, to hear, to feel or taste—this sensory intelligence that seems so immediate to us as to be simple and given—comes about in a formal organization so complicated that it remains obscure to our investigation in all but its crudest aspects. To be alive itself is a form involving organization in time and space, continuity and body, that exceeds clearly our conscious design. "It is by avoiding the rapid decay into the inert state of 'equilibrium,' that an organism appears so enigmatic," Schrödinger writes, "so much so, that from the earliest times of human thought some special nonphysical or supernatural force was claimed to be operative in the organism."[6]

There is not a phase of our experience that is meaningless, not a phrase of our communication that is meaningless. We do not make things meaningful, but in our making we work towards an awareness of meaning; poetry reveals itself to us as we obey the orders that appear in our work. In writing I do not organize words but follow my consciousness of—but it is also a desire that goes towards—orders in the play of forms and meanings toward poetic form. This play is like the play of actors upon a stage. Becoming conscious, becoming aware of the order of what is happening is the full responsibility of the poet. The poem that always seems to us such a highly organized event is in its very individuality ("idiocy" the classical Greek would have said), in its uniqueness, crude indeed compared with the subtlety of organization which in the

[6] Schrödinger, *op. cit.*, p. 70.

range of contemporary linguistic analysis the study of syntax, morphology, etymology, psychology reveals in the language at large from which the poem is derived. The materials of the poem—the vowels and consonants—are already structured in their resonance, we have only to listen and to cooperate with the music we hear. The storehouse of human experience in words is resonant too, and we have but to listen to the reverberations of our first thought in the reservoir of communal meanings to strike such depths as touch upon the center of man's nature.

Man's nature? Man's speech? Carlyle in his essay "The Hero as Poet" saw the inherent music of our common speech:

> All speech, even the commonest speech, has something of song in it: not a parish in the world but has its parish-accent;—the rhythm or *tune* to which the people there *sing* what they have to say! Accent is a kind of chanting; all men have accent of their own,—though they only *notice* that of others. Observe too how all passionate language does of itself become musical. All deep things are Song. It seems somehow the very central essence of us, Song; as if all the rest were but wrappages and hulls! The primal element of us; of us, and of all things. The Greeks fabled of Sphere-Harmonies; it was the feeling they had of the inner structure of Nature; that the soul of all her voices and utterances was perfect music. Poetry, therefore, we will call *musical* thought. The Poet is he who *thinks* in that manner. See deep enough, and you see musically; the heart of Nature *being* everywhere music, if you can only reach it.[7]

This music of men's speech that has its verity in the music of the inner structure of Nature is clearly related to that beauty of mathematics that Schrödinger and Dirac feel relates to the beauty of the inner structure of the physical universe.

The dancer comes into the dance when he loses his consciousness of his own initiative, what *he* is doing, feeling, or thinking, and enters the consciousness of the dance's initiative, taking feeling and thought there. The self-consciousness is not lost in a void

[7] *Heroes and Hero-Worship* (1840).

but in the transcendent consciousness of the dance. "Night and Day address each other in their swift course, crossing the great brazen threshold," Hesiod sings in his *Theogony;* "the one will go inside, the other comes out." As consciousness is intensified, all the exciting weave of sensory impression, the illustration of time and space, are "lost" as the personality is "lost"; in focus we see only the dancer. We are aware only in the split second in which the dance is present. This presentation, our immediate consciousness, the threshold that is called both *here-and-now* and *eternity,* is an exposure in which, perilously, identity is shared in resonance between the person and the cosmos.

In 1950, with his essay "Projective Verse,"[8] Charles Olson called for a new consideration of form in the poem where the poet as he worked had to be "instant by instant, aware."

> And if you also set up as a poet, USE USE USE the process at all points, in any given poem always, always one perception must must must MOVE, INSTANTER, ON ANOTHER!

In the poem this instant was the attention of "the HEAD, by way of the EAR, to the SYLLABLE." The mind was not to be diverted by what it wanted to say but to attend to what was happening immediately in the poem.

> With this warning, to those who would try: to step back here to this place of the elements and minims of language is to engage speech where it is least careless and least logical.

At the same time the poem demanded a quickening of "the HEART, by way of the BREATH, to the LINE." Here Olson too was thinking of the dance:

> Is it not the PLAY of a mind we are after, is it not that that shows whether a mind is there at all? . . . And the threshing floor for the dance? Is it anything but the LINE?

This play of heart and mind we see as the play of life itself in the extension of our language as life plays in the extension of our

[8] "Projective Verse" (New York: Totem Press, 1959).

lifetime upon the threshold of consciousness between what man is
and his Cosmos—the very fire of Heraclitus upon the hearth where
the imagination of what man is and what the cosmos is burns. Our
gods are many as our times are many, they are the cast and events
of one play. There is only this one time; there is only this one
god.

If the sea is first mother of the living, the sun is first father, and
fire is his element. Here too death and life, the heat of our blood
and the light of our mind, in one reality. That I have seen in poems
as the fire upon the hearth, the genius of the household, as if the
secret of our warmth and companionship were hidden in a wrath-
ful flame.

FOOD FOR FIRE, FOOD FOR THOUGHT[9]

> good wood
that all fiery youth burst forth from winter,
> go to sleep in the poem.
Who will remember the green flame,
> thy heart's amber?

Language obeyd flares tongues in obscure matter.

> We trace faces in clouds: they drift apart,
> palaces of air—the sun dying down
> > sets them on fire;

> descry shadows on the flood from its dazzling mood,
> or at its shores read runes upon the sand
> > from sea-spume.

This is what I wanted for the last poem,
a loosening of conventions and return to open form.

> Leonardo saw figures that were stains upon a wall.
> Let the apparitions containd in the ground
> > play as they will.

[9] From Robert Duncan, *The Opening of the Field* (New York: New Direc-
tions, 1960). © 1960 by Robert Duncan.

You have carried a branch of tomorrow into the room.
Its fragrance has awakened me—no,

> it was the sound of a fire on the hearth,
> leapt up where you bankt it, sparks of delight.
>   Now I return the thought

> to the red glow, that might-be-magical blood,
> palaces of heat in the fire's mouth

—*"If you look you will see the salamander"*—
> to the very elements that attend us,
> fairies of the fire, the radiant crawling.

That was a long time ago.
No, they were never really there,

> tho once I saw—did I stare
> into the heart of desire burning
> and see a radiant man? like those
> fancy cities from fire into fire falling?

We are close enough to childhood, so easily purged
of what we thought we were to be,

> flamey threads of firstness go out from your touch,

> flickers of unlikely heat
> at the edge of our belief bud forth.

There is an emotion, a realization, but it is also a world and a self, that impends in the first stirrings of a poem. In a poem like "A Storm of White" or "Food for Fire, Food for Thought," the voice may seem to rise directly from or to the incoming breakers that had become a moving whiteness into which I stared or the flickering light and shadow cast upon a wall by a fire on the hearth I had forgotten, waking in the night, still close enough to the sleeping mind that I dreamed in what was happening. In "A Poem Beginning with a Line by Pindar," the germ of the poem quickened as I was reading one evening the *Pythian Odes* translated by H. T. Wade-Grey and C. M. Bowra. I have an affinity with Pindar, but here it was my inability to understand that began the work or it was the work beginning that proposed the words I was reading in such a way that they no longer belonged to Pindar's *Pythian I:* "The light foot hears you, and the brightness begins." In Pindar it is the harp of Apollo that the light foot of the dancer hears, but something had intruded, a higher reality for me, and it was the harp that heard the dancer. "Who is it that goes there?" the song cried out.

I had mistaken the light foot for Hermes the Thief, who might be called The Light Foot, light-fingered, light-tongued. The Homeric Hymns tell us that he devised the harp of Apollo and was first in the magic, the deceit, of song. But as Thoth, he is Truth, patron of poets. The infant Hermes, child of Zeus and the lady Maia—Alexandrian gnostics of the second century saw Zeus as the One God and the lady as Maya, name and personification of the Buddha's mother and also of the Great Illusion—this genius of childhood in his story resolves: "I too will enter upon the rite that Apollo has. If my father will not give it me, I will seek—and I am able—to be a prince of robbers." First crossing the threshold of the Sun, he steals a tortoise. "Living, you shall be a spell against mischievous witchcraft," he says: "but if you die, then you shall make sweetest song." Then staring at the shell, he conceives song's instrument: "As a swift thought darts through the heart of a man when thronging cares haunt him, or as bright glances flash from the eye, so glorious Hermes planned both thought and deed at once."[10]

The poet is such a child in us. And the poem, the instrument of music that he makes from men's speech, has such a hunger to live, to be true, as mathematics has. Numbers and words were both things of a spell. To dream true, to figure true, to come true. Here poetry is the life of the language and must be incarnate in a body of words, condensed to have strength, phrases that are sinews, lines that may be tense or relaxed as the mind moves. Charles Olson in his essays toward a physiology of consciousness has made us aware that not only heart and brain and the sensory skin but all the internal organs, the totality of the body is involved in the act of a poem, so that the organization of words, an invisible body, bears the imprint of the physical man, the finest imprint that we feel in

[10] *The Homeric Hymns,* Hugh Evelyn-Whik, trans. (Cambridge: Loeb Library, 1908).

our own bodies as a tonic consonance and dissonance, a being-in-tune, a search for the as yet missing scale. Remembering Schrö-dinger's sense that the principle of life lies in its evasion of equilibrium, I think too of Goethe's Faust, whose principle lies in his discontent, not only in his search but also in his search beyond whatever answer he can know. Our engagement with knowing, with craft and lore, our demand for truth is not to reach a conclusion but to keep our exposure to what we do not know, to confront our wish and our need beyond habit and capability, beyond what we can take for granted, at the borderline, the light finger-tip or thought-tip where impulse and novelty spring.

This exposed, open form ("Projective Verse," Olson named it in poetry) began to appear in the 1940's. With the *Pisan Cantos* of Ezra Pound and *Paterson* of William Carlos Williams, with the *Symphony in Three Movements* of Stravinsky, I began to be aware of the possibility that the locus of form might be in the immediate minim of the work, and that one might concentrate upon the sound and meaning present where one was, and derive melody and story from impulse not from plan. I was not alone, for other poets—Louis Zukofsky, Charles Olson, Denise Levertov, Robert Creeley—following seriously the work of Pound and Williams, became aware, as I was, that what they had mastered opened out upon a new art where they were first ones working. In music John Cage, Pierre Boulez, or Karlheinz Stockhausen seem in the same way to realize that Stravinsky, Schonberg, and Webern stand like doors, mastering what music was, opening out upon what music must be.

It is a changing aesthetic, but it is also a changing sense of life. Perhaps we recognize as never before in man's history that not only our own personal consciousness but also the inner structure of the universe itself has only this immediate event in which to be realized. Atomic physics has brought us to the threshold of such a—I know not whether to call it certainty or doubt.

The other sense that underlies the new form is one that men have come to again and again in their most intense or deepest vision, that the Kingdom is here, that we have only now in which to live—that the universe has only now in which to live. "The present contains all that there is," Whitehead says in *The Aims of Education:*

It is holy ground; for it is the past, and it is the future. . . . The communion of saints is a great and inspiring assemblage, but it has only one possible hall of meeting, and that is the present; and the mere lapse of time through which any particular group of saints must travel to reach that meeting-place, makes very little difference.[11]

[*1966*]

[11] *The Aims of Education* (1929).

JACK SPICER

Jack Spicer to Federico Garcia Lorca

DEAR LORCA,

When I translate one of your poems and I come across words I do not understand, I always guess at their meanings. I am inevitably right. A really perfect poem (no one yet has written one) could be perfectly translated by a person who did not know one word of the language it was written in. A really perfect poem has an infinitely small vocabulary.

It is very difficult. We want to transfer the immediate object, the immediate emotion to the poem—and yet the immediate always has hundreds of its own words clinging to it, short-lived and tenacious as barnacles. And it is wrong to scrape them off and substitute others. A poet is a time mechanic not an embalmer. The words around the immediate shrivel and decay like flesh around the body. No mummy-sheet of tradition can be used to stop the process. Objects, words must be led across time not preserved against it.

I yell "Shit" down a cliff at an ocean. Even in my lifetime the immediacy of that word will fade. It will be dead as "Alas." But if I put the real cliff and the real ocean into the poem, the word "Shit" will ride along with them, travel the time-machine until cliffs and oceans disappear.

Most of my friends like words too well. They set them under the blinding light of the poem and try to extract every possible connotation from each of them, every temporary pun, every direct or indirect connection—as if a word could become an object by mere addition of consequences. Others pick up words from the streets, from their bars, from their offices and display them proudly

226

in their poems as if they were shouting, "See what I have collected from the American language. Look at my butterflies, my stamps, my old shoes!" What does one do with all this crap?

Words are what sticks to the real. We use them to push the real, to drag the real into the poem. They are what we hold on with, nothing else. They are as valuable in themselves as rope with nothing to be tied to.

I repeat—the perfect poem has an infinitely small vocabulary.

LOVE
JACK

[*1957*]

Excerpts from the Vancouver Lectures

Yeats is probably the first modern who took the idea of dictation seriously. He was on a train back in 1918—a train oddly enough going through San Bernardino to Los Angeles—when his wife suddenly began to have trances and spooks came to her. She was in the tradition of the Psychic Research Society and so they would naturally come in a form the Psychic Research Society would think spooks would come in. And she started automatic writing as they were going through the orange groves between San Berdoo and Los Angeles. Yeats didn't know what to make of it for a while but it was a slow train and he started getting interested. He finally decided he'd ask a question or two of the spooks while Georgie was in a trance. And he asked a rather good question. He asked "What are you here for?" And the spooks replied, "We are here to give metaphors for your poetry." It was the first thing since Blake on the business of taking poetry as coming from the outside rather than from the inside. In other words, instead of the poet being a beautiful machine which manufactured the current for itself, did everything for itself—almost a perpetual motion machine, of emotion, until the poet's heart broke, or was burned on the beach like Shelley's—instead there was something from the outside coming in.

.   .   .

I think that the first kind of hint that one has as a poet, after having written poems for a while and struggled with them, a poem comes through in just about one-eighth the time that the poem usually does and you say "Well, gee, it's going to be much easier if I can just have this happen very often." And so then you write 17 or 18 different things which are just what you're thinking about at the particular moment and are lousy. It isn't simply the matter of being able to get a fast take. Its something else. But the fast take is a good sign that you're hooked up to some source of power, some source of energy.

.   .   .

So one day, after you have this first experience, suddenly there comes a poem which you just hate and would like to get rid of that says just exactly the opposite of what you mean, of what you have to say. You want to say something about your beloved's eyebrows and the poem says the eyes should fall out. And you don't really want the eyes to fall out. Or, you're trying to write a poem about Viet Nam and you write a poem about Vermont. These things, again, begin to show you just exactly where the road to dictation leads.

.   .   .

The third stage comes when you get some idea that there is a difference between you and the outside of you which is writing poetry. Then you start seeing—if you can clear your mind away from the things which are you, the things which you want—that you are something which is being transmitted into. It's as if a Martian comes into a room with children's blocks, with A, B, C, D, and E, which are in English, and he tries to convey a message. This is the way the source of energy goes. But the blocks on the other hand are always resisting it. You are stuck with language, you are stuck with words, you are stuck with the things you know. It's a very nice thing and a very difficult thing. The more you know, the more languages you know, the more building blocks the Martians have to play with. But the more building blocks you have to arrange the more temptation to say, "Oh, yes, yes, yes, I remember this has to do with the Trojan war, and this has to do with this, and this has to do with that." And you spoil what the Martian was trying to say. But, given the cooperation between the host poet and the visitor—the thing from outside—the more things you have in the room the better if you can handle them in such a way that you don't impose your will on the thing coming through.

.   .   .

You then say, "Oh, I'll just write this thing and I'll take a line from something or other, or use dada or surrealism, the French surrealist way of placing things together, and that won't be what *I* want to say. Unfortunately, that doesn't work too well either.

.   .   .

[Robert] Creeley talks about the poem following the dictation of language. It seems to me that's not—it's part of the furniture of the room. Language isn't anything of itself. It's something that is in the mind of the host. Five languages just makes the room structure more difficult, also possibly more usable. It certainly doesn't have to do with any mystique of English. [Robert] Duncan's business of words and their shadows and sounds and their shadows seems to me again taking things which are in the room rather than things coming into the room. When you get a beautiful thing which uses the words and shadows of words—the fact "silly" once meant blessed instead of "silly" as it now does—you ought to be distrustful, although the thing which invades you from the outside can use it.

.   .   .

Language is a complex system that involves words, gesture and all that sort of thing, and it's a higher abstraction than words. Words are things which just happen to be in you head or someone else's head just like memories are. Various pieces of furniture in the room that this Martian has to put the clues in. Language is a more complicated thing. But at the same time it is a structure that hasn't yet been described and it's doubtful if any two people have the same language. I'm now speaking as a professional linguist and not as a poet and it seems to me that it simply is another layer of stuff that the Martians have to penetrate and have to work with. Please don't get me wrong, "Martians" is just a word for X. I am not saying that the little green men are coming in saucers into my bedroom and helping me write poetry. I think that [language] is just a higher level of abstraction than [words] and is less useful.

.   .   .

Pound simply uses history . . . in the sense of everything connected to everything else. And when Duncan talks about words he sees it the same way, follow back the words, etc. You can follow back the word as far as you can but it is still furniture the way history is. The business of history is an important thing but essentially it's furniture. I just think essentially that it is an accident that I have this history in my skull instead of some other history which is absolutely alien to me. Then you have someone like Eliot who was completely hung up by this and wasn't able to write any poetry after "The Wasteland" on account of it, because he thought he didn't know enough history. He had gotten a few historical things and so he thought I'd better write plays because I don't know enough about what my muse is.

.   .   .

I think myself from what I've seen that there's no question that objective events can be caused in order for poems to be written. Robin Blaser in *The Moth Poem* has moths just coming in the wildest places where the odds would be about a million to one against the moths being in just exactly the place where he wanted the poems written. But I've been there a couple of times when it happened. And I think that it is certainly possible that the objective universe can be affected by the poet. You recall Orpheus made the trees and stones dance, and this is something which is in almost all primitive cultures and it has some definite basis to it. I'm not sure what. It's like telekinesis, which I know very well on a pinball machine is perfectly possible. But again, with the physical world reacting, you don't know exactly. But yes, I do think that you can have things happen simply because the poem wants them to happen. No question about it.

.   .   .

If you have an idea that you want to develop, don't write a poem about it. Because it's almost bound to be a bad poem. You can have an idea that you want to develop and the poem has an idea that is a little bit different. Say like Pope's *Essay on Man,* which was supposed to have pleased Bolingbroke enormously and didn't—and didn't please Pope. And I'm using just about the so-called most disciplined poet there is. I mean you can start out with an idea that you want to write about how terrible it is that President Johnson is an asshole and you can come up with a good poem. But it will be just by chance and will undoubtedly not just say that President Johnson is an asshole and will really have a meaning different from what you started with. I mean, if you want to write a letter to the editor than it seems to me the thing to do is write a letter to the editor. It doesn't seem to me that poetry is for that. Ron Loewinsohn is a typical example in San Francisco and he's written some very good poems. He would tell me the plot of the poem he was writing. He was going to write a poem about Willie McCovey and there was going to be this, and this, and this, and be this sequence—without having written the poem. Well, jeez Ron, why don't you write a short story? A letter to the editor? And usually it doesn't work out. Occasionally it does. And occasionally the thing gets through and the poem about Willie McCovey doesn't turn out to be about Willie McCovey at all, and doesn't have the same point he [the poet] wanted. I don't know, it just seems to me a bass-ackward way of doing things to try to get your ideas in first and then let the ghost knock them down. But I don't know. I haven't the vaguest notion of whether that's the only way to write poetry. For Duncan and Creeley, Olson and me, and Ginsberg when he was writing poetry, that was the way. And Williams too, in his own funny sense, where he thought of the objects as the source of energy, the magickers, rather than anything else, but especially in "The Desert Music" where the objects where taken over by something else. I don't know. I don't think there's one formula. But I do think that the simplest thing for the poet is not to say I have this great metaphor I'm going to put down on paper and expand it. But well, the only good poet who I think does it to some extent is Denise Levertov, and the poems I like of hers are all poems that have scared her and that she didn't really want to have written.

.   .   .

I don't think the messages are for the poet any more than a radio program is for the radio set. And I think that the radio set doesn't really worry about whether anyone is listening to it or not, and neither does the poet. And I don't know what the poem does. The poem may have some Neilsen ratings of its own that it carries on in the middle distance. But I don't think the poet ought to worry about that. On the other hand, I think the poet ought to read poems to an audience because often he can find things in the audience's reactions that he didn't understand the poem said which tell him something about it. I mean it's just as important to understand your own poetry as it is to understand someone else's. And most poets I know, including some I admire, don't read their own poems. I mean they read them aloud to audiences but they very seldom read them back to see what the things are that scare them about them. They just put them in orphan asylums. You know, they grow depressed and that kind of thing. Just leave them there and get fifteen bucks for them. You know, baby farms.

.   .   .

It's just a question that we disagree on what a younger poet should concentrate on, and I don't think it should be technique. I think he ought to do just exactly what somebody would do in some one of those mystical Asian sects that Ginsberg likes so well, trying to get his personality out of himself and let something else come in, whatever the hell it is. And I think that the first thing of becoming a poet is a kind of spiritual exercise. Its emptying yourself as a vessel, and then the language is one of the pieces of furniture. The language is there and it has to be learned and you have to really know the shadows of the words and all of that eventually. But the first thing, if you're going to build a house and furnish it and set a table, the first thing is to make sure you have a guest. I mean it's like the recipe for rabbit stew, first catch a rabbit.

.   .   .

A serial poem, in the first place, has the book as its unit as an individual poem has the poem as its unit, the actual poem that you write at the actual time, the single poem. And there is a dictation of form as well as a dictation of the individual form of the individual poem. And you have to go into a serial poem not knowing what the hell you're doing. That's the first thing. You have to be tricked into it. It has to be some path that you've never seen on a map before. I think all of my books as far as they're successful have just followed the bloody path to see where it goes, and sometimes it doesn't go anywhere. What I'm saying is you have a unit, one unit the poem, which is taken by dictation, and another unit, the book, which is a more structured thing. But it should be structured by dictation and not by the poet. And when the poet gets some idea—oh, this is going to amount to this or going to amount to that, and he starts steering the poem himself—then he's lost in the woods. And the brambles are all about. Or else he pulls out a boy scout compass and goes back to the nearest bar.

.   .   .

Robin Blaser once said in talking about a serial poem that it's as if you go into a room, a dark room, the light is turned on for a minute, then it's turned off again, and then you go into a different room where a light is turned on and turned off. And I suspect one of the reasons that makes people write serial poems is the business if you can get focused on the individual part enough you have a better chance of dictation, you have a better chance of being an empty vessel, being filled up by whatever's outside. You don't when you're writing a long poem because when you're writing a long poem not composed of separate parts but a long poem say five or ten pages, well naturally you can't write a five or ten-page poem if you're a good poet within a humanly recognizable period of one sitting. And it does seem to me that it's much easier to write a dictated poem if you can write it in one sitting because the next morning you've had great ideas of what the poem means and it's you not the poem that's talking. I think this business of the take from one room to another, from one frame to another, is not because that's particularly attractive aesthetic form but simply because it's easier on the poet.

.   .   .

There's plenty of fudging that's allowed in this kind of thing. But the old thing that René Char said, he said the poet should have a sign on his wall saying, "CHEAT AT THIS GAME." And this is true enough if you know the right time to cheat. But if you don't you get clobbered. Somebody pulls out a gun from his boot and shoots you with all of the five aces you have in your hand.

[*1965*]

ROBIN BLASER

The Fire

---

especially for Ebbe Borregaard

I am here writing about my poetry in relation to poetry. The writing had an occasion: for a few in San Francisco, where I read it last March 8th [1967]. I want to talk about the personalism and the so-called obscurity of my poems in relation to the *sight, sound* and *intellect* that compose them. "The test of poetry," in Zukofsky's words, "is the range of pleasure it affords as sight, sound, and intellection."

One difficulty I want to describe is that I'm haunted by a sense of the invisibility of everything that comes into me (aware that nothing is more invisible than emotion—by emotion, I mean the heat of one's sense of the war, or a place, or a body, or of the extensions of these, the earth, the existence of gods, and so forth—the I-have-seen-what-I-have-seen, recorded by Pound in "Canto II"). I believe there is a reality, which, given the leisure to live for it, is neither conceptual and systemized in the ordinary sense of these words—or imageless. There are many times when, forced by exhaustion, I take the lazy way of the conceptual and imageless, but it is a kind of desire which leads me to write of that other, outside world. Because the personal stake in companionship becomes so great in the way I live, I am sometimes lost when a reader finds me uninteresting or too obscure, his interest too soon exhausted to come to any meeting. I am literal about that other reality. It is, I think, the purest storytelling to try to catch that light—and the difficulty of it, the loss of it, is personal. If I see the light, even fragmentarily, and lose it, that too is subject matter, and leads to a kind of heartless poem, for it is not the elegiac loss which interests me, but the difficulty, the activity, of holding on to it. Burning up myself, I would leave fire behind me.

To hold an image within the line by sound and heat is to have caught something that passed out there. The psychological accuracy of this perception is not enough; the sculptural imagistic quality is not enough; and the very aesthetic quality of taking the one image, or even three images as a whole, the beauty of the idea that you can write a single poem, is a lie. The processional aspect of the world has to be caught in the language also. The body hears the world, and the power of the earth over the body, the city over the body, is in terms of rhythms, meters, phrasing, picked up—the body's own rhythms compose those or it would shake to pieces. —The music of the spheres is quite real, but the sound of the earth must meet it. I suppose I want to say that the real business of poetry is cosmology, and I'm claiming my own stake in this. And this is the activity of telling the story—the necessity is chemical— it is *not* invented, but it is original, personal, singular, and even domestic. If one man gives up his life for the world, the energy of it is not symbolical: it is the story of one man tied to the heaven and hell he recognizes. No symbols.

My friend Stan Persky was reading to me one night when a passage turned up that is so much to my purpose, slightly reworded, that I won't give the author credit: it is in that meeting entirely mine: "What we describe as imagination is no free play of the soul, but a real meeting with real elements that are outside of us, and what matters is not the surrender to the images of fantasy that appear, but to redeem those elements themselves. What we suppose we effect merely in our souls, in reality we effect on the destiny of the world." —Here, I wish to say that it is not language which is the source: it is the record of the meeting, and the magical structure of sight, sound, and intellect is indeed a personal responsibility. Language is given to us and in the most insidious way it controls sight, sound and intellect, but it is also the medium which can be shaped. —Metaphor as a focus is an immediate escape from the ordinary focus, which rots for some reason I can't explain, and keeps me always from using the word we, though there is a kind of we that I hope to earn the right to use. But the poem offers a field of energy and activity—to be met by whatever companion can be found. If you imagine, as I do, that, at any waking moment, you are a corpuscle in the left wrist of god, then any reality is precisely to be found in the flow of corpuscles in that vast body.

In the constant interruption that it is to go to work every day, to talk in generalities of things that can only be known in specifics, this time guiding others through American writing, I'm struck by this thing called cosmology: Poe wanders off into a long prose piece, "Eureka," which he calls a poem, and it is, drawing on all the contemporary science he can digest to record a cosmology; Emerson drops poetry and heads into poetically structured essays, wherein he can describe a cosmology; Thoreau drops poetry to write two strangely structured books, where, as in *Walden,* the detailed attention given to the seasons is cosmological; Melville goes about it backwards—in *Moby-Dick,* myths had to be reset so that they could say what they should say about origins, where he is, then later the poetry clanks along unable to hold on to what he wants; Whitman comes in with a new line, as open as he could make it; Henry Adams moves from the well-formed novel to the work on the great Virgin of the 13th century to tell in detail the story of a unified world; Pound puts it in the *Cantos* when he says the first thing was to break the iambic pentameter. It seems to me that the whole marvelous thing of open form is a traditional and an American problem—"hung up" on form because it was so difficult to open it. The whole thing came in a geography where the traditional forms would no longer hold our purposes. I was very moved when, some years ago, I was reading a scholarly book by Jo Miles in which she is making an argument for the sublime poem, which oddly has something to do with the public poem, and she begins to talk about the narrative of the spirit. I think the key word here is narrative—the story of persons, events, activities, images, which tell the tale of the spirit.

I'm interested in a particular kind of narrative—what Jack Spicer and I agreed to call in our own work the serial poem—this is a narrative which refuses to adopt an imposed story line, and completes itself only in the sequence of poems, if, in fact, a reader insists upon a definition of completion which is separate from the activity of the poems themselves. The poems tend to act as a sequence of energies which run out when so much of a tale is told. I

like to describe this in Ovidian terms, as a *carmen perpetuum,* a
continuous song in which the fragmented subject matter is only
apparently disconnected. Ovid's words are:

> to tell of bodies
> transformed
> into new shapes
> you gods, whose power
> worked all transformations,
> help the poet's breathing,
> lead my continuous song
> from the beginning   to the present world

> «In nova ferat animus mutatas dicere formas
> corpora: di, coeptis (nam vos mutastia et illas)
> aspirate meis, primaque ab origine mundi
> ad meo *perpetuum* deducite tempora *carmen!*»

The sequence of energies may involve all kinds of things—anger
may open a window, a sound from another world may completely
reshape the present moment, the destruction of a friendship may
destroy a whole realm of language or the ability to use it—each
piece is in effect an extended metaphor (another word is probably
needed), because in the serial poem the effort is to hold both the
correspondence and the focus that an image is, and the process of
those things coming together—so that the light from a white linen
tablecloth reflects on the face of one's companion, becomes light,
fire, and the white moth which happens to be in the room is also
light in the dark around the table, and is thus both the light and the
element of light that destroys it. I ask you to remember that every
metaphor involves at least four elements—which are a story, and
the bringing them together is an activity, a glowing energy if
stopped over, if entered. If the joy one feels in the sunny morning
comes out as: the boat on the fire of the sea moves slowly to burn
out—the story is of a boat on the sea—the fire is the sun on the
water and the movement is of the boat, of the flow of the sun, and
of the passing of the sun toward night. The joy of the movement is
held a moment, then unfolds the story of the four elements, the
boat and where it is, and the sun and what it is doing.

I wish now to extend these remarks by referring to some

sources, which, in this case, were brought to me by Stan Persky, who has turned anthropologist, and who offers the pleasures of a real discourse. The gift is a passage in Edith Cobb. She says, "I became acutely aware that what a child wanted to do most of all was to make a world in which to find a place to discover a self. This ordering reverses the general position that self-exploration produces a knowledge of the world." Furthermore, while observing the *"passionate world-making behavior* of the child," she noted that "accompanied by a population of toys, fauna and flora, and artifacts that do duty as figures of speech," she became "keenly aware of those processes which the genius in particular in later life seeks to recall." Edith Cobb in her interest in biological psychology moves to describe what she names a "cosmic sense," which in a separate essay, Margaret Mead describes as "a human instinctual need for a perceptual relation to the universe." This is the scientific basis for the proprioceptive process which Charles Olson speaks of. In this context, I am arguing not for my pretensions as a poet, but for what the poetry reflects, if it is entered. That the poet does the job of entering this world and continues through his life to record that entrance is a fact, not pretense—that it is personal, original, and singular is also fact. And here I want to quote the ethnologist Frank Speck on the Naskapi Indians (Labrador). He says that among them the form of the earth is like a hill and floats upon the water. He calls this a general concept, which is not true; it is a well-known image among them, and his informant, Charley Metowecic said that the earth's form comes to be known only from the testimony of a man about to die. "In the vision that comes at this time the mind can view the universe and sees all around the earth as it rises above the water. And he feels it rocking." This is a statement which draws my attention because it is my own belief that any vision of the world is not complete until a man dies. I mean here that imagination is more a power to take in and hold than it is a power of making up, though it must in its activity take responsibility for the uncreated.

I want now to describe some very personal matters—as indications of the singularity—the personalness of language and form. I want here to create the image of a field which is true history, and autobiography, as well as land, place, and presence. I come to poetry with a definite sense of foreignness. Spicer once said that I was the only person he had ever met who could speak quotation marks, and these always appeared around the slang words I used. Now that given thing language comes to me through a combination of settled Americans on the one hand and from immigrants on the other. On the paternal side, a grandfather, born in the south of France, and a grandmother born in Wales, who was deeply ashamed of any non-English elements. On the maternal side, a great grandmother, whom I knew, from Springfield, Mass., who came west with the Mormons, and was named West, and who had been secretary to Brigham Young. That grandfather arrived in New York in the 1880s and came west to Sage, Wyoming, as a laborer for the railroad, and he was to work his way up to the exalted position of roadmaster and bishop of the Church of the Latter-day Saints. My own Roman Catholic thing comes from that great grandmother's hatred of Mormons, so that my mother and I were in turn sent to the Catholics—with whom we were both to learn "The Star-Spangled Banner" in Latin. In the midst of this interplay of talk about the revelation of God here on the American continent, somewhere on the Great Plains was my sense of it, and of the ritual mystery of the Catholic Church, performed for kneeling and rising men and women, we lived in houses that were always by the railroad tracks, sometimes between two railbeds— the houses were remodeled railway cars, sometimes dining cars— with window after window where the tables had been. These were painted yellow and placed upon cement foundations. There was always a vast desert of sagebrush, and in one's place a small garden, watered from a well—of poplar trees, goldenrod, and—— the garden was one's own population. Shoshone and Blackfoot passed at a distance walking beside their wagons or dragloads. The people who lived and worked in this land were largely foreign— Greeks, Italians, Mexicans, and so on. Their hold on the land, the houses, the work, and the language was like that of migratory birds. Cities were dreams—I have never forgotten the early morning hum of the city waking up in the first city I had ever seen— Boise, Idaho. Towns I lived in had populations of 8 persons, 14, seldom 20—Kimima, Wapai, Orchard. Cities were imaginary— like oceans. The name of a man would be a town. Blaser, Idaho has, according to the current Rand McNally Commercial Atlas, no population. In this setting, that force to be English and American, settled, not migratory, forced that paternal grandfather to whisper any French words he wished to remember. And so far as I know, in this, I was his only companion. If we were alone listening to the radio, we would play at translating the words of popular songs:

> Tu es la crême de mon café
> Tu es le pois de ma soupe

Outwardly, to others, he was not foreign; the long southern a's and trilled r's of his French were secrets between us. He sported a goatee, and told me with increasing detail the strange tale that he was the lost Dauphin of France. This story and this language are fragmentarily preserved by me. None of his children knew it; my father denies his father was foreign born. When that grandfather was dying, riddled with cancer, I was called home from college to speak with him because the only words he knew were a childish French. And no member of the family knew enough to keep him company. That English and American thing had such force that the other English which most people spoke, more like Woody Guthrie's, was also forbidden sound and thought:

> I been doin' some hard travelin'
> I thought you knowed

There was a step-grandfather besides, who was German, with one eye, and could not hide his accent. Because of his talk of the Kaiser, though the war was long over, they painted the house yellow, which was funny because the house was already yellow. But this was a bright yellow and when they threw a bucket of it over a window, the beautiful color was there, though it killed the verbenas in the window box. But the deer would have come to eat them anyway. Around this, like a circle with two circumferences, the house was surrounded by talk of Joseph Smith's golden tablets, and the hatred of that talk. The laughter that a prophet could be named Smith still rings in my head.

I think every poet has a favorite imagery which helps him to explain the preoccupations of his work. I have repeatedly chosen the Orphic, and in so doing, I will remind you of certain elements of Orpheus' story. Unfortunately, the usual reference to him covers his power in song over animals and rocks, and this has become thoroughly sentimentalized—the magic that it represents cheapened by the view that one wants power over rather than entrance to. There is fairly good evidence that Orpheus was a man, another Greek hero, of early date, pre-Homeric, and that his life is closely attached to the realm of Dionysus, who precedes Apollo at Delphi and later shares the oracle with him. Orpheus' death is recorded in the story, his journey to hell, which he was able to complete only once, though at least four entrances to hell were well known in ancient Greece. One part of his story has to do with the power of death over love and the power of death over the dead. The other part has to do with his death at the hands of the Bacchantes, when he is torn to pieces. His head floats down a river or over a stretch of Ocean and continues to speak in prophecies, but this is stopped by jealous Apollo, when he becomes really dead. Clearly, the Orphic Dionysus is being edited. In some peculiar sense, Orpheus is really repeating the life of Dionysus, the god who is both joyous and terrible, who is bringer of wine, who can be defeated, thrown into the sea by a mortal, locked in a chest, torn to pieces by giants, and who dies. That he holds within himself all the contradictions, the change and process of the world as it is known, and the terror that goes with that process, as Orpheus contradicts his power, has the power to charm with his music, but cannot charm the Bacchantes, has the power to bring Eurydice back from the dead, at least metaphorically, but cannot look at her. It is precisely in the image of the scattered body and mind of Orpheus that I place whatever I know about the poetic process— that scattering is a living reflection of the world.

I am thirty years old before I begin even tentatively to accept the title of poet. In San Francisco, I was tied to two other poets, who, it was my superstition, wrote my poems for me. When that notion became sentimental, I dropped it, and became another poet. I have worked since 1955 to find a line which will hold what I see and hear, and which will tie a reader to the poems, not to me. This fascination precedes my great debt to Charles Olson, for it is in a schoolbook problem, Plato's description of the power of music over the body and the dangers of poetry in *The Republic,* and it was the fantastic pull of hearing [Arthur] Brodeur read *Beowulf,* 100 lines at a whack on a good day, which led Spicer and me to compete in our translations to bring over the heat of that story.

I am greatly moved by what is received and held with force in a poet's work. And sometimes that work promises that a great deal more will be held. In 1945, August, when Jack Spicer came to Berkeley from Los Angeles, and wound up living with me, I had read little philosophy, and Jack soon led me into that mess (though he later turned violently against it). He was soon reading Leibnitz and Spinoza. I can't say that a very great deal of this came over to me, nor did it seem to stick in detail with Jack, but I do remember discussions of monads and reflections. Recently, reading an exciting book by Frances Yates, *The Art of Memory,* I ran into a passage which brought back part of those dialogues with Jack. " . . . the monads, when they are human souls having memory, have as their chief function the representation of reflections of the universe of which they are living mirrors." Her book contains a description of the Memory Theater, a box with tiers, where the initiate would take the place of the stage and look out on the tiers, which in an ordinary theater would hold the audience—here there are images upon images, so that a man could hold the whole world in view. The idea is that the best means of memory is by image, and the image will hold best when it is given a place. Here the place itself is built to hold the images. Were I in this theater, and before I could take responsibility for the images of the whole universe or hold them, I would have to hold on to those images first, to dwell upon them, which hold the nature of two stars eminently important in my life:

Taurus: *A man ploughing, a man bearing a key, a man holding a serpent and a spear.* This is almost clear, but I can't say in which hands he holds the snake and spear, so the memory is incomplete, or uncreated.

and Saturn: *A man with a stag's head on a dragon, with an owl which is eating a snake in his right hand.* It is my view that the nature of this star cannot be held in a poem until the uncreated dragon is created.

I am trying to describe the foreignness, the outsideness, as a kind of metaphor for the sense I have of the process that leads to a poem, which again is outside, when made, and it is akin to translation, a word which in its parts holds the meaning of the word metaphor, the bringing over. This is here a problem of describing the process of inclusions, which as a man's work extends, enlarges and must take in both earth and sky. The heat I'm after is not simply the personal heat of the meeting, the recognition, but a heat and a passion which are of the nature of existence itself. The personal, yes, but then the translation of the personal to correspond with larger and larger elements, images of earth, is a process of inclusion—a growth of sensibility, in Valéry's phrase, but also a making which is not self-expressive. To be included, to be caught, to be brought over. Though I consider most of my work as a kind of translation, I have moved toward translation in the ordinary sense. My Nerval is an effort to bring over the chimeras of another poet, because the recognition was word for word. In doing so, I spent months trying to find the words in English to carry the heat of the Nerval world, which is cosmic, but also most personal. And it is this content which must be translated—not the word for word crib, but the actual heat of the process which gave form to the poems. Nerval begins in a real image of loss—the women of his world who disappear into the earth, and if they continue to exist, the realms of death have to be seen in terms of change and in images which hold that change. All this is most clear in one of Nerval's dreams, from which I took my lead:

> The lady I followed, displaying her slender form in a movement that caused the folds in her dress of changing taffeta to glisten, gracefully placed her bare arm around a long stalk of hollyhock, then under a clear ray of light, she began to grow in such a manner that little by little the garden took her form, and the flowerbeds and the trees became the roses and garlands of her garment, while her figure and her arms printed their contours on the violet clouds in the sky. In this way I lost sight of her in a process of transfiguration, for she seemed to disappear into her own grandeur. "Oh!, do not leave me! I cried . . . for nature dies with you."

Nerval took the ultimate responsibility for the other side of the world, like the old idea, before it was photographed, of the other side of the moon. He saw and recorded a world in which the sun is black, the alchemical sol niger, under the earth yes, but in addition an in FORM ing vision. How personal the first vision of this was is

seen in an early poem, which Nerval had adapted from a poem by
Bürger, and which I translated:

THE BLACK SPOT

whoever has stared directly into the sun
thinks he sees before him,   unyielding,
flying around   in the air   an ashen spot

really young once   and a lot braver,
I dared to fix my eyes on glory
for an instant:
what my eyes craved left a black point

since then, mingling with everthing
like a token of grief,   everywhere,
in places where my eyes rest
I see it perch also,   a black spot

ask me if this is always true   it is
between me and fortune constantly
this bad luck and shared sorrow
if only an eagle looks in the Sun
and the Glory   without punishment

Here, I wish to point to the responsibility of the poet for the
experience of power as it is seen and felt in the world. And no
more ultimate vision is possible than the one which tells the tale
and holds the cost of the vision of the other side, the way down,
sometimes the way up, the realms of deadness both in and out of
the world—held in image, not a tract full of wisdom, but a reality
created, held by image and sound. This is seen in the first poem of
Nerval's sequence, *Les Chimères,* a serial poem, in his use of myth,
original in his recognition—the tale behind the sirens—that they
are indeed cursed muses, forced to be birds of the sea, which is the
realm of love and eros. The siren is a sea bird from her origin in
this very ancient story. The image holds it absolutely. When I
come to a work, like *The Moth Poem,* which is not a translation in
this sense, it is, however, a translation of the record of the burning
light and death of certain presences. I believe that all men live in
this realm, the serious, intense kingdom, funny as it is at times,
with its passionate thought.

And it is just here that an accusation is leveled at many poets. "He writes for a coterie, the poets talk only among themselves. They live in a world of flattery and selfhood." It is my belief that it is somewhere in this messy denial of the thought of poetry that an explanation can be found for the importance of community. That poets do band together. I am demonstrably bad at the kind of communism one dreams of, yet I have repeatedly worked in and added to a community of that sort. The reason is that only in such communities is the necessary talk of this high, serious realm possible. Such communities tend to build a structure for men who wish to keep, hold, and record the passionate relation with the outside that the world, the nation, need. This is the only place where such talk goes on. That we have reached a point now here where such discourse must include the nation, our politics, the scholarship in which we tend to lay down the images of poetic thought—is obvious. This is a kind of memory theater in which the poet with his craft is after not some thing or place remembered, but present. Nothing would be more painful or more costly to the mind, and ugly in a sense that great poetry may be very ugly, than a poetry in which the present war was present, held in sight and sound and intellect. Not opinion or reflection or dialectic about the presence. Few poets have caught the terror, which is the other side of the world. Those who have, Spicer, Pound and Olson, for example, took a long time to burn—and their lives are of different lengths.

[*1967*]

ROBERT CREELEY

A Note on Ezra Pound

For my generation the fact of Ezra Pound and his work is inescapable, no matter what the particular reaction may be. But it should equally be remembered that during the forties, that time in which we came of age, Pound's situation was, in all senses, most depressed. To the young of that period he was often simply a traitor, an anti-Semite, an obscurantist, a money crank—and such courses in universities and colleges as dealt with modern poetry frequently avoided all mention of the *Cantos*. For example, I remember in my shyness going to F. O. Mathiessen at Harvard, to ask why we had not used the *Cantos* in his own course on contemporary poetry. His answer was that he understood Pound's work too poorly, that he felt Pound's political attitudes most suspect, and that he could not finally see the value of the work in a course such as ours was.

It is hard to see, in one sense, how we were not frightened away from Pound—there was so much to persuade us of his difficulties and of those he would surely involve us with. But who else could responsibly teach us that "nothing matters but the quality of the affection," that "only emotion endures"? The work we were otherwise given was, on the one hand, Auden—wherein a socially based use of irony became the uselessly exact rigor of repetitive verse patterns—or perhaps Stevens, whose mind one respected, in the questions it realized, but again whose use of poetry had fallen to the questionable fact of a device.

Pound, on the other hand, brought us immediately to the context of how to write. It was impossible to avoid the insistence he put on *precisely* how the line *goes*, how the word *is*, in its context,

247

what *has been* done, in the practice of verse—and what *now* seems possible to do. It was, then, a *measure* he taught—and a measure in just that sense William Carlos Williams insisted upon:

> . . . The measure itself
> has been lost
> and we suffer for it.
> We come to our deaths
> in silence. . . .

To the attacks upon Pound as bigot merely, Charles Olson—speaking in the guise of Yeats in defence of Pound, in 1946—makes the relevant answer:

> It is the passivity of you young men before Pound's work as a whole, not scripts alone, you who have taken from him, Joyce, Eliot and myself the advances we made for you. There is a court you leave silent—history present, the issue the larger concerns of authority than a state, Heraclitus and Marx called, perhaps some consideration of descents and metamorphoses, form and the elimination of intellect.

For my own part I came first to the earlier poems, *Personae,* and to the various critical works, *Make It New, Pavannes and Divisions, ABC of Reading, Guide to Kulchur,* and *Polite Essays.* It was at that time the critical writing I could most clearly use, simply that my own limits made the *Cantos* a form intimidating to me. As a younger man, I wanted to know in a "formal" sense where it was I was going, and had a hard time learning to admit that the variousness of life is as much its quality as its quantity. Or rather—akin to the anecdote Pound tells of Agassiz's student not really *looking* at the fish—I wanted the categories prior to the content which might in any sense inform them.

But it is again the sense of *measure,* and how actively it may be proposed, that I found insistently in Pound's work. Rather than tell me *about* some character of verse, he would give the literal instance side by side with that which gave it context. This method is, of course, an aspect of what he calls the *ideogrammic*—it *presents,* rather than comments upon. That emphasis I feel to be present in all his work, from the rationale of imagism, to the latest *Cantos*.

In the same sense he directed a real attention to characters of verse in the early discriminations he offered as to its nature. For example, he spoke of "three chief means" available to the man wanting to "charge language with meaning to the utmost possible degree"—in the context that "Literature is language charged with meaning":

    I throwing the object (fixed or moving) on to the visual imagination.

    II inducing emotional correlations by the sound and rhythm of the speech.

    III inducing both of the effects by stimulating the associations (intellectual or emotional) that have remained in the receiver's consciousness in relation to the actual words or word groups employed.

        (phanopoeia, melopoeia, logopoeia)

Such location of attention meant an active involvement with what was happening in the given poem—and not a continuingly vague discussion of its aesthetic "value," or its "period," or all that area of assumption which finds place in unrealized generality. Pound's discriminations were located in the poem's literal activity.

How large he was then for us, is more simply stated than described. He took the possibility of writing to involve more than descriptive aesthetics. He defined sincerity as Kung's "man standing by his word." He moved upon the active principle of intelligence, the concept of *virtu,* so that, as Charles Olson has written:

    . . . his single emotion breaks all down to his equals or inferiors (so far as I can see only two, possibly, are admitted, by him, to be his betters—Confucius, & Dante. Which assumption, that there are intelligent men whom he can outtalk, is beautiful because it destroys historical time, and

    thus creates the methodology of the *Cantos,* viz, a space-field where, by inversion, though the material is all time material, he has driven through it so sharply by the beak of his ego, that, he has turned time into what we now must have, space & its live air. . . .

Beyond that sense of principle—if such "beyonds" can exist—there is the effect of reading Pound, of that experience of an energy, of ear and mind, which makes a language man's primary act. A sound:

> And then went down to the ship,
> Set keel to breakers, forth on the godly sea. . . .

> [*1965*]

Louis Zukofsky: *All:*
The Collected Short Poems, 1923-1958

In his preface to *A Test of Poetry* (1948) Louis Zukofsky notes at the outset, "The test of poetry is the range of pleasure it affords as sight, sound, and intellection. This is its purpose as art . . ." In his long poem *"A"* he qualifies its occasion as *"Out of deep need*. . . ."" Then, continuing:

> Who had better sing and tell stories
> Before all will be abstracted.
> So goes: first, *shape*
> The creation—
> A mist from the earth,
> The whole face of the ground:
> Then *rhythm*—
> And breathed breath of life;

> Then *style*—
> That from the eye its function takes—
> "Taste" we say—a living soul.
> First, glyph; then syllabary,
> Then letters. Ratio after
> Eyes, tale in sound. First, dance. Then
> Voice. First, body—to be seen and to pulse
> Happening together.
>
>   (*"A"* 12)

It is a sense that proposes poetry to be evidence as to its own activity, apart from any other sense of description or of a convenience to some elsewise considered reality of things. More, it is a belief, deeply committed, that what is said says "what-is-said"—a complexity of no simple order. For example, the first poem in *All* notes by the fact of its activity that any *said* thing exists in its saying and cannot be less than said—each time it is. It is interesting that this poem is called "Poem beginning 'The' "—which article is itself a determined emphasis upon what is defined in speech. In this case, a method as well takes form in this poem, as William Carlos Williams points out in his essay "Zukofsky," included in *"A."** It is based, I feel, upon the premise that all that is, as whatever has spoken it, may occur as it is, each time it is spoken. In other words, there is nothing which anything so existent is "about," that will go away in time, so as to embarrass the actuality of such existence. Zukofsky makes a lovely note of *time* in the 28th of *"29 Songs,"* which is pertinent to all such facts of *factness:* ". . . And for years it was four o'clock,—not time which would have broken the hour and placed a statue of David in history, but an ornamental herb of that name,—with flowers that grow in Peru of a great variety of color. So that for years it was four o'clock and the same as bloom from 4 P.M. till the next morning."

There is one poem which I would feel very useful for many senses of Zukofsky's poems, both in that character with which I have been concerned and also, very much, in the full complexity of their involvement with the man who is writing them. The poem is "Mantis" and there is a note as to its date of writing, November 4,

* Origin Press edition (1959).

1934. At a time when so much concern has come to center on assumptions of form, and remembering also that Empson's *Seven Types of Ambiguity,* for one such instance, was published in the early thirties—this poem makes clear a context of possibility and response itself a manifest of the poem's writing. The ostensible form of the poem is a sestina, and in " 'Mantis,' An Interpretation"—a close response to the poem's writing and concerns which follows in the next—Zukofsky says:

> The sestina, then, the repeated end words
> Of the lines' winding around themselves,
> Since continuous in the Head, whatever has been read,
> > whatever is heard,
> > > whatever is seen
> Perhaps goes back cropping up again with
> Inevitable recurrence again in the blood
> Where the spaces of verse are not visual
> But a movement,
> With vision in the lines merely a movement . . .
>
> One feels in fact inevitably
> About the coincidence of the mantis lost in the subway,
> About the growing oppression of the poor—
> Which is the situation most pertinent to us—
> With the fact of the sestina:
> Which together fatally now crop up again
> To twist themselves anew
> To record not a sestina, post Dante,
> Nor even a mantis.

What I am most intent to point out here is that Zukofsky feels form as an intimate presence, whether or not that form be the use of issue of other feelings in other times, or the immediate apprehension of a *way* felt in the moment of its occurrence. The distinction is, then, against what appropriates the outline sans an experience of its intimate qualities—as Zukofsky notes in this same section:

> What is most significant
> Perhaps is that C— and S— and X—of the 19th century

Used the "form"—not the form but a Victorian
Stuffing like upholstery
For parlor polish,
And our time takes count against them
For their blindness and their (unintended?) cruel smugness.
Again: as an experiment, the sestina would be wickerwork—
As a force, one would lie to one's feelings not to use it.

There is no reason I would credit to prevent a man's walking down
a road another has made use of—unless the road, by such use, has
become a "road," an habituated and unfelt occasion. But as
"force" its possibility is timeless.

Given the briefness of these notes, I am embarrassed to deal
with all that in this poem excites and informs me. It is a peculiar
virtue of Zukofsky's work that it offers an extraordinary handbook
for the writing of poems. His particular sensitivity to the qualities
of poetry as "sight, sound, and intellection" mark the significance
of his relation to Ezra Pound, who dedicated *Guide to Kulchur*
"To Louis Zukofsky and Basil Bunting, strugglers in the desert." It
is Bunting who says that his own first experience of poetry as an
unequivocal possibility for himself came with the recognition that
the order and movement of *sound* in a poem might itself create a
coherence of the emotions underlying. In this respect, the follow-
ing note by Zukofsky merits much thought:

> How much what is sounded by words has to do with what
> is seen by them, and how much what is at once sounded
> and seen by them crosscuts an interplay among them-
> selves—will naturally sustain the scientific definition of
> poetry we are looking for. To endure it would be com-
> pelled to integrate these functions: time, and what is
> seen in time (as held by a song), and an action whose
> words are actors or, if you will, mimes composing steps
> as of a dance that at proper instants calls in the vocal
> cords to transform it into plain speech.
>
>   ("Poetry," in *"A"* [Origin Press edition])

The brilliance, then, of these poems is their grace in such a recogni-
tion, that they can move so articulately in all the variables of a life.
I can make no selection because, as their author has said, one

writes one poem all one's life, and there can be no significant division. But as one moment, this may stand as token of all:

> Strange
> To reach that age,
> remember
> a tide
> And full
> for a time
> be young.
>
> (36, *Anew*)
>
> [*1966*]

Introduction to
The New Writing in the USA

Nothing will fit if we assume a place for it. To attempt to classify writing before one has had the experience of its activity will be to misplace it altogether. What can be said is something itself particular—to senses of form, to the literal nature of living in a given place, to a world momently informed by what energies inhabit it.

1

The forties were a hostile time for the writers here included. The colleges and universities were dominant in their insistence upon an *idea* of form extrinsic to the given instance. Poems were equivalent to cars insofar as many could occur of similar pattern—although each was, of course, "singular." But it was this assumption of a *mold,* of a means that could be gained beyond the literal fact of the writing *here and now,* that had authority.

It is the more ironic to think of it, remembering the incredible pressure of *feeling* also present in these years—of all that did want "to be said," of so much confusion and pain wanting statement in its own terms. But again, it is Karl Shapiro's *Essay on Rime* (written in the South Pacific at a military base, "without access to books," in iambic pentameter) which is successful, and Auden is the measure of competence. In contrast Ezra Pound, H.D., William Carlos Williams (despite the token interest as *Paterson* begins to be published), Hart Crane, and especially Walt Whitman are largely disregarded.

The situation of prose I remember as much the same. Despite the apparent insistence of *digression* in the work of Joyce, Faulkner, Céline and others who are valued, there is nonetheless the attempt to shape all discussion of their "form" to the context of an overt pattern, a symbolism, an explanation again anterior to the instance. In short, it is a period when criticism enjoys control of literary reference—so much so, that it can propose itself to be of primary value quite apart from its "subjects."

The sense of *form* which comes of this insistence is defined by Robert Duncan in an essay, "Ideas of the Meaning of Form":

> Form, to the mind obsessed by convention, is significant insofar as it shows control. What has nor rime nor reason is a bogie that must be dismissed from the horizons of the mind. . . . Wherever the feeling of control is lost, the feeling of form is lost. The reality of the world and men's habits must be constricted to a realm—a court or a salon or a rationale—excluding whatever is feared. . . . Metaphor must be fumigated or avoided (thought of as displaying the author's fancy or wit) to rid the mind of the poetic where metaphor had led dangerously towards Paracelsus' universe of psychic correspondences, towards a life where men and things were beginning to mix and cross boundaries of knowledge. Poets, who had once had dreams and epiphanies, now admit only to de-

vices and ornaments. Love, that had been a passion, had best be a sentiment or a sensible affection. . . . The struggle was to have ideas and not to let ideas have one. Taste, reason, rationality rule, and rule must be absolute and enlightened, because beyond lies the chiaroscuro in which forces co-operate and sympathies and aversions mingle. The glamor of this magic haunts all reasonable men today, surrounding them with, and then protecting them from, the darkness of possibilities that controls cannot manage, the world of thought and feeling in which we may participate but not dominate, where we are used by things even as we use them.

Confronting such *rule,* men were driven back upon the particulars of their own experience, the literal *things* of an immediate environment, wherewith to acknowledge the possibilities of their own lives. This alternative must now be familiar, but at that time there were few indeed to propose it. It is first found for me in Williams' introduction to *The Wedge* (1944):

Therefore each speech having its own character the poetry it engenders will be peculiar to that speech also in its own intrinsic form. . . . When a man makes a poem, makes it, mind you, he takes words as he finds them interrelated about him and composes them—without distortion which would mar their exact significances—into an intense expression of his perceptions and ardors that they may constitute a revelation in the speech that he uses. . . .

It is, in fact, a congruence of "the darkness of possibilities that control cannot manage" and that "revelation in the speech" that Williams emphasizes, which informs the first major work of Allen Ginsberg, *Howl*. He writes of its composition as follows:

By 1955 I wrote poetry adapted from prose seeds, journals, scratchings, arranged by phrasing or breath groups into little short-line patterns according to ideas of measure of American speech I'd picked up from W. C. Williams' imagist preoccupations. I suddenly turned aside in San Francisco, unemployment compensation leisure, to follow my romantic inspiration—Hebraic-Melvillean bardic breath. I thought I wouldn't write a *poem,* but just write what I wanted to without fear, let my imagination go, open secrecy, and scribble magic lines from my real mind—sum up my life—something I wouldn't be able to show anybody, writ for my own soul's ear and a few other golden ears. So the first line of *Howl.* . . .

It is relevant that he says, "I thought I wouldn't write a *poem,* but just write what I wanted to without fear . . ."—as does Duncan so emphasize that it was fear that felt "The reality of the world and men's habits must be constricted to a realm . . . excluding whatever is feared. . . ." The need becomes, then, literally:

> . . . to recreate the syntax and measure of poor human
>   prose and stand before you speechless and intelligent
>   and shaking with shame, rejected yet confessing out
>   the soul to conform to the rhythm of thought in his
>   naked and endless head,
> the madman bum and angel beat in Time, unknown, yet
>   putting down here what might be left to say in time
>   come after death,
> and rose reincarnate in the ghostly clothes of jazz in the
>   goldhorn shadow of the band and blew the suffering of
>   America's naked mind for love into an eli eli lamma
>   lamma sabacthani saxophone cry that shivered the
>   cities down to the last radio
> with the absolute heart of the poem of life butchered out
>   of their own bodies good to eat a thousand years.
>
> (*Howl,* Part 1)

2

The usual critical vocabulary will not be of much use in trying to locate the character of writing we have now come to. If one depends on the dichotomy of *romantic* and *classical,* he is left with, too simply, an historical description, itself a remnant from an earlier "period."

The question becomes, *what is real*—and what is of that nature? The most severe argument we can offer against the "value" of some thing or act, is that it is *not* real, that is has no given place in what our world has either chosen or been forced to admit. So it is the *condition* of reality which becomes our greatest concern—in which relation the following notes by Charles Olson are most useful:

> All things did come in again, in the 19th century. An idea shook loose, and energy and motion became as important a structure of things as that they are plural, and, by matter, mass. It was even shown that in the infinitely small the older concepts of space ceased to be valid at all. Quantity—the measurable and numerable—was suddenly as shafted in, to any thing, as it was also, as had been obvious, the striking character of the external world, that all things do extend out. Nothing was now inert fact, all things were there for feeling, to promote it, and be felt; and man, in the midst of it, knowing well how he was folded in, as well as how suddenly and strikingly he could extend himself, spring or, without even moving, go, to far, the farthest—he was suddenly possessed or repossessed of a character of being, a thing among things, which I shall call his physicality. It made a re-entry of or to the universe. Reality was without interruption, and we are still in the business of finding out how all action, and thought, have to be refounded. . . .
>
> ("Equal, That Is, to the Real Itself")

This recognition had come primarily from scientific thinking, as it might be called—but its evidence in the way in which the world occurs in *Moby-Dick* (the object of Olson's discussion) is very striking. What happens to "plot" or all such instance of "category"—the assumption of action as *contained,* for example—when all is continuous, "when the discrete [isn't] any longer a good enough base for discourse. . . ."? The sentence itself—as Fenollosa had proposed in *The Chinese Written Character as a Medium for Poetry,* and Olson reasserts—has become "an exchange of force" in no way a "completed thought," since such "completion" is impossible in the context of that *real* which Melville had apprehended, Olson notes, as "the absolute condition of present things . . ." Let it be stressed:

[Melville] put it altogether accurately himself, in a single sentence of a letter to Hawthorne, written when he was writing *Moby-Dick* (1851): "By visible truth we mean the apprehension of the absolute condition of present things."

(*Ibid.*)

The context so defined will include such present statement as this one taken from William Burroughs' *Naked Lunch:*

There is only one thing a writer can write about: *what is in front of his senses at the moment of writing* . . . . I am a recording instrument . . . . I do not presume to impose "story" "plot" "continuity" . . . .

What has been criticized as a loss of coherence in contemporary American prose—specifically that of Burroughs and Kerouac—has been, rather, evidence of this character of the *real* with which we are involved. In "Kerouac's Sound" Warren Tallman makes a parallel distinction:

In conventional fiction the narrative continuity is always clearly discernible. But it is impossible to create an absorbing narrative without at the same time enriching it with images, asides, themes and variations—impulses from within. It is evident that in much recent fiction—Joyce, Kafka, Virginia Woolf, and Faulkner are obvious examples—the narrative line has tended to weaken, merge with, and be dominated by the sum of variations. Each narrative step in Faulkner's work is likely to provoke many sidewinding pages before a next narrative step is taken. More, a lot of Faulkner's power is to be found in the sidewindings. In brief, what happens in jazz when the melody merges with the improvisations and the improvisations dominate, has been happening in fiction for some time now.

Not only have the earlier senses of "form" been rejected, but equally "subject" as a conceptual focus or order has given place to the literal activity of the writing itself.

The objects which occur at every given moment of composition (of recognition, we can call it) are, can be, must be treated exactly as they do occur therein and not by any ideas or preconceptions from outside the poem, must be handled as a series of objects in field in such a way that a series of tensions (which they also are) are made to *hold,* and to hold exactly inside the content and the context of the poem which has forced itself, through the poet and them, into being.

(Charles Olson, *Projective Verse*)

But is is in the nature of the writing itself that this thinking finds its most active definition—as here in the final section of John Wieners' "A Poem for Painters":

. . . At last. I come to the last defense.

My poems contain no
wilde beestes, no
lady of the lake, music
of the spheres, or organ chants.

Only the score of a man's
struggle to stay with
what is his own, what
lies within him to do.

Without which is nothing.
And I come to this
knowing the waste,
leaving the rest up to love
and its twisted faces,
my hands claw out at
only to draw back from the
blood already running there.

3

Finally, there seems so much that might be said. The American condition has much to do with *place,* an active spatial term which differs in that way from what has been assumed its European equivalent. Space, as physical ground, not sky, I feel to be once again politically active—as it has always been for the American from the outset. It is useless, for example, to acknowledge the growing political weight of either Africa or China without seeing the literal measure these *places* effect in relation to all senses of the European continuum—in which the American takes its place, at least in part.

But more than that—since "place" is not now more than activity—there is the question of *all* terms of relationship, and of the possible continuities of that relationship in a *time* which is continuous and at all moments "present"—else it never was.

The point seems that we cannot, as writers—or equally as readers—assume such content in our lives, that all presence is defined as a history of categorical orders. If the nature of the writing is to move in the field of its recognitions, the "open field" of Olson's *Projective Verse,* for example, then the nature of the life it *is* demands a possibility which no assumption can anticipate.

In such a situation the entity of oneself becomes more than a cultural "program" and the attempt to recognize its potential has led to experiment with "consciousness expanding" drugs such as mescaline, and writing which attempts to record such states, as Michael McClure's "Peyote Poem."

The impulse is also clear in attempts to rediscover the viable content of terms of life which precede the "categorical" defined by Aristotle. One does not want to go "back," merely. But I feel it true, as Duncan writes, "We have come so far that all the old stories/ whisper once more . . ." History, as "progress," seems quite dead.

Otherwise—*things* as they have taken place so consistently with us in this country are relevant, both as condition and as presence. They have been, always, a basic company, and they involve, with persistence, our uses of space. Further, I do not feel that Allen Ginsberg's insistent equation of states of feeling or being with so-called "material" things is surreal and/or a dimension of reality less present in one of its aspects than in another. There is a persistent literalness in American writing—very much so in the tradition with which we are concerned—and it has never been easily "symbolic." "All the accumulations of life, that wear us out—clocks, bodies, consciousness, shoe, breasts—begotten sons—your

Communism—'Paranoia' into hospitals . . ." is literal reality and literally apprehended. It is—as Denise Levertov notes from Jung for the title of one of her poems—that "everything that acts is actual," and the context may be a street in broad daylight where reality is just as pervasive "as a dream"—in fact, *is* "the dream" equally with consciousness.

One cannot describe it, so to speak. Either one acts in an equal sense—becomes the issue of a term "as real as real can be"—or else there is really nothing to be said. Again, the writing here collected seems to me distinct in point of its distance from the usual habit of *description*—by which I mean that practice that wants to "accompany" the *real* but which assumes itself as "objectively" outside that context in some way. Certainly it is possible to minimize or otherwise distort one's concern in a given matter or relation. Yet one is either there or not, and being there, cannot assume some "not being" so as to "talk about it."

I feel, however, that what I am trying to say here comes clearer in Edward Dorn's discussion of Olson's *Maximus Poems* (with their center in the town of Gloucester, Massachusetts):

> when the Place is brought forward fully in form conceived entirely by the activation of a man who is under its spell it is a resurrection for us and the investigation even is not extractable. And it is then the only *real* thing. I am certain without ever having been there, I would be bored to sickness walking through Gloucester. Buildings as such are not important. The wash of the sea is not interesting in itself, that is luxuria, a degrading thing, people as they stand, must be created, it doesn't matter at all they have reflexes of their own, they are casual, they do more than you could hope to know, it is useful, it is a part of industry. It has an arrogance of intention. This is the significance of Olson's distrust of Thucydides and his care for Herodotus. It is the significance of Blake's "the practice of art is anti-christ." Which further means that if you are not capable of the non-functional striking of a World, you are not practicing art. Description, letting things lay, was reserved for not necessarily the doubtful, but the slothful, or the merely busy.

4

To tell the story, is all one can do. What accumulates as the tradition of a craft—its means, its sophistications—must each time be reapprehended, not for "style." Because as Louis Zukofsky has taken care to say, of poetry:

> This does not presume that the style will be the man, but rather that the order of his syllables will define his awareness of order. For his . . . major aim is not to show himself but that order that of itself can speak to all men.
>
> ("Poetry")

That undertaking most useful to writing as an art is, for me, the attempt to *sound* in the nature of the language those particulars of time and place of which one is a given instance, equally present. I find it here.

[*1965*]

"I'm Given to Write Poems"

I'm *given* to write poems. I cannot anticipate their occasion. I have used all the intelligence that I can muster to follow the possibilities that the poem "under hand," as Olson would say, is declaring, but I cannot anticipate the necessary conclusions of the activity, nor can I judge in any sense, in moments of writing, the significance of that writing more than to recognize that it is being *permitted* to continue. I'm trying to say that, in writing, at least as I have experienced it, one is *in* the activity, and that fact itself is what I feel so deeply the significance of anything that we call poetry.

For some sense, then, of how it was I came to be involved with poetry, at the outset I was much more interested in *writing* apart from its designated modes, and perhaps I am characteristically American in that respect. To begin with, I was shy of the word "poet" and all its associations in a world I was then intimate with. It was not, in short, a fit attention for a young man raised in the New England manner, compact of Puritanically deprived senses of speech and sensuality. Life was real and life was earnest, and one had best get on with it. The insistent preoccupation with words did begin for me early, just that I did want so much to know what people were saying, and what, more precisely, they meant by it.

I think the most significant encounter for me as a young man trying to write was that found in the work of William Carlos Williams. He engaged language at a level both familiar and active to my own senses, and made of his poems an intensively *emotional* perception, however evident his intelligence. Despite his insistence on his Mediterranean connections, so to speak, he was as Puritan as I—or Lawrence, or Thoreau or the Melville of *Pierre*.

Otherwise, the forties—the time in which I came of age—were complicated in many bitter ways indeed. Not the least of the problems then evident for someone trying to realize him or herself in the world was the confusion about the very nature of "literature" itself. Coming from New England, I felt awkwardness about books to begin with, because they were for me often instances of social mark or measure, even at times a privilege of intellectual order—just as Hardy speaks of them in *Jude the Obscure*. I was very shy about communicating my own commitments in reading, and yet I used books as a very real *place* to be. Not merely an escape from the world—the difficulty was how to get *into* it, not away—books proved a place very deeply open to me, at moments of reading, in a sense few others were ever to be.

Thinking of that, let me note kinship with another writer—Robert Duncan—who has played a very important role in my life, both as mentor, very often, and as one whom I feel to share with me this particular sense of world, and writing, and poetry, which I most deeply respect. In a collection of his called *The Opening of the Field,* significantly enough, the first poem begins:

OFTEN I AM PERMITTED TO RETURN TO A MEADOW

Then continues:

> as if it were a scene made-up by the mind,
> that is not mine, but is a made place,
>
> that is mine, it is so near to the heart,
> an eternal pasture folded in all thought
> so that there is a hall therein
>
> that is a made place, created by light
> wherefrom the shadows that are forms fall.

This sense of a poem—that *place,* that *meadow*—has echoes of so many things that are intimate to my own sense of the reality experienced in writing. One would find that field or "meadow" in Whitman also, and it would be equally the sense of place I feel Allen Ginsberg many times to be entering, to be speaking of or longing for. Charles Olson too possesses its occasion in his sense of "open" verse or that *open field,* as he insists upon it, in composition. I have found it deeply in H.D.'s writing: "I go where I love and am loved. . . ." And in Pound's "What thou lovest well remains,/the rest is dross. . . ."

> What thou lov'st well shall not be reft from thee
> What thou lov'st well is thy true heritage
> Whose world, or mine or theirs
>   or is it of none?
> First came the seen, then thus the palpable
>   Elysium, though it were in the halls of hell,
> What thou lovest well is thy true heritage. . . .

All of these are, to my own mind, not only tokens but evidences of a place, a very distinct and definite *place,* that poetry not only creates but itself issues from—and one in writing is, as Duncan says, "permitted to return," to go there, to be in that reality. There is a poem by Allen Ginsberg which has always moved me deeply. He calls it simply "Song" and it is included in the first collection of his poetry, *Howl.* The closing lines of this poem are:

yes, yes,
　　　　that's what
I wanted,
　　　　I always wanted,
I always wanted,
　　　　to return
to the body
　　　　where I was born.

That body is the "field" and is equally the experience of it. It is, then, to "return" not to oneself as some egocentric center, but to experience oneself as *in* the world, thus, through this agency or fact we call, variously, "poetry."

In the same passage quoted from Duncan, there is another sense of much interest to me in the emphasis he puts upon "made": "a scene," as he says, "made-up by the mind,/ that is not mine, but is a made place,/ that is mine. . . ." And again, two lines following: "there is a hall therein/ that is a made place. . . ." This emphasis takes its occasion from the sense of poet as maker, going back to the Greek root, *poiein,* "to make."

One of the few books I've ever had that was stolen—not by me, as it happened, but by a girl I persuaded to steal it for me—was William Carlos Williams' *The Wedge.* It proved *fire* of a very real order, and, for the record, was subsequently stolen from me in turn when I was teaching at Black Mountain in the mid-fifties. In 1944, when it was first published and shortly after which I got hold of it, its content was a revelation to me. In the preface Williams makes this statement:

> When a man makes a poem, makes it, mind you, he takes words as he finds them interrelated about him and composes them—without distortion which would mar their exact significances—into an intense expression of his perceptions and ardors that they may constitute a revelation in the speech that he uses. It isn't what he *says* that counts as a work of art, it's what he makes, with such intensity of perception that it lives with an intrinsic movement of its own to verify its authenticity.

I think this is very much the way Americans are given to speak— not in some dismay that they haven't another way to speak, but,

rather, that they feel that they, perhaps more than any other group
of people upon the earth at this moment, have had both to imagine
and thereby to *make* that reality which they are then given to live
in. It is as though they had to *realize* the world anew. They are, as
Charles Olson says, "the last first people." Now, in contemporary
fact, they are also the oldest issue of that imagination—even in
some ways bitterly so, because they have thus inherited the world
as not only a place to live in, but also as that reality for which they
are responsible in every possible sense.

However, I would mistake my own experience of poetry if I
were to propose it as something merely *intentional,* and what men
may imagine, either as worlds or poems, is not simply a *purpose*
either may satisfy. Williams also had no sense of patness in the
making of a poem, or of a world—but felt, as he says in one of his
own poems:

> Be patient that I address you in a poem,
>> there is no other
>>> fit medium.
> The mind
>> lives there. It is uncertain,
>>> can trick us and leave us
> agonized. But for resources
>> what can equal it?
>>> There is nothing. We
> should be lost
>> without its wings to
>>> fly off upon.
> The mind is the cause of our distresses
>> but of it we can build anew.
>>> Oh something more than
> it flies off to:
>> a woman's world,
>>> of crossed sticks, stopping
> thought. A new world
>> is only a new mind.
>>> And the mind and the poem
> are all apiece.

To put it simply indeed, it is not the intention to write that matters, but that _one can_—that such a possibility _can_ exist in which the mind may make evident its resources apart from the limits of intention and purpose.

In "The Desert Music"—for myself the loveliest form he left us—Williams makes further qualifications of the poem in its peculiar and singular function of _making real:_

>   Only the poem
> only the made poem, to get said what must
> be said, not to copy nature, sticks
> in our throats
>
> The law? The law gives us nothing
> but a corpse, wrapped in a dirty mantle.
> The law is based on murder and confinement,
> long delayed,
> but this, following the insensate music,
> is based on the dance:
>
>   an agony of self-realization
> bound into a whole
> by that which surrounds us
>
>   I cannot escape
> I cannot vomit it up
>
> Only the poem!
> Only the made poem, the verb calls it
>   into being.

Act becomes the primary issue of "verb," or _verbum,_ a word. "In the beginning was the Word"—and the word was the _reality of the imagination._ The "music," which the poem's title emphasizes and which becomes so central a content in the poem's activity is that which vivifies, the _anima mundi,_ lifeness and/or life itself. Our response to it or what it creates, its effects in the reality we are given, is the "dance."

> Now the music volleys through as in
> a lonely moment I hear it. Now it is all

> about me. The dance! The verb detaches itself
> seeking to become articulate

Poems are very specific kinds of *dancing,* because language is that possibility most specific to our condition as human beings. But I do not speak easily of these things because I feel, always, a timidity and confusion trying to isolate a sense that can only be experienced in the literal fact of the poem itself. It is as though I were trying to make actual a sense of wetness apart from water itself.

It is possible, nonetheless, to continue now to use those men I have used so much, to make evident what senses of poetry have been for me insistent. In "Maximus, to Gloucester" Charles Olson gives measure of the occasion in a way that informs my own:

> He left him naked,
> the man said, and
> nakedness
> is what one means
>
> that all start up
> to the eye and soul
> as though it had never
> happened before

My sense of his statement is this: in the fact of our lives we are brought to primary situations, primary terms of experience—what they might have meant by "first things first" but probably didn't. "Nakedness" is to stand manifestly in one's own condition, in that necessary *freshness,* however exposed, because all things are particular and reality itself is the specific content of an instant's possibility. In poems we realize, not in discursive or secondary manner, but with this implicit and absolutely consequential fact of *firstness,* terms of our own life, manifestations of that life which, otherwise, are most awkwardly acknowledged. It is, again, that "field" that Robert Duncan speaks of as being "permitted" to enter. First things. We arrive in poems at the condition of life most viable and most primal in our own lives.

I've said that I feel myself to be a poet who is *given* to write. And I'm even awkward about using that designation, that is, to call myself so, a poet—because I do not feel I have that decision in it. Yet the complexity of the dilemma seems to me a very real one. How shall we understand Williams' painfully marked insistence just before the close of "The Desert Music":

> I *am* a poet! I
> am. I am. I am a poet, I reaffirmed, ashamed

In America, we are certainly not poets simply, nor much of the time.

The saints of my own calendar are saints of this exposure, beginning with Columbus and like men whose imagination realized, *reified,* one might say, the world I live in. They are Poe—who, as Williams makes clear, forced the *local* to yield him a world apart from the habits of English manner; Whitman—for the *permission* of life he insisted upon; Melville—the primary *imagination* of the isolation of our condition; Pound—who, like any Yankee, makes *intelligence* an invention of necessity; Hart Crane —whose "failure" regained the *possibility* of our response to what we are given to feel. It may well be that in the absence of such allusive society as European literature, in its own condition, has necessarily developed, that the American in contrast must so realize each specific thing of his own—"as though it had never/ happened before." I think of Williams' sharply contemptuous answer to the British English professor, met with in Seattle, Washington, of all places, who asked him after a reading, "where he got his language"—to which Williams replied, "Out of the mouths of Polish mothers"—meaning not Polish, but the harsh, crude, blocked "poor English" of those immigrant women he had as patients in his profession as a doctor. My "saints," then, are those men who defined for me an explicit possibility in the speech that I was given to use, who made the condition of being American not something chauvinistically national but the intimate fact of one life in one place at one time.

To speak then of the writing itself, which I can do only tentatively—just that I am persuaded by Heisenberg that "observation impedes function"—I have again much depended upon senses of procedure and examples (which are, of course, the point) given me by such men. In the forties there was so much talk *about* the poem, about levels of meaning, ambiguities, symbols, allusions. It was even felt that criticism itself would prove the most significant literary activity of the time.

Pound, in contrast, spoke of the literal condition of the writing, and it was he I used as guide—and continue to now, twenty years later, because his advice proved facts of perception as active to my mind now as when I first came to them. For example, his quotation from Remy de Gourmont, "Freely to write what one chooses is the sole pleasure of a writer," continues for me the only actual measure of the occasion I am aware of. He gave me the experience of integrity as "Man standing by his word." More, he spoke so clearly of the explicit situation of writing:

> In making a line of verse (and thence building the lines into passages) you have certain primal elements:
> That is to say, you have the various "articulate sounds" of the language, of its alphabet, that is, and the various groups of letters in syllables.
> These syllables have differing weights and durations
> A. original weights and durations
> B. weights and durations that seem naturally imposed on them by the other syllable groups around them.
>
> Those are the medium wherewith the poet cuts his design in TIME.

Against the arguments of taste and opinion which criticism so largely depends upon, Pound called attention to the character of the activity:

> Rhythm is a form cut into TIME, as a design is determined SPACE. . . .
> LISTEN to the sound that it makes . . .

However, it is really Charles Olson I must thank for whatever *freedom* I have as a poet, and I would value him equally with Pound and Williams and those others I have mentioned. *Freedom* has always been for me a difficult experience in that, when younger, I felt it had to propose senses of experience and of the world I was necessarily *not* in possession of—something in that way one might escape to. I mistook, I think, the meaning of "freely to write what one chooses," which both de Gourmont and Pound may well have had in mind, because I took "freely" to mean "without significant limit" and "chooses" to be an act of will. I therefore was slow in realizing the nature of Olson's proposal, that "Limits/ are what any of us/ are inside of," just that I had taken such "limits" to be a frustration of possibility rather than the literal possibility they in fact must provoke. Despite Pound—or rather, because I could not hope to gain such means as he had—I had to find my own way, and at first I was completely ignorant of what it might be.

In consequence, what Olson made clear to me during the late forties and early fifties was of very great use. I am speaking of the *kind* of thinking that is evident in his essay, "Projective Verse," written during the same time. Let me quote an instance:

> The objects which occur at every given moment of composition (of recognition, we can call it) are, can be, must be treated exactly as they do occur therein and not by any ideas or preconceptions from outside the poem, must be handled as a series of objects in field in such a way that a series of tensions (which they also are) are made to *hold,* and to hold exactly inside the content and the context of the poem which has forced itself, through the poet and them, into being.

Not long ago, in conversation, Robert Duncan qualified his sense of *choice* as being *recognition,* that is, choice is significantly the act of recognition, and I believe it. What one "chooses" in writing is importantly of this nature, for me, and composition is the fact and effect of such activity. One isn't putting things *into* poems, then, at least not as my own experience of writing informs me. There is never a "subject" *about* which one constructs an activity called "poetry." Nor can one, as Williams says, "copy nature," take from that which is elsewise informed some felicitious appearance, whether a rhyme or a so-called sentiment.

However best it might be put, what Olson made evident to me was that writing could be an intensely specific revelation of one's own content, and of the world the fact of any life must engage. It has nothing to do with "personalism"—which, like personality, is a mirror or reflective image sense, a cosmetic of intentions. To the contrary, what emerges in the writing I most value is a content which cannot be anticipated, which "tells you what you don't know," which you subvert, twist, or misrepresent only on peril of death.

What I have written I knew little of until I had written it. If at times I have said that I enjoy what I write, I mean that writing is for me the most viable and open condition of possibility in the world. Things have happened there, as they have happened nowhere else—and I am not speaking of "make-believe," which, be it said, is "as real as real can be." In poems I have both discovered and born testament to my life in ways no other possibility has given me. Can I *like* all that I may prove to be, or does it matter? Am I merely living for my own approval? In writing it has seemed to me that such small senses of existence were altogether gone, and that, at last, the world "came true." Far from being its limit or director, the wonder is that I have found myself to be there also.

[Lecture delivered at the Literarisches Colloquium, Berlin, January 1967]

Linda Wagner:
An Interview with Robert Creeley

Q: We hear frequently that this is an excellent period for poetry, that from all the present experimentation will come strong new modes. As a poet, do you feel that these are peak years?

A: I feel that we have been party to an extraordinary experimentation and a building on the possibilities offered by Ezra Pound,

William Carlos Williams, and . . . Whitman—I think that these last ten or fifteen years in American poetry have been perhaps the most rich of any, or certainly will prove to be as rich as those in the earlier part of the century. What's now happening is something else again; I find that there's an extraordinary interest in poetry, and certainly many, many people writing it—but I've as yet not seen, except in a few instances, a clear significance of its effect. For example, recently in San Francisco at the Berkeley Poetry Conference, I was very interested in the poems of Ted Berrigan. Now they come from a mode that has been developed partly by Frank O'Hara, more by John Ashbery, and perhaps even more significantly by Mac Low, Jackson Mac Low. In Berrigan's poems, words are returned to an almost primal circumstance, by a technique that makes use of feed-back, that is, a repetitive relocation of phrasing, where words are curiously returned to an almost objective state of presence so that *they* speak rather than someone speaking with them. It is something that Gertrude Stein had been concerned with. But these people are using it for a most interesting possibility, and I'm interested in that sense in what they are doing, very much so. I feel that this is probably one of the most interesting new possibilities in writing to have occurred in some time. Otherwise, I think that there is the usual activity, but I don't really find much distinction in it. I do not mean to criticize those persons now writing, but—this may be simply an instance of my own age at this point.

I feel that these are peak years, however, in regard to the demand that society now makes upon poetry. That demand has never been more insistent. Therefore, let's say the occasion is certainly here. The time is right, in all possible senses. At the same time, perhaps the very wealth of possibilities is itself a slight confusion to people trying to decide which of many things is that most akin to their own circumstance.

I feel for myself that these are peak years indeed. I have everything I want, for example. I think most poets writing must feel somewhat the same, that there's no reason to sit and grouch about not having something because—my God—there's incredible possibility in all senses. Again, what I did find out in

Germany was this, that German poets and prose writers also are very interested in what they call "the American vernacular." That is, we are blessed by having a literary language which easily makes use of the so-called "vernacular." Either we can use a highly developed rhetorical mode or else we can use a very commonly situated vernacular. And we have no diminution of the literary possibility in either case.

Q: In Germany, then, that's not so?

A: No, there the language of poetry has been primarily a literary language so that poets like Enzensberger and others have been interested to translate poets like Williams simply that in Williams they find this vernacular in such intensity that they hope by translation to gain its use, in the German context. So that there, you see, the modes are much more limited at present. This is even more recognizably true in France, where poetic language has definitely limited the articulation possible to poetry. I was talking to Claude Gallimard about whether or not there were many French poets of interest, and the only one he really remarked upon was, unhappily, a young poet whose name I cannot remember—a Belgian, I think, significantly enough. He was then about eighteen. But he was the *only* one they really had come upon. In this country, it's possible to find at least ten or fifteen persons who are writing with extraordinary qualification.

Q: Would you consider them major poets? In other words, have these strong new modes appeared?

A: Yes, they've appeared. Pound alone has provided so many possibilities in his work that it will be a long time indeed before they're exhausted. I feel that Pound will take his place in the context of literature in the same way that Chaucer did, in offering the possibility of iambic pentameter or actually the iamb as a measure for verse. In other words, setting a mode in the technical performance of the craft that stays for all subsequent time. Spenser, in his modulations or inventions, would be another figure. Bunting, Basil Bunting, is right I think when he draws a parallel between Pound and Spenser as two great innovators in the art of poetry, whose work may then be built upon for years and years. I think that these modes—coming both from such men as Pound and Williams and from more contemporary figures like Charles Olson—are evident and that now their particular use is really up to the qualification of each person who attempts to make use of them.

Q: Perhaps we should continue into the big questions at once. Talking about "strong modes," what in your estimation is a strong, or a good, poem?

A: Well, a "good" poem . . . I've come in the past few months at least—whether from fatigue or from a kind of ultimately necessary conservatism—to feel that there can be at least one kind of primary measure for the activity of poetry; and perhaps this statement will seem oblique, but in any case what really sticks in my head through the years as a measure of literature is a pair of statements made by Pound—years ago, I would think. One is, simply, "Only emotion endures." And the other is, "Nothing matters save the quality of affection." Now these offer to me two precise terms of measure for the possibility of a poem. I feel that what the poem says in a didactic or a semantic sense —although this fact may be very important indeed—is not what a poem is about primarily; I think this is not its primary fact. I believe, rather, that it is that complex of emotion evident by means of the poem, or by the response offered in that emotion so experienced, that is the most signal characteristic that a poem possesses. So, the measure of poetry is that emotion which it offers, and further, the quality of the articulation of that emotion —how it is felt, the fineness of its articulation.

I would add two things. One, the sense of poetry that's evident in Williams' introduction to *The Wedge* where he says. " . . . a man makes a poem, *makes* it, mind you," so that it has "an intrinsic movement of its own to verify its authenticity" —in other words, so that it is not simply a wish on the part of the writer (or not simply a communication, saying, "I'm telling you this"), but has within it all that it needs to survive in its own statement. This wherewithal for survival is a condition necessary to a poem that's active.

Two, I would take Zukofsky's sense of enjoying poetry with reference to the pleasure it offers as sight, sound, and intellection. These would offer for me three primary conditions of a poem's activity. And I would much respect them. I would also—for my own work at least—respect Zukofsky's sense of poetry as a function, with its upper limit being music and its lower limit speech.

Q: Would your answer be any different had I said a good *contemporary* poem?

A: No. I have no interest in *contemporary* as a sense of *the latest*. I remember reading years ago in the work of a linguist, Joshua Whatmough—a very simple book called *Language*—a comment that poetry had said nothing new for the last 6000 years. And perhaps now that we can go back farther in time, we will find that poetry has not said anything genuinely new in the past 20,000 or 30,000 years. Its concerns have always been war, the love between man and woman or man and man, friendship, and the land—planting and harvest. They have been a curiously insistent set of themes. I don't know, war is the most intense and perhaps the largest political possibility ever experienced by men —and then the most intimate measure of his life is his love for woman or that of woman for man, or man for man.

I would use the word, "contemporary," as Stendhal did. (I might say that Stendhal is probably the one writer whom I've had consistent regard for since I was reading anything at all. I'm just now rereading some of his work, and I'm struck again by the incredible clarity and fluidity of his thinking.) That is, it's necessary to articulate these kinds of possibility in the intimate language of one's own reality. That is what it is to be modern he felt. To borrow the language of other times and places when it is not intimate is to risk faking—even though one be very sincere. It is like making old furniture. Even though the piece may be an exact replica, the situation of the authentic is always particular. When that element of time and place is removed from it, it becomes a curiously vacant thing. So I don't think that I would have spoken differently of a good contemporary poem, because a poem that is active in the ways that I've tried to suggest is always active in these ways, if it can be understood at all. Its language may simply be lost to us by some effect of time or by a shift in the dialect. But, that aside, I would feel that a poem is continually active and that time, in the historical sense, is of no interest in any measure of a poem's activity.

Q: I should like to solicit your opinions of prose here, if I may. Too often, I think, you are considered a "poet"; and, therefore the short stories and your recent novel, *The Island,* are overlooked. Yet your prose seems to approximate your poetry, not only in its careful, polished style, but in its themes of love, hate, human concern. Do you feel that all your work is of a piece?

A: Effectively so, by no means intentionally so, but insofar as any one man is this kind of thing we've been talking about—or does have this insistence of his own organism and his own organization as such—all that issues from him is particular to himself. I don't mean "style." I mean, if it's the issue of him, then it will have a continuity, whether he intends it or not.

I remember years ago, again in a letter from Louis Zukofsky about one of my books which I had sent him—after talking about the various poems in it, he said, "We write one poem all our lives." In other words, any one part of that poem may or may not have individual significance, but it is, in all, one continuous work. To make divisions in it is a little specious because it does in that way necessarily cohere. I find, then, that I can't write outside of my own "givens." These are the things that I'm given to work with. I can try to escape them, but I never succeed in any interesting fashion. For me the novel is an issue of the continuous work that I've been trying to do now for almost —what?—twenty years. It doesn't take a place apart from the poems, nor is it different from the poems in its concerns. It's all an attempt to articulate some complex of feelings gained through the writing, that are not otherwise to be gained. I remember one time in conversation with Ramon Sender, he was saying, "Well, anyone, an eleven-year-old school boy can write a poem. The emotional equipment is there even that early. But," he said, "now think of the problem of gaining an articulation and an actual placing for each word in a novel—that's 50,000 to 75,000 to 100,000 words which one is responsible for, the conduct of each word.

Now a novelist whom I respect does feel that way about what

he is doing, and I certainly felt that way about this novel: I felt that each word had to have as much justification in its own position as, say, any word in a poem. I'm not here claiming that the novel is a poem—they are very different modes—but I think that a novel is responsible to words in just the same way that a poem is responsible, and that the conduct of words in either situation has to be the responsibility of the writer in all possible senses.

Q: With all this personal feeling in a work, how can the writer avoid writing a "true confession" story? The age-old problem, how does he maintain the proper perspective, whatever that may be?

A: There is no "proper perspective." Really, I can remember in writing classes in college, one professor would tell us, avoid all autobiographical reference because you will have such a subjective sense of it that you will not be able to approach it coolly or objectively. Therefore you'll find yourself involved with distortions because of your writing about yourself. It will be disastrous, etc., etc. Then I'd go into another class and be told there that all one could really use was autobiographical material because that's all one really knew. All the rest was too removed from the intimacies or intensities of one's own experience. You see now, either of those adamant rules is a little specious.

One *knows* in writing, I don't know quite how, but one knows what one needs and one takes it, without embarrassment and increasingly with a demand that's not to be gainsaid. So that there's no reason why one shouldn't write a true confession story. Again I'm thinking of Stendhal, who wrote a brilliant true confession story, *The Life of Henri Brulard,* and of something like *Lucien Leuwen.* Or there's a quote to the effect that Stendhal said, "Julien Sorel, c'est moi." Again, writing makes its own demands, its own articulations, and it is its own activity—so that to say, "Why, he's simply telling us the story of his life," the very fact that he is telling of his life will be a decisive modification of what that life is. The life of the story will not so simply be the life of the man. The modifications occurring in the writing will be evident and will be significant.

I feel that a proper perspective is of no use except in cases where there is a clear need for it—that is, to keep your head while others all about you, etc., etc. There are circumstances evidently where that kind of coolness or objectivity is much required. Or there are kinds of writing in which it is. But in writing it doesn't really matter whether one is literally out of one's head with the insistence of what's being said, with the emotional demand of it; or whether one is working at a cool and quiet and objective remove from what the material suggests as emotional possibility. Again, you see, Rousseau's *Confessions*—that to my mind is an extraordinary work. I'll never know Rousseau, any more than anyone else will, but that book is a great purge of human feelings. Therefore their admission into the writing with such intensity and clarity is already a great relief from all that surrounds him. To read that book is to be relieved.

In other words, I've never felt that writing was fiction, that it was something made up about something. I've felt that it was direct evidence of the writer's engagement with his own feelings and with the possibilities that words offered him.

Q: The issue of "distance," then, is an invalid one?

A: The distance is dictated by the poem, not by the writer or by the assumptions he may bring to it. The writer may begin writing coolly about something in which he feels no possibility of involvement exists, though why he should want to write about such a thing I don't really know, but suppose he does so begin. To me, it's a large absurdity; it would be like living with someone from whom one could maintain a discreet distance. What would be the point of that? Writing to me is the most intimate of all acts; why should I want to maintain a distance from that which engages me? True, there are times in writing when I want the sight of something, or when I want to gain the view of it that will eradicate my assumptions about it. But that distance, you see, is dictated by something very intimate in the writing. It's not to be proposed prior to the writing unless one is writing instructions for assembling washing machines. But, again, the circumstance will dictate that need much more ably than the writer can propose, and much more significantly.

Q: I've been interested in this matter of the difference between poetry and prose, Bob. Since you have been writing both for many years—with the short stories coming first, of course—what do you find to be the major differences between the two modes?

A: Well, again let me speak personally. The differences as they exist for me are these. Poetry seems to be written momently—that is, it occupies a moment of time. There is, curiously, no time in writing a poem. I seem to be given to work in some intense moment of whatever possibility, and if I manage to gain the articulation necessary *in* that moment, then happily there is the poem. In prose there's a coming and going. Much more of a gathering process is evident in prose writing. In fact I think I undertook prose because it gave me a more extended opportunity to think *in* something—to think around and about and in something which was on my mind. It hardly gave me this sense of objective distance we've just been talking about, but it gave me the possibility of stating the thing that occupied me in a variety of ways.

For example, an early story like "Three Fate Tales" would be an instance of this. It's fairly clear what's on my mind there—how is one in the world?—and these three takes on that sense of situation are really what the story consists of. Also, I was involved at the time I wrote the novel . . . well, I was very interested to gain the use of something that would go on, that would give me a kind of day-to-day possibility. Now in the actual writing I found that it occurred quite otherwise; that is, in some ways I was back to a circumstance which I had come to know in poems. And I must note here that stories were usually written the same way—in one sitting; so that I wasn't really aware of how much time they were taking until I'd finished and looked at the clock. Maybe two hours or four hours had gone by, and I'd been writing.

But those stories too had the same kind of context, and the same sense of demand in them that the poems came to have for me. I think that I was probably more articulate in prose than in poetry at first, in the early 50s, as the second issue of *Origin* will probably show. You can see from that kind of evidence that prose was much on my mind; I was more at home with its possibilities at that time than I was with poetry's. In any case, prose lets me tinker rather than work in the adamant necessity of its demand upon me. I come and go from it. I can work at many levels of response and can articulate these many levels—whether I am intense or quite relaxed or even at times inattentive. Prose, as Williams says, can carry a weight of "ill-defined matter." Well, I don't know if it's necessarily ill-defined, but it can be random and even at times indecisive. It doesn't have to say everything, so to speak, in one intense moment.

Q: And poetry does.

A: Usually. And also this sense of continuity, of having something there day after day was something for which I've had a great longing. I had distinctly envied Olson the possibility of the *Maximus* poems—that they could provide—this is what Olson calls Pound's *Cantos*—a kind of "walker" for all that one could feel in writing, or by means of writing. Robert Duncan had had this also, I felt, in poems like "A Poem Beginning with a Line by Pindar" and very much in "The Venice Poem," which was the first poem of his that really seemed to me major. So I tried to write a novel earlier, when I was living in France in the early 50s, but there the program of the writing became so intrusive that the actual possibility of the writing leaked out—I was so intent upon how to make a transition from one chapter to another that this is really all the writing amounted to. I did get from one chapter to another with some grace, but the actual writing was largely lax and ineffectual.

Q: Any explanation for this state of affairs?

A: Well, I wasn't really under much pressure, or much necessity. The stories of that same period, "The Grace" and "The Party," were much more intensive and, I would feel now, much more a result of the things I was confronting in my life.

About the differences. For me, personally, poetry is an intense instant which is either gained or lost in the actual writing. Prose is much more a coming and going, though my own habits in writing prose are very much like those I do have in writing poetry: I don't revise as a rule, I find it necessary to begin at the beginning, to go forward, so to speak. I recall another conversation with Sender. He asked, "Why don't you simply begin at some point that's of intense interest to you, to what you think to be dealing with?" I said, "Well, I can't really do it that way. I can only come to that. I can't anticipate it by going to it directly. I have to arrive at it, and I don't even—curiously—know what that point will be. I'll have to find it." Not at all to be sentimental, but I think again that writing for me is a process of discovery, and I mean that very literally: a way of finding things, a way of looking for things, a way of gaining recognition of them as they occur in the writing.

Prose offers me a more variable way of approaching that kind of experience than poetry does, but then I do have the sense that Pound speaks of: that one chafes, if something in prose is of interest, to have it, frankly, articulated in poetry. Poetry offers the finer and the more intense articulation. Now this isn't always true. Unquestionably there are moments in prose (as in the writing of Stendhal again) which are as intense and as charged as any I've ever experienced. This is certainly obvious in Lawrence, and indeed in many prose writers who have this ability to articulate a very intense emotion; but the finer articulation is possible for me in poetry. There is one exception: I am embarrassed as yet to manage in poems the kind of coming and going that I've been given to manage only in prose.

Q: One question that's fairly relevant here, this issue of using so-called prose rhythms in poetry, of taking the language of poetry from natural speech: How does the poet himself decide what is poetry and what is conversation?

A: If we think of Zukofsky's poetics as being "a function with upper limit music and lower limit, speech," perhaps that will help to clarify what the distinctions are. Really, the organization of poetry has moved to a further articulation in which the rhythmic and sound structure now becomes not only evident but a primary coherence in the total organization of what's being experienced. In conversation, you see, this is not necessarily the case. It largely isn't, although people speaking (at least in American speech) do exhibit clusters or this isochronous pattern of phrase groups with one primary stress; so there is a continuing rhythmic insistence in conversation. But this possibility has been increased in poetry so that now the rhythmic and sound organization have been given a very marked emphasis in the whole content. Prose rhythms in poetry are simply one further possibility of articulating pace; these so-called prose rhythms tend to be slower so that therefore they give perhaps a useful drag.

I would like to make the point that it isn't that poets are using common words or common vocabulary. This kind of commonness is deceptive. For example, if one reads Williams carefully, he finds that the words are not largely common. What is common is the *mode* of address, the way of speaking that's commonly met with in conversations. But when that occurs in poetry, already there's a shift that is significant: that fact in a poem is very distinct from that fact in conversation. And I think what really was gained from that sense of source in common speech was the recognition that the intimate knowing of a way of speaking—such as is gained, as Olson says, with the mother's milk—offers the kind of intensity that poetry peculiarly admits.

Q: You have written recently that it is not the single word choices so much as it is the sound of rhythm of entire passages that determines the immediacy of the language.

A: Last fall Basil Bunting told me that his own grasp of what poetry might be for him was first gained when he recognized that the sounds occurring in a poem could carry the emotional content of the poem as ably as anything "said." That is, the modifications of sounds—and the modulations—could carry this emotional content. He said, further, that, while the lyric gives an inclusive and intense singularity, usually, to each word that is used, in a longer poem such as his own "The Spoils," there's an accumulation that can occur much more gradually so that sounds are built up in sustaining passages and do not, say, receive an individual presence but accumulate that presence as a totality. So that one is not aware, let us say, that the word *the* is carrying its particular content; but as that *e* sound or *th* sound accumulates, it begins to exert an emotional effect that is gained not by any insistence on itself as singular word but as accumulation. To quote Pound again, "Prosody consists of the total articulation of the sound in a poem"—and that's what I'm really talking about.

Q: Is line and stanza arrangement still used to indicate what the poet intends, rhythmically? Are poets today more concerned with the sound or with the visual appearance *per se* of their work?

A: For myself, lines and stanzas indicate my rhythmic intention. I don't feel that any poet of my acquaintance whose work I respect is working primarily with the visual appearances except for Ian Finlay; and Finlay is working in a very definite context of language which has to do with the fact that there have been *printed* words for now, say, 400 years. The experience of words as printed has provided a whole possibility of that order as visual as opposed to oral or audible. Ian conceives language as what one sees on signboards, stop signs, titles of books—where the words *are* in that sense; and there is an increasing school of poets who are involved with concrete poetry in that way. But for myself the typography of poetry is still simply a means of scoring— in a musical sense—of indicating how I want the poem to be read.

Q: I have noticed in your own readings that you pause after each line, even though many of the lines are very short. You're not just creating quatrains of fairly even shape, then?

A: No, I tend to pause slightly after each line. Those terminal endings give me a way of both syncopating and indicating a rhythmic measure. I think of those lines as something akin to the bar in music—they state the rhythmic modality. They indicate the basic rhythm of the poem.

The quatrain, to me, operates somewhat like the paragraph in prose. It is both a semantic measure and a rhythmic measure. It's the full unit of the latter. I remember Pound in a letter one time saying, "Verse consists of a constant and a variant." The quatrain, for me, is the constant. The variant, then, can occur in the line, but the basic rhythm also has a constant which the quatrain in its totality indicates. I wanted something stable, and the quatrain offered it to me, as earlier the couplet form had. This, then, allows all variability of what could be both said and indicated as rhythmic measure.

Q: Where in this whole discussion does your often-quoted statement, "Form is never more than an extension of content," fall?

A: Olson had lifted that statement from a letter I had written him, and I'm very sure it was my restatement of something that he had made clear to me. It's not at all a new idea. I find it in many people, prose writers as well as poets—Flaubert, for example. I would now almost amend the statement to say, "Form is what happens." It's the fact of things in the world, however they are. So that form in that way is simply the presence of any thing.

What I was trying then to make clear was that I felt that form —if removed from that kind of intimacy—became something static and assumptional. I felt that the way a thing was said would intimately declare *what* was being said, and so therefore, form was never more than an extension of what it was saying. The what of what was being said gained the how of what was being said, and the how (the mode) then became what I called "form." I would again refer the whole question to Olson's "Projective Verse." It's the attempt to find the intimate form of what's being stated as it's being stated.

A few weeks ago I was moved to hear Morgenthau in the teach-in which was televised saying, "Facts have their own dynamic." In other words, content has its own form.

Q: Let's move to a somewhat different issue now. Recent happenings have made many of us question what the artist's responsibility actually is to his culture. Lowell's refusal to attend the White House Culture-fest, the Artists' and Writers' Protest against policies in Vietnam—what *should* the artist be doing, politically?

A: Well, it's impossible that a man should be only a "fact" in himself. I suppose what Robert Lowell was saying was, among other things, that he simply didn't want to be part of a group of people who were not only admitting but making use of a social occasion that was also a demonstration of commitment to a way of thinking that he himself found very suspect. I know that many of my fellow writers, for example, Allen Ginsberg, Charles Olson, and Robert Duncan in his recent poems (*Passages*), have undertaken a very direct involvement with contemporary political events—as Duncan's poem called "The Multiversity" and the two or three poems that follow it in the cycle show. These as very abrupt and highly articulate attacks upon modern political contexts.

Q: Today's artist should not be an ivory-tower iconoclast, then?

A: No. It's impossible that a man should be indifferent to what qualifies his existence. That is, my ability to live and make a living and secure the possibility of family for myself—this is political. Its *polis* is the fact of people living together in some common place and time. And all that relates to it is a large part of life indeed. I can no more avoid political concerns than I can avoid the fact that it's raining outside.

Now what I'm going to do about it is a question intimate to my own nature and decisions involved with that nature. I have, for example, joined in the protest that you mention. And in my conduct both as a teacher and as a writer, I would like to think that any time these concerns confront me I am not only prepared, in some specious sense, but also obliged to say what I feel. I will lend whatever time and support I can give to a protest. But I'm not often able to involve a political context in my writing; consequently I have felt at times a kind of dismay that I was being irresponsible. But I have found reassurance in a statement that Williams made some time ago (early 50s) on receiving the National Book Award.

It goes something like this. "In dreams, as the poet W. B. Yeats has told us, begin responsibilities. The government of the words is our responsibility since it is of all governments the archetype." And then he notes the fact that in this conduct of words many poets have as a result been killed outright or driven into exile. That is, language is a political act. Anything that enters into the world as decision of this order involves the political context.

So that I have felt that if, in my own conduct as a writer, I could propose commitment as a "man standing by his word," and if I would not be blocked or shamed or coerced (as Allen would say) out of my natural skin—then possibly I would be making my contribution to the political reality of the time during which I lived.

I would hate, however, to confuse political reality with what one can call "topicality." That is, I am dismayed that so soon after the assassination of President Kennedy there was a proposal by two men, very sincere and well meaning in their suggestion, to edit a collection of poems on the death of President

Kennedy. And I questioned their project when I got their letter. I said, first of all, that I had no poems that were involved directly with his death and therefore couldn't contribute; but, further, that I thought they were making capital so to speak of an event that was much more profound in its implications than this use of it would indicate. I felt they were rushing this thing into print almost too conveniently.

You see, we're back again to Williams' sense of the government of the words as our responsibility. What outrages the articulation of feeling in language, what subverts language to the meager reality of distorted and finally criminal acts against men, what distorts and beguiles and coerces by means of language can only, I think, be confronted by a use of language which makes obvious that criminal distortion on the part of those who make use of it. In other words, it's impossible either to ignore or to separate oneself from such a circumstance. It means for me personally that language must be more insistent in its articulations than ever, must be more articulate in all ways, so as not to lose the possibility of saying what one feels in a world which has been given such assumptions that at times it's a nightmare to think how to confront them with sufficient energy and definition, to embarrass them in their own place.

Q: In return for this concern, then, should there be any state or federal responsibility to the arts?

A: I feel, no. I have never wanted the patronage of any state or federal government. I feel that it's a very great danger. Allen Ginsberg, for example, reporting his conversations with Yevtushenko and the other poets in Russia recently, said that one of the largest dilemmas they have concerning the circumstances of American writers is the fact that American writers seem to work outside of the structure of the government they have. Not that they are indifferent to that structure, but that they work apart from it. The state in Russia, Allen was saying, is such an admitted fact that it is impossible for them to think any articulation can occur apart from its structure. Yevtushenko, for example, had just written a very long poem, and was then asked by the censors to make some four hundred corrections. Now he did that because, for him, it's impossible to think of how a poem can occur in his situation without being subject to this limitation.

Q: Without government assistance, what is the financial answer for today's artists? How can the poet support himself and his family, and still have adequate time to write? You have taught in various colleges; do you feel that teaching is compatible with writing?

A: I've known so many writers with so many various jobs that I think there's no single answer. I was listening to a discussion recently in which it was pointed out that Ives, after all, was a very wealthy man and that his music is certainly very significant; yet that some other composer might be poor indeed. In short, the conditions for writing aren't so simply defined. Each man makes whatever solution is possible. I've found myself often embarrassed by the fact that when I do have time provided for me, as by grants, then I'm almost shut up. Simply having the time designated as time "in which to write" seems to make that writing impossible. This is not a plea *not* to be given such grants, because I have other uses for them; and I feel the rest and the accumulation of things that they make possible is very useful to me. But no, I am living as I find I can, and I assume all other men to do the same thing. Some can't; then it's a question of who can help, but there's no easy solution.

Poets have been so many kinds of persons that there is no one solution that will apply to even three of them. They've been so many things. As we know of Williams in his own life, being a doctor obviously was of great importance to him. I don't know what being an insurance executive meant to Wallace Stevens, but it apparently gave him the possibilities he was after. On the other hand, someone like Lew Welch, whom I met recently in San Francisco—the jobs he's done in his life have been important to him: working on fishing boats or for the Forestry Service. Each man comes to a solution.

I find for my own case that teaching is compatible with writing; it gives me a way of living in the world. It earns me the living I need, and it's an activity that I can respect. No matter how often I find individual instances that I don't respect, it gives me an active voice in something I can respect myself in doing. It's compatible with writing in that it lets me find the world, and it allows me admission to a world that's constantly coming into being—that is, as I understand it, as of next year fifty percent of the population of this country will be 25 years old or younger. Many of those people are in colleges or universities; that is the context for their activities—for example, the Free Speech Movement in Berkeley. So it's a very interesting place to be now.

Q: Speaking of place, Bob—as you do frequently in your work —what is the influence of geography on an artist? What I'm thinking of specifically is that at one time artists clustered in a few large cities. Today, however, there are many *isolatos*— Vassar Miller, Robert Bly, James Wright, and yourself. Why?

A: Unlike painting, for example, which does require some kind of location (if you want to see what's going on in painting you live in Los Angeles or New York, simply because the galleries and museums in those places are active referents), writing can be sent to somebody who lives ten thousand miles away. Writing doesn't require that you be present. When one's young it is extremely important to be in close contact with stimulating people. You must try to find what's particular to your own possibility. But by the age of 35 or 40 one goes about one's own work in a more decisive and more determined fashion. Once that happens, it is not necessary to be so closely in touch with others. I, for example, like isolation, or at least I find it useful to me. At times I balk against it very much. But I like it in that it gives me long uninterrupted periods when I can work, no matter what I may be doing for a living. I find I can pay attention to what's really confronting me more simply in this environment than I can in the city where I'm distracted by both curiosity and sympathy, by all that's going on around me. And it isn't so much that it won't be of use to me, but I mean, I can't—I've got my work to do just as these other men have their work to do; and in order to do it, I need a time and privacy that's particular to myself.

Q: Could we return to associations for a moment? You've mentioned Olson and Duncan and Ginsberg frequently. I know you are friends, but what influence has the writing of, say, Olson had on your poetry? Have any poets really been important in the development of your art?

A: It's almost impossible to qualify that sufficiently. Olson was the first reader I had, the first man both sympathetic and articulate enough to give me a very clear sense of what the effect of my writing was, in a way that I could make use of it. His early reading of my stories particularly was very, very helpful to me. I found him the ideal reader, and have always found him so. At the same time, his early senses of how I might make the line intimate to my own habits of speaking—that is, the groupings and whatnot that I was obviously involved with—was a great release for me. I had been trying to write in the mode of Wallace Stevens and it just hadn't worked. The period, the rhythmic period that he was using, just wasn't intimate to my own ways of feeling and speaking. And so, much as I respected him I couldn't use him at all. Williams came in too and he had large influence, but it was Olson curiously enough in the "Projective Verse" piece (I think I'm right in saying that the first section of that is taken in part at least from letters that Olson wrote me, the part about from the heart to the line, where he's explaining his sense of the line and the relation to breath) who really made clear to me what the context of writing could be in a way that no other man had somehow ever quite managed.

Denise Levertov certainly in those early years was very important to me. We talked so much and exchanged so much sense of mutual concern while living in France. She's very important to me; we share both a respect for Williams and an interest in problems of writing. Paul Blackburn in the same period also. Robert Duncan is one of the most warm and sympathetic friends I've ever had. And Allen equally, because Allen reassured me as Williams had that my emotions were not insignificant, that their articulation was really what I was given to be involved with. Ed Dorn—many, many men. It's impossible to list them all.

Q: One last question, Bob: of all the great poets America has seen in this century, which do you think will have the greatest influence in the years to come?

A: Very difficult—that's future, and I don't live in the future.

At present it would seem to me—and I can only speak of my own condition—the most singular poet of this time known to me is, of course, Ezra Pound. And then from my own personal terms, my own nature leads me to Williams. Williams and Pound are the great centers for my own sources. And then there is Louis Zukofsky very much akin to my own nature and therefore very instructive to me; Basil Bunting in England, who happily is now enjoying an increasingly insistent reputation; Charles Olson—I would feel that these five men were absolutely singular and absolutely to be respected. And then Robert Duncan. It's awfully hard to say more. These are the men I've most learned from. I'm now, in effect, rediscovering Bunting after having read his first and only book years ago when I was too young or too inept to make much use of it.

So, in the immediate American context, I would feel that Olson and Zukofsky, and then the two who to my mind come just before them, Pound and Williams, are the centers of the world I live in. Whether that world will survive or not is, of course, something I have no ability either to propose or even, perhaps, to understand.

[*1965*]

EDWARD DORN

What I See in *The Maximus Poems*

_____

PART I: THERE ARE PLACES

There are a handful of places in America today where artists gather, in all their varieties, and some of them, New York, San Francisco, are large cities, with all the commitments to that size, i.e., streets that are busy over most of the day, traffic problems, buildings filled with other people, and generally, the so-called frenzy of specially concentrated peoples. Suburbs where it is said the really important people like computers live, and so on. Other towns, Santa Fe, Taos, Aspen, perhaps a place or two in Missouri, and the ones in New England, are much smaller, the buildings, streets, parties, private libraries and public, don't come on so fabulously. It is dangerous to imply that artists are either numerous or plentiful, no matter how true it is they are widespread. This doesn't at all depend on what one's *taste* is.

I find myself in one such particular place. Right now, this evening, there are some very nice bells coming from Christo Rey. Across the Santa Fe River. Perhaps a half-mile away. The sound fading into groves of cottonwood. There are departures like this that belie all the other grossnesses of this town, and for a brief period the sense is changed, and you feel as it is possible to feel about Santa Fe, not as the various literatures tell you you should. One really *is* in New Mexico. One really *is* 7000 feet high. The threading Rio Grande really *is* off to the right, though many miles, down through what is to this day, a desolate and very breathtaking country. But the sweep-out of that land one can see standing here, where it runs down all the way more and more barren, away from

293

the pine breaks of the mountains, to a moon-land, to Albuquerque, and below. And then at this time once in a while, I walk up to the ridge back of the house and can see the most standing thing on any of the horizons: the bulwark of the Sandias which is opposite Albuquerque. Or as Meline said, Albuquerque lies at the foot of . . . 60 miles south. For all of it is clearness, visibility, the sky itself is variation, accompanying the landscape.

Artists and skies, the range of the Sandias, later, the Indians and a few other things. This is perhaps a harsh way to talk, throwing the components of this place together, human and nonhuman, all together in the same bag. I certainly don't do this because I am impelled toward that basis from a wish to be modern and cold, "dehumanized." Not at all. In those terms, I know what I am doing. The reason is: it is not in my hands to do otherwise. As everyone knows, places vary widely. In spite of the fact the earth is reputed to be a ball, the formality stops there. And that man is of one species and can interbreed, endlessly, is not the same thing. Man makes his true hybrids manifest in the acts of men. Ultimately the general mass of men act the same from a desire, but as you come up, there is a smaller way of looking at it. For instance, Kemerer is not the same as Santa Fe, which is not the same as Biloxi. But all men try to act the same, there is the generality. "Nature is less indulgent. After the mule comes nothing." said Gauguin.

So that place has to shift for itself, largely. It is all *there*, certainly, and presumably, always was, but that isn't enough. Man, who is distinct from nature, will attempt almost anything. This has, unfortunately, a limited interest, for the rest of us. Because, though the direction, even stated intent, may differ, be a nuance, the place he comes back to, to show the rest of us, the spot as a motivation, his very maligning reason, does not change, it officially is always the same. And when he takes off from the green and grey earth, from wherever, Kemerer or Santa Fe, he returns with the news, not surprising, that the planets are inhabited by the same creatures he is, with the same propensities for the half-cocked, the same deception in his well-stated motives. Finds, and brings back specimens we are already shy of, alas. But the trip out was ostentatious. That is not rewarding, either. Because place, as a nonhuman reality, is simply outside the presentments of human meaning. And not interesting. Although sometimes it may be. But I doubt it.

No. Where the depth, the strata are, that we as human beings require it, to be satisfied with the revelation, the recurring nouns that pronounce our lives, these are wilder places, not cast indefinitely upon the earth any more than gold is. Prose flounders now because it seeks to celebrate indiscriminately, out of a need for relief (we have gotten so far from catharsis the word can't be used), but the relief doesn't come on a continuing plane, and it is rather pitiful to see its aspects of commentary dwindle to the size of sociologist apprehensions. Invention is not the point. That Indians and artists and the mountains are the same here as the merchants the artists and the mountains, all lying in the strata of promotion I would never argue with. Because, having a flagging patience, I won't bring forth something which balks at coming. Not that it depends on me and my ability. It is that I refuse to be a party to any sort of obscurity.

Places, the geographic and oceanic tidal surgings which have been common ground for man since time, are built, not rebuilt (that refers to ruins, for which there is no hope) or they are birthed again. There is no loss implied although I can't seem to shake a term that implies *second* or *following*. . . . Anyway a beautiful thing is occurring in America, today. By the way, I don't use the term Place as a mannerism, as an indiscriminate word, covering the "doings of man," at all. Not in any of the senses of the usability of anything, there is no functionalism meant, we mustn't have anything to do with arrangements put into people's hands, with reports or accounts, at the same time not discounting it is a Place, where the din, of everything that happened there, and is, comes to the ear, and eye, the building front, the woman's smile influenced by the school she attended etc., but that man standing at the side of the street shouting in Navajo, at the police cars, shaking his fist, going back and forth in a frenzy across the plaza to stand there, shaking his fist screaming in abrupt Navajo, at the passing cars.

The beautiful thing is the writing now of *The Maximus Poems*. This is all that I am saying Santa Fe would only hypocritically yield. I.e., one could force it out, carry it farther than Vestal would, but it would be a trick, and interesting as that might be, it wouldn't at all serve to spring immensities of reality, of art, because they were never here. I am aware that at any time such a statement can be "disproven." Men came into this area governed on the one hand by what they distinctly found—Indians & raw space in front of them, and carrying, a principle—Spanish Christianity, which produced at most some interesting carved doors and Santos. That's about it. That isn't good enough to support a structure of place. Indeed it propagates a condition for the effete, not the human art; the latter is dreadfully more deep and wide than the first. That is precisely why you found that the archaeologist, the anthropologist and the sociologist, take them all as one, flocked here. There was from the start a superabundance of the effete condition, surface, large thin space, and a principle just dead enough and known enough to make a likeable and easy complication in what they found. Which was *things,* which are effete. This is not a generality. It is awfully particular, it takes a very exacting registration, such as *Maximus* is capable of, to make *things* not effete, effects. The same thing, superficiality, probably explains too why opera is so popular here. And at the same time a predicament. Everyone wants an Art. But they want it too easily and casually, and they subscribe to very spurious people to get it sometimes. There is a series of letters in the local newspaper disputing the quality of reviews of the Opera. Naturally, when the local newspaper proceeded on its own account, for the first two or three performances it handled the thing as a social occasion. Which I comply with, opera has no possibility of art, it *is* a social occasion. But the ringer came when cultured people recognized this as a poor reflection on the *Place,* hence themselves, since they make up a disproportionate number. They wanted critical reviews, strictures, saying in effect, that this or that was or was not so etc., treating the thing seriously, analyzing, cribbing the procedures of art. Of course it is indisputable that these people are art lovers. But what is that? This is the point: you don't have a place just because you barge in on it as a literal physical reality, or want it to prosper because you live there. Instead go see the Grand Canyon, that's what it was made for. Place, you have to have a man bring it to you. You are *casual.* This is a really serious business, and *not* to be tampered with. You might just as well live in Buenos Aires or Newfoundland, it doesn't make a damn bit of difference. But being casual, you have to be patient and intelligent.

Now, once we have got our place, or hope for it, the fine reliev- ing quality and discrimination, Gloucester, the thing is then art, and you can never go to it, by any other route. It is the complex instrument I at least never cease to carry with me and be kept alive by, live under, and feel myself very damn glad to be on this lovely earth, having been given this gift. This is probably the only sense in which I am a child. It seems to me the way Homer must have worked. Not to be underneath the writing, not to have to pay attention to that. Olson is a master in the normal sense, i.e., there is no trafficking possible with his means, so tied to the source is he with his art. Nor can we learn anything of use from him. When other poets, those who exchange terms, whose mechanisms in a sense overlap, or make sense in a functional procedural way to one another, address him "for Charles Olson" it isn't necessarily improper, who is to say that, but it is beautifully senseless. As a man he is in Gloucester, that is definitely something else. One takes uses from minor writers. This is their availability and to some extent their value, they are not deeply tied and the display of their talent is thinly spread, covered with bubbles, temporarily available to the eyes. They come to realizations late, and as an afterthought to their art. Wilde is an example. They never resur- rect, theirs is a technology of the senses. It isn't that Olson doesn't manifest the same recognizable properties that mark writing. It is that the terms are not extractable from the whole art: there are no terms, but there is the term of the form. It isn't just a piece of logic to say that for the total art of Place to exist there has to be this coherent form, the range of implication isn't even calculable. I know *master* is a largish word. I don't mean my master. I mean Dostoevsky, Euripides. The power. It is a removal from the effete and at the same time the aesthetic. There was a certain fascism (not the political term) that existed in american writing for the last 35 years or more or less, in which the zeal for material effect was the cardinal quality, material effect being something that impresses itself by virtue of itself, per se, in which the springing is neither inward nor outward, but merely within. Images suffer. Techné is brought in.

Well, that is ended now, even though it is still practiced. Here in

Santa Fe. The indians are down in the plaza, some of them prob-
ably don't have a way home, but there seem to be many pick-up
trucks. My man is probably there too, screaming in his off-reserva-
tion world. Haniel Long has been dead three years. Somewhere out
there, I don't know where the cemetery is, the wind is blowing over
his grave, blowing the grass and weeds, I must find out where he is
buried.

Long was the only man concerned himself with art, here in the
place, concerned with place. He never had one. He is a minor
writer. A great minor writer, in America, and he had the radical
mind it takes for that kind of art. He was involved with aesthetics,
like minor art is, because the components themselves, the members
that come together to make their art are always on the outside, as
though the building were reversed in its construction, showing its
structure first, enclosing its content, interiorly and arbitrarily. For
want of the aspects of total place. The elements he brings forward
would normally be those given elements that gracefully go together
in an accordance which one could retain the mystery and buoy-
ancy of and thus have the timelessness of the effect, which is what
is lingering, and knows no tenses, the now, the then, the will be.
Cabeza de Vaca and Haniel Long. And, his wandering Christ figure,
who traversed the Southwest barefoot from Denver to the border,
and cured, cast lovely spells, who had long hair, was a man full of
grace and humility, a violent kind, who talked too much, walked,
was lonely, and had meaning and cognizance, was followed, there
was an awe. Would normally have been his elements, had, as I say,
there been a concordance of place for him to work, but reality is
not manysided like a prism here, here geology is, and the excava-
tions will never cease. It was no loss to him probably. I love
Long's writing for this abstraction of fulfillment. It *was* a loss to
us. *Piñon Country* is the specimen of a radical mind with no home,
no anchorage; as artist this is the one factor outside our control.

But when the Place is brought forward fully in form conceived
entirely by the activation of a man who is under its spell it is a
resurrection for us and the investigation even is not extractable.
And it is then the only *real* thing. I am certain, without ever having
been there, I would be bored to sickness walking through Glouces-
ter. Buildings as such are not important. The wash of the sea is not
interesting in itself, that is luxuria, a degrading thing, people as

they stand, must be created, it doesn't matter at all they have reflexes of their own, they are casual, they do more than you could hope to know, it is useful, it is a part of industry. It has an arrogance of intention. This is the significance of Olson's distrust of Thucydides and his care for Herodotus. It is the significance of Blake's "the practice of art is anti-christ." Which further means that if you are not capable of the nonfunctional striking of a World, you are not practicing art. Description, letting things lay, was reserved for not necessarily the doubtful, but the slothful, or the merely busy.

> The places still
> half-dark, mud,
> coal-dust.
>
> There is no light
> east
> of the bridge
>
> Only on the headland
> toward the harbor
> from Cressy's
>
> have I seen it (once
> when my daughter ran
> out on a spit of sand
>
> isn't even there). Where
> is Bristow? when does I-A
> get me home? I am caught
>
> in Gloucester. (What's buried
> behind Lufkin's
> Diner? Who is
>
> Frank Moore?

—"The Librarian"

This is toward the most acute possible measurement. All the arrogance of intention that pervades Place is left out of "The Librarian" poem. The beginning of the poem, right down through the first two stanzas, is the key to this code of location, as of now.

We can come home. From the Pacific or out west. And the ending fragment beginning, "The places still . . . ," is my reunion with the nouns and questionings, of my life, it makes me weep, there is no loss suffered, I am very much excited, what next, who is Frank Moore? When does I-A get me home?

The singular problem is difficult to come at. There is no contention that things, in the sense that one holds them, material things, but that is rather limiting, because utensils aren't only meant, or santos, or carved doors, or the "I" and all its predicament, its environment, inclement and unhappy, and in general the ranges upon ranges of materially disposed things that contain the mines of our lives, there is no contention that these things are really permanently deadening to us, they *are* grotesque in their deathly confrontation. I am perhaps a little suspicious about their strength, but that's all right. The important thing is that the only quarantine we have from them now is this new discovery of a total disposition of them in the human inherited sense. Coming all at once, and large, it is a morphology that up to now has been lacking. There is no aesthetic to bring us back into a social world of intention, delaying by way of modern functionalism our grasp, shortening our vision, putting us back outside again, where we spend so much time traveling the hall of distraction and apportionment, not ever coming to rest in cognizance and lingering mystery. Mystery, as it stands, is not a good word to apply to *Maximus,* because what I see in *The Maximus Poems* is the compelling casting of light over the compounds that make it up. I.e., regardless of their own distinct natures. There is a gain for me since there is nothing I detest so much as objectivity. So my sense of the mystery is: awelike, something unknown but more importantly, cognizant, a crest, by which our common histories are made human again, and thrilling, for *no* other motive than they are ours.

PART II: HOW THE TWO PARTS OF THE
WORLD DO NOT COME TOGETHER.

The minute anything is illustrated for me, a point, a religion, a doctrine etc., I immediately lose interest. Any validities I am able to pick up, I pick up through my own peculiar senses, and I must say it took me long enough to become sufficiently bored with understanding and reason, to abandon them altogether. Haniel Long said, "The nucleus of free People is a matter so delicate that I wonder if we can ever see it except through the eyes of the spirit." Well, I am not considering people so much as I am everything I meet.

It is one of the lovely qualities of Western Man that he is abstract. What I mean by abstract is, as far purely away from nature as he can get, thus bringing into fruition all the properties of man, simply. This same abstraction is the background for his intense ugliness too, and generates such men as scientists, and the men who hire them. It seems a necessary dual. When the Oriental Philosophy scholar uses as an illustration of the "difference between east and west" the construction of a paper flower, taking the petals and stamen from a box and placing them on a wire stem, with his sickening laborious smile, as an example of the way the west makes a flower, Materialism, Process, Power, Arbitrary, you see, Dominion, removing the components from a box and arranging them by Will, as, say, against, the other illustration, now to come in which the flower (the same damn paper flower by the way, always) grows: this is a photographic trick (which is still the west, because that's where the lecture occurs) but in spite of your eyes, this is the flower growing, unfolding itself before your very eyes gents, and it is cynical to see the transfer for what it is and not very kind to the current propaganda for the east. With its tradition of multiple armed gods. But Materialism, Power, Dominion etc. are the ischial callosities (those things that hang down on an orangutan) of the West which are promptly kicked by anyone anywhere who has even a pretense of education.

I imagine some people do believe that in the one example the flower is built out of the force of the "ego" of Western man ("who never lets anything lay") and that in the other the flower really does grow all by itself, a kind of immaculate conception of the universe. Well, whatever happens in immaculate conceptions, I don't trust the universe. I would kick it in the teeth if it came near me. Because I have thus far seen the universe to be in the hands of such men who would parry such examples. Of course it isn't to be imagined that *anyone* is talking about the stars. No, no. This is for much bigger game, the winning and welding, the cohesion of men's souls. The stars are fixed, more or less, already. Whatever the benign outward gesture, only the individual (I don't mean the word in the old doctrinal sense of a way to be a liberal, but as "anyone") has the carrying power of the soul and its responsibilities of the community, also those historical. The consequence of all this is that I don't find the "ego" at all obnoxious, but am aware it is an undesirable word now; what I want though is its centrality. There are other words perhaps less committed one could use in talking of what goes on in *The Maximus Poems*. Enough qualification to say I am not using it as a personal limitation, nor in its political senses. It reverts to my insistence that a creation of the order of *Maximus* comes exclusively from a man, and if dependencies are evident, it is the man we go to for their explication, not the so-called source. But the ego has been dangerous only since Freud defiled it at the same time he saved puritanism, after the latter had nearly died in the late 19th century: by simply and deftly shifting the field of taboo from the body to the mind. Fortunately though, there's no harm done, because the reality and the art remain the same, "only man can make a tree" . . . God's business is subject to mood, and wars with the times.

If I am irrelevant to bring in the ego, you will correct me. But this is what I fully mean: No matter how much I may want ego to be a centrality, it is practically worthless as "center." In the senses of self and center the ego lacks meaning, and this class of senses disintegrates immediately into something cheap and commercial and psychiatric. A center existing within any periphery is simple enough. It is a bore. Its location is a little more interesting but only utilitarianly so, and that, as a pursuit, is a chief method of keeping clever people busy. The technology of the senses. Taking the ear as preparatory opposite of speech, I suppose it plays its part in necessity, but it disturbs me, and I would never give that organ a place other than as a deviant, much like a messenger, who goes about among the princely senses, carrying data which is very often drab in its accuracy and practicality. "I couldn't believe my ears." And seldom do.

There is a term of ego in Maximus, and although I know it as a general thing it branches from specific places. Melville: *Redburn*: What Redburn saw in Launcelott's-Hey: "It's none of my business, Jack. I don't belong to that street." "Who does then?" "I don't know. But what business is it of yours? Are you not a

Yankee?" "Yes," said I, "But come, I will help you remove that woman, if you say so." This could be reduced to nothing more than a "personal concern" but what would be the value of such a point as that? I prefer it in the light of one of the minor workings of Melville's ego, which in other places roamed a much wider pasture. In some senses it is a method, but again that's not what I am taking it as. Rather the great vivid homage, placing a zebra amongst elk, banding with elk. Not as a value concerning either elk or zebra. But as a placement on this earth, as an environment in which things are pronounced, otherwise, I suppose everyone is familiar with the defense of uniformity and placid reason.

And if there is a "good" for mankind as a whole it is in just such an isolation that he gains it for the whole, not, as the decipherers of the problem of how to bring the two halves of the world together "East & West" would have us believe, that we will gain the whole more directly by forsaking Will and Ego, first, become a window through which things, a channel, etc. It isn't so bad that men wish to dominate us, because in a cliché they do anyway, but the realm of thought that seeks to make it "natural" is what I cry out against. Granted that men have a beautiful oceanic sense of their predicament, and that it is common, and that this very sense rests absolutely on the existence of the thing that separates him from and makes him more than the equal of nature (not in the active sense of course, but it is a recent discovery that he must match an earthquake to make his point) there is a terrifying proposition that he abandon the only thing he has with the promise that he later will regain it, even better. And in the interim, when he has his guard down? What will happen? You know goddamn well what will happen, he will never see himself again, but will see the universe or some other ice-cream cone, and then when he is most down they will slip him a bowl of *merde* about having eight arms, and three faces. As if this, finally, isn't a beastly limitation anyway!

Which is enough to say the ego is a dangerous thing. I can't see that Whitman did anything but degenerate it again with his line. I mean in his line. The line is not distinctly responsible for what happened. Its peculiar length and sway is not the working of what is real and birth-giving, the nonargumentative edification of human event. Rather it is the helpless output length of an ego which wasn't practically able to terminate itself in a relationship with nature, so that his participation, his own determinant lagged always before the onslaught of the so-called outside world. It seems an odd time to trot Whitman in. His value is the study of the expansion of the ego. I don't know when ego became personal, but it was an unfortunate thing. But probably it was *made* personal. And that fencing produces only expansion. Expansion has a way of instantly becoming an echo, and is compulsive like Echo. The scream makes its point the first time, which is all right, but it then by rudeness abolishes the recurrence in the mind, which factor is, in fact, about the only thing one has left, granted we are alive. Which is to say, the energy of beauty consumes itself. This is not a valuable suicide.

I know of only two kinds of historic gods. The first are seemingly spontaneous men who appear on the earth and are rather direct in their talents, more or less wise in their ways. And the touching thing about them is that we love them very much and they are figures of great suffering, sympathy and tenderness. And something political happens to them, or they become the property of political intrigue, for civil jurisdiction, then, for centuries. Christ is the most prominent victim, the most prominent of this kind of god. The other kind of god isn't political at all necessarily. But he might be incidentally, and it isn't his suffering that is so important about him. And it is impossible to use him as a force of deception because his clarity rests in beauty. And he remains unexploited in his existence in us, because he is abstract and illustrates nothing tending to be lowly. Hector. He could not be farther from the example of the flower, because again, flowers mean nothing to man except his own flowers, those he has brought forth, and he loves them as does nature love her flowers. This isn't to say he also can't love nature's flowers. A poet created Hector. In a sense Christ wasn't created. This made possible his resurrection, and the resurrection harks back to the immaculate nonhuman conception. Hector is not resurrectable. He lives in the manor of the mind and stands for unalienated beauty. And certainly man has a nature in that sense. Hector died in battle with the natural ugliness of the world, symbolized as the state in the form of Achilles. The death was final. And the abstraction this event drifted to is the pure abstract. Which is to say it is free from the commitments life in general, life in the Everyday, life in its mechanics, has made. Christ is hopelessly involved in the secrets of the State, because his ego was perverted for its use. Hector still possesses a free ego, the kind of circuit which stays in the human breast in the form of beauty (even such a thing as behavior was once beauty), but the ego, as well as beauty, and things abstract, are pagan. Whereas Christ was quickly utilized out of existence, Hector remained, precisely because he wasn't chosen. The chosen is the blackest fate of all, and that's why my heart still yearns over Christ. The Roman world rose on the shoulders of a god which is cut on the secular pattern, because beauty is isolated and abstract, while virtue and grace are infinitely manipulatable. *Maximus* returns to a pre-Christian ordering of the ego, or however, comes forward to a non-Christian ordering—thus journeying out to prepare the day for a new look at man, and what I have thus far read thrills in me as a song about man, from a spirit which has an unerring knowledge of what is decent and lovely and dignified in man.

It would be too much to say that all this is being offered as a strict knowledge of anything. It, needless to say, has a validity only in the sense that it is the quick casting of the world I am in as I look at *Maximus*.

PART III: A LOOK AT THE POEMS: A NON TECHNICAL NOTE

Actually, I'm not going to look at the poems because I already have, many times. There is no point in talking about the way they are put together, in a subtotal sense, because, in the first place, I never had a taste for analysis, and in so far as technique goes, there is Olson's projective verse essay, and besides, any man ought to do that work for himself. Offhand I would say the best single poem to go to to test his own statements about verse is "On first Looking out through Juan de la Cosa's Eyes." I say this to mean it has more exactly the particular turnings, springs, shutters, the weavings, and the riding away, that I take it this verse has when it works best. But picking out that one poem is not the point either, because I at least find a consistency of success which will enable

306 POETICS OF THE NEW AMERICAN POETRY

you to go anywhere to find what might be the very best of the
whole. Which is just great. Because I read, to use an opposite, I
read spontaneously. I.e., I am probably interested in the language
at all times, just because I am. I don't particularly care the way it
is arranged. I like the way it is, on the page, and find great sense in
the way it is, and relevantly, in the way Olson says it ought to be.
But I don't depend on it. In one sense, I am completely anticriti-
cal. But maybe I mean not critical at all. The distinction of
whether a thing is verse or poetry or indeed prose bores me. I hate
the term *verse,* though. Which seems to me so small and clerkish
and embarrassed in the face of Poetry. Poetry is currently put
squeamishly down as a term, as though we are all embarrassed and
afraid of our own knowledges about what it is and what it is not.
To me, by their ring, there is not misunderstanding of such famil-
iar terms. They have no meaning in a literal sense, you always
mean them emotionally anyway, and if this is the case I un-
abashedly say, Poetry. But I, for a niceness, take "The Twist" as
the highest achievement of *The Maximus Poems,* prior to "The
Librarian" (which I understand is not, strictly speaking, a *Maxi-
mus* poem). And the low quarter exists for me in the first line of
all: "By ear, he sd/." This is not a fussing of the given dogma,
because I will leave alone what is necessary for Olson. To me it is
simply a false preamble to a work which I feel vastly, and subse-
quently doesn't comprise the remaining substance of the poem. I
bring it up only because it is a tenet, and as held, the poem takes
its rising from there. And breaks out of that conch wherein the
sound merely, of the sea is heard, along about "The Song and
Dance of," which is the stage setting for "The Twist," to come,
and by that time is definitely off the singular pole of Ear. I say this
not because I notice a clicking change of metrics, or anything that
neat. But because I sense a turning of the human attitude. Already
in "Juan de la Cosa."

And in "The Twist" is the seed sown from which springs "The
Librarian," and if I am correct, what is now to come. The nouns
seem to calm themselves first here, and take on the sheerings and
simplicity of immediate knowledge which resides together in what
is more felt, the searching substantives of the inscribed field of
Gloucester. Are the measure of where we are always. It has a nice
closeness. The compounds, Olson and me, or whoever. Beginning

"Trolley-cars/ are my inland waters" the compound is spoken quite distinctly as in the first person: "Or he and I distinguish/" "It rained,/ the day we arrived." "She was staying,/ after she left me," "When I found her" "When I woke." And then follows the two beautiful letters 19 and 20, with the same attendant breathing of the first person nominative, out into reality, "the opening out/ of my countree." And this generosity is essentially different, these pronoun beginnings, than the more or less quick benevolence of "you sing, you/who also/wants." Anyway, it must be obvious, it is the matrix which interests me rather than the metrics.

[*1960*]

DENISE LEVERTOV

An Admonition

———————

And indeed what are the heavens, the earth, nay, every creature, but Hieroglyphics and Emblems of his glory?

FRANCIS QUARLES

You cannot crack a myth as you can crack Minoan. In hieroglyphic the meaning is embodied in the figure itself.

ELIZABETH SEWELL in *The Orphic Voice*

Deliberately to encode knowledge so as to hide it from the vulgar is the task of cipher but never of myth or poetry . . . "This stands for that" . . . is cipher and not myth.

IBID

"No ideas but in things" does not mean "No ideas." Nor does it specify:
"No ideas but in everyday things
modern things
urban things." No! It means that:
poetry appears when meaning is embodied in the figure.

Language is not the dress but the incarnation of thought.

WORDSWORTH

Life is no less complex and mysterious than it has always been. That we dwell in enormous cities, and invent and use astonishing machinery, does not simplify it, but continually reveals the dissolution of limit after limit to physical possibility. Our still tentative

308

awareness of the great gulfs of the unconscious, in constant trans-
formation like the marvellous cloudscapes one sees from a jet
plane, must surely lead to awe, not to supposed simplicity. There-
fore if our poetry is to seek ᵛtruth—and it must, for that is a
condition of its viability, breath to its lungs—then it cannot
confine itself to what you, the editors of *things,* in your prospectus,
have called *direct statement,* but must allow for all the dazzle,
shadow, bafflement, leaps of conjecture, prayers and dream-
substance of that quest.

"Allusions to Acteon do not speak to us of pain and terror,"
you say. I know there have been many poems on mythological
themes written by subject-seeking poets not seriously engaged with
the life of art. Right. But if a poet within himself identifies with
Acteon; or has felt the hand of any god on his shoulder; or has
himself been steeped in the cosmogony and mythological history of
any place and time; then (if he *is* a poet) he can write of it so that
his pain and terror, or delight, will be felt by the reader whether or
not that reader's education has given him specific clues to the
allusion. Or rather, yes, you are right, *allusions* tell one nothing:
Acteon (or any other personage of the imagination) must be
present in the poem. It is that *presentness* that is the "direct state-
ment" I *do* believe in; not the banishment of Acteon. *"A poetry
denies its end in any* descriptive *act, I mean any act which leaves
the attention outside the poem,"* Robert Creeley wrote in "To
Define." (And this—the attention being put or left outside of the
work: given allusions, references, only, to things not present in the
substance of the work—is not the same as having the attention *led
to awareness* of things that though not named, not visible, exist
within the universe of the work.)

"We shall not publish lyrics about Love, because each experi-
ence of love differs from every other experience." But the idea of
Love, the seeking to understand it, may be a passion in a man.
Will you write off Dante, will you write off George Herbert? Will
you write off Robert Duncan today, when he writes for instance,

> for I went down into the end of all things
> to bring up the spirit of Man before me
> > to the beginnings of Love

or:

> The light that is Love
> rushes on toward passion. It verges upon Dark.
> Roses and blood flood the clouds.
> Solitary first riders advance into legend.

Or:

> It is life
> that tenders   green shoots of
> hurt and healing

> we name Love.

"We shall look for innovation in the content and language of a poem, not in its form. There are no new forms: free verse is merely another vehicle available to capable craftsmen." This intention reveals a basic misunderstanding of the nature of form. Form exists only *in* the content and language. The visual shape of a poem is not its form but a result of the notation of its form. Oh, not to quibble, it is true that the set forms exist abstractly, too; sonnet, sestina, etc., have their rules, and one can invent rules for new "forms" in this sense ad infinitum. But this is a rudimentary view. In fact—and not only in organic poetry and "free verse"— form is the total interactive functioning of content and language, including every contributing element. The form of a man is not that he has 2 legs, 2 arms, a head and body and no tail, but the sum of his anatomical, physiological, mental, textural, moral, motor, etc., structure. And the form of a poem comprises all the equivalent components you can think of.

Form is never more than the extension of content. At the Vancouver poetry conference this summer (63) I proposed to Robert Creeley, the originator of this now famous formula, that it should be changed to read:

Form is never more than the revelation *of content*—(to which he agreed).

Against the editorial statement that "There are no new forms: free verse is merely another vehicle," etc., I pose my belief that the poet, not the poem, is a vehicle.

All poetry is experimental poetry. WALLACE STEVENS

Robert Duncan (in *The Day Book,* part of a work in progress centered in a study of the poetry of H.D.,—see a recent issue of *Origin*) has pointed out how the poets and critics of the school of Rational Imagination—and we still have them with us—have regarded words "not as powers but as counters." A misinterpretation of "No ideas but in things" can lead to a similar stance. But the poem leaves the room the moment the poet begins to use its fallen eyelashes, its nailparings, its frozen tears, its drops of blood and eventually its fingers and toes in his checker-game. No, sir.

"Ornament does not interest us." Here again you oversimplify. The "ornaments" in a harpsichord piece show how ornament can be functional. A lapel without a buttonhole, a buttonhole without a flower, are no more virtuous than those whose hole invites a flower, whose flower invites a smile.

We need a poetry not of *direct statement* but of *direct evocation:* a poetry of hieroglyphics, of embodiment, incarnation; in which the personages may be of myth or of Monday, no matter, if they are of the living imagination.

You asked for my "moral support," and how could I *not* give it to a magazine [*Things*] that takes its title from *Paterson,* and from a line that has always meant so much to me? You will know, I think, that it is given with genuine interest, just because, not in spite of, its being in the form of admonition.

[*1964*]

Some Notes on Organic Form

For me, back of the idea of organic form is the concept that there is a form in all things (and in our experience) which the poet can discover and reveal. There are no doubt temperamental differences between poets who use prescribed forms and those who look for new ones—people who need a tight schedule to get anything done, and people who have to have a free hand—but the difference in their conception of "content" or "reality" is functionally more important. On the one hand is the idea that content, reality, experience, is essentially fluid and must be given form; on the other, this sense of seeking out inherent, though not immediately apparent, form. Gerard Manley Hopkins invented the word *inscape* to denote intrinsic form, the pattern of essential characteristics both in single objects and (what is more interesting) in objects in a state of relation to each other; and the word *instress* to denote the experiencing of the perception of inscape, the *apperception* of inscape. In thinking of the process of poetry as I know it, I extend the use of these words, which he seems to have used mainly in reference to sensory phenomena, to include intellectual and emotional experience as well; I would speak of *the inscape of an experience* (which might be composed of any and all of these elements, including the sensory) or of the inscape of a sequence or constellation of experiences.

A partial definition, then, of organic poetry might be that it is a *method of apperception,* i.e., of recognizing what we perceive, and is based on an intuition of an order, a form beyond forms, in which forms partake, and of which man's creative works are analogies, resemblances, natural allegories. Such a poetry is exploratory.

How does one go about such a poetry? I think it's like this: First there must be an experience, a sequence or constellation of perceptions of sufficient interest, felt by the poet intensely enough to demand of him their equivalence in words: he is *brought to speech*. Suppose there's the sight of the sky through a dusty window, birds and clouds and bits of paper flying through the sky, the sound of music from his radio, feelings of anger and love and amusement roused by a letter just received, the memory of some long ago thought or event associated with what's seen or heard or felt, and an idea, a concept, he has been pondering, each qualifying the other; together with what he knows about history; and what he has been dreaming—whether or not he remembers it—working in him. This is only a rough outline of a possible moment in a life. But the condition of being a poet is that periodically such a crosssection, or constellation, of experiences (in which one or another element may predominate) demands, or wakes in him this demand, *the poem*. The beginning of the fulfillment of this demand is to contemplate, to meditate; words which connote a state in which the heat of feeling warms the intellect. To contemplate comes from "templum, temple, a place, a space for observation, marked out by the augur." It means, not simply to observe, to regard, but to do these things in the presence of a god. And to meditate is "to keep the mind in a state of contemplation"; its synonym is "to muse," and to muse comes from a word meaning "to stand with open mouth"—not so comical if we think of "inspiration"—to breathe in.

So—as the poet stands open-mouthed in the temple of life, contemplating his experience, there come to him the first words of the poem: the words which are to be his *way in* to the poem, if there is to be a poem. The pressure of demand and the meditation on its elements culminate in a moment of vision, of crystallization, in which some inkling of the correspondence between those elements occurs; *and it occurs as words*. If he forces a beginning before this point, it won't work. These words sometimes remain the first, sometimes in the completed poem their eventual place may be elsewhere, or they may turn out to have been only forerunners, which fulfilled their function in bringing him to the words which are the actual beginning of the poem. It is faithful attention to the experience from the first moment of crystallization that allows those first or those forerunning words to rise to the surface: and with that same fidelity of attention the poet, from that moment of being *let in* to the possibility of the poem, must *follow through,* letting the experience lead him through the world of the poem, its unique inscape revealing itself as he goes.

During the writing of a poem the various elements of the poet's being are in communion with each other, and heightened. Ear and eye, intellect and passion, interrelate more subtly than at other times; and the "checking for accuracy," for precision of language, that must take place throughout the writing is not a matter of one element supervising the others but of intuitive interaction between all the elements involved.

In the same way, content and form are in a state of dynamic interaction; the understanding of whether an experience is a linear sequence or a constellation raying out from and in to a central focus or axis, for instance, is discoverable only *in the work,* not before it.

Rhyme, chime, echo, repetition: they not only serve to knit the elements of an experience but often are the very means, the sole means, by which the density of texture and the returning or circling of perception can be transmuted into language, apperceived. A may lead to E directly through $B, C,$ and D: but if then there is the sharp remembrance or revisioning of $A,$ this return must find its metric counterpart. It could do so by actual repetition of the words that spoke of A the first time (and if this return occurs more than once, one finds oneself with a refrain—not put there because one decided to write something with a refrain at the end of each stanza but directly because of the demand of the content). Or it may be that since the return to A is now conditioned by the journey through $B, C,$ and $D,$ its words will not be a simple repetition but a variation. . . . Again, if B and D are of a complementary nature, then their thought- or feeling-rhyme may find its corresponding word-rhyme. Corresponding images are a kind of non-aural rhyme. It usually happens that within the whole, that is between the point of crystallization that marks the beginning or onset of a poem and the point at which the intensity of contemplation has ceased, there are distinct units of awareness; and it is—for me anyway—these that indicate the duration of stanzas. Sometimes these units are of such equal duration that one gets a whole poem of, say, three-line stanzas, a regularity of pattern that looks like, but is not, pre-determined.

When my son was eight or nine I watched him make a crayon drawing of a tournament. He was not interested in the forms as such but was grappling with the need to speak in graphic terms, to say, "And a great crowd of people were watching the jousting knights." There was a need to show the tiers of seats, all those people sitting in them. And out of the need arose a formal design that was beautiful—composed of the rows of shoulders and heads. It is in very much the same way that there can arise, out of fidelity to instress, a design that is the form of the poem—both its total form, its length and pace and tone, and the form of its parts (e.g., the rhythmic relationships of syllables within the line, and of line to line; the sonic relationships of vowels and consonants; the recurrence of images, the play of associations, etc.). "Form follows function" (Frank Lloyd Wright).

Frank Lloyd Wright also wrote that the idea of organic architecture is that "the reality of the building lies in the space within it, to be lived in." And he quotes Coleridge: "Such as the life is, such is the form." (Emerson says, "Ask the fact for the form.") The Oxford Dictionary quotes Huxley (Thomas, presumably) as stating that he used the word *organic* "almost as an equivalent for the word 'living.' "

In organic poetry the metric movement, the measure, is the direct expression of the movement of perception. And the sounds, acting together with the measure, are a kind of *extended onomatopoeia*—i.e., they imitate, not the sounds of an experience (which may well be soundless, or to which sounds contribute only incidentally)—but the feeling of an experience, its emotional tone, its texture. The varying speed and gait of different strands of perception within an experience (I think of strands of seaweed moving within a wave) result in counterpointed measures.

Thinking about how organic poetry differs from free verse, I wrote that "most free verse is failed organic poetry, that is, organic poetry from which the attention of the writer had been switched off too soon, before the intrinsic form of the experience had been revealed." But Robert Duncan pointed out to me that there is a "free verse" of which this is not true, because it is written not with any desire to seek a form, indeed perhaps with the longing to *avoid* form (if that were possible) and to express inchoate emotion as purely as possible. There is a contradiction here, however, because if, as I suppose, there is an inscape of emotion, of feeling, it is impossible to avoid presenting something of it if the rhythm or tone of the feeling is given voice in the poem. But perhaps the difference is this: that free verse isolates the "rightness" of each line or cadence—if it seems expressive, O.K., never mind the relation of it to the next; while in organic poetry the peculiar rhythms of the parts are in some degree modified, if necessary, in order to discover the rhythm of the whole.

But doesn't the character of the whole depend on, arise out of, the character of the parts? It does; but it is like painting from nature: suppose you absolutely imitate, on the palette, the separate colors of the various objects you are going to paint; yet when they are closely juxtaposed in the actual painting, you may have to lighten, darken, cloud, or sharpen each color in order to produce an effect equivalent to what you see in nature. Air, light, dust, shadow, and distance have to be taken into account.

Or one could put it this way: in organic poetry the *form sense,* the *tragic sense,* as Stefan Wolpe speaks of it, is ever present *along with* (yes, paradoxically) fidelity to the revelations of meditation. The form sense is a sort of Stanislavsky of the imagination: putting a chair two feet downstage there, thickening a knot of bystanders upstage left, getting this actor to raise his voice a little and that actress to enter more slowly; *all in the interest of a total form he intuits.* Or it is a sort of helicopter scout flying over the field of the poem, taking aerial photos and reporting on the state of the forest and its creatures—or over the sea to watch for the schools of herring and direct the fishing fleet towards them.

A manifestation of form sense is the sense the poet's ear has of some rhythmic norm peculiar to a particular poem, from which the individual lines depart and to which they return. I heard Henry Cowell tell that the drone in Indian music is known as the *horizon note.* Al Kresch, the painter, sent me a quotation from Emerson: "The health of the eye demands a horizon." This sense of the beat or pulse underlying the whole I think of as the horizon note of the poem. It interacts with the nuances or forces of feeling which determine emphasis on one word or another, and decides to a great extent what belongs to a given line. It relates the needs of that feeling-force which dominates the cadence to the needs of the surrounding parts and so to the whole.

Duncan also pointed to what is perhaps a variety of organic poetry: the poetry of linguistic impulse. It seems to me that the absorption in language itself, the awareness of the world of multiple meaning revealed in sound, word, syntax, and the entering into this world in the poem, is as much an experience or constellation of perceptions as the instress of non-verbal sensuous and psychic events. What might make the poet of linguistic impetus appear to be on another tack entirely is that the demands of his realization may seem in opposition to truth as we think of it; that is, in terms of sensual logic. But the apparent distortion of experience in such a poem for the sake of verbal effects is actually a precise adherence to truth since the experience itself was a verbal one.

Form is never more than a *revelation* of content.

"The law—one perception must immediately and directly lead to a further perception." I've always taken this to mean, no *loading of the rifts with ore,* because there are to be no rifts. Yet, alongside of this truth is another truth (that I've learned from Duncan more than from anyone else)—that there must be a place in the poem for rifts too—(never to be stuffed with imported ore). Great gaps between perception and perception which must be leapt across if they are to be crossed at all. The X factor, the magic, is when we come to those rifts and make those leaps. A religious devotion to the truth, to the splendor of the authentic, involves the writer in a process rewarding in itself; but when that devotion brings us to undreamed abysses and we find ourselves sailing slowly over them and landing on the other side—that's ecstasy.

[*1965*]

ALLEN GINSBERG

Notes for *Howl and Other Poems*

By 1955 I wrote poetry adapted from prose seeds, journals, scratchings, arranged by phrasing or breath groups into little short-line patterns according to ideas of measure of American speech I'd picked up from W. C. Williams' imagist preoccupations. I suddenly turned aside in San Francisco, unemployment compensation leisure, to follow my romantic inspiration—Hebraic-Melvillian bardic breath. I thought I wouldn't write a *poem,* but just write what I wanted to without fear, let my imagination go, open secrecy, and scribble magic lines from my real mind—sum up my life—something I wouldn't be able to show anybody, write for my own soul's ear and a few other golden ears. So the first line of *Howl,* "I saw the best minds," etc. the whole first section typed out madly in one afternoon, a huge sad comedy of wild phrasing, meaningless images for the beauty of abstract poetry of mind running along making awkward combinations like Charlie Chaplin's walk, long saxophone-like chorus lines I knew Kerouac would hear the *sound* of—taking off from his own inspired prose line really a new poetry.

I depended on the word "who" to keep the beat, a base to keep measure, return to and take off from again onto another streak of invention: "who lit cigarettes in boxcars boxcars boxcars," continuing to prophesy what I really knew despite the drear consciousness of the world: "who were visionary indian angels." Have I really been attacked for this sort of joy? So the poem got serious, I went on to what my imagination believed true to Eternity (for I'd had a beatific illumination years before during which I'd heard Blake's ancient voice & saw the universe unfold in my brain), &

318

what my memory could reconstitute of the data of celestial experience.

But how sustain a long line of poetry (lest it lapse into prosaic)? It's natural inspiration of the moment that keeps it moving, disparate thinks put down together, shorthand notations of visual imagery, juxtapositions of hydrogen juke-box—abstract haikus sustain the mystery & put iron poetry back into the line: the last line of "Sunflower Sutra" is the extreme, one stream of single word associations, summing up. Mind is shapely, Art is shapely. Meaning Mind practiced in spontaneity invents forms in its own image & gets to Last Thoughts. Loose ghosts wailing for body try to invade the bodies of living men. I hear ghostly Academics in Limbo screeching about form.

Ideally each line of *Howl* is a single breath unit. Tho in this recording it's not pronounced so, I was exhausted at climax of 3 hour Chicago reading with Corso & Orlovsky. My breath is long— that's the Measure, one physical-mental inspiration of thought contained in the elastic of a breath. It probably bugs Williams now, but it's a natural consequence, my own heightened conversation, not cooler average-dailytalk short breath. I got to mouth more madly this way.

So these poems are a series of experiments with the formal organization of the long line. Explanations follow. I realized at the time that Whitman's form had rarely been further explored (improved on even) in the U.S. Whitman always a mountain too vast to be seen. Everybody assumes (with Pound?) (except Jeffers) that his line is a big freakish uncontrollable necessary prosaic goof. No attempt's been made to use it in the light of early XX Century organization of new speech-rhythm prosody to *build up* large organic structures.

I had an apt on Nob Hill, got high on Peyote, & saw an image of the robot skullface of Moloch in the upper stories of a big hotel glaring into my window; got high weeks later again, the Visage was still there in red smokey downtown Metropolis, I wandered down Powell Street muttering, "Moloch Moloch" all night & wrote *Howl* II nearly intact in cafeteria at foot of Drake Hotel, deep in the hellish vale. Here the long line is used as a stanza form broken within into exclamatory units punctuated by a base repetition, Moloch.

The rhythmic paradigm for Part III was conceived & half-written same day as the beginning of *Howl,* I went back later & filled it out. Part I, a lament for the Lamb in America with instances of remarkable lamblike youths; Part II names the monster of mental consciousness that preys on the Lamb; Part III a litany of affirmation of the Lamb in its glory: "O starry spangled shock of Mercy." The structure of Part III, pyramidal, with a graduated longer response to the fixed base.

A lot of these forms developed out of an extreme rhapsodic wail I once heard in a madhouse. Later I wondered if short quiet lyrical poems could be written using the long line. "Cottage in Berkeley" & "Supermarket in California" (written same day) fell in place later that year. Not purposely, I simply followed my Angel in the course of compositions.

What if I just simply wrote, in long units & broken short lines, spontaneously noting prosaic realities mixed with emotional upsurges, solitaries? "Transcription of Organ Music" (sensual data), strange writing which passes from prose to poetry & back, like the mind.

What about poem with rhythmic buildup power equal to *Howl* without use of repeated base to sustain it? "The Sunflower Sutra" (composition time 20 minutes, me at desk scribbling, Kerouac at cottage door waiting for me to finish so we could go off somewhere party) did that, it surprised me, one long Who . . .

Last, the Proem to *Kaddish* (NY 1959 work)—finally, completely free composition, the long line breaking up within itself into short staccato breath units—notations of one spontaneous phrase after another linked within the line by dashes mostly: the long line now perhaps a variable stanzaic unit, measuring groups of related ideas, marking them—a method of notation. Ending with a hymn in rhythm similar to the synagogue death lament. Passing into dactyllic? says Williams? Perhaps not: at least the ear hears itself in Promethian natural measure, not in mechanical count of accent.

I used Chicago Big Table readings (Jan. 1959) of *Howl,* "Sunflower" and *Kaddish* on this record because they're the best I can find. Though the tapes were coarse. And hope the reproduction of that reading will permanently give lie to much philistine slander by the capitalist press and various brain-washed academies. And convince the Lamb. I tried recording *Howl* under better mechanical conditions in studio but the spirit wasn't in me by then. I'm not in control. The rest of the poems were recorded in June '59 Fantasy Studios in SF. "Footnote to *Howl*" may seem sick and strange, I've included it because I trust it will be heard in Heaven, though some cruel ear in U.S. may mock. Let it be raw, there is beauty. These are recorded as best I can now, though with scared love, imperfect to an angelic trumpet in mind, I quit reading in front of live audiences for while. I began in obscurity to communicate a live poetry, it's become more a trap and duty than the spontaneous ball it was first.

A word on Academies; poetry has been attacked by an ignorant & frightened bunch of bores who don't understand how it's made, & the trouble with these creeps is they wouldn't know Poetry if it came up and buggered them in broad daylight.

A word on the Politicians: my poetry is Angelical Ravings, & has nothing to do with dull materialistic vagaries about who should shoot who. The secrets of individual imagination—which are transconceptual & non-verbal—I mean unconditioned Spirit—are not for sale to this consciousness, are of no use to this world, except perhaps to make it shut its trap & listen to the music of the Spheres. Who denies the music of the spheres denies poetry, denies man, & spits on Blake, Shelley, Christ & Buddha. Meanwhile have a ball. The universe is a new flower. America will be discovered. Who wants a war against roses will have it. Fate tells big lies, & the gay Creator dances on his own body in Eternity.

[*Independence Day 1959*]

Introduction to *Gasoline*

Open this book as you would a box of crazy toys, take in your hands a refinement of beauty out of a destructive atmosphere. These combinations are imaginary and pure, in accordance with Corso's individual (therefore universal) DESIRE.

All his own originality! What's his connection, but his own beauty? Such weird haiku-like juxtapositions aren't in the American book. Ah! but the real classic tradition—from Aristotle's description of metaphor to the wildness of his Shelley—and Apollinaire, Lorca, Mayakovsky. Corso is a great word-slinger, first naked sign of a poet, a scientific master of mad mouthfuls of language. He wants a surface hilarious with ellipses, jumps of the strangest phrasing picked off the streets of his mind like "mad children of soda caps."

This is his great *sound:* "O drop that fire engine out of your mouth!"

Crazier: "Dirty Ears aims a knife at me, I pump him full of lost watches."

What nerve! "You, Mexico, you have no Chicago, no white-blonde moll." ("H. G. Wells," unpublished.)

He gets pure abstract poetry, the inside sound of language alone.

But what is he *saying?* Who cares?! It's said! "Outside by a Halloween fire, wise on a charred log, an old man is dictating to the heir of the Goon."

This heir sometimes transcribes perfect modern lyrics anyone can dig: "Italian Extravaganza," "Birthplace Revisited," "Last Gangster," "Mad Yak," "Furnished Room," "Haarlem," "Last Night I Drove a Car," "Ecce Homo," "Hello."

A rare sad goonish knowledge with reality—a hip piss on reality

also—he prefers his dreams. Why not? His Heaven is Poetry. He
explains at length in the great unpublished "Power":

> I do not sing of dictatorial power.
> The stiff arm of dictatorship is symbolic of awful power.
> In my room I have gathered enough gasoline and evi-
>   dence to allow dictators inexhaustible power.
> Am I the stiff arm of Costa Rica?
> Do I wear red and green in Chrysler Squads?
> Do I hate my people?
> Will they forgive me their taxes?
> Am I to be shot at the ràcetrack? Do they plot now?
>
> . . . .
>
> Beautiful people, you too are power. I remember your
>   power.
> I have not forgotten you in the snows of Bavaria skiing
>   down on the sleeping village with flares and car-
>   bines,
> I have not forgotten you rubbing your greasy hands on
>   my aircraft, signing your obscure names on the
>   blockbuster!
> No!
> I have not forgotten the bazooka you decked with palm
>   fastened on the shoulder of a black man aimed at
>   a tank full of Aryans!
> Nor have I forgotten the grenade, the fear and emer-
>   gency it spread throughout your brother's trench.
> You are power, beautiful people!
>
> . . . .
>
> Power is not to be dropped from a plane
> A hat is power
> The world is power
> Being afraid is power
> Standing on a streetcorner waiting for no one is power
> The demon is not as powerful as walking across the
>   street
> The angel is not as powerful as looking and then not
>   looking.

What a solitary dignitary! He's got the angelic power of making autonomous poems, like god making brooks.

"With me automaticism is an entranced moment in which the mind accelerates a constant hour of mind-foolery, mind-genius, mind-madness . . .

"When Bird Parker or Miles Davis blow a standard piece of music, they break off into other own-self little unstandard sounds—well, that's my way with poetry—X Y & Z, call it automatic—I call it a standard flow (because at the offset words are standard) that is intentionally distracted diversed into my own sound. Of course many will say a poem written on that order is unpolished, etc.—that's just what I want them to be—because I have made them truly my own—which is inevitably something NEW—like all good spontaneous jazz, newness is acceptable and expected—by hip people who listen."

"Don't Shoot The Warthog!" The mind has taken a leap in language. He curses like a brook, pure poetry. "I screamed the name: Beauty!" We're the fabled damned if we put it down. He's probably the greatest poet in America, and he's starving in Europe.

[*Amsterdam, Holland Oct 57*]

"When the Mode of the Music Changes the Walls of the City Shake"

Trouble with conventional form (fixed line count & stanza form) is, it's too symmetrical, geometrical, numbered and pre-fixed— unlike to my own mind which has no beginning and end, nor fixed measure of thought (or speech—or writing) other than its own cornerless mystery—to transcribe the latter in a form most nearly representing its actual "occurrence" is my "method"—which requires the Skill of freedom of composition—and which will lead Poetry to the expression of the highest moments of the mind-body—mystical illumination—and its deepest emotion (through tears—love's all)—in the forms nearest to what it actually looks like (data of mystical imagery) & feels like (rhythm of actual speech & rhythm prompted by direct transcription of visual & other mental data)—plus not to forget the sudden genius-like Imagination or fabulation of unreal & out of this world verbal constructions which express the true gaiety & excess of Freedom—(and also by their nature express the First Cause of the world) by means of spontaneous irrational juxtaposition of sublimely related fact,

by the dentist drill singing against the piano music; or pure construction of imaginaries, hydrogen jukeboxes, in perhaps abstract images (made by putting together two things verbally concrete but disparate to begin with)—

always bearing in mind, that one must verge on the unknown, write toward the truth hitherto unrecognizable of one's own sincerity, including the avoidable beauty of doom, shame and embarrassment, that very area of personal self-recognition (detailed individual is universal remember) which formal conventions, internalized, keep us from discovering in ourselves & others—For if we write with an eye to what the poem should be (has been), and do not get lost in it, we will never discover anything new about ourselves in the process of actually writing on the table, and we lose the chance to live in our works, & make habitable the new world which every man may discover in himself, if he lives—which is life itself, past present & future.

Thus the mind must be trained, i.e. let loose, freed—to deal with itself as it actually is, and not to impose on itself, or its poetic artifacts, an arbitrarily preconceived pattern (formal or Subject) —and *all* patterns, unless discovered in the moment of composition—all remembered and *applied* patterns are by their very nature arbitrarily preconceived—no matter how wise & traditional—no matter what sum of inherited experience they represent—The only pattern of value or interest in poetry is the solitary, individual pattern peculiar to the poet's moment & the poem *discovered* in the mind & in the process of writing it out on the page, as notes, transcriptions—reproduced in the fittest accurate form, at the time of composition. ("Time is the essence" says Kerouac.) It is this personal discovery which is of value to the poet & to the reader—and it is of course more, not less, communicable of actuality than a pattern chosen in advance, with matter poured into it arbitrarily to fit, which of course distorts & blurs the matter . . . Mind is shapely, art is shapely.

II

The amount of blather & built-in misunderstanding we've encountered—usually in the name of good taste, moral virtue or (at most presumptuous) civilized value—has been a revelation to me of the absolute bankruptcy of the Academy in America today, or that which has set itself up as an academy for the conservation of literature. For the Academy has been the enemy and Philistine host itself. For my works will be taught in the schools in 20 years, or sooner—it is already being taught for that matter—after the first screams of disgruntled mediocrity, screams which lasted 3 years before subsiding into a raped moan.

They should treat us, the poets, on whom they make their livings, more kindly while we're around to enjoy it. After all we are poets and novelists, not Martians in disguise trying to poison man's mind with anti-earth propaganda. Tho to the more conformist of the lot this beat & Buddhist & mystic & poetic exploration may seem just that. And perhaps it is. "Any man who does not labor to make himself obsolete is not worth his salt."—Burroughs.

People take us too seriously & not seriously enough—nobody interested in what *we* mean—just a lot of bad journalism about beatniks parading itself as highclass criticism in what are taken by the mob to be the great journals of the intellect.

And the ignorance of the technical accomplishment & spiritual interests is disgusting. How often have I seen my own work related to Fearing & Sandburg, proletarian literature, the 1930's—by people who don't *connect* my long line with my own obvious reading: Crane's "Atlantis," Lorca's *Poet in NY*, Biblical structures, psalms & lamentations, Shelley's high buildups, Apollinaire, Artaud, Myakovsky, Pound, Williams & the American metrical tradition, the new tradition of measure. And Christopher Smart's *Rejoice in the Lamb*. And Melville's prose-poem *Pierre*. And finally the spirit & illumination of Rimbaud. Do I have to be stuck with Fearing (who's alright too) by phony critics whose only encounter with a long line has been anthology pieces in collections by Oscar Williams? By intellectual bastards and snobs and vulgarians and hypocrites who have never read Artaud's *Pour en finir avec le jugement de Dieu* and therefore wouldn't begin to know that this masterpiece which in 30 years will be as famous as *Anabasis* is the actual model of tone for my earlier writing? This is nothing but a raving back at the false Jews from Columbia who have lost memory of the Shekinah & are passing for middleclass. Must I be attacked and contemned by these people, I who have heard Blake's own ancient voice recite me the Sunflower a decade ago in Harlem? and who say *I* don't know about "poetic tradition"?

The only poetic tradition is the Voice out of the burning bush. The rest is trash, & will be consumed.

If anybody wants a statement of values—it is this, that I am ready to die for Poetry & for the truth that inspires poetry—and will do so in any case—as all men, whether they like it or no—. I believe in the American Church of Poetry.

And men who wish to die for anything less or are unwilling to die for anything except their own temporary skins are foolish & bemused by illusion and had better shut their mouths and break their pens until they are taught better by death—and I am sick to death of prophesying to a nation that hath no ears to hear the thunder of the wrath & joy to come—among the "fabled damned" of nations—& the money voices of ignoramuses.

We are in American Poetry & Prose still continuing the venerable tradition of compositional self exploration & I would say the time has not come, historically, for any effort but the first sincere attempts at discovering those natural structures of which we have been dreaming & speaking. Generalizations about these natural patterns may yet be made—time for the Academies to consider this in all technical detail—the data, the poetry & prose, the classics of original form, have already been written or are about to be—there is much to learn from them and there may be generalizations possible which, for the uninitiated, the non-poets, may be reduced to "rules & instructions" (to guide attention to what is being done)—but the path to freedom of composition goes through the eternal gateless gate which if it has "form" has an indescribable one—images of which are however innumerable.

There is nothing to agree or disagree with in Kerouac's method —there is a statement of fact (1953) of the method, the conditions of experiment, which he was pursuing, what he thought about it, how he went about it. He actually did extend composition in that mode, the results are apparent, he's learned a great deal from it & so has America. As a proposed method of experiment, as a completed accomplishment, there is nothing to agree or disagree with, it is a fact—that's what he was interested in doing, that's what he did—he's only describing his interest (his passion) for the curious craftsman or critic or friend—so be it. Why get mad and say he's in "error"? There's no more error here than someone learning how to build a unicorn table by building one. He's found out (rare for a writer) *how* he really wants to write & he is writing that way, courteously explaining his way.

Most criticism is semantically confused on this point—should & shouldn't & art is & isn't—trying to tell people to do something other than that which they basically & intelligently want to do, when they are experimenting with something new to them (and actually in this case to U.S. literature).

I've had trouble with this myself, everybody telling me or implying that I shouldn't really write the way I do. What do they want, that I should write some other way I'm not interested in? Which is the very thing which doesn't interest me in their prose & poetry & makes it a long confused bore?—all arty & by inherited rule & no surprised no new invention—corresponding inevitably to their own dreary characters—because anyway most of them have no character and are big draggy minds that don't *know* and just argue from abstract shallow moral principles in the void? These people are all too abstract, when it comes down to the poetry facts of poetry— and I have learned in the past 2 years that argument, explanation, letters, expostulation are all vain—nobody listens anyway (not only to what I say, to what I *mean*), they all have their own mental ax to grind. I've explained the prosodaic structure of *Howl* as best I can, often, and I still read criticism, even favorable, that assumes that I am not interested in, have no, form—they just don't recognize any form but what they have heard about before & expect & what they want (they, most of them, being people who don't write poetry even & so have no idea what it involves & what beauty they're violating).—And it is also tiresome & annoying to hear K or myself or others "Beat" described because of our art as Incoherent, we are anything but. After all.

But so far we have refused to make arbitrary abstract generalizations to satisfy a peculiar popular greed for Banality. I perhaps lose some of this ground with this writing. I occasionally scream with exasperation (or giggles); this is usually an attempt to communicate with a blockhead. And Kerouac sometimes says "Wow" for joy. All this can hardly be called incoherence except by ververbal madmen who depend on longwinded defenses of their own bad prose for a livelihood.

The literary problems I wrote of above are explained at length in Dr. Suzuki's essay Aspects of Jap Culture (*Evergreen Review*) & placed in their proper aesthetic context. Why should the art of spontaneity in the void be so, seem so, strange when applied in the U.S. prosepoetry context? Obviously a lack of intuitive spirit and/or classical experience on the part of these provincial frauds who have set themselves up as conservators of tradition and attack our work.

A sort of philistine brainwashing of the public has taken place. How long the actual sense of the new poetry will take to filter down, thru the actual writing and unprejudiced sympathetic reading of it, is beyond my power to guess & at this point beyond my immediate hope. More people take their ideas from reviews, newspapers & silly scholarly magazines than they do from the actual texts.

The worst I fear, considering the shallowness of Opinion, is that some of the poetry & prose may be taken too familiarly, and the ideas accepted in some dopey sociological platitudinous form—as perfectly natural ideas & perceptions which they are—and be given the same shallow treatment, this time sympathetic, as, until recently, they were given shallow unsympathy. That would be the very woe of fame. The problem has been to communicate the very spark of life, and not some opinion about that spark. Most negative criticism so far has been fearful overanxious obnoxious opinionation about this spark—and most later "criticism" will equally dully concern itself with favorable opinions about that spark. And that's not art, that's not even criticism, that's just more dreary sparkless blah blah blah—enough to turn a poet's guts. A sort of cancer of the mind that assails people whose loves are eaten by their opinions, whose tongues are incapable of wild lovely thought, which is poetry.

The brainwashing will continue, tho the work be found acceptable, and people will talk as emptily about the void, hipness, the drug high, tenderness, comradeship, spontaneous creativity, beat spiritual individuality & sacramentalism, as they have been talking about man's "moral destiny" (usually meaning a good job & full stomach & no guts and the necessity of heartless conformity & putting down your brother because of the inserviceability of love as against the legal discipline of tradition because of the unavailability of God's purity of vision & consequent souls angels—or anything else worthwhile). That these horrible monsters who do nothing but talk, teach, write crap & get in the way of poetry, have been accusing us, poets, of lack of "values" as they call it is enuf to make me vow solemnly (for the second time) that pretty soon I'm going to stop even trying to communicate coherently to the majority of the academic, journalistic, mass media & publishing trade & leave them stew in their own juice of ridiculous messy ideas. SQUARES SHUT UP & LEARN OR GO HOME. But alas the square world will never and has never stopt bugging the hip muse.

That we have begun a revolution of literature in America, again, without meaning to, merely by the actual practice of poetry—this would be inevitable. No doubt we knew what we were doing.

[*1961*]

Poetry, Violence,
and The Trembling Lambs

Recent history is the record of a vast conspiracy to impose one
level of mechanical consciousness on mankind and exterminate all
manifestations of that unique part of human sentience, identical in
all men, which the individual shares with his Creator. The suppres-
sion of contemplative individuality is nearly complete.

The only immediate historical data that we can know and act on
are those fed to our senses through systems of mass communi-
cation.

These media are exactly the places where the deepest and most
personal sensitivities and confessions of reality are most prohib-
ited, mocked, suppressed.

At the same time there is a crack in the mass consciousness of
America—sudden emergence of insight into a vast national sub-
conscious netherworld filled with nerve gases, universal death
bombs, malevolent bureaucracies, secret police systems, drugs that
open the door to God, ships leaving Earth, unknown chemical
terrors, evil dreams at hand.

Because systems of mass communication can communicate only
officially acceptable levels of reality, no one can know the extent of
the secret unconscious life. No one in America can know what will
happen. No one is in real control. America is having a nervous
breakdown.

Poetry is the record of individual insights into the secret soul of
the individual—and, because all individuals are One in the eyes of
their Creator, into the soul of the World. The world has a soul.

America is having a nervous breakdown. San Francisco is one
of many places where a few individuals, poets, have had the luck

and courage and fate to glimpse something new through the crack in mass consciousness; they have been exposed to some insight into their own nature, the nature of the governments, and the nature of God.

Therefore there has been great exaltation, despair, prophecy, strain, suicide, secrecy, and public gaiety among the poets of the city.

Those of the general populace whose individual perception is sufficiently weak to be formed by stereotypes of mass communication disapprove and deny the insight. The police and newspapers have moved in, mad movie manufacturers from Hollywood are at this moment preparing bestial stereotypes of the scene.

The poets and those who share their activities, or exhibit some sign of dress, hair, or demeanor of understanding, or hipness, are ridiculed. Those of us who have used certain benevolent drugs (marijuana) to alter our consciousness in order to gain insight are hunted down in the street by police. Peyote, an historic vision-producing agent, is prohibited on pain of arrest. Those who have used opiates and junk are threatened with permanent jail and death. To be a junky in America is like having been a Jew in Nazi Germany.

A huge sadistic police bureaucracy has risen in every state, encouraged by the central government, to persecute the illuminati, to brainwash the public with official lies about the drugs, and to terrify and destroy those addicts whose spiritual search has made them sick.

Deviants from the mass sexual stereotype, quietists, those who will not work for money, or fib and make arms for hire, or join armies in murder and threat, those who wish to loaf, think, rest in visions, act beautifully on their own, speak truthfully in public, inspired by Democracy—what is their psychic fate now in America? An America, the greater portion of whose economy is yoked to mental and mechanical preparations for war?

Literature expressing these insights has been mocked, misinterpreted, and suppressed by a horde of middlemen whose fearful allegiance to the organization of mass stereotype communication prevents them from sympathy (not only with their own inner nature but) with any manifestation of unconditioned individuality. I mean journalists, commercial publishers, book-review fellows, multitudes of professors of literature, etc., etc. Poetry is hated. Whole schools of academic criticism have risen to prove that human consciousness of unconditioned Spirit is a myth. A poetic renaissance glimpsed in San Francisco has been responded to with ugliness, anger, jealousy, vitriol, sullen protestations of superiority.

And violence. By police, by customs officials, post-office employees, by trustees of great universities. By anyone whose love of Power has led him to a position where he can push other people around over a difference of opinion—or Vision.

The stakes are too great—an America gone mad with materialism, a police-state America, a sexless and soulless America prepared to battle the world in defense of a false image of its Authority. Not the wild and beautiful America of the comrades of Whitman, not the historic America of Blake and Thoreau where the spiritual independence of each individual was an America, a universe, more huge and awesome than all the abstract bureaucracies and Authoritative Officialdoms of the World combined.

Only those who have entered the world of Spirit know what a vast laugh there is in the illusory appearance of worldly authority. And all men at one time or other enter that Spirit, whether in life or death.

How many hypocrites are there in America? How many trembling lambs, fearful of discovery? What Authority have we set up over ourselves, that we are not as we Are? Who shall prohibit an art from being published to the world? What conspirators have power to determine our mode of consciousness, our sexual enjoyments, our different labors and our loves? What fiends determine our wars?

When will we discover an America that will not deny its own God? Who takes up arms, money, police and a million hands to murder the consciousness of God? Who spits in the beautiful face of Poetry which sings of the Glory of God and weeps in the dust of the world?

[*1959*]

Prose Contribution
to Cuban Revolution

I have been sitting in lovely club-bar across the street where Greek boys congregate, they are friendly & they make love between men like in Plato, the whole classic love scene preserved intact with no faggotry involved, a huge relief to find it's really true & good as an Ideal, but for real. Tho I find myself now shy & so except for a few not so satisfactory flings with boys I dug for cock but not really in love with, have not been very promiscuous or don't get too deep involved, but dig watching the scene & being in presence of men who are open, that is, where my feelings are not *queer* but something out of old human love story.

This will have to be long junk letter so might as well relax & get to the point that's bothering me, you, maybe right now, jump in, what to do about politics, Cuba, human history, what I should do, what you are doing. I didn't know I was your monster that much, meaning in your respect and conscience, tho that's what I've tried to be for a lot of people, that's the image I had of myself as Poet-prophet friend on side of love & the Wild Good. That's the karma I wanted, to be Saint. That's what I told Van Doren* anyway and dreamed of myself; although wanting to get into heaven without paying ugly Prices as of yore. Prophesy without Death as a consequence, giggle into Paradise, that was the dream Peter and I had together; that was the ideal mellow feeling I had respecting Kerouac & other Heroes for me, Neal, Bill, including Huncke; and

---

* This is Mark Van Doren, Columbia University professor. Other persons mentioned in this paragraph are American writers Peter Orlovsky, Neal Cassady, William Burroughs, Herbert Huncke, and Columbia professor Lionel Trilling.

anybody that dug that scene with us. Already it's an exclusive club; and my measure at the time was the sense of personal genius and acceptance of all strangeness in people as their nobility; staying *out* of conflict and politics, staying with sort of dostoyevskian-shakespearean *know,* ken, of things as mortal, tearful, transient, sacred—not to join one side or other for an Idea, however serious, realizing the relativity & limitation of all judgments and discriminations, relying on the angel of wide consciousness in us to always sympathize or empathize with anybody, even hitler, because that's natural as in Whitman it's natural to be everybody at once, as it is in Dostoyevsky to understand the weirdness of everybody, even if it seems to conflict or lead to conflicts; wanting to stay sympathetic, even to Trilling, as to thieves or suicides or murderers. All this in the free atmosphere of US & appropriate to it, where we are not directly faced with threat of starve or extermination; except private deaths suicides faced and touched & for me shied away from. Now Bill and Jack were my monsters in that, that is they were the broad funny minds in which I recognized this sense of life, thru whose eyes I saw; Jack always telling me I was a "hairy loss," chiding my attempts to be vain, control moralities thru my mind, seeing in me vanities of wanting to Howl on stages and be Hero, be famous, or be a leader or intellectual, be superior thru mind-intelligence, criticize, get involved in politics, which in his-my eyes is always vanity trying to have power & impress other people which finally leads to big Decisions & Executions & unkindnesses and loss of the mortal empathy. I.e. if you take sides you make others enemies and can't see them any more; and you become like them, a limited identity. Well all this very sympatico and true in its way, except I did have this desire to be labor leader people's hero, that is, with my Jewish left wing atheist Russian background I even made a vow (not ever to be broken) on the ferryboat when I went to take entrance exam at Columbia, Vow Forever that if I succeeded in the scholarship test and got a chance I would never betray the Ideal—to help the masses in their misery. At the time I was very political and just recovering from Spanish Civil War which obsessed me in Jersey age 11 or 13. First upset of this idealism I had, entering to study Law as per plan of becoming pure Debs, was being mocked and shamed at my idea structure of the time by Lu. C. in workman's cafeteria on 125 Street, where as a

trembling Columbia intellectual, hardly "one of the roughs" I
found I was actually so self-conscious & mental I was scared of the
workmen in the cafeteria—that having to do with my complete
inexperience of life and also sensitive homosexual virginity & gen-
eral naivete—scared that is, in sense of feeling strange, an out-
sider, superior-inferior, I couldn't have a conversation with any of
the soup eaters—I was obviously too gauche to fit in in any way,
and yet I had this image of myself as a *leader* of these imaginary
masses. So then my direction turned to getting experience, working
on ships & as welder and kicked out of school & hanging around
lumpen & Times Sq. scene & dishwashing & mopping up cafeterias
& all that till some rough external edges were smoothed out & I
could at least fade into the landscape of the common world, so
that by 20 I took pride in this wholly or part imaginary accom-
plishment of, tho being a Columbia genteel type, at least being able
to get along with non-intellectuals and poor people & knowing the
argot of jazz & Times Sq. & varying my social experience more
than is usually, or was, varied in most Law students—not realizing
partly that most people were not as crazy as myself and didn't
make it all a big problem like I did, not being homosexual virgins
like myself. Meanwhile developing with Jack a sense of Poesy as
mellow as could be, reading Rimbaud, and with Burroughs, a
sense of Spenglerian history & respect for the "irrational" or un-
conscious properties of the soul & disrespect for all Law. Some-
thing broader than formalistic anarchism, that is, that you can
make a law as good as you want & it can be, but that still doesn't
cover what you will feel when someone's trapped in yr law. So a
distrust of mental decisions, generalizations, sociology, a hip sense;
plus then experience with love & with drugs actually causing
telepathic & what were to me "mystic" experiences, i.e. feelings
outside of anything I ever felt before. Meanwhile for a sense of the
rightness of life I trusted people most, that is Friendship & the
recognition of the light in people's eyes; and from then on I pur-
sued & idealized friendship especially in Poesy which was the
manifestation of this light of friendship secret in all man, open in
some few.

Then as I've said but never fully described nor in context of
development, came a time when college-days were o'er and I had
to depend on myself, and Jack and Bill went their ways in the

world—tho I felt bound to them by sacramental mellow lifelong-to-be ties—and the one idealistic love affair I had with Neal came to end because it was impractical & he was married & not really the same thing I was after—which was lifelong sex-soul union—he was willing but not to the extreme all out homo desire I had—anyway I realized I was alone & not ever to be loved as I wanted to be loved—Tho I'd had with him some great Pathos love-bed scenes which surpassed in tenderness anything I'd ever be handed on earth—so that the loss was even more utterly felt, as a kind of permanent doom of my desires as I knew them since childhood—I want somebody to love me, want somebody to carry me Hoagy tenderness—and at that point living alone eating vegetables, taking care of Huncke who was too beat to live elsewhere—I opened my book of Blake (as I've said before, it's like the Ancient Mariner repeating his obsessional futile tale to every guest he can lay his hand on) and had a classical hallucinatory-mystical experience, i.e. heard his voice commanding & prophesying to me from eternity, felt my soul open completely wide all its doors & windows and the cosmos flowed thru me, and *experienced* a state of altered apparently total consciousness so fantastic & science-fictional I even got scared later, at having stumbled on a secret door in the universe all alone. Meanwhile immediately made vow No. 2 that henceforth, no matter what happened in later decades, always to be faithful to that Absolute Eternal X I had thru destiny seen face to face—several times that week. As per usual it made my social behavior frantic, but I saw I was in danger of being considered mad—and possibly (what horror) was mad—so I kept cool enough to continue somewhat normal life. However the crash came within the visions themselves, as, one time, when I summoned the Great Spirit, this Great Spirit did appear but with a sense of Doom & Death so universal, vast & living that it felt to me as if the universe itself had come alive and was a hostile entity in which I was trapped and by which I would be eaten consciously alive.

So these are the deepest sense experiences I have had, and the only things I can know. I can't get around them any way yet, and they are in some form or other my own destiny, any move I make I always meet that Depth in new guise. At the same time afraid of meeting Eternity face to face, like tempted and fearful, like Hound of

Heaven or moth to flame. Later somewhat similar experiences tho weaker, and approximations of almost equal intensity with Peyote, Mescaline, Ayahuasca, Lysergic Acid, Hashish concentrates, & Psylocybin Mushrooms & Strobiscopic lights; also at intervals of tranquillity or changes of life & personal crises, all open out to the same vastness of consciousness in which all I know and plan is annihilated by awareness of Hidden Being-ness.

For that reason then, all loves, poetries & politics and intellectual life & literary scenes and all travels or stay-home years, are by me pursued as much spontaneously, without plan, without restrictive regulation of Rules & Rights and Wrongs & Final Judgments, without fixed ideas—as much as possible; and I do get into ruts that lead to Habit that thin my consciousness, being actually always careful to keep myself together and pursue Poesy & have a forwarding address.

However various basic rules have evolved, as far as my instincts & feelings, which is that all creation & poesy as transmission of the message of eternity is sacred and must be free of any rational restrictiveness; because consciousness has no limitations. And this led to experiments with new kinds of writings and literary renaissances and new energies & compositional techniques—most of which I got from Kerouac who all along let himself go to ball with his spontaneous Art, to tell the secrets of his memory. And I expected that, given this widening of belief and tolerance & empathy, some touch of natural basic consciousness would emanate from Poesy & my activities and serve to remind others outside me of human original wide nature, and thus affecting their consciousness little tho it be, serve the general uplift of Man and the purpose of Vow No. 1, to aid the Masses in their suffering. But if that end were approached directly, I always felt it would become a surface idea & get tangled in limited sometimes mistaken front-brain judgments (such as Kerouac warns about when he laments my being what seems to him involved in politics); (and that way he makes sense).

Another basic generalization that emerged was to finally trust my natural love feelings and that led to now almost decade alliance with Peter whom I thought a saint of lovely tolerance & joy—for me, strange tender ambulance driver, is what I wrote Jack announcing his presence in our company; Jack later Pronounced him to be the guard at gate of heaven, "but he's so goofy he lets everybody in."

And so, on Poesy and Peter and all described before, I began to get a fixed identity and creational life, with sort of basic sentiments and some ideas, which, as far as public "pronouncements" I kept to just urging freedom, of Meter & technique in Poesy, to follow the shape of the mind, and laws (narcotic) to follow thru to wider consciousness, & love, to follow natural desire.

However, taking drugs, and in solitude, I still was faced with omnivorous oblivion, chills of isolation and sterility not having met the woman half of the universe and progenied new babes, natural dissatisfactions with the incompleteness of the comes we could have together being men, and it made me vomit to realize the whole identity now built around me, Poetry, Peter, me, visions, consciousness, all my life, were destined by dissolution of time (a la Buddha) to be separated from me, and I would later if not willingly sooner be faced with having it all taken away with my corpse.

In fact in Peru with witch doctors taking Ayahuasca one night I came face to face with what appeared to be the Image of Death come to warn me again as 12 years before in Harlem, that all this me-ness of mine was mere idea vanity & hollow & fleeting as the mosquitos I was killing in the tropic night. In fact, tho I'd made a principle of Non-identity, I was scared to have my identity taken away, scared to die—clinging to the self-doomed (transient by nature) pleasures of dependable love, sex, income, cigarettes, Poesy, fame, face & cock—clinging, frightened, to *stay in* this identity, this body, vomiting as it was—and seeing its doom as a living monster *outside* of me that would someday EAT ME ALIVE.

Thus faced with human limitation I turned back from Eternity again and wanted to stay the Allen I was & am.

At this point frightened, seeing my basic saint-desire might be death & madness, I wrote Burroughs long letter from Peru asking for advice—Burroughs who had kicked junk habit and thus in very real way kicked his own identity habit, as can be seen in *Naked Lunch* hints.

His answer, go right ahead, into space, outside of Logos, outside of time, outside of concepts of Eternity & God & Faith & Love I'd built up as an identity—Cancel all your messages, said he, and I also cancel mine—.

Then thinking of wandering East with Peter & Gregory we looked into Bill in Tangier this year, and I met *someone I didn't know;* who rejected me, as far as Allen & Bill were concerned and all previous relationships they built up. And if I don't know Bill I sure don't know myself, because he was my rock of Tolerance & Friendship & true Art. And what was he doing with his art? He was cutting it up with a razor as if it weren't no sacred texts at all, just as he was cutting up all known human feelings between us, and cutting up the newspapers, and cutting up Cuba & Russia & America & making collages; he was cutting up his own consciousness & escaping as far as I can tell outside of anything I could recognize as his previous identity. And that somewhat changed my identity since that had been something built I had thought and permanently shared with him. And Peter and I suddenly broke thru the automaton Love-Faith habit we were junked-up and comfortable in, and looked in each others eyes—and nobody was there but a couple robots talking words and fucking. So he left for Istanbul and I stayed in Tangier and vomited off the roof.

Now the serious technical point that Burroughs was making by his cut-ups, which I resisted and resented since it threatened everything I depend on—I could stand the loss of Peter but not the loss of Hope & Love; & could maybe even stand the loss of them, whatever they are, if Poesy were left, for me to go on being something I wanted, sacred poet however desolate; but Poesy itself became a block to further awareness. For further awareness lay in dropping every fixed concept of self, identity, role, ideal, habit & pleasure. It meant dropping language itself, *words,* as medium of consciousness. It meant literally altering consciousness outside of what was already the fixed habit of language-inner-thought-monologue - abstraction - mental - image - symbol - mathematical abstraction. It meant exercising unknown & unused areas of the physical brain. Electronics, science fiction, drugs, strobiscopes, breathing exercises, exercises in thinking in music, colors, no thinks, entering and believing hallucinations, altering the neurologically fixated habit pattern Reality. But that's what I thought Poetry was doing all along! *But* the poetry I'd been practicing depended on living inside the structure of language, depended on words as the medium of consciousness & therefore the medium of conscious being.

Since then I've been wandering in doldrums, still keeping habit up with literature but uncertain if there is enough Me left to continue as some kind of Ginsberg. I can't write, except journals and dreams down; as the next step if any for Poetry, I can't imagine— Perhaps we've reached point in human or unhuman evolution where art of words is oldhat dinosaur futile, & must be left behind. I also stopped reading newspapers 2 months ago. Also the paranoid fear that I'm degenerate robot under the mind-control of the mad spectre of Burroughs. Except that it finally seems (after dreams of killing him) that he has only taken the steps, or begun to take, steps toward actual practice of expanded consciousness that were in the cards for me anyhoo, since the first days of mind break-up with Blake, and of which I was repeatedly reminded in drug trances.

A side effect of loss of dependence on words is the final breakup of my previously monotheistic memory-conception of one holy eternity. One God. Because all that conceptualization depends on the railroad track of language. And actual experience of consciousness is not Nameable as One. I suppose this is all in sophisticated form in Wittgenstein.

Meanwhile I am carrying for the last few months a dose of mushroom pills which I have been too fearful to take. Waiting for a day to look into that, or *be* that, THING, again. And operating still on language, thus this letter.

What to do about Cuba? Can the world Reality (as we know it through consciousness controlled by the Cortex part of the brain) be improved? Or, with expanded population & increasing need for social organization and control & centralization & standardization & socialization & removal of hidden power controllers (capitalism), will we in the long run doom man to life within a fixed and universal monopoly on reality (on materialist level) by a unison of cortex-controlled consciousness that will regulate our Being's evolution? Will it not direct that evolution toward stasis of preservation of its own reality, its idea of reality, its own identity, its Logos? But this is not the problem of socialism, this is the problem of Man. Can any good society be founded, as all have been before & failed, on the basis of old-style human consciousness? Can a vast human-teeming world "democratically" regulate itself at all in future with the kind of communications mechanism this present known & used consciousness has available? How escape rigidification and stasis of consciousness when man's mind is only words and these words and their images are flashed on every brain continuously by the interconnected networks of radio television newspapers wire services speeches decrees laws telephone books manuscripts? How escape centralized control of Reality of the masses by the few who want and can take power, when this network is now so interconnected, and the state so dominant, and the leaders of the state have decision over the Network? Democracy as previously sentimentally conceived now perhaps impossible (as proved in U.S.) since a vast feed-back mechanism, mass media, inescapably orients every individual, especially on subliminal levels. Same problem for Russia, China, Cuba.

I have no notion of future state or Government possible for man, I don't know if continuance of machine civilization is even possible or desirable. Perhaps science may have to dismantle itself (or kill the race)—this is parallel to individual intellectual experience of cycles of reasoning leading back to non-intellectual "natural" life. However I assume (for no good reason yet) the latest cycle of human evolution is irreversible except by atomic apocalypse, so I suppose Science is here to stay in one form or other, and civilizations too. I think the possible direction of development, then, to solve problems created by vast population & centralized network control, is toward increasing the efficiency and area of brain use, i.e. widening the area of consciousness in all directions feasible. I.e. telepathy might annihilate mass media power centers of control. In any case the old sense of identity of human consciousness, the sense of separate identity, self & its limited language, may alter. Individuals may have to step into hitherto unrecognizable areas of awareness, which means, for practical purposes, unrecognizable or undiscovered areas of BEING.

The change may be so far out as to be unimaginable to present day 2-dimensional political consciousness, or even 2-dimensional Poet's consciousness. I may have to (willingly) give up say being me, being Poet A.G., (or unwillingly depending on how fixed my cravings for security & the old life are). The social changes I can't even guess. It may be that we find the material reality we take for granted was literally an illusion all along. We may not *have* bodies. Nothing can be assumed, everything is UNKNOWN.

Space exploration is secondary and only triumphant in limited areas of consciousness; whereas an evolution or scientific exploration of consciousness itself (the brain & nervous system) is the inevitable route for man to take.

I see no reason why no government on earth is really alive in this evolutionary direction. All governments including the Cuban are still operating within the rules of identity forced on them by already outmoded modes of consciousness. I say outmoded since it has brought all Govts. to edge of world destruction. No govt., not even the most Marxian revolutionary & well-intended like Cuba presumably, is guiltless in the general world mess, no one can afford to be righteous any more. Righteous and right & wrong are still fakes of the old suicidal identity.

Next day continued:

Now the Cuban Revolutionary government as far as I can tell is basically occupied by immediate practical problems & proud of that, heroic resistances, drama, uplift, reading & teaching language, and totally unoccupied as yet with psychic exploration in terms which I described above. When I talked with Franqui of *Revolución* in NY he parroted the U.S. imperialist line against marijuana and added, "It should be easier for a poet to understand a revolution than for a revolution to understand poetry." Poetry here meaning my contention that poet had right to use marijuana. He gave me all sorts of rationalistic arguments against social use of marijuana—tho he added liberally that he himself was not personally opposed to it. And also I see that there has been no evidence of real technical revolution in Poesy or language in recent Cuban poetry—it still is old hat mechanistic syntax & techniques. So that it is obvious that any, meaning ANY, mediocre bureaucratic attempt to censor language, diction or direction of psychic exploration is the same old mistake made in all the idiot academies of Russia and America. Arguments about immediate practical necessities are as far as I can tell from afar strictly the same old con of uninspired people who don't know what the writing problem is, and don't have any idea of the consciousness problems I'm talking about.

Re censorship of language. I wrote an article for *Show Business Illustrated* on the Cannes film festival which they accepted and paid 450 for, using the word shit (describing use of it in "The Connection"); now they want to chicken out on the single use of Shit in one sentence. I wrote back no, same day I got your letter, thus pledging myself to repay them 450 dollars I've already spent—over one little Shit. Censorship of language is direct censorship of consciousness; and if I don't fit in I can't change the shape of my mind. No. No revolution can succeed if it continues the puritanical censorship of consciousness imposed on the world by Russia and America. Succeed in what? Succeed in liberating the masses from domination by secret Monopolists of communication.

I'm NOT down on the Cubans or anti their revolution, it's just that it's important to make clear *in advance, in front,* what I feel about life. Big statements saying Viva Fidel are/would be/ meaningless and just 2-dimensional politics.

Publish as much of this letter as interests you, as prose contribution to Cuban Revolution.

[Oct. 16, 1961]
Athens, Greece

How *Kaddish* Happened

First writing on *Kaddish* was in Paris '58, several pages of part IV which set forth a new variation on the litany form used earlier in *Howl*—a graduated lengthening of the response lines, so that the *Howl* litany looks like a big pyramid on the page. *Kaddish* IV looks like three little pyramids sitting one on top of another, plus an upside-down pyramid mirror-reflected at the bottom of the series. Considered as breath, it means the vocal reader has to build up the feeling-utterance three times to climax, and then, as coda, diminish the utterance to shorter and shorter sob. The first mess of composition had all these elements, I later cut it down to look neat and exact. (Further extension of this form, litany, can be found in poem 4 years later, "The Change.")

Sometime a year later in New York I sat up all night with a friend who played me Ray Charles genius classics—I'd been in Europe two winters and not heard attentively before—also we chippied a little M and some then new-to-me meta-amphetamine—friend showed me his old bar-mitzvah book of Hebrew ritual & read me central Kaddish passages—I walked out in early blue dawn on to 7th Avenue & across town to my Lower East Side apartment—New York before sunrise has its own celebrated hallucinatory unreality. In the country getting up with the cows and birds hath Blakean charm, in the megalopolis the same nature's hour is a science-fiction hell vision, even if you're a milkman. Phantom factories, unpopulated streets out of Poe, familiar nightclubs bookstores groceries dead.

I got home and sat at desk with desire to write—a kind of visionary urge that's catalyzed by all the strange chemicals of the City—but had no idea what Prophecy was at hand—poetry I figured. I began quite literally assembling recollection data taken from the last hours—"Strange now to think of you gone without corsets and eyes while I walk etc." I wrote on several pages till I'd reached a climax, covering fragmentary recollections of key scenes with my mother ending with a death-prayer imitating the rhythms of the Hebrew Kaddish—"Magnificent, Mourned no more, etc."

But then I realized that I hadn't gone back and told the whole secret family-self tale—my own one-and-only eternal child-youth memories which no one else could know—in all its eccentric detail. I realized that it would seem odd to others, but *family* odd, that is to say, familiar—everybody has crazy cousins and aunts and brothers.

So I started over again into narrative—"this is release of particulars"—and went back chronologically, sketching in broken paragraphs all the first recollections that rose in my heart—details I'd thought of once, twice often before—embarrassing scenes I'd half amnesiaized—hackle-raising scenes of the long black beard around the vagina—Images that were central to my own existence such as the mass of scars on my mother's plump belly—all archetypes.

Possibly subjective archetypes, but archetype is archetype, and properly articulated subjective archetype is universal.

I sat at same desk from six AM Saturday to ten PM Sunday night writing on without moving my mind from theme except for trips to the bathroom, cups of coffee and boiled egg handed into my room by Peter Orlovsky (Peter the nurse watching over his beloved madman), and a few dexedrine tablets to renew impulse. After the twentieth hour attention wandered, the writing became more diffuse, dissociations more difficult to cohere, the unworldly messianic spurts more awkward, but I persevered till completing the chronological task. I got the last detail recorded including my mother's death-telegram. I could go back later & clean it up.

I didn't look at the handwritten pages for a week—slept several days—and when I reread the mass I was defeated, it seemed impossible to clean up and revise, the continuous impulse was there messy as it was, it was a patient scholar's task to figure how it could be more shapely.

Standing on a streetcorner one dusk another variation of the litany form came to me—alternation of Lord Lord and Caw Caw ending with a line of pure Lord Lord Lord Caw Caw Caw—pure emotive sound—and I went home and filled in that form with associational data. The last 3 lines are among the best in the poem—the *most* dissociated, on the surface, but, given all the detail of the poem, quite coherent—I mean it's a very great jump from the broken shoe to the vast highschool caw caw—and in that gap's the whole Maya-Dream-Suchness of existence glimpsed.

It took me a year—trip to South America half that time—to have the patience to type poem up so I could read it. I delayed depressed with the mess, not sure it was a "poem." Much less interesting to anyone else. Defeat like that is good for poetry—you go so far out you don't know what you're doing, you lose touch with what's been done before by anyone, you wind up creating a new poetry-universe. "Make it new" saith Pound, "Invention," said W. C. Williams. That's the "Tradition"—a complete fuck-up so you're on your own.

The poem was typed, I had to cut down & stitch together the last sections of narrative—didn't have to change the expression, but did have to fit it together where it lapsed into abstract bathos or got mixed in time or changed track too often. It was retyped by Elise Cowen, a girl I'd known for years and had fitful lovers' relations with. When she gave me the copy she said, "You still haven't finished with your mother." Elise herself had been reading the bible and heard voices saying her own mind was controlled by outside agent-machinery, and several years later she died by jumping off her family apartment or roof.

By 1963 looking back on woman and on the poem for new City Lights edition I tried to make Amen: In the midst of the broken consciousness of mid twentieth-century suffering anguish of separation from my own body and its natural infinity of feeling its own self one with all self, I instinctively seeking to reconstitute that blissful union which I experienced so rarely I took it to be supernatural and gave it holy Name thus made hymn laments of longing and litanies of triumphancy of Self over the mind-illusion mechano-universe of un-feeling Time in which I saw my self my own mother and my very nation trapped desolate our worlds of consciousness homeless and at war except for the original trembling of bliss in breast and belly of every body that nakedness rejected in suits of fear that familiar defenseless living hurt self which is myself same as all others abandoned scared to own our unchanging desire for each other. These poems almost unconscious to confess the beatific human fact, the language intuitively chosen as in trance & dream, the rhythms rising thru breath from belly to breast, the hymn completed in tears, the movement of the physical poetry demanding and receiving decades of life while chanting Kaddish the names of Death in many mind-worlds the self seeking the Key to life found at last in our self.

[March 20, 1966]

Some Metamorphoses
of Personal Prosody

Much earlier training in versification & time sense modeled after pages of Wyatt resulted in overwritten coy stanzas permutating abstract concepts derived secondhand from Silver Poets, which carefulness managed to suppress almost all traces of native sensibility diction concrete fact & personal breath on my own *vers de collège*. "In this mode perfection is basic," W.C. Williams reproved me correctly; simultaneously he responded with enthusiasm to short fragments of personal notation drawn from diaries & rearranged in lines emphasizing crude breath-stop syncopations. Later practice in this mode (Kerouac urging "speak now or ever hold thy peace") trained my sensibility to the eccentric modulations of long-line composition displayed by Smart, Blake, Whitman, Jeffers, Rimbaud, Artaud & other precursors including now Edward Carpenter (whose *Towards Democracy* read me this year by his later lover Gavin Arthur struck me as the combine of Blake-visionary & Whitmanic-direct-notation nearest my own intuition that I'd ever stumbled upon). (In fact I decided ruefully for 24 hours that I was like Carpenter just another fine minor Whitman necessary but forgettable.)

But young minstrels have now arisen on the airwaves whose poetic forms outwardly resemble antique verse including regular stanzas refrains and rhymes: Dylan and Donovan and some fragments of the Rolling Stones because they *think* not only in words but also in music simultaneously have out of the necessities of their own space-age media and electric machinery tunes evolved a natural use of—a personal realistic imaginative rhymed verse. Principle of composition here is, however, unlike antique literary form, primarily spontaneous & improvised (in the studio if need be at the last minute), and prophetic in character in that tune and language are invoked shamanistically on the spot from the unconscious. This new ear is not dead only for eye-page, it's connected with a voice improvising, with hesitancies aloud, a living musician's ear. The old library poets had lost their voices; natural voice was rediscovered; and now natural song for physical voice. Oddly this fits Pound's paradigm tracing the degeneration of Poesy from the Greek dance-foot chorus thru minstrel song thru 1900 abstract voiceless page. So now returned to song and song forms we may yet anticipate inspired Creators like Shiva Krishna Chaitanya Mirabai & Ramakrishna who not only composed verse in ecstatic fits, but also chanted their verse in melody, and lifted themselves off the floor raised their arms and danced in time to manifest Divine Presence. Mantra repetition—a form of prayer in which a short magic formula containing various God names is chanted hypnotically—has entered Western consciousness & a new Mantra-rock is formulated in the Byrds & Beatles.

Not being a musician from childhood my own Japa and Kirtan is home-made but not without influence on verbal composition practice. Introduction of tape recorder also catalyses changes in possibilities of composition via improvisation. "Wichita Vortex Sutra," a short fragment of longer trans-american voyage poetries, is therefore composed directly on tape by voice, and then transcribed to page: page arrangement notates the thought-stops, breath-stops, runs of inspiration, changes of mind, startings and stoppings of the car.

Sept 10, 1966

On Improvised Poetics

First thought best thought.

ALLEN GINSBERG
Independence Day 1973

JOHN WIENERS

The Address of the Watchman to the Night

Watchman, what of the night, always semed an order to me in my own life, even though I never knew the phrase until I was 29 or 30. To explore those dark eternals of the nightworld: the prostitute, the dope addict, thief and pervert. These were the imagined heroes of my world: and the orders of my life. What they stood for, how they lived, what they did in the daytime were the fancies of my imagination. And I had to become every one of them until I knew. Until I know now that they are only deprivations of the self, not further extensions of its being: manifestations of want, denial and betrayal.

They assumed no dreamlike poses or positions of the hero; they expressed no noble sentiments; they banded together out of fear and in need. The night was their palace, their working ground; its neighbor was the dawn and that never to be known. Daylight was only to be endured. And the night war never ended. There was no declaration of peace or armistice. And love only a casual happening or accident. When it occurred, salvation and a change of life for the instant. But it never seemed to be of any permanence. And one went on, shunning mirrors and the sun.

Love was to profit by; a night's warmth, a new suit, a week's lodging, a full meal, a soft pillow under the head; but to the heart and soul only a remembrance or memory out of childhood, a tune played on a tinny piano in someone else's house.

Morning found us sick, dawn exhausted, night an exhilaration and excursion. Who wanted to be seen in the daylight, when the drudges were out, lazy to do their lives justice. The lames abound on weekends, so use them, find them out. Houses and villages of money, furs and jewels. Yet such it was, we became who let life exhaust us by 30 or before we felt burnt out, and truly were; only to re-kindle later, we hope, by rest, relief and redemption.

In the form of a poem, with its order, expressions and release. Touching on subjects once remote, now familiar, as the song of birds in the backyard where before there was snow and the drift of rain.

Communion also with the ordinary things of life, removal of and from excitement, ordering externals and interior beliefs, mingled with a cohesion of world and its cosmos down to the single syllable. There let live the divine reign and the mysterious manifest itself in the hard touch of wood upon the bottom. The bottom! the depths reached, the sounding of the ocean swell in the empty plains of the heart, reaching to the sky with forests of the country filling the horizon. The world revealed in a word.

Saturday April 27th 1963

FRANK O'HARA

Personism: A Manifesto

Everything is in the poems, but at the risk of sounding like the poor wealthy man's Allen Ginsberg I will write to you because I just heard that one of my fellow poets thinks that a poem of mine that can't be got at one reading is because I was confused too. Now, come on. I don't believe in god, so I don't have to make elaborately sounded structures. I hate Vachel Lindsay, always have, I don't even like rhythm, assonance, all that stuff. You just go on your nerve. If someone's chasing you down the street with a knife you just run, you don't turn around and shout, "Give it up! I was a track star for Mineola Prep."

That's for the writing poems part. As for their reception, suppose you're in love and someone's mistreating (*mal aimé*) you, you don't say, "Hey, you can't hurt me this way, I *care!*" you just let all the different bodies fall where they may, and they always do may after a few months. But that's not why you fell in love in the first place, just to hang onto life, so you have to take your chances and try to avoid being logical. Pain always produces logic, which is very bad for you.

I'm not saying that I don't have practically the most lofty ideas of anyone writing today, but what difference does that make? they're just ideas. The only good thing about it is that when I get lofty enough I've stopped thinking and that's when refreshment arrives.

But how can you really care if anybody gets it, or gets what it means, or if it improves them. Improves them for what? for death? Why hurry them along? Too many poets act like a middle-aged mother trying to get her kids to eat too much cooked meat, and potatoes with drippings (tears). I don't give a damn whether they eat or not. Forced feeding leads to excessive thinness (effete). Nobody should experience anything they don't need to, if they don't need poetry bully for them, I like the movies too. And after all, only Whitman and Crane and Williams, of the American poets, are better than the movies. As for measure and other technical apparatus, that's just common sense: if you're going to buy a pair of pants you want them to be tight enough so everyone will want to go to bed with you. There's nothing metaphysical about it. Unless, of course, you flatter yourself into thinking that what you're experiencing is "yearning."

Abstraction in poetry, which Allen recently commented on in *It is,* is intriguing. I think it appears mostly in the minute particulars where decision is necessary. Abstraction (in poetry, not in painting) involves personal removal by the poet. For instance, the decision involved in the choice between "the nostalgia of the infinite" and "the nostalgia *for* the infinite" defines an attitude towards degree of abstraction. The nostalgia *of* the infinite representing the greater degree of abstraction, removal, and negative capability (as in Keats and Mallarmé). Personism, a movement which I recently founded and which nobody yet knows about, interests me a great deal, being so totally opposed to this kind of abstract removal that it is verging on a true abstraction for the first time, really, in the history of poetry. Personism is to Wallace Stevens what *la poésie pure* was to Béranger. Personism has nothing to do with philosophy, it's all art. It does not have to do with personality or intimacy, far from it! But to give you a vague idea, one of its minimal aspects is to address itself to one person (other than the poet himself), thus evoking overtones of love without destroying love's life-giving vulgarity, and sustaining the poet's feelings towards the poem while preventing love from distracting him into feeling about the person. That's part of personism. It was founded by me after lunch with LeRoi Jones on August 27, 1959, a day in which I was in love with someone (not Roi, by the way, a blond). I went back to work and wrote a poem for this person. While I was writing it I was realizing that if I wanted to I could use the telephone instead of writing the poem, and so Personism was born. It's a very exciting movement which will undoubtedly have lots of adherents. It puts the poem squarely between the poet and the person, Lucky

Pierre style, and the poem is correspondingly gratified. The poem is at last between two persons instead of two pages. In all modesty, I confess that it may be the death of literature as we know it. While I have certain regrets, I am still glad I got there before Alain Robbe-Grillet did. Poetry being quicker and surer than prose, it is only just that poetry finish literature off. For a time people thought that Artaud was going to accomplish this, but actually, for all its magnificence, his polemical writings are not more outside literature than Bear Mountain is outside New York State. His relation is no more astounding than Dubuffet's to painting.

What can we expect of Personism? (This is getting good, isn't it?) Everything, but we won't get it. It is too new, too vital a movement to promise anything. But it, like Africa, is on the way. The recent propagandists for technique on the one hand, and for content on the other, had better watch out.

[9/3/59]

About Zhivago and His Poems

We are used to the old saw that poets cannot write great novels or indeed any novels. The adherents of this cliché, hoping to perpetuate a mystery-distinction between two kinds of writing, are cheered on by the novelists who hate "poetic" novels and the poets who hate "prosaic" poems. Virginia Woolf gets hers from one quarter and William Carlos Williams gets his from the other. The argument is usually bolstered by phrases like "Joyce *turned to* prose," which would have been an amusing scene, but never occurred. For what poetry gave to Joyce, as to Pasternak, is what painting gave to Proust: the belief that high art has a communicability far superior in scope and strength to any other form of human endeavor. The Nobel Prize committee was correct in making the award include Pasternak's poetry as well as the novel. To admirers of his poetry *Doctor Zhivago* is the epic expression of many of the themes first found in individual lyrics and short stories; the present epic form is the poet's response to the demand of his time for its proper expression.

With one prose masterpiece behind him, *Safe Conduct* (1931), Pasternak insists in *Doctor Zhivago* on identifying poetry with truth to the supreme extent: in no other work of modern literature do we wait for the final revelation of meaning to occur in the hero's posthumous book of poems. The political ramifications of the novel's publication have thrust the poet (author *and* hero) into dramatic relief for a vast international public and established the efficacy of the poet's stance in realms far beyond personal lyricism. The clamor over *Doctor Zhivago* has been denounced by various literary figures as damaging to Pasternak personally, but let there be no mistake about this clamor: it comes not from anything Pasternak has said in the press, nor from the phrasing of the Nobel Prize citation, nor from Western or Soviet political commentaries on the novel's content, it comes from the nature of the work itself. Of the critics only Edmund Wilson has seen this quality in its proper perspective. Pasternak has written a revolutionary and prophetic work which judges contemporary society outside as well as within the Iron Curtain. And if Pasternak is saying that the 1917 Revolution failed, he must feel that the West never even made an attempt. Far from being a traitorous work, *Doctor Zhivago* is a poem on the nobility of the Soviet failure to reconstruct society *in human terms,* and it is not without hope. The two disillusioning heroes of *Safe Conduct,* Scriabin and Mayakovsky, give way to the triumphant hero of *Doctor Zhivago.*

It is plain that this hero must be an artist; to Pasternak the artist is the last repository of individual conscience, and in his terms conscience is individual perception of life. This is not at all a counterrevolutionary attitude based on an intellectual-aristocratic system. It has not to do with a predilection for "culture." The lesson comes from life. Zhivago himself becomes a doctor, but he finds that his usefulness to society is everywhere stymied, that his

social efficacy is incomplete and does not contribute to his under-
standing of his own predicament. To be a twentieth-century hero
Zhivago must leave for subsequent generations a living testament.
It does not suffice that he "live in the hearts of his countrymen" by
remembered deeds alone. It is a question of articulation: the epic
events of Doctor Zhivago demand from their participants articu-
late perception or mute surrender. Pasternak's epic is not the
glorification of the plight of the individual, but of the accomplish-
ment of the individual in the face of almost insuperable sufferings
which are personal and emotionally real, never melodramatic and
official. And it is the poet's duty to accomplish this articulation.

Everywhere in the work of Pasternak published in English, we
saw this meaning growing. It is a world very like that of Joyce's
characters as we meet them in *Dubliners* and *The Portrait of the
Artist as a Young Man* and find them later older, clearer, changed,
in *Ulysses* and *Finnegans Wake*. Obviously the young Larisa
Feodorovna bears this kind of resemblance to the adolescent
Zhenia Luvers of the early story (mistakenly printed as two dis-
tinct stories under separate titles by New Directions); several
scenes in "Aerial Ways" anticipate events in the novel, and indeed
Pasternak draws attention to this aspect of his writing in the
opening passages of "A Tale" (called "The Last Summer" in
English). It is the writer of the "Letters to Tula" who bears the
strongest resemblance to Zhivago himself: "Everything that hap-
pens happens from the nature of the place. This is an event on the
territory of conscience, it occurs on her own ore-bearing regions.
There will be no 'poet.' " In this passage Pasternak reveals early
(1918) his belief that the poet must first be a person, that his
writings make him a poet, not his acting the role. I cannot agree
with Elsa Triolet when she recently attacked Pasternak for having
betrayed Mayakovsky in writing *Doctor Zhivago*. On the contrary,
the principles which were later to seduce Mayakovsky had been
exposed in "Letters to Tula" already:

> . . . I swear to you that the faith of my heart is
> greater than ever it was, the time will come—no, let
> me tell you about that later. Tear me to pieces, tear me
> to pieces, night, burn to ashes, burn, burn brilliantly,
> luminously, the forgotten, the angry, the fiery word

"Conscience"! Burn maddening, petrol-bearing tongue of the flame . . .

This way of regarding life has come into being and now there is no place on earth where a man can warm his soul with the fire of shame: shame is everywhere watered down and cannot burn. Falsehood and dissipation. Thus for thirty years all who are singular live and drench their shame, old and young, and already it has spread through the whole world, among the unknown . . .

The poet, henceforward inscribing this word, until it is purged with fire, in inverted commas, the "poet" observes himself in the unseemly behavior of actors, in the disgraceful spectacle which accuses his comrades and his generation. Perhaps he is only playing with the idea. No. They confirm him in the belief that his identity is in no way chimerical . . .

This passage is like a rehearsal of the talks Zhivago has with his uncle when they discuss principles. That it also bears on Pasternak's relationship with Mayakovsky is witnessed by the following passage from *Safe Conduct*:

But a whole conception of life lay concealed under the Romantic manner which I was to deny myself from henceforth. This was the conception of life as the life of the poet. It had come down to us from the Romantics, principally the Germans.

This conception had influenced Blok but only during a short period. It was incapable of satisfying him in the form in which it came naturally to him. He could either heighten it or abandon it altogether. He abandoned the conception. Mayakovsky and Esenin heightened it.

In the poet who imagines himself the measure of life and pays for this with his life, the Romantic conception manifests itself brilliantly and irrefutably in his symbolism, that is in everything which touches upon Orphism and Christianity imaginatively. In this sense something inscrutable was incarnate both in the life of Mayakovsky and in the fate of Esenin, which defies all epithets, demanding self-destruction and passing into myth.

But outside the legend, the Romantic scheme is false. The poet who is its foundation, is inconceivable without the nonpoets who must bring him into relief, because this poet is not a living personality absorbed in the study of moral knowledge, but a visual-biographical "emblem," demanding a background to make his contours visible. In contradistinction to the Passion plays which needed a Heaven if they were to be heard, this drama needs the evil of mediocrity in order to be seen, just as Romanticism always needs philistinism and with the disappearance of the petty bourgeoisie loses half its poetical content.

What then, after rejecting the concept of the Romantic "pose" in relation to his own life and art, does Pasternak's position become? He had already moved towards this decision in the poems written previous to 1917 and in a later volume he chooses the title from a poem, "My Sister Life." This expresses very clearly his position: the poet and life herself walk hand in hand. Life is not a landscape before which the poet postures, but the very condition of his inspiration in a deeply personal way: "My sister, life, is in flood today . . ." This is not the nineteenth-century Romantic identification, but a recognition. In the later work Zhivago says to the dying Anna Ivanovna:

. . . But all the time, life, one, immense, identical throughout its innumerable combinations and transformations, fills the universe and is continually reborn. You are anxious about whether you will rise from the dead or not, but you rose from the dead when you were born and you didn't notice it . . .

So what will happen to your consciousness? *Your* consciousness, yours, not anyone else's. Well, what are you? There's the point. Let's try to find out. What is it about you that you have always known as yourself? What are you conscious of in yourself? Your kidneys? Your liver? Your blood vessels? No. However far back you go in

your memory, it is always in some external, active mani-
festation of yourself that you come across your identity
—in the work of your hands, in your family, in other
people. And now listen carefully. You in others—this is
your soul. This is what you are. This is what your con-
sciousness has breathed and lived on and enjoyed through-
out your life—your soul, your immortality, your life in
others. And what now? You have always been in others
and you will remain in others. And what does it matter
to you if later on that is called your memory? This will
be you—the you that enters the future and becomes a
part of it . . .

There is every reason to believe that Pasternak's recognition of
self was accompanied by great pain. He adored Mayakovsky at the
time and indeed was forced to this decision of self by Mayakov-
sky's presence in that time, ". . . because poetry as I understand
it flows through history and in collaboration with real life."
Mayakovsky made a fatal error and became a tragic hero. Like
Strelnikov in the novel, he succumbed to a belief in the self-created
rhetoric of his own dynamic function in society. That society
needed him and benefited from this rhetoric is obvious. But both
he and the character in *Doctor Zhivago* ended in suicide when
their usefulness in this function came to an end, and while their
response to social demand seems shortsighted to Pasternak, he
also condemned society for the temptation:

> The great Soviet gives to the highest passions
> In these brave days each one its rightful place,
> Yet vainly leaves one vacant for the poet.
> When that's not empty, look for danger's face.

The chair of poetry must remain empty, for poetry does not
collaborate with society, but with life. Soviet society is not alone in
seducing the poet to deliver temporary half-truths which will
shortly be cast aside for the excitement of a new celebration of
nonlife. The danger is that life does not allow any substitute for
love.

It is not surprising then that this sense of poetry and its intimate
connection with his relationship to life is one of the strongest

elements in Zhivago's nature. It makes of Zhivago one of the most original heroes in Western literature, a man who cannot be interpreted by nineteenth-century standards, which I suspect Lionel Abel attempts to do when he says, writing in *Dissent*, ". . . how can he not have understood that in yielding to the impulse to write of his beloved immediately after his loss of her, he was taking a practical attitude toward his grief, trying to get something out of it, literature, maybe even glory?" What Mr. Abel misses finding here is the grief-expression of the romantic hero, which had been eschewed by Pasternak himself in an early poem which fits oddly well into the present scene of loss:

> . . . O miraculous obit, beckon, beckon! You may
> Well be astonished. For—look—you are free.
>
> I do not hold you. Go, yes, go elsewhere,
> Do good. *Werther* cannot be written again,
> And in our time death's odor is in the air;
>
> To open a window is to open a vein.

Far from shallow or opportunistic in his grief (being left alone in the Urals with the wolves closing in would hardly raise hopes for literary fame), Zhivago weeps, drinks vodka, scribbles poems and notes, is subject to hallucinations, and begins the decline which will end in his death. But at this crucial period of his life in which he unexpectedly suffers the ultimate loss, that of Larisa Feodorovna, the period in which he had hoped to accomplish his poetic testament, his creativity does not desert him. We must remember that the events of the post-revolution period have robbed him of the time to think, the time to write. He saves his sanity by crowding the writing and the speculations of a lifetime into these days of isolation, coming to conclusions about certain events, and thus approaching once again, after this interval of grief, his "sister, life":

> . . . Mourning for Lara, he also mourned that distant summer in Meliuzeievo when the revolution had been a god come down to earth from heaven, the god of the summer when everyone had gone crazy in his own way, and when everyone's life had existed in its own right, and

not as an illustration for a thesis in support of the right-
ness of a superior policy.

As he scribbled his odds and ends, he made a note re-
affirming his belief that art always serves beauty, and
beauty is delight in form, and form is the key to organic
life, since no living thing can exist without it, so that
every work of art, including tragedy, expresses the joy of
existence. And his own ideas and notes also brought him
joy, a tragic joy, a joy full of tears that exhausted him
and made his head ache.

He decides to forego the virtual suicide of his retreat in the
snowy wilderness, in the abandoned house which has offered him,
for the first time since he was a student, the solitude for his poetry,
and to return to Moscow. The inverted commas have been purged
from the word poet. And unlike Chekhov's *Three Sisters* he does
reach Moscow. And there he has a tangible reality even after his
death, as recognized by his two childhood friends as they read at
dusk the posthumous poems which Zhivago's mysteriously angelic
half brother Evgraf has collected:

> . . . And Moscow, right below them and stretching into
> the distance, the author's native city, in which he had
> spent half his life—Moscow now struck them not as the
> stage of the events connected with him but as the main
> protagonist of a long story, the end of which they had
> reached that evening, book in hand.
>
> Although victory had not brought the relief and free-
> dom that were expected at the end of the war, neverthe-
> less the portents of freedom filled the air throughout the
> postwar period, and they alone defined its historical sig-
> nificance.
>
> To the two old friends, as they sat by the window, it
> seemed that this freedom of the soul was already there,
> as if that very evening the future had tangibly moved into
> the streets below them, that they themselves had entered
> it and were now part of it . . .
>
> And the book they held seemed to confirm and en-
> courage this feeling.

This is Zhivago's triumph over the terrible vicissitudes of love and circumstance which we have witnessed, the "active manifestation" of himself—his soul, his immortality, his life in others.

Though the greatness of scale in *Doctor Zhivago* bears a resemblance to Tolstoy's achievement, this is not a massively documented and described war-novel like those we have had from American, French and Russian neo-Tolstoyans, where the scheme is that of nineteenth-century prototypes swamped by the events of their time. On the contrary, one of the great beauties of Pasternak's technique is that of portraying events through the consciousness of principal and minor characters. In this he resembles Joyce and Proust; often we hear of an event from a character *after* it has changed him, so that we apprehend both the event and its consequences simultaneously. The intimacy which this technique lends to the epic structure, particularly when the character is relatively unknown to us, and the discretion with which it is handled, reminds one of two other works of perfect scale, Lermontov's *A Hero of Our Times* and Flaubert's *A Sentimental Education*.

Nowhere in the novel is this method more rewarding than in the presentation of the hero, and here it is varied beyond what I have described. Of Yurii Andreievich Zhivago we know a great deal as we progress through the novel. We not only know his feelings and his response to and attempted evaluation of events, but also his longings. We even know what he considers the most important elements in his life and how he intends to evaluate them in his work. But here Pasternak's devastating distrust of the plane of action in human affairs becomes clearest and makes its strongest point. In the post-epilogue book of poems we find that Zhivago has not written the poems he wanted to, nor the poems we expected (except for the one on St. George); in the course of creating the poems he has become not the mirror of the life we know, but the instrument of its perceptions, hitherto veiled. This is the major expression of a meaning which Pasternak has implied often in the novel proper. The human individual is the subject of historical events, not vice versa; he is the repository of life's force. And while he may suffer, may be rendered helpless, may be killed, if he has the perceptiveness to realize this he knows that events require his participation to occur. In this context we find another revolutionary reinterpretation of the human condition: Strelnikov, the "active" Red Army Commissar, is rendered passive by his blind espousal of principles whose needful occasion has passd; Zhivago, passively withdrawn from action which his conscience cannot sanction, finds the art for which an occasion will continue to exist. This qualitative distinction between two kinds of significance is as foreign to our own society as it is to that of the U.S.S.R.

The poems with which the novel culminates are truly Zhivago's own, not Pasternak's. They deliver us a total image of the hero's life which is incremented by details of that life from the prose section. While we recognize the occasions of many, we find their expression different from what we, or Zhivago, expected. As an indication of how different they are from Pasternak's own poems, we need only compare two poems on a similar theme, Pasternak's lyric "If only when I made my début" and Zhivago's "Hamlet." In the one, Pasternak deals with one of his central themes which is mentioned above in relation to Mayakovsky. The poem is full of the tragedy of human involvement, but in a pure, nonsymbolic manner: it is the role taking over the actor, of course, but it is also the word consuming the poet, the drama of the meaning, which the poet has found through the act of creating this meaning, transporting him to an area of realization beyond his power, where he has been joined to the *mortal* presence of life:

> A line that feeling sternly dictates
> Sends on the stage a slave, and, faith,
> It is good-bye to art forever
> Then, then things smack of soil and Fate.

How different is Zhivago's poem on this theme. Not only does he assume a "masque," that of Hamlet, but before we are through the second stanza he has made the symbolic connection of Hamlet with the Hebraic-Christian myth of father-and-son positive by reference to Christ in the Garden of Olives. The poem ends on a reference to Zhivago's own physical circumstance, a personal note that has saved many a Symbolist poem:

> I stand alone. All else is swamped in Pharisaism.
> To live life to the end is not a childish task.

Because of the novel, we cannot resist the idea that this poem was written in the snowy forests of Varykino after Lara's departure, where Zhivago endures his agonizing "vigil" and decides to forego suicide and to return to Moscow.

The Christian poems are extraordinary achievements as poems, and also reveal how complicated the structure of the novel is. In reading them we realize for the first time how enormously influential on Zhivago was the interpretation of Christ's significance by a minor character who was speaking to Lara and overheard by him from the next room. It becomes clear that Zhivago's Christianity is no hieratic discipline, but a recognition of social change: ". . . you have a girl—an everyday figure who would have gone unnoticed in the ancient world—quietly, secretly bringing forth a child . . .

"Something in the world had changed. Rome was at an end. The reign of numbers was at an end. The duty, imposed by armed force, to live unanimously as a people, as a whole nation, was abolished. . . . Individual life became the life story of God . . ." For those who have interpreted *Doctor Zhivago* with some smugness as a return to Christianity as the Western World knows it, it should be pointed out that this historical interpretation bears roughly the same analogy to Protestantism and Catholicism as they are practiced that Marxism does to Capitalism. It is not only based on historical distinctions, but "faith" is further set aside by the distinctions made in the poems between human life and nature, and the ambiguities of this relationship as they affect the Christ legend. When the fig tree is consumed to ashes in "Miracle," Zhivago writes:

If at that point but a moment of free choice had been granted
To the leaves, the branches, to the trunk and roots
The laws of nature might have contrived to intervene.

And in "Holy Week" our dependency on nature becomes the rival of God:

And when the midnight comes
All creatures and all flesh will fall silent
On hearing spring put forth its rumor
That just as soon as there is better weather

> Death itself can be overcome
> Through the power of the Resurrection.

It is not difficult to ascertain that for Pasternak the interdependency of man and nature is far from theological. It is in these clarifications of feelings and thoughts, in these poems, that Zhivago becomes a true hero. Here we find his inner response to his wife's moving letter from exile which also contains his reasons for not joining her outside Russia ("Dawn"), in other poems his ambivalences and his social nobility. In the most revealing of all, the love poems to Lara (including the superb "Autumn," "Parting," "Encounter" and "Magdalene"), we find the intensity which had so moved her and which Zhivago himself reveals nowhere else except in the secrecy of their own intimate hours. Her greatness in responding to this love becomes even more moving in retrospect than it was when one first read her thoughts at his bier, one of the greatest scenes in literature:

> . . . Oh, what a love it was, utterly free, unique, like nothing else on earth! Their thoughts were like other people's songs.
>
> They loved each other, not driven by necessity, by the "blaze of passion" often falsely ascribed to love. They loved each other because everything around them willed it, the trees and the clouds and the sky over their heads and the earth under their feet. Perhaps their surrounding world, the strangers they met in the street, the wide expanses they saw on their walks, the rooms in which they lived or met, took more delight in their love than they themselves did.

And the posthumous response to her love is on as grand a scale:

> You are the blessing in a stride toward perdition,
> When living sickens more than sickness does itself;
> The root of beauty is audacity,
> And that is what draws us to each other

It is this inevitability which makes *Doctor Zhivago* great, as if we, not Pasternak, had willed it. And if love lives at all in the cheap tempestuousness of our time, I think it can only be in the unrelenting honesty with which we face animate nature and inanimate things and the cruelty of our kind, and perceive and articulate and, like Zhivago, choose love above all else.

[*1959*]

Larry Rivers: A Memoir

I first met Larry Rivers in 1950. When I first started coming to New York from Harvard for weekends Larry was in Europe and mutual friends had said we would like each other. Finally, at for me a very literary cocktail party at John Ashbery's we did meet, and we did like each other: I thought he was crazy and he thought I was even crazier. I was very shy, which he thought was intelligence; he was garrulous, which I assumed was brilliance—and on such misinterpretations, thank heavens, many a friendship is based. On the other hand perhaps it was not a misinterpretation: certain of my literary "heroes" of the *Partisan Review* variety present at that party paled in significance when I met Larry, and through these years have remained pale while Larry has been somewhat of a hero to me, which would seem to make me intelligent and Larry brilliant. Who knows?

The milieu of those days, and it's funny to think of them in such a way since they are so recent, seems odd now. We were all in our early twenties. John Ashbery, Barbara Guest, Kenneth Koch and I, being poets, divided our time between the literary bar, the San Remo, and the artists' bar, the Cedar Tavern. In the San Remo we argued and gossiped: in the Cedar we often wrote poems while listening to the painters argue and gossip. So far as I know nobody painted in the San Remo while they listened to the writers argue. An interesting sidelight to these social activities was that for most of us non-academic and indeed non-literary poets in the sense of the American scene at the time, the painters were the only generous audience for our poetry, and most of us read first publicly in art galleries or at The Club. The literary establishment cared about as much for our work as the Frick cared for Pollock and de Kooning, not that we cared any more than they did about establishments, all of the disinterested parties being honorable men.

Then there was great respect for anyone who did anything marvelous: when Larry introduced me to de Kooning I nearly got sick, as I almost did when I met Auden; if Jackson Pollock tore the door off the men's room in the Cedar it was something he just did and was interesting, not an annoyance. You couldn't see into it anyway, and besides there was then a sense of genius. Or what Kline used to call "the dream." Newman was at that time considered a temporarily silent oracle, being ill, Ad Reinhardt the most shrewd critic of the emergent "art world," Meyer Schapiro a god and Alfred Barr right up there alongside him but more distant, Holger Cahill another god but one who had abdicated to become more interested in "the thing we're doing," Clement Greenberg the discoverer, Harold Rosenberg the analyzer, and so on and so on. Tom Hess had written the important book. Elaine de Kooning was the White Goddess: she knew everything, told little of it though she talked a lot, and we all adored (and adore) her. She is graceful.

Into this scene Larry came rather like a demented telephone. Nobody knew whether they wanted it in the library, the kitchen or the toilet, but it was electric. Nor did he. The single most important event in his artistic career was when de Kooning said his painting was like pressing your face into wet grass. From the whole jazz scene, which had gradually diminished to a mere recreation, Larry had emerged into the world of art with the sanction of one of his own gods, and indeed the only living one.

It is interesting to think of 1950–52, and the styles of a whole group of young artists whom I knew rather intimately. It was a liberal education on top of an academic one. Larry was chiefly involved with Bonnard and Renoir at first, later Manet and Soutine. Joan Mitchell—Duchamp; Mike Goldberg—Cezanne-

Villon-de Kooning; Helen Frankenthaler—Pollock-Miro; Al Leslie
—Motherwell; De Niro—Matisse; Nell Blaine—Helion; Harti-
gan—Pollock-Guston; Harry Jackson—a lot of Matisse with a
little German Expressionism; Jane Freilicher—a more subtle com-
bination of Soutine with some Monticelli and Moreau appearing
through the paint. The impact of THE NEW AMERICAN
PAINTING on this group was being avoided rather self-con-
sciously rather than exploited. If you live in the studio next to
Brancusi, you try to think about Poussin. If you drink with Kline
you tend to do your black and whites in pencil on paper. The
artists I knew at that time knew perfectly well who was Great and
they weren't going to begin to imitate their works, only their spirit.
When someone did a false Clyfford Still or Rothko, it was talked
about for weeks. They hadn't read Sartre's *Being and Nothingness*
for nothing.

Larry was especially interested in the vast range of possibilities
of art. Perhaps because of his experience as a jazz musician, where
everything can become fixed so quickly in style, become "the
sound," he has moved restlessly from phase to phase. Larry always
wanted to see something when he painted, unlike the then-preva-
lent conceptualized approach. No matter what stylistic period he
was in, the friends he spent most time with were invariably
subjects in some sense, more or less recognizable, and of course
his two sons and his mother-in-law who lived with him were the
most frequent subjects (he was separated from his wife, Augusta).
His mother-in-law, Mrs. Bertha Burger, was the most frequent
subject. She was called Berdie by everyone, a woman of infinite
patience and sweetness, who held together a Bohemian household
of such staggering complexity it would have driven a less great
woman mad. She had a natural grace of temperament which over-
came all obstacles and irritations. (During her fatal illness she
confessed to me that she had once actually disliked two of Larry's
friends because they had been "mean" to her grandsons, and this
apologetically!) She appears in every period: early Soutinesque
painting with a cat; at an Impressionistic breakfast table; in the
semi-abstract paintings of her seated in a wicker chair; as the
double nude, very realistic, now in the collection of the Whitney
Museum; in the later "The Athlete's Dream," which she especially
enjoyed because I posed with her and it made her less self-

conscious if she was in a painting with a friend; she is also all the figures in the Museum of Modern Art's great painting "The Pool." Her gentle interestedness extended beyond her own family to everyone who frequented the house, in a completely incurious way. Surrounded by painters and poets suddenly in mid-life, she had an admirable directness with esthetic decisions: "it must be very good work, he's such a wonderful person." Considering the polemics of the time, this was not only a relaxing attitude, it was an adorable one. For many of us her death was as much the personal end of a period as Pollock's death was that of a public one.

I mention these details of Rivers' life because, in the sense that Picasso meant it, his work is very much a diary of his experience. He is inspired directly by visual stimulation and his work is ambitious to save these experiences. Where much of the art of our time has been involved with direct conceptual or ethical considerations, Rivers has chosen to mirror his preoccupations and enthusiasms in an unprogrammatic way. As an example, I think that he personally was very awed by Rothko and that this reveals itself in the seated figures of 1953–54; at the same time I know that a rereading of *War and Peace,* and his idea of Tolstoy's life, prompted him to commence work on "Washington Crossing the Delaware," a non-historical, non-philosophical work, the impulse for which I at first thought was hopelessly corny until I saw the painting finished. Rivers veers sharply, as if totally dependent on life impulses, until one observes an obsessively willful insistence on precisely what he is interested in. This goes for the father of our country as well as for the later Camel and Tareyton packs. Who, he seems to be saying, says they're corny? This is the opposite of Pop Art. He is never naive and never over-sophisticated.

Less known that his jazz interests are Larry's literary ones. He has kept, sporadically, a fairly voluminous and definitely scandalous journal, has written, in addition to articles and lectures, some good poems of a diaristic (boosted by surrealism) nature, and collaborated with several poets (including myself) who have posed for him, mainly I think to keep them quiet while posing and to relax himself when not painting or sculpting. The literary side of his activity has resulted mainly in the poem-paintings with Kenneth Koch, a series of lithographs with me, and our great collaborative play *Kenneth Koch, a Tragedy* which cannot be printed because it is so filled with 50s art gossip that everyone would sue us. This latter work kept me amused enough to continue to pose for the big nude which took so many months to finish. That is one of Larry's strategies to keep you coming back to his studio, or was when he couldn't afford a professional model. The separation of the arts, in the "pure" sense, has never interested him. As early as 1952, when John Myers and Herbert Machiz were producing the New York Artists Theatre, Larry did a set for a play of mine, *Try! Try!*. At the first run-through I realized it was all wrong and withdrew it. He, however, insisted that if he had done the work for the set I should be willing to rewrite to my own satisfaction, and so I rewrote the play for Anne Meacham, J.D. Cannon, Louis Edmonds and Larry's set, and that is the version printed by Grove Press. Few people are so generous toward the work of others.

As I said earlier, Larry is restless, impulsive and compulsive. He loves to work. I remember a typical moment in the late 50s when both Joan Mitchell and I were visiting the Hamptons and we were all lying on the beach, a state of relaxation Larry can never tolerate for long. Joan was wearing a particularly attractive boating hat and Larry insisted that they go back to his studio so he could make a drawing of her. It is a beautiful drawing, an interesting moment in their lives and Joan was not only pleased to be drawn, she was relieved because she is terribly vulnerable to sunburn. As Kenneth Koch once said of him, "Larry has a floating sub-conscious—he's all intuition and no sense."

That's an interesting observation about the person, but actually Larry Rivers brings such a barrage of technical gifts to each intuitive occasion that the moment is totally transformed. Many of these gifts were acquired in the same manner as his talents in music and literature, through practice. Having been hired by Herbie Fields' band in his teens he became adept at the saxophone, meeting a group of poets who interested him he absorbed, pro or con, lots of ideas about style in poetry, and attending classes at Hans Hofmann's school plunged him into activities which were to make him one of the best draughtsmen in contemporary art and one of the most subtle and particular colorists. This has been accomplished through work rather than intellection. And here an analogy to jazz can be justified: his hundreds of drawings are each like a separate performance, with its own occasion and subject, and what has been "learned" from the performance is not just the technical facility of the classical pianists' octaves or the studies in a Grande Chaumière class, but the ability to deal with the increased skills that deepening of subject matter and the risks of anxiety-dictated variety demand for clear expression. When Rivers draws a nose, it is my nose, your nose, his nose, Gogol's nose, and the nose from a drawing instruction manual, and it is the result of highly conscious skill.

There is a little bit of Hemingway in his attitude toward ability, toward what you do to a canvas or an armature. His early painting, "The Burial," is really, in a less arrogant manner than Hemingway's, "getting into the ring" with Courbet ("The Funeral at Ornans"), just as his nude portrait of me started in his mind from envy of the then newly acquired Gericault slave with the rope at the Metropolitan Museum, the portrait "Augusta" from a Delacroix; and even this year he is still fighting it out, this time with David's "Napoleon." As with his friends, as with cigarette and cigar boxes, maps, and animals, he is always engaged in an esthetic athleticism which sharpens the eye, hand and arm in order to beat the bugaboos of banality and boredom, deliberately invited into the painting and then triumphed over.

What his work has always had to say to me, I guess, is to be more keenly interested while I'm still alive. And perhaps this is the most important thing art can say.

[*1965*]

LEROI JONES
(IMAMU AMIRI BARAKA)

Expressive Language

Speech is the effective form of a culture. Any shape or cluster of human history still apparent in the conscious and unconscious habit of groups of people is what I mean by culture. All culture is necessarily profound. The very fact of its longevity, of its being what it is, *culture,* the epic memory of practical tradition, means that it is profound. But the inherent profundity of culture does not necessarily mean that its *uses* (and they are as various as the human condition) will be profound. German culture is profound. Generically. Its uses, however, are specific, as are all uses . . . of ideas, inventions, products of nature. And specificity, as a right and passion of human life, breeds what it breeds as a result of its context.

Context, in this instance, is most dramatically social. And the social, though it must be rooted, as are all evidences of existence, in culture, depends for its impetus for the most part on a multiplicity of influences. Other cultures, for instance. Perhaps, and this is a common occurrence, the reaction or interreaction of one culture on another can produce a social context that will extend or influence any culture in many strange directions.

Social also means *economic,* as any reader of nineteenth-century European philosophy will understand. The economic is part of the social—and in our time much more so than what we have known as the spiritual or metaphysical, because the most valuable canons of power have either been reduced or traduced into stricter economic terms. That is, there has been a shift in the actual meaning of the world since Dante lived. As if Brooks Adams were right. Money does not mean the same thing to me it must mean to a rich

373

man. I cannot, right now, think of one meaning to name. This is not so simple to understand. Even as a simple term of the English language, *money* does not possess the same meanings for the rich man as it does for me, a lower-middle-class American, albeit of laughably "aristocratic" pretensions. What possibly can "money" mean to a poor man? And I am not talking now about those courageous products of our permissive society who walk knowledgeably into "poverty" as they would into a public toilet. I mean, The Poor.

I look in my pocket; I have seventy cents. Possibly I can buy a beer. A quart of ale, specifically. Then I will have twenty cents with which to annoy and seduce my fingers when they wearily search for gainful employment. I have no idea at this moment what that seventy cents will mean to my neighbor around the corner, a poor Puerto Rican man I have seen hopefully watching my plastic garbage can. But I am certain it cannot mean the same thing. Say to David Rockefeller, "I have money," and he will think you mean something entirely different. That is, if you also dress the part. He would not for a moment think, "Seventy cents." But then neither would many New York painters.

Speech, the way one describes the natural proposition of being alive, is much more crucial than even most artists realize. Semantic philosophers are certainly correct in their emphasis on the final dictation of words over their users. But they often neglect to point out that, after all, it is the actual importance, *power,* of the words that remains so finally crucial. Words have users, but as well, users have words. And it is the users that establish the world's realities. Realities being those fantasies that control your immediate span of life. Usually they are not your own fantasies, *i.e.,* they belong to governments, traditions, etc., which, it must be clear by now, can make for conflict with the singular human life all ways. The fantasy of America might hurt you, but it is what should be meant when one talks of "reality." Not only the things you can touch or see, but the things that make such touching or seeing "normal." Then words, like their users, have a hegemony. Socially—which is final, right now. If you are some kind of artist, you naturally might think this is not so. There is the future. But *immortality* is a kind of drug, I think—one that leads to happiness at the thought of death. Myself, I would rather live forever . . . just to make sure.

The social hegemony, one's position in society, enforces more specifically one's terms (even the vulgar have "pull"). Even to the mode of speech. But also it makes these terms an available explanation of any social hierarchy, so that the words themselves become, even informally, laws. And of course they are usually very quickly stitched together to make formal statutes only fools or the faithfully intrepid would dare to question beyond immediate necessity.

The culture of the powerful is very infectious for the sophisticated, and strongly addictive. To be any kind of "success" one must be fluent in this culture. Know the words of the users, the semantic rituals of power. This is a way into wherever it is you are not now, but wish, very desperately, to get into.

Even speech then signals a fluency in this culture. A knowledge at least. "He's an educated man," is the barest acknowledgment of such fluency . . . in any time. "He's hip," my friends might say. They connote a similar entrance.

And it is certainly the meanings of words that are most important, even if they are no longer consciously acknowledged, but merely, by their use, trip a familiar lever of social accord. To recreate instantly the understood hierarchy of social, and by doing that, cultural, importance. And cultures are thought by most people in the world to do their business merely by being hierarchies. Certainly this is true in the West, in as simple a manifestation as Xenophobia, the naïve bridegroom of anti-human feeling, or in economic terms, Colonialism. For instance, when the first Africans were brought into the New World, it was thought that it was all right for them to be slaves because "they were heathens." It is a perfectly logical assumption.

And it follows, of course, that slavery would have been an even stranger phenomenon had the Africans spoken English when they first got here. It would have complicated things. Very soon after the first generations of Afro-Americans mastered this language, they invented white people called Abolitionists.

Words' meanings, but also the rhythm and syntax that frame and propel their concatenation, seek their culture as the final reference for what they are describing of the world. An A flat played twice on the same saxophone by two different men does not have to sound the same. If these men have different ideas of what they want this note to do, the note will not sound the same. Culture is the form, the overall structure of organized thought (as well as emotion and spiritual pretension). There are many cultures. Many ways of organizing thought, or having thought organized. That is, the form of thought's passage through the world will take on as many diverse shapes as there are diverse groups of travelers. Environment is one organizer of *groups,* at any level of its meaning. People who live in Newark, New Jersey, are organized, for whatever purpose, as Newarkers. It begins that simply. Another manifestation, at a slightly more complex level, can be the fact that blues singers from the Midwest sing through their noses. There is an explanation past the geographical, but that's the idea in tabloid. And singing through the nose does propose that the definition of singing be altered . . . even if ever so slightly. (At this point where someone's definitions must be changed, we are flitting around at the outskirts of the old city of Aesthetics. A solemn ghost town. Though some of the bones of reason can still be gathered there.)

But we still need definitions, even if there already are many. The dullest men are always satisfied that a dictionary lists everything in the world. They don't care that you may find out something *extra,* which one day might even be valuable to them. Of course, by that time it might even be in the dictionary, or at least they'd hope so, if you asked them directly.

But for every item in the world, there are a multiplicity of definitions that fit. And every word we use *could* mean something else. And at the same time. The culture fixes the use, and usage. And in "pluralistic" America, one should always listen very closely when he is being talked to. The speaker might mean something completely different from what we think we're hearing. "Where is your pot?"

I heard an old Negro street singer last week, Reverend Pearly Brown, singing, "God don't never change!" This is a precise thing he is singing. He does not mean "God does not ever change!" He means "God don't never change!" The difference, and I said it was crucial, is in the final human reference . . . the form of passage through the world. A man who is rich and famous who sings, "God don't never change," is confirming his hegemony and good fortune . . . or merely calling the bank. A blind hopeless black

American is saying something very different. He is telling you about the extraordinary order of the world. But he is not telling you about his "fate." Fate is a luxury available only to those fortunate citizens with alternatives. The view from the top of the hill is not the same as that from the bottom of the hill. Nor are most viewers at either end of the hill, even certain that, in fact, there is any other place from which to look. Looking down usually eliminates the possibility of understanding what it must be like to look up. Or try to imagine yourself as not existing. It is difficult, but poets and politicians try every other day.

Being told to "speak proper," meaning that you become fluent with the jargon of power, is also a part of not "speaking proper." That is, the culture which desperately understands that it does not "speak proper," or is not fluent with the terms of social strength, also understands somewhere that its desire to gain such fluency is done at a terrifying risk. The bourgeois Negro accepts such risk as profit. But does *close-ter* (in the context of "jes a close-ter, walk wi-thee") mean the same thing as *closer?* Close-ter, in the term of its user is, believe me, exact. It means a quality of existence, of actual physical disposition perhaps . . . in its manifestation as a *tone* and *rhythm* by which people live, most often in response to common modes of thought best enforced by some factor of environmental emotion that is exact and specific. Even the picture it summons is different, and certainly the "Thee" that is used to connect the implied "Me" with, is different. The God of the damned cannot know the God of the damner, that is, cannot know he is God. As no Blues person can really believe emotionally in Pascal's God, or Wittgenstein's question, "Can the concept of God exist in a perfectly logical language?" Answer: "God don't never change."

Communication is only important because it is the broadest root of education. And all cultures communicate exactly what they have, a powerful motley of experience.

[*1963*]

Hunting Is Not Those Heads
on the Wall

Thought is more important than art. Without thought, art could certainly not exist. Art is one of many products of thought. An impressive one, perhaps the most impressive one, but to revere art, and have no understanding of the process that forces it into existence, is finally not even to understand what art is.

The artist is cursed with his artifact, which exists without and despite him. And even though the process, in good art, is everywhere perceptible, the risk of perfection corrupts the lazy public into accepting the material *in place of* what it is only the remains of.

The academic Western mind is the best example of the substitution of artifact worship for the lightning awareness of the art process. Even the artist is more valuable than his artifact, because the art process goes on in his mind. But the process itself is the most important quality because it can transform and create, and its only form is possibility. The artifact, because it assumes one form, is only that particular quality or idea. It is, in this sense, after the fact, and is only important because it remarks on its source.

The academician, the aesthete, are like deists whose specific corruption of mysticism is to worship things, thinking that they are God (thought, the process) too. But art is not capable of thought. Just as things are not capable of God, but the reverse is what we mean by the God function, the process I am talking about.

The Supermaker, is what the Greeks identified as "Gods." But here the emphasis is still muddled, since it is what the God can do that is really important, not the fact that he is the God. I speak of the *verb process,* the doing, the coming into being, the at-the-time-of. Which is why we think there is particular value in live music, contemplating the artifact as it arrives, listening to it emerge. *There* it is. And *There*.

But even this is after the fact. Music, the most valuable of artifacts, because it is the most abstract, is still not the activity that makes itself possible. Music is what is left after what? *That* is important.

A museum is a curious graveyard of thinking. But we can go through one hoping to get some inkling of what those various creators who made the creations were thinking. What was he thinking when he did That? is a common question. The answer is obvious, though: That.

Formal art, that is, artifacts made to cohere to preconceived forms, is almost devoid of this verb value. Usually a man playing Bach is only demonstrating his music lessons; the contemporary sonneteer, his ability to organize intellectual materials. But nothing that already exists is *that* valuable. The most valuable quality in life is the will to existence, the unconnected zoom, which finally becomes in anyone's hands whatever part of it he could collect. Like dipping cups of water from the falls. Which is what the artist does. Fools want to dictate what kind of dipper he uses.

Art is like speech, for instance, in that it is at the end, and a shadowy replica, of another operation, thought. And even to name something, is to wait for it in the place you think it will pass. Thought, "I've written"—understanding even this process is recording. Art-ing is what makes art, and is thereby more valuable. But we speak of the Muse, to make even the verb a thing.

If we describe a man by his life we are making him a verb, which is the only valid method since everything else is too arbitrary. The clearest description of now is the present participle, which if the activity described continues is always correct. Walking is not past or future. Be-ing, the most complex, since it goes on as itself, as adjective-verb, and at the moment of. Art is not a be-ing, but a Being, the simple noun. It is not the verb, but its product. Worship the verb, if you need something. Then even God is after the fact, since He is the leavings of God-ing. The verb-God, is where it is, the container of all possibility. Art, like time, is the measurement of. Make no mistake.

Even "sense" is clearly a use some energy is put to. No one should fool around with art who is only trying to "make sense."

We are all full of meaning and content, but to make that wild grab for more! To make words surprise themselves. Some more of the zoom trembling in its cage, where some fool will be impressed by its "perfection." This is what should be meant by a "primitive" mind, that which is satisfied with simple order. But "using" words denies the full possibility of expression, which is, we must suppose, impossible, since it could not be stopped and identified. Art is identification, and the slowing-down for it. But hunting is *not* those heads on the wall.

The imitator is the most pitiful phenomenon since he is like a man who eats garbage. A saxophonist who continues to "play like" Charlie Parker cannot understand that Charlie Parker wasn't certain that what had happened had to sound like that. But if a man tries to understand *why* Parker sounded like he did, the real value of his music begins to be understood.

Form is simply *how* a thing exists (or what a thing exists as). When we speak of man, we ask, "How does he make it?" Content is *why* a thing exists. Every thing has both these qualities; otherwise it could not (does not) exist. The art object has a special relationship between these two qualities, but they are not separable in any object.

The recent concern in the West for the found object and chance composition is an attempt to get closer to the non-Western concept of natural expression as an Art object, since of course such an object has form and content in special relationship like any thing a man made. Because a man cannot make a thing that is in this sense unnatural. The unnatural aspect of the man-made object is that it seems to exist only as a result of man, with no other real connection with the nonhuman world. *Artificial,* in this sense, is simply *made.* "Bad art" is usually unnatural, *i.e.,* it seems as if it could not exist without being made by a man. It is strictly artificial.

Western men have always been more concerned with the artifact, the made thing, as "an art" separated from some natural use. Art as a separate category of concern is first seen when? Functional art is as old as man was when he made *anything.* To posit the idea that you will make a thing whose sole value and function is that you will make it, is a different emphasis.

God (which is separate, and before, A God) is in one sense an art object and was probably the first. In the secular West, God is a nonfunctional (literally) art object. But earlier, God was simply the naming of force, in the same sense I meant earlier of naming a thing by its life. God was "the force out of which the world (and life) issued." The *naming,* nominalization, of that force is finally a step at making it artificial. The arbitrary assignment of content (which means nothing in a strictly local context, *i.e.,* Who will object?) based very likely on need, is the beginning of God as an art object.

But think about this, "the force out of which the world (and life) issued" exists everywhere, as we can see, and this is the basic form (and content) of God. Everything else is most likely to be nationalism. Nothing else exists. But again the confusing of process with artifact, or rather the substitution of process for artifact. When God gets to be a thing, it is an artifact. When the lightning was "the force out of which the world issued," the emphasis was on natural evidence, the natural thing. And lightning is curiously apt, since in its natural form, it is a process, a happening, as well as an artifact. Duplicating God signs was simple education.

When God started to *look like* a human being, men had gotten very sure of themselves. (That is, once the dog, the wolf, the fish, the bear, the leopard, etc., had all been God, and the fallacy of this reasoning, in whatever turn of environmental circumstance, became traditional. Some of the things we have seen are animals, possibly one of them is God. Men next.) But *naming* is the first appropriation, the earliest humanist trend. Jane Harrison says the Greeks took the fear away by not only making all the various qualities known in the world men, but understandable, knowable, men. They began to make lives for their Gods, so those Gods could only exist in that certain way. From the unknown verb, to the familiar artifact. Greek Gods are beautiful Greeks, which finally in social/political terms is the beginning of modern nationalism. What the Western white man calls the beginning of democracy was the positing of the sovereign state, wherein everyone was free. The rest of the world could be exploited. *Logos,* then, is not merely thought, but belief. Greeks were Greeks because they had the same beliefs. A Greek was a man who believed the Gods were Greeks.

Humanism is good in this sense, that it puts the emphasis on what we actually have, but there is a *loss* with the loss of the unspecific imagination because knowing man was all there was enabled the less imaginative to show up fully armed. Man's mind is revered and, in the ugliest emphasis, man's inventions. Again the hideous artifact, to replace the valuable process. The most stupid man ought to know he is more important than what he can make. But he will never understand that what moves him is even more important, because of the contemporary (post-Renaissance) loss of prestige for the unseen. When God had a rep, his curious "workings" were given deference. But now that everything is grounded or lodged in the sweaty palm, men only believe in what, as Auden inferred, "takes up space."

Thinking, in the most exalted humanist terms, is God, the force out of which the world issued. Nature, we make a "natural" process. Darwinian determinism provided the frame. From the Renaissance, the boost of the industrial revolution, and man surrounded by his artifacts. Machines, which are completely knowable.

[*1964*]

State/Meant

The Black Artist's role in America is to aid in the destruction of America as he knows it. His role is to report and reflect so precisely the nature of the society, and of himself in that society, that other men will be moved by the exactness of his rendering and, if they are black men, grow strong through this moving, having seen their own strength, and weakness; and if they are white men, tremble, curse, and go mad, because they will be drenched with the filth of their evil.

The Black Artist must draw out of his soul the correct image of the world. He must use this image to band his brothers and sisters together in common understanding of the nature of the world (and the nature of America) and the nature of the human soul.

The Black Artist must demonstrate sweet life, how it differs from the deathly grip of the White Eyes. The Black Artist must teach the White Eyes their deaths, and teach the black man how to bring these deaths about.

> We are unfair, and unfair.
> We are black magicians, black art
> s we make in black labs of the heart.
>
> The fair are
> fair, and death
> ly white.
>
> The day will not save them
> and we own
> the night.

[*1965*]

Statement

———————————

An "anarchist" does not believe, as some wrongly have put it, in social chaos. He believes in a state of society wherein there is no frozen power structure, where all persons may make significant initiatory choices in regard to matters affecting their own lives. In such a society coercion is at a minimum & lethal violence practically non-existent. Certainly, there will still be situations where coercion may have to be exercised to prevent something worse, but, as Ammon Hennacy has demonstrated in life, even maniacs with knives may be sometimes pacified without violent coercion. A "pacifist" believes that better methods than violence may almost always be found to solve social difficulties & resolve differences between individuals & groups. While not all anarchists are pacificists even now, & many pacificists are not anarchists, I think all agree in regarding the individual person as being infinitely precious & as being capable of cooperating with others for the good of all. Let us add to these attitudes that of the Taoist, Zen Buddhist, or Kegon Buddhist, wherein the elementary actions of the world itself & of "all sentient beings" are regarded as being on a level with those of human beings in the narrower sense. One comes to a situation wherein "even plants have rights" (one doesn't chop down a tree unless there's a damn good reason to). How better to embody such ideas in microcosm than to create works wherein both other human beings & their environments & the world "in general" (as represented by such objectively hazardous means as random digits) are all able to act within the general framework & set of "rules" given by the poet, "the maker of plots or fables," as Aristotle insists—the poet is pre-eminently the maker of the plot, the framework—not necessarily of everything that takes place within that framework! The poet creates a *situation* wherein he invites other persons & the world in general to be co-creators with him! He does not wish to be a dictator but a loyal co-initiator of action within the free society of equals which he hopes his work will help to bring about.

That such works themselves may lead to new discoveries about the nature of the world & of man I have no doubt. I have learned, for instance, that it is often very difficult to tell, in many cases, what is "chance" & what is "cause." There are kinds of inner & hidden causation that are very difficult to distinguish, on the one hand, from "chance" or "coincidence," & on the other, from "synchronicity": "meaningful acausal interconnection." Also, absolutely unique situations may arise during performances of such works, & the experiences of those participating in them (whether as performers, audience or both) cannot help but be of new *aesthetic* (experiential) meanings. That is, not only do the works embody & express certain metaphysical, ethical, & political meanings, but they also bring into being new aesthetic meanings.

Some Remarks to the Dancers*

(HOW THE DANCES ARE TO BE
PERFORMED & HOW THEY WERE MADE)

The Pronouns is "A *Collection* of 40 Dances"—not a *series*. That is, despite the fact that the dances are numbered, each is a separate & complete work in itself & may be performed on a program before or after any or none of the other dances in the collection. Also,

* From *The Pronouns—A Collection of 40 Dances—For the Dancers—6 February—22 March 1964.*

any number of different realizations of one or more of the dances may succeed or follow each other during a particular performance. For example, a program might have on it such a succession of the dances as the following, in which each reappearance of a dance's number stands for a different realization of that dance: 5, 7, 10, 5, 22, 40, 33, 33, 11, 7, 1, 7, 1, 1, 10, 28, 18, 6, 22, 5.

By suggesting a *succession* of realizations of dances, I do not intend to rule out entirely the possibilities of simultaneous or over-lapping performances of various of the dances on a program. However, I do wish to *de-emphasize* these possibilities (which might seem most appropriate in view of the fact that so much of my past work—my simultaneous poems & other simultaneities—involves the simultaneous &/or overlapping performance of sepa-rate works that are also members of non-ordered collections, e.g., the "Asymmetries") in order to encourage performances in which some or all of the dances are realized *one at a time* in various orders of succession. The important thing is that (even in overlap-ping realizations or the like) the *integrity* of each dance—its hav-ing a definite beginning, middle, & end—ought to be completely clear in every performance.

The dances require various numbers of performers. Some are obviously solos or duets, & some will be found to require a group of a definite number that will probably be the same in any realiza-tion, but the sizes of the groups required in many of them are somewhat indefinite & are to be decided for each realization by the dancers themselves by careful interpretation of the given text.

In realizing any particular dance, the individual dancer or group of dancers has a very large degree of freedom of interpretation. However, although they are to interpret the successive lines of each of these poems-which-are-also-dance-instructions as they see fit, dancers are required to find *some definite interpretation* of the *meaning* of *every* line of the dance-poems they choose to realize. Above all, no line or series of lines may be left uninterpreted & unrealized simply because it seems too complicated or obscure to realize as movement (&/or sound or speech).

In addition to finding concrete meanings as actions for every line of each dance-poem realized, the dancers must carefully work out the time-relations between the various actions, as indicated by their positions in the poems & by the particular conjunctions &

adverbs used to connect them together within the sentence-length strophes, & to connect these strophes together. For example, if a poem indicates that someone "has the chest between thick things *while* he says things about making gardens," a dancer may realize each of these actions as he sees fit, but they must take place simultaneously, *not* one after the other.

There is a seemingly unlimited multiplicity of possible realizations for each of these dances because the judgments of the particular dancers will determine such matters as degrees of literalness or figurativeness in interpreting & realizing instructions. Each dancer or group of dancers must decide for itself whether, &/or to what extent, to use or avoid props, miming, &c., & whether, &/or to what extent, to be consistent in such use or avoidance—one might, for instance, within the same realization, sometimes use props & sometimes dispense with them, even in different appearances of the same action in a poem. Thus, while the text of each dance-poem is completely determinate, &, if realized, is to be realized in its entirety, the actual movements & actions constituting any particular realization are very largely unpredictable from the text of the poem of which it is a realization.

I first conceived these dance-instruction-poems as *either* being read aloud as poems (& I have read many of them at various poetry readings already) *or* as being realized as dances. Lately, however, I have come to agree with a number of persons who've heard me read them that the poems themselves might well be read aloud during *some* of their realizations as dances. A program might include, then, some realizations accompanied by the reading aloud of the poems & some not so accompanied.

In any case, the sounds of the reading of the poems, when they are read, &/or any other sounds used as "accompaniment" to the dances must never get in the way of the sounds produced by the dancers themselves in accordance with those instructions calling for sound or speech. It is to be emphasized that wherever a line calls for sound-production or speech, this instruction must be taken literally, at least insofar as the dancer must produce some definite sound or speak some words or other, as he finds appropriate.

I might well note here that, as in the line above, "he" & "himself" are used throughout *The Pronouns* (except in the "1st

Dance—Making Things New") *generically;* that is, they are used to refer to persons of *either* sex, in order to avoid the use of awkward & unnecessary locutions such as "he or she" & "himself or herself."

Now, as to HOW THEY WERE MADE: The actions of the 40 dances comprised in *The Pronouns* were drawn by a systematic "chance" method (outlined below) from a "pack" of 56 filing cards, on each of which are typed one to five actions, denoted by gerunds or gerundial phrases, e.g., "jumping," "having a letter over one eye," & "giving the neck a knifing or coming to give a parallel meal, beautiful & shocking." 170 different actions are each named once in this pack of cards, & three more, "jumping," "mapping," & "questioning," are each named twice. (That is, in the 56 sets of one to five actions, there are, in all, 176 "places" filled by 173 *different* actions, three of which actions occur in two of the sets, the rest each only in one.)

This pack of actions was composed in May 1961. At that time, these 56 sets of one to five actions were typed on another set of filing cards, on each of which one to ten single words were also typed. Both these single words & all the definite lexical words among the words & phrases denoting actions were drawn, with the help of the Rand table of a million random digits, from the 850-word Basic-English Word List. In the action-naming phrases, each Basic-English word was used in any desired form (i.e., as verb, adverb, adjective, or noun, in the singular or the plural, &c.). For example, if I drew the word "beautiful" from the list, I might use it as "beauty," "beautify," "beautiful," "beautifully," "beauties," "beauty's," "beautifying," "beautified," &c. Structure words (conjunctions, prepositions, pronouns, indefinite nouns, &c.) were freely used in connecting these Basic-English "nuclei" into phrases. However, the number & order of succession of the Basic-English "nuclei" in each action-phrase were determined by systematic "chance" although their grammatical forms & connections were freely chosen by the author.

This pack of cards having both one to ten unconnected words & one to five action-naming gerunds & gerundial phrases on them have been used in two kinds of performances: as a play, *Nuclei,* in which the performers used the unconnected words on each card as nuclei around which to improvise speeches while they performed the actions in various realizations, & as a vehicle for solo improvisation, *Nuclei for Simone Morris*, now called *Nuclei for Simone Forti*, in which the performer used each single card as the basis upon which to construct a separate improvisation incorporating the words & actions typed on that card.

Both of these were performed in June 1961 at the AG Gallery (then on Madison Avenue near 74th Street in New York). On 17 June 1961, *Nuclei for Simone Forti* was performed by the dedicatee, a most inspired dancer, as a series of about five short improvisations, each based on one card, during a program consisting mainly of my non-verbal musical works. & on 30 June 1961, the play *Nuclei* was performed by a group of poets & composers as part of a program consisting mainly of my poems. Two years later, on 11–12 May 1963, as part of the Yam Festival, a continuous two-day presentation of music, plays, poetry, happenings, &c., at the Hardware Poets Playhouse (on 54th Street near 6th Avenue in New York), Trisha Brown performed *Nuclei for Simone Forti* as a couple of series of short improvisations, each based on a single card from that pack.

In addition to that pack, I prepared two packs, each of 56 filing cards, that have on them only the sets of actions, not the additional separated words. In 1961, at Les Deux Megots, a coffeehouse on East 7th Street, New York, I read this entire pack of actions as a poem in its own right, & one of the packs of filing cards was exhibited at the Smolin Gallery during the Yam Festival in May 1963. It was one of these packs having only the actions in them that was used as the source of *The Pronouns*.

The "1st Dance—Making Things New" was composed after the late Fred Herko, a marvelous dancer, had asked me several times for the loan of the *Nuclei for Simone Morris (Forti)* pack. He had seen Trisha Brown's realizations during the Yam Festival of May 1963 & wished to improvise from the pack himself. Unfortunately, Trisha had borrowed the pack after her performances & had taken it to California, where she had been using it with her students & other dancers, & had not had the time to copy & return the pack to me. Thus after Fred's last request, I conceived the idea of using the pack of 56 sets of actions as the source of a dance-instruction-poem for him to realize. After having written the "he" poem for Fred, it was natural that I thought of writing a "she" poem for

Trisha (& possibly for Simone, although she was not performing at the time). After that I decided to write a dance-instruction-poem for every word listed as a pronoun in the Merriam-Webster Dictionary (most linguists would now call such words as "everybody" nouns rather than pronouns, but I went by the book). After having written 40 of them, I thought I'd written enough of them, so there are no poems for some of the less-used pronouns (or pronounlike nouns). [New paragraph added to London edition 4 January 1971.]

In composing each dance, I would first shuffle the pack & then cut it & point blindly to one of the actions on the card cut to. This action became the title of the dance. Before or after determining the title I would also choose which *pronoun* was to be the subject of all the sentences in that dance-poem. The title was then used as a "through-acrostic index" to determine the successive actions of the dance & also, necessarily, their number. That is, the letters of the title determined the actions drawn for the dance: turning the filing cards over, one at a time, with occasional shufflings, I let the title letters "select" the successive actions from the sets of one to five actions as they showed up. For example, in the "37th Dance— Banding," the "B" selected "*b*eing flies," the "A," "h*a*ving examples," the "N," "doing something co*n*sciously," the "D," "saying things about making gar*d*ens," &c. In some dances I gave myself the rule that the actions had to have the title letters not only in corresponding places in *any one* of the words (as in the example) but also in corresponding words. That is, if the 2nd word of the title had an "H" in the 2nd place (e.g., in "T*h*e"), the corresponding action-phrase had also to have an "H" in the 2nd place of the 2nd word, & so on.

As each action—word or phrase—was arrived at, it was either modified grammatically, or used unmodified, as part of a sentence of which the pronoun chosen for that dance was the subject. While punctuation, & thus sentence length & the number, & often the kinds, of clauses in sentences, was largely determined by the punctuation already on the filing cards, the various conjunctions & adverbs used to connect the action-lines into sentence-strophes, & to connect the sentence-strophes with each other, were freely chosen. In short, although systematic "chance" determined many features of each dance, a few crucial features, such as which pronoun was to be the subject of all sentences in that dance, & how the actions were to be connected—& thus, incidentally, the time-relations persisting between the actions of the dance—were matters of free choice.

The Pronouns is "For the *Dancers*"—all the dancers every-where—& it is my hope that many of these dances will receive as many entirely different realizations as possible.

[*17–30 March 1964*]

[Note on performances added to London edition 4 January 1971 & completed 7 July 1973:]

On 10 September 1965 during the 3rd Annual New York Avant-Garde Festival, eight of the poems were realized by a group co-ordinated by Meredith Monk & including Kenneth King, Judith Kuemmerle, Al Kurchin, Phoebe Neville, Ms. Monk, & myself. I also read the eight poems as a "reading dance" in which I appeared at a different place in the theatre (after a sound-filled blackout) for each poem. In February 1967 a student group at the University of Kansas at Lawrence performed several realizations while I read the corresponding poems as part of a reading by David Antin, Ted Berrigan, Jerome Rothenberg, Armand Schwerner, & myself. In July 1971 Christine Loizeaux performed several of the dances while I read the corresponding poems as part of the poetry environment I made for the end of the National Poetry Festival at Thomas Jefferson College of Grand Valley State Colleges, Allendale, Michigan.

GARY SNYDER

Buddhism and the Coming Revolution

Buddhism holds that the universe and all creatures in it are intrinsically in a state of complete wisdom, love and compassion; acting in natural response and mutual interdependence. The personal realization of this from-the-beginning state cannot be had for and by one-"self"—because it is not fully realized unless one has given the self up; and away.

In the Buddhist view, that which obstructs the effortless manifestation of this is Ignorance, which projects into fear and needless craving. Historically, Buddhist philosophers have failed to analyze out the degree to which ignorance and suffering are caused or encouraged by social factors, considering fear-and-desire to be given facts of the human condition. Consequently the major concern of Buddhist philosophy is epistemology and "psychology" with no attention paid to historical or sociological problems. Although Mahayana Buddhism has a grand vision of universal salvation, the *actual* achievement of Buddhism has been the development of practical systems of meditation toward the end of liberating a few dedicated individuals from psychological hangups and cultural conditionings. Institutional Buddhism has been conspicuously ready to accept or ignore the inequalities and tyrannies of whatever political system it found itself under. This can be death to Buddhism, because it is death to any meaningful function of compassion. Wisdom without compassion feels no pain.

No one today can afford to be innocent, or indulge himself in ignorance of the nature of contemporary governments, politics and social orders. The national polities of the modern world maintain their existence by deliberately fostered craving and fear: monstrous protection rackets. The "free world" has become economically dependent on a fantastic system of stimulation of greed which cannot be fulfilled, sexual desire which cannot be satiated and hatred which has no outlet except against oneself, the persons one is supposed to love, or the revolutionary aspirations of pitiful, poverty-stricken marginal societies like Cuba or Vietnam. The conditions of the Cold War have turned all modern societies— Communist included—into vicious distorters of man's true potential. They create populations of "preta"—hungry ghosts, with giant appetites and throats no bigger than needles. The soil, the forests and all animal life are being consumed by these cancerous collectivities; the air and water of the planet is being fouled by them.

There is nothing in human nature or the requirements of human social organization which intrinsically requires that a culture be contradictory, repressive and productive of violent and frustrated personalities. Recent findings in anthropology and psychology make this more and more evident. One can prove it for himself by taking a good look at his own nature through meditation. Once a person has this much faith and insight, he must be led to a deep concern with the need for radical social change through a variety of hopefully non-violent means.

The joyous and voluntary poverty of Buddhism becomes a positive force. The traditional harmlessness and refusal to take life in any form has nation-shaking implications. The practice of meditation, for which one needs only "the ground beneath one's feet" wipes out mountains of junk being pumped into the mind by the mass media and supermarket universities. The belief in a serene and generous fulfilment of natural loving desires destroys ideologies which blind, maim and repress—and points the way to a kind of community which would amaze "moralists" and transform armies of men who are fighters because they cannot be lovers.

Avatamsaka (Kegon) Buddhist philosophy sees the world as a vast interrelated network in which all objects and creatures are necessary and illuminated. From one standpoint, governments, wars, or all that we consider "evil" are uncompromisingly contained in this totalistic realm. The hawk, the swoop and the hare are one. From the "human" standpoint we cannot live in those terms unless all beings see with the same enlightened eye. The

Bodhisattva lives by the sufferer's standard, and he must be effective in aiding those who suffer.

The mercy of the West has been social revolution; the mercy of the East has been individual insight into the basic self/void. We need both. They are both contained in the traditional three aspects of the Dharma path: wisdom (prajña), meditation (dhyāna), and morality (śīla). Wisdom is intuitive knowledge of the mind of love and clarity that lies beneath one's ego-driven anxieties and aggressions. Meditation is going into the mind to see this for yourself— over and over again, until it becomes the mind you live in. Morality is bringing it back out in the way you live, through personal example and responsible action, ultimately toward the true community (sangha) of "all beings." This last aspect means, for me, supporting any cultural and economic revolution that moves clearly toward a free, international, classless world. It means using such means as civil disobedience, outspoken criticism, protest, pacifism, voluntary poverty and even gentle violence if it comes to a matter of restraining some impetuous redneck. It means affirming the widest possible spectrum of non-harmful individual behavior—defending the right of individuals to smoke hemp, eat peyote, be polygynous, polyandrous or homosexual. Worlds of behavior and custom long banned by the Judaeo-Capitalist-Christian-Marxist West. It means respecting intelligence and learning, but not as greed or means to personal power. Working on one's own responsibility, but willing to work with a group. "Forming the new society within the shell of the old"—the I. W. W. slogan of fifty years ago.

The traditional cultures are in any case doomed, and rather than cling to their good aspects hopelessly it should be remembered that whatever is or ever was in any other culture can be reconstructed from the unconscious, through meditation. In fact, it is my own view that the coming revolution will close the circle and link us in many ways with the most creative aspects of our archaic past. If we are lucky we may eventually arrive at a totally integrated world culture with matrilineal descent, free-form marriage, natural-credit communist economy, less industry, far less population and lots more national parks.

Poetry and the Primitive
NOTES ON POETRY AS AN ECOLOGICAL SURVIVAL TECHNIQUE

BILATERAL SYMMETRY

"Poetry" as the skilled and inspired use of the voice and language
to embody rare and powerful states of mind that are in immediate
origin personal to the singer, but at deep levels common to all who
listen. "Primitive" as those societies which have remained non-
literate and non-political while necessarily exploring and develop-
ing in directions that civilized societies have tended to ignore.
Having fewer tools, no concern with history, a living oral tradition
rather than an accumulated library, no overriding social goals, and
considerable freedom of sexual and inner life, such people live
vastly in the present. Their daily reality is a fabric of friends and
family, the field of feeling and energy that one's own body is, the
earth they stand on and the wind that wraps around it; and various
areas of consciousness.

At this point some might be tempted to say that the primitive's
real life is no different from anybody else's. I think this is not so.
To live in the "mythological present" in close relation to nature
and in basic but disciplined body/mind states suggests a wider-
ranging imagination and a closer subjective knowledge of one's
own physical properties than is usually available to men living (as
they themselves describe it) impotently and inadequately in "his-
tory"—their mind-content programmed, and their caressing of
nature complicated by the extensions and abstractions which
elaborate tools are. A hand pushing a button may wield great

power, but that hand will never learn what a hand can do. Unused capacities go sour.

Poetry must sing or speak from authentic experience. Of all the streams of civilized tradition with roots in the paleolithic, poetry is one of the few that can realistically claim an unchanged function and a relevance which will outlast most of the activities that surround us today. Poets, as few others, must live close to the world that primitive men are in: the world, in its nakedness, which is fundamental for all of us—birth, love, death; the sheer fact of being alive.

Music, dance, religion, and philosophy of course have archaic roots—a shared origin with poetry. Religion has tended to become the social justifier, a lackey to power, instead of the vehicle of hair-raising liberating and healing realizations. Dance has mostly lost its connection with ritual drama, the miming of animals, or tracing the maze of the spiritual journey. Most music takes too many tools. The poet can make it on his own voice and mother tongue, while steering a course between crystal clouds of utterly incommunicable non-verbal states—and the gleaming daggers and glittering nets of language.

In one school of Mahayana Buddhism, they talk about the "Three Mysteries." These are Body, Voice, and Mind. The things that are what living *is* for us, in life. Poetry is the vehicle of the mystery of voice. The universe, as they sometimes say, is a vast breathing body.

With artists, certain kinds of scientists, yogins, and poets, a kind of mind-sense is not only surviving but modestly flourishing in the twentieth century. Claude Lévi-Strauss (*The Savage Mind*) sees no problem in the continuity: ". . . it is neither the mind of savages nor that of primitive or archaic humanity, but rather mind in its untamed state as distinct from mind cultivated or domesticated for yielding a return. . . . We are better able to understand today that it is possible for the two to coexist and interpenetrate in the same way that (in theory at least) it is possible for natural species, of which some are in their savage state and others transformed by agriculture and domestication, to coexist and cross . . . whether one deplores or rejoices in the fact, there are still zones in which savage thought, like savage species, is relatively protected. This is the case of art, to which our civilization accords the status of a national park."

MAKING LOVE WITH ANIMALS

By civilized times, hunting was a sport of kings. The early Chinese emperors had vast fenced hunting reserves; peasants were not allowed to shoot deer. Millennia of experience, the proud knowledges of hunting magic—animal habits—and the skills of wild plant and herb gathering were all but scrubbed away. Much has been said about the frontier in American history, but overlooking perhaps some key points: the American confrontation with a vast wild ecology, an earthly paradise of grass, water, and game—was mind-shaking. Americans lived next to vigorous primitives whom they could not help but respect and even envy, for three hundred years. Finally, as ordinary men supporting their families, they often hunted for food. Although marginal peasants in Europe and Asia did remain part-time hunters at the bottom of the social scale, these Americans were the vanguard of an expanding culture. For Americans, "nature" means wilderness, the untamed realm of total freedom—not brutish and nasty, but beautiful and terrible. Something is always eating at the American heart like acid: it is the knowledge of what we have done to our continent, and to the American Indian.

Other civilizations have done the same, but at a pace too slow to be remembered. One finds evidence in T'ang and Sung poetry that the barren hills of central and northern China were once richly forested. The Far Eastern love of nature has become fear of nature: gardens and pine trees are tormented and controlled. Chinese nature poets were too often retired bureaucrats living on two or three acres of trees trimmed by hired gardeners. The professional nature-aesthetes of modern Japan, tea-teachers and flower-arrangers, are amazed to hear that only a century ago dozens of species of birds passed through Kyoto where today only swallows and sparrows can be seen; and the aesthetes can scarcely distinguish those. "Wild" in the Far East means uncontrollable, objectionable, crude, sexually unrestrained, violent; actually ritually polluting. China cast off mythology, which means its own dreams, with hairy cocks and gaping pudenda, millennia ago; and modern Japanese families participating in an "economic miracle" can have daughters in college who are not sure which hole babies come out of. One of the most remarkable intuitions in Western thought was Rousseau's Noble Savage: the idea that perhaps civilization has something to learn from the primitive.

Man is a beautiful animal. We know this because other animals admire us and love us. Almost all animals are beautiful and paleolithic hunters were deeply moved by it. To hunt means to use your body and senses to the fullest: to strain your consciousness to feel what the deer are thinking today, this moment; to sit still and let your self go into the birds and wind while waiting by a game trail. Hunting magic is designed to bring the game to you—the creature who has heard your song, witnessed your sincerity, and out of compassion comes within your range. Hunting magic is not only aimed at bringing beasts to their death, but to assist in their birth—to promote their fertility. Thus the great Iberian cave paintings are not of hunting alone—but of animals mating and giving birth. A Spanish farmer who saw some reproductions from Altamira is reported to have said, "How beautifully this cow gives birth to a calf!" Breuil has said, "The religion of those days did *not* elevate the animal to the position of a god . . . but it was *humbly entreated* to be fertile." A Haida incantation goes:

> The Great One coming up against the current
>   begins thinking of it.
> The Great One coming putting gravel in his mouth
>   thinks of it
> You look at it with white stone eyes—
>   Great Eater begins thinking of it.

People of primitive cultures appreciate animals as other people off on various trips. Snakes move without limbs, and are like free penises. Birds fly, sing, and dance; they gather food for their babies; they disappear for months and then come back. Fish can breathe water and are brilliant colors. Mammals are like us, they fuck and give birth to babies while panting and purring; their young suck their mothers' breasts; they know terror and delight, they play.

Lévi-Strauss quotes Swanton's report on the Chickasaw, the

tribe's own amusing game of seeing the different clans as acting out the lives of their totemic emblems: "The Raccoon people were said to live on fish and wild fruit, those of the Puma lived in the mountains, avoided water of which they were very frightened and lived principally on game. The Wild Cat clan slept in the daytime and hunted at night, for they had keen eyes; they were indifferent to women. Members of the Bird clan were up before daybreak: 'They were like real birds in that they would not bother anybody . . . the people of this clan have different sorts of minds, just as there are different species of birds.' They were said to live well, to be polygamous, disinclined to work, and prolific . . . the inhabitants of the 'bending-post-oak' house group lived in the woods . . . the High Corncrib house people were respected in spite of their arrogance: they were good gardeners, very industrious but poor hunters; they bartered their maize for game. They were said to be truthful and stubborn, and skilled at forecasting the weather. As for the Redskunk house group: they lived in dugouts underground."

We all know what primitive cultures don't have. What they *do* have is this knowledge of connection and responsibility which amounts to a spiritual ascesis for the whole community. Monks of Christianity or Buddhism, "leaving the world" (which means the games of society) are trying, in a decadent way, to achieve what whole primitive communities—men, women, and children—live by daily; and with more wholeness. The Shaman-poet is simply the man whose mind reaches easily out into all manners of shapes and other lives, and gives song to dreams. Poets have carried this function forward all through civilized times: poets don't sing about society, they sing about nature—even if the closest they ever get to nature is their lady's queynt. Class-structured civilized society is a kind of mass ego. To transcend the ego is to go beyond society as well. "Beyond" there lies, inwardly, the unconscious. Outwardly, the equivalent of the unconscious is the wilderness: both of these terms meet, one step even farther on, as *one*.

One religious tradition of this communion with nature which has survived into historic Western times is what has been called Witchcraft. The antlered and pelted figure painted on the cave wall of Trois Frères, a shaman-dancer-poet, is a prototype of both Shiva and the Devil.

Animal marriages (and supernatural marriages) are a common motif of folklore the world around. A recent article by Lynn White puts the blame for the present ecological crisis on the Judaeo-Christian tradition—animals don't have souls and can't be saved; nature is merely a ground for us to exploit while working out our drama of free will and salvation under the watch of Jehovah. The Devil? "The Deivill apeired vnto her in the liknes of ane prettie boy in grein clothes . . . and at that tyme the Deivil gaive hir his markis; and went away from her in the liknes of ane blak dowg." "He wold haw carnall dealling with ws in the shap of a deir, or in any vther shap, now and then, somtyme he vold be lyk a stirk, a bull, a deir, a rae, or a dowg, etc, and haw dealling with us."

The archaic and primitive ritual dramas, which acknowledged all the sides of human nature, including the destructive, demonic, and ambivalent, were liberating and harmonizing. Freud said *he* didn't discover the unconscious, poets had centuries before. The purpose of California Shamanism was "to heal disease and resist death, with a power acquired from dreams." An Arapaho dancer of the Ghost Dance came back from his trance to sing:

> I circle around, I circle around
>
> The boundaries of the earth,
> The boundaries of the earth
>
> Wearing the long wing feathers as I fly
> Wearing the long wing feathers as I fly.

THE VOICE AS A GIRL

"Everything was alive—the trees, grasses, and winds were dancing with me, talking with me; I could understand the songs of the birds." This ancient experience is not so much—in spite of later commentators—"religious" as it is a pure perception of beauty. The phenomenal world experienced at certain pitches is totally living, exciting, mysterious, filling one with a trembling awe, leaving one grateful and humble. The wonder of the mystery returns direct to one's own senses and consciousness: inside and outside; the voice breathes, "Ah!"

Breath is the outer world coming into one's body. With pulse—

the two always harmonizing—the source of our inward sense of rhythm. Breath is spirit, "inspiration." Expiration, "voiced," makes the signals by which the species connects. Certain emotions and states occasionally seize the body, one becomes a whole tube of air vibrating; all voice. In mantra chanting, the magic utterances, built of seed-syllables such as OM and AYNG and AH, repeated over and over, fold and curl on the breath until—when most weary and bored—a new voice enters, a voice speaks through you clearer and stronger than what you know of yourself; with a sureness and melody of its own, singing out the inner song of the self, and of the planet.

Poetry, it should not have to be said, is not writing or books. Non-literate cultures with their traditional training methods of hearing and reciting, carry thousand of poems—death, war, love, dream, work, and spirit-power songs—through time. The voice of inspiration as an "other" has long been known in the West as The Muse. Widely speaking, the muse is anything other that touches you and moves you. Be it a mountain range, a band of people, the morning star, or a diesel generator. Breaks through the ego-barrier. But this touching-deep is as a mirror, and man in his sexual nature has found the clearest mirror to be his human lover. As the West moved into increasing complexities and hierarchies with civilization, Woman as nature, beauty, and The Other came to be an all-dominating symbol; secretly striving through the last three millennia with the Jehovah or Imperator God-figure, a projection of the gathered power of anti-nature social forces. Thus in the Western tradition the Muse and Romantic Love became part of the same energy, and woman as nature the field for experiencing the universe as sacramental. The lovers' bed was the sole place to enact the dances and ritual dramas that link primitive people to their geology and the Milky Way. The contemporary decline of the cult of romance is linked to the rise of the sense of the primitive, and the knowledge of the variety of spiritual practices and paths to beauty that cultural anthropology has brought us. We begin to move away now, in this interesting historical spiral, from monogamy and monotheism.

Yet the muse remains a woman. Poetry is voice, and according to Indian tradition, voice, vāk (vox)—is a Goddess. Vāk is also called Sarasvati, she is the lover of Brahma and his actual creative energy; she rides a peacock, wears white, carries a book-scroll and a vīna. The name Sarasvati means "the flowing one." "She is again the Divine in the aspect of wisdom and learning, for she is the Mother of Veda; that is of all knowledge touching Brahman and the universe. She is the Word of which it was born and She is that which is the issue of her great womb, Mahāyoni. Not therefore idly have men worshipped Vāk, or Sarasvati, as the Supreme Power."

As Vāk is wife to Brahma ("wife" means "wave" means "vibrator" in Indo-European etymology) so the voice, in everyone, is a mirror of his own deepest self. The voice rises to answer an inner need; or as BusTon says, "The voice of the Buddha arises, being called forth by the thought of the living beings." In esoteric Buddhism this becomes the basis of a mandala meditation practice: "In their midst is Nayika, the essence of *Ali,* the vowel series—she possesses the true nature of Vajrasattva, and is Queen of the Vajra-realm. She is known as the Lady, as Suchness, as Void, as Perfection of Wisdom, as limit of Reality, as Absence of Self."

The conch shell is an ancient symbol of the sense of hearing, and of the female; the vulva and the fruitful womb. At Koptos there is a bas-relief of a four-point buck, on the statue of the god Min, licking his tongue out toward two conches. There are many Magdalenian bone and horn engravings of bear, bison, and deer licking abstract penises and vulvas. At this point (and from our most archaic past transmitted) the mystery of voice becomes one with the mystery of body.

How does this work among primitive peoples in practice? James Mooney, discussing the Ghost Dance religion, says "There is no limit to the number of these [Ghost Dance] songs, as every trance at every dance produces a new one, the trance subject after regaining consciousness embodying his experience in the spirit world in the form of a song, which is sung at the next dance and succeeding performances until superseded by other songs originating in the same way. Thus a single dance may easily result in twenty or thirty new songs. While songs are thus born and die, certain ones which appeal especially to the Indian heart, on account of their mythology, pathos, or peculiar sweetness, live and are perpetuated."

Modern poets in America, Europe, and Japan, are discovering

the breath, the voice, and trance. It is also for some a discovery to realize that the universe is not a dead thing but a continual creation, the song of Sarasvati springing from the trance of Brahma. "Reverence to Her who is eternal, Raudrī, Gaurī, Dhātri, reverence and again reverence, to Her who is the Consciousness in all beings, reverence and again reverence. . . . Candī says."

HOPSCOTCH AND CATS' CRADLES

> The clouds are "Shining Heaven" with his
> different bird-blankets on
>
> —*Haida*

The human race, as it immediately concerns us, has a vertical axis of about 40,000 years and as of 1900 AD a horizonal spread of roughly 3000 different languages and 1000 different cultures. Every living culture and language is the result of countless cross-fertilizations—not a "rise and fall" of civilizations, but more like a flowerlike periodic absorbing—blooming—bursting and scattering of seed. Today we are aware as never before of the plurality of human life-styles and possibilities, while at the same time being tied, like in an old silent movie, to a runaway locomotive rushing headlong toward a very singular catastrophe. Science, as far as it is capable of looking "on beauty bare" is on our side. Part of our being modern is the very fact of our awareness that we are one with our beginnings—contemporary with all periods—members of all cultures. The seeds of every social structure or custom are in the mind.

The anthropologist Stanley Diamond has said "The sickness of civilization consists in its failure to incorporate (and only then) to move beyond the limits of the primitive." Civilization is so to speak a lack of faith, a human laziness, a willingness to accept the perceptions and decisions of others in place of your own—to be less than a full man. Plus, perhaps, a primate inheritance of excessive socializing; and surviving submission/dominance traits (as can be observed in monkey or baboon bands) closely related to exploitative sexuality. If evolution has any meaning at all we must hope to slowly move away from such biological limitations, just as it is within our power to move away from the self-imposed limitations of small-minded social systems. We all live within skin, ego, society, and species boundaries. Consciousness has boundaries of a different order, "the mind is free." College students trying something different because "they do it in New Guinea" is part of the real work of modern man: to uncover the inner structure and actual boundaries of the mind. The third Mystery. The charts and maps of this realm are called mandalas in Sanskrit. (A poem by the Sixth Dalai Lama runs "Drawing diagrams I measured / Movement of the stars / Though her tender flesh is near / Her mind I cannot measure.") Buddhist and Hindu philosophers have gone deeper into this than almost anyone else but the work is just beginning. We are now gathering all the threads of history together and linking modern science to the primitive and archaic sources.

The stability of certain folklore motifs and themes—evidences of linguistic borrowing—the deeper meaning of linguistic drift— the laws by which styles and structures, art-forms and grammars, songs and ways of courting, relate and reflect each other are all mirrors of the self. Even the uses of the word "nature," as in the seventeenth-century witch Isobel Gowdie's testimony about what it was like to make love to the Devil—"I found his nature cold within me as spring-well-water"—throw light on human nature.

Thus nature leads into nature—the wilderness—and the reciprocities and balances by which man lives on earth. Ecology: "eco" (*oikos*) meaning "house" (cf. "ecumenical"): Housekeeping on Earth. Economics, which is merely the housekeeping of various social orders—taking out more than it puts back—must learn the rules of the greater realm. Ancient and primitive cultures had this knowledge more surely and with almost as much empirical precision (see H. C. Conklin's work on Hanunoo plant-knowledge, for example) as the most concerned biologist today. Inner and outer: the Brihadāranyaka Upanishad says, "Now this Self is the state of being of all contingent beings. In so far as man pours libations and offers sacrifice, he is in the sphere of the gods; in so far as he recites the Veda he is in the sphere of the seers; in so far as he offers cakes and water to the ancestors, in so far as he gives food and lodging to men, he is of the sphere of men. In so far as he finds grass and water for domestic animals, he is in the sphere of domestic animals; in so far as wild beasts and birds, even down to ants, find something to live on in his house, he is of their sphere."

The primitive world view, far-out scientific knowledge and the poetic imagination are related forces which may help if not to save the world or humanity, at least to save the Redwoods. The goal of Revolution is Transformation. Mystical traditions within the great religions of civilized times have taught a doctrine of Great Effort for the achievement of Transcendence. This must have been their necessary compromise with civilization, which needed for its period to turn man's vision away from nature, to nourish the growth of the social energy. The archaic, the esoteric, and the primitive traditions alike all teach that beyond transcendence is Great Play, and Transformation. After the mind-breaking Void, the emptiness of a million universes appearing and disappearing, all created things rushing into Krishna's devouring mouth; beyond the enlightenment that can say "these beings are dead already; go ahead and kill them, Arjuna" is a loving, simple awareness of the absolute beauty and preciousness of mice and weeds.

Tsong-kha-pa tells us of a transformed universe:

1. This is a Buddha-realm of infinite beauty
2. All men are divine, are subjects
3. Whatever we use or own are vehicles of worship
4. All acts are authentic, not escapes.

Such authenticity is at the heart of many a primitive world view. For the Anaguta of the Jos plateau, Northern Nigeria, North is called "up"; South is called "down." East is called "morning" and West is called "evening." Hence (according to Dr. Stanley Diamond in his *Anaguta Cosmography*), "Time flows past the permanent central position . . . they live at a place called noon, at the center of the world, the only place where space and time intersect." The Australian aborigines live in a world of ongoing recurrence—comradeship with the landscape and continual exchanges of being and form and position; every person, animals, forces, all are related via a web of reincarnation—or rather, they are "interborn." It may well be that rebirth (or interbirth, for we are actually mutually creating each other and all things while living) is the objective fact of existence which we have not yet brought into conscious knowledge and practice.

It is clear that the empirically observable interconnectedness of nature is but a corner of the vast "jewelled net" which moves from without to within. The spiral (think of nebulae) and spiral conch (vulva/womb) is a symbol of the Great Goddess. It is charming to note that physical properties of spiral conches approximate the Indian notion of the world-creating dance, "expanding form"— "We see that the successive chambers of a spiral Nautilus or of a straight Orthoceras, each whorl or part of a whorl of a periwinkle or other gastropod, each additional increment of an elephant's tusk, or each new chamber of a spiral foraminifer, has its leading characteristic at once described and its form so far described by the simple statement that it constitutes a *gnomon* to the whole previously existing structure." (D'Arcy Thompson)

The maze dances, spiral processions, cats' cradles, Micronesian string star-charts, mandalas and symbolic journeys of the old wild world are with us still in the universally distributed children's game. Let poetry and Bushmen lead the way in a great hop forward:

> In the following game of long hopscotch, the part marked H is for Heaven: it is played in the usual way except that when you are finishing the first part, on the way up, you throw your tor into Heaven. Then you hop to 11, pick up your tor, jump to the very spot where your tor landed in Heaven,
> and say, as fast as you can,
> the alphabet forwards and backwards,
> your name, address and telephone number (if you have one), your age,
> and the name of your boyfriend or girlfriend (if you have one of those).

—Patricia Evans, *Hopscotch*
[*XII. '67*]

Passage to More Than India

It will be a revival, in higher form, of the liberty, equality,
and fraternity of the ancient gentes.

—Lewis Henry Morgan

THE TRIBE

The celebrated human Be-In in San Francisco, January of 1967,
was called "A Gathering of the Tribes." The two posters: one
based on a photograph of a Shaivite sadhu with his long matted
hair, ashes and beard; the other based on an old etching of a Plains
Indian approaching a powwow on his horse—the carbine that had
been cradled in his left arm replaced by a guitar. The Indians, and
the Indian. The tribes were Berkeley, North Beach, Big Sur, Marin
County, Los Angeles, and the host, Haight-Ashbury. Outriders
were present from New York, London and Amsterdam. Out on the
polo field that day the splendidly clad ab/originals often fell into
clusters, with children, a few even under banners. These were the
clans.

Large old houses are rented communally by a group, occupied
by couples and singles (or whatever combinations) and their
children. In some cases, especially in the rock-and-roll business
and with light-show groups, they are all working together on the
same creative job. They might even be a legal corporation. Some
are subsistence farmers out in the country, some are contractors
and carpenters in small coast towns. One girl can stay home and
look after all the children while the other girls hold jobs. They will

all be cooking and eating together and they may well be brown-rice vegetarians. There might not be much alcohol or tobacco around the house, but there will certainly be a stash of marijuana and probably some LSD. If the group has been together for some time it may be known by some informal name, magical and natural. These house-holds provide centers in the city and also out in the country for loners and rangers; gathering places for the scattered smaller hip families and havens for the questing adolescent children of the neighborhood. The clan sachems will sometimes gather to talk about larger issues—police or sheriff department harassments, busts, anti-Vietnam projects, dances and gatherings.

All this is known fact. The number of committed total tribesmen is not so great, but there is a large population of crypto-members who move through many walks of life undetected and only put on their beads and feathers for special occasions. Some are in the academies, others in the legal or psychiatric professions—very useful friends indeed. The number of people who use marijuana regularly and have experienced LSD is (considering it's all illegal) staggering. The impact of all this on the cultural and imaginative life of the nation—even the politics—is enormous.

And yet, there's nothing very new about it, in spite of young hippies just in from the suburbs for whom the "beat generation" is a kalpa away. For several centuries now Western Man has been ponderously preparing himself for a new look at the inner world and the spiritual realms. Even in the centers of nineteenth-century materialism there were dedicated seekers—some within Christianity, some in the arts, some within the occult circles. Witness William Butler Yeats. My own opinion is that we are now experiencing a surfacing (in a specifically "American" incarnation) of the Great Subculture which goes back as far perhaps as the late Paleolithic.

This subculture of illuminati has been a powerful undercurrent in all higher civilizations. In China it manifested as Taoism, not only Lao-tzu but the later Yellow Turban revolt and medieval Taoist secret societies; and the Zen Buddhists up till early Sung. Within Islam the Sufis; in India the various threads converged to produce Tantrism. In the West it has been represented largely by a string of heresies starting with the Gnostics, and on the folk level by "witchcraft."

Buddhist Tantrism, or Vajrayana as it's also known, is probably the finest and most modern statement of this ancient shamanistic-yogic-gnostic-socioeconomic view: that mankind's mother is Nature and Nature should be tenderly respected; that man's life and destiny is growth and enlightenment in self-disciplined freedom; that the divine has been made flesh and that flesh is divine; that we not only should but *do* love one another. This view has been harshly suppressed in the past as threatening to both Church and State. Today, on the contrary, these values seem almost biologically essential to the survival of humanity.

THE FAMILY

Lewis Henry Morgan (d. 1881) was a New York lawyer. He was asked by his club to reorganize it "after the pattern of the Iroquois confederacy." His research converted him into a defender of tribal rights and started him on his career as an amateur anthropologist. His major contribution was a broad theory of social evolution which is still useful. Morgan's *Ancient Society* inspired Engels to write *Origins of the Family, Private Property and the State* (1884, and still in print in both Russia and China), in which the relations between the rights of women, sexuality and the family, and attitudes toward property and power are tentatively explored. The pivot is the revolutionary implications of the custom of matrilineal descent, which Engels learned from Morgan; the Iroquois are matrilineal.

A schematic history of the family:

Hunters and gatherers—a loose monogamy within communal clans usually reckoning descent in the female line, i.e., matrilineal.

Early agriculturalists—a tendency toward group and polyandrous marriage, continued matrilineal descent and smaller-sized clans.

Pastoral nomads—a tendency toward stricter monogamy and patrilineal descent; but much premarital sexual freedom.

Iron-Age agriculturalists—property begins to accumulate and the family system changes to monogamy or polygyny with patrilineal descent. Concern with the legitimacy of heirs.

Civilization so far has implied a patriarchal, patrilineal family. Any other system allows too much creative sexual energy to be released into channels which are "unproductive." In the West, the clan, or gens, disappeared gradually, and social organization was ultimately replaced by political organization, within which separate male-oriented families compete: the modern state.

Engels' Marxian classic implies that the revolution cannot be completely achieved in merely political terms. Monogamy and patrilineal descent may well be great obstructions to the inner changes required for a people to truly live by "communism." Marxists after Engels let these questions lie. Russia and China today are among the world's staunchest supporters of monogamous, sexually turned-off families. Yet Engels' insights were not entirely ignored. The Anarcho-Syndicalists showed a sense for experimental social reorganization. American anarchists and the I. W. W. lived a kind of communalism, with some lovely stories handed down of free love—their slogan was more than just words: "Forming the new society within the shell of the old." San Francisco poets and gurus were attending meetings of the "Anarchist Circle"—old Italians and Finns—in the 1940's.

THE REDSKINS

In many American Indian cultures it is obligatory for every member to get out of the society, out of the human nexus, and "out of his head," at least once in his life. He returns from his solitary vision quest with a secret name, a protective animal spirit, a secret song. It is his "power." The culture honors the man who has visited other realms.

Peyote, the mushroom, morning-glory seeds and Jimson-weed are some of the best-known herbial aids used by Indian cultures to assist in the quest. Most tribes apparently achieved these results simply through yogic-type disciplines: including sweat-baths, hours of dancing, fasting and total isolation. After the decline of the apocalyptic fervor of Wovoka's Ghost Dance religion (a pan-Indian movement of the 1880's and 1890's which believed that if all the Indians would dance the Ghost Dance with their Ghost shirts on, the Buffalo would rise from the ground, trample the white men to death in their dreams, and all the dead game would return; America would be restored to the Indians), the peyote cult spread and established itself in most of the western American tribes.

Although the peyote religion conflicts with pre-existing tribal religions in a few cases (notably with the Pueblo), there is no doubt that the cult has been a positive force, helping the Indians maintain a reverence for their traditions and land through their period of greatest weakness—which is now over. European scholars were investigating peyote in the twenties. It is even rumored that Dr. Carl Jung was experimenting with peyote then. A small band of white peyote users emerged, and peyote was easily available in San Francisco by the late 1940's. In Europe some researchers on these alkaloid compounds were beginning to synthesize them. There is a karmic connection between the peyote cult of the Indians and the discovery of lysergic acid in Switzerland.

Peyote and acid have a curious way of tuning some people in to the local soil. The strains and stresses deep beneath one in the rock, the flow and fabric of wildlife around, the human history of Indians on this continent. Older powers become evident; west of the Rockies, the ancient creator-trickster, Coyote. Jaime de Angulo, a now-legendary departed Spanish shaman and anthropologist, was an authentic Coyote-medium. One of the most relevant poetry magazines is called *Coyote's Journal*. For man, the invisible presence of the Indian, and the heartbreaking beauty of America work without fasting or herbs. We make these contacts simply by walking the Sierra or Mohave, learning the old edibles, singing and watching.

THE JEWEL IN THE LOTUS

At the Congress of World Religions in Chicago in the 1890's, two of the most striking figures were Swami Vivekananda (Shri Ramakrishna's disciple) and Shaku Soyen, the Zen Master and Abbot of Engaku-ji, representing Japanese Rinzai Zen. Shaku Soyen's interpreter was a college student named Teitaro Suzuki. The Ramakrishna-Vivekananda line produced scores of books and established Vedanta centers all through the Western world. A small band of Zen monks under Shaku Sokatsu (disciple of Shaku Soyen) was raising strawberries in Hayward, California, in 1907. Shigetsu Sasaki, later to be known as the Zen Master Sokei-an, was roaming the timberlands of the Pacific Northwest just before World War I, and living on a Puget Sound Island with Indians for neighbors. D. T. Suzuki's books are to be found today in the libraries of biochemists and on stone ledges under laurel trees in the open-air camps of Big Sur gypsies.

A Californian named Walter Y. Evans-Wentz, who sensed that the mountains on his family's vast grazing lands really did have spirits in them, went to Oxford to study the Celtic belief in fairies and then to Sikkim to study Vajrayana under a lama. His best-known book is *The Tibetan Book of the Dead*.

Those who do not have the money or time to go to India or Japan, but who think a great deal about the wisdom traditions, have remarkable results when they take LSD. The *Bhagavad-Gita*, the Hindu mythologies, *The Serpent Power*, the *Lankavatara-sūtra*, the *Upanishads*, the *Hevajra-tantra*, the *Mahanirvana-tantra* —to name a few texts—become, they say, finally clear to them. They often feel they must radically reorganize their lives to harmonize with such insights.

In several American cities traditional meditation halls of both Rinzai and Soto Zen are flourishing. Many of the newcomers turned to traditional meditation after initial acid experience. The two types of experience seem to inform each other.

THE HERETICS

> When Adam delved and Eve span,
> Who was then a gentleman?

The memories of a Golden Age—the Garden of Eden—the Age of the Yellow Ancestor—were genuine expressions of civilization and its discontents. Harking back to societies where women and men were more free with each other; where there was more singing and dancing; where there were no serfs and priests and kings.

Projected into future time in Christian culture, this dream of the Millennium became the soil of many heresies. It is a dream handed down right to our own time—of ecological balance, classless society, social and economic freedom. It is actually one of the possible futures open to us. To those who stubbornly argue "it's against human nature," we can only patiently reply that you must know your own nature before you can say this. Those who have gone into their own natures deeply have, for several thousand years now, been reporting that we have nothing to fear if we are willing to train ourselves, to open up, explore and grow.

One of the most significant medieval heresies was the Brotherhood of the Free Spirit, of which Hieronymus Bosch was probably a member. The Brotherhood believed that God was immanent in everything, and that once one had experienced this God-presence in himself he became a Free Spirit; he was again living in the Garden of Eden. The brothers and sisters held their meetings naked, and practiced much sharing. They "confounded clerics with the subtlety of their arguments." It was complained that "they have no uniform . . . sometimes they dress in a costly and dissolute fashion, sometimes most miserably, all according to time and place." The Free Spirits had communal houses in secret all through Germany and the Lowlands, and wandered freely among them. Their main supporters were the well-organized and affluent weavers.

When brought before the Inquisition they were not charged with witchcraft, but with believing that man was divine, and with making love too freely, with orgies. Thousands were burned. There are some who have as much hostility to the adepts of the subculture today. This may be caused not so much by the outlandish clothes and dope, as by the nutty insistence on "love." The West and Christian culture on one level deeply wants love to win—and having decided (after several sad tries) that love can't, people who still say it will are like ghosts from an old dream.

Love begins with the family and its network of erotic and responsible relationships. A slight alteration of family structure will project a different love-and-property outlook through a whole culture . . . thus the communism and free love of the Christian heresies. This a real razor's edge. Shall the lion lie down with the lamb? And make love even? The Garden of Eden.

WHITE INDIANS

The modern American family is the smallest and most barren family that has ever existed. Each newly-married couple moves to a new house or apartment—no uncles or grandmothers come to live with them. There are seldom more than two or three children. The children live with their peers and leave home early. Many have never had the least sense of family.

I remember sitting down to Christmas dinner eighteen years ago in a communal house in Portland, Oregon, with about twelve others my own age, all of whom had no place they wished to go home to. That house was my first discovery of harmony and community with fellow beings. This has been the experience of hundreds of thousands of men and women all over America since the end of World War II. Hence the talk about the growth of a "new society." But more; these gatherings have been people spending time with each other—talking, delving, making love. Because of the sheer amount of time "wasted" together (without TV) they know each other better than most Americans know their own family. Add to this the mind-opening and personality-revealing effects of grass and acid, and it becomes possible to predict the emergence of groups who live by mutual illumination—have seen themselves as of one mind and one flesh—the "single eye" of the heretical English Ranters; the meaning of sahajiya, "born together"—the name of the latest flower of the Tantric community tradition in Bengal.

Industrial society indeed appears to be finished. Many of us are, again, hunters and gatherers. Poets, musicians, nomadic engineers and scholars; fact-diggers, searchers and re-searchers scoring in rich foundation territory. Horse-traders in lore and magic. The super hunting-bands of mercenaries like Rand or CIA may in some ways belong to the future, if they can be transformed by the ecological conscience, or acid, to which they are very vulnerable. A few of us are literally hunters and gatherers, playfully studying the old techniques of acorn flour, seaweed-gathering, yucca-fiber, rabbit snaring and bow hunting. The densest Indian population in pre-Columbian America north of Mexico was in Marin, Sonoma and Napa Counties, California.

And finally, to go back to Morgan and Engels, sexual mores and the family are changing in the same direction. Rather than the "breakdown of the family" we should see this as the transition to a new form of family. In the near future, I think it likely that the freedom of women and the tribal spirit will make it possible for us to formalize our marriage relationships in any way we please—as groups, or polygynously or polyandrously, as well as monogamously. I use the word "formalize" only in the sense of make public and open the relationships, and to sacramentalize them; to see family as part of the divine ecology. Because it is simpler, more natural, and breaks up tendencies toward property accumulation by individual families, matrilineal descent seems ultimately indicated. Such families already exist. Their children are different in personality structure and outlook from anybody in the history of Western culture since the destruction of Knossos.

The American Indian is the vengeful ghost lurking in the back of the troubled American mind. Which is why we lash out with such ferocity and passion, so muddied a heart, at the black-haired young peasants and soldiers who are the "Viet Cong." That ghost will claim the next generation as its own. When this has happened, citizens of the USA will at last begin to be Americans, truly at home on the continent, in love with their land. The chorus of a Cheyenne Indian Ghost dance song—"hi-niswa' vita'ki'ni"—"We shall live again."

> Passage to more than India!
> Are thy wings plumed indeed for such far flights?
> O soul, voyagest thou indeed on voyages like those?

Phi Upsilon Kappa

I've been through personal agonies that all men must go through. Writing this is a kind of pain as well as a joy at the chance to make a new liberty. Gregory Corso asked me to join him in a project to free the word FUCK from its chains and strictures. I leap to make some new freedom. I believe in a visionary philosophy that demands I take this chance and make a personal speech and statement. I know no languages but words of French, German, Latin and Greek that come from smatterings of school and reading. In my own investigations the Anglo Saxon language, Old English, is the most perfect tower and cavern of words I've yet discovered. I have emerged from a dark night of the soul. I entered into it by peyote and a propensity within myself that was brought to extreme by the cactus drugs. I emerged but still felt a fear that arose when I saw light radiating from the inorganic universe—the light that gleams from a plaster wall, or a brick, or chair, or old stool of dark wood. Constantly I saw all lights that flare and glisten stilly from objects. There were visions of man freed of time and born again as the beast and titan that he is within each Olympian set of genes-unique. Delusions and fear accompanied the sight.

Sometimes I would find myself snapped into a state of partial hallucination and tormented sight. Part of my suffering was that recognizing the timelessness of the Universe and man, I damned fear of mortality as contemptible sickness. I felt all cowardly acts to be fear of death. Life is not sacred only boldness is—*I thought*. The death we know is the gestures that are undone by fear. All actions are perfect and immortal. They can only be judged by intent and boldness. I envisioned Eternity as an infinite statuary of

416

acts. My inability to perform any act of desire or want, and my fear to live out the concepts that I dreamed of, added to my anguish. The light-from-objects reminding me of worse times caused exhaustion and more fear. The memory itself was a new and damning fright. Childlike blankness would settle on my mind and strike out both fear and human feelings. The image of my body wavered and became inexact. I swelled to soul hugeness and delusions of physical grandeur and vacuity. With my dark night vision had come the knowledge that we have no minds and are only spiritmeat. Meat, spirit, and *gene* are one and there is no time or size! I hallucinated that there is no *time* because it is a tool invented by corruption and domestication, of gene and spirit. I knew there is no mind because body is all. I no longer believe these things as I say them here. I am amazed at the pain and yearning of the search for total spirit and new universes of spirit. . . . I sweated into a tiny and infinite void.

As it all ended I saw my soul and found that I lived once before and that I had been a killer whale. I have had but one life before. At the end of this one I shall be free of the chain of meat. When I saw this I wept for long-lived men and for my daughter. (My freedom I know is a coincident of Time & Space.) I saw that there is no evolution in a single life. Death is good and black and painless and beautiful. I shook with the urge to die, staring through my black October window. I would have died but I realized that if all is good, and painless, and ecstatic sweet, and black on the other side of death, then this side of death is good also. There is no evolution in the personal sense. There is no graduation through suffering. The soft, soft, beauties of Anacreon and Jesus are as true as blacker ecstasies and are of the same matter and fleshmeat. I say these things as I have just turned 28 and I speak them while still suffering sometimes from a blankness that causes me anguish. But I have found idealism and sight of beauty that I cherish in deepest new depths.

I felt inspiration coming. I was shaken by it and realized I had no words to speak what was growing in me. I mulled in the books of Melville (his holy novel *Pierre*) and read the works of great poets of our language and other men I knew. Still I could not find more than beginnings of the words I needed. I looked in the plays of Shakespeare and found his sweet wise imagewords, and the behemoth metaphors he makes with use or turn of word—how he gives everything noble stature by his suddenness and humor. I could not find in words anywhere the counterpart of what I felt within myself that lay unspoken and building in intensity. By instinct while searching through books of words, because of a memory of great sounds I heard in poetry of that language, I turned to Anglo Saxon and I began leafing in dictionaries of that speech.

Almost first I opened to the word *aelf-scin—shining like an elf.* The reference was to the light that gleams from objects! This is the light I saw at many moments and for extended lengths of time. It threw me into fear and blankness. It was the real visionary horror of the inert world about to become hallucinatory vision. BUT if those great Anglo Saxon men saw the light and named it—natural phenomena—*then what is there to fear from it? What is there to fear from elf-light? From elf-scimmer?*

THE AELF-SCIN, THE SHINING SCIMMER,
THE GLEAM, THE SHINING
color of walls, of scratches, of cracks, of brightness.
The cold mystery the (Philip calls it) Weir. The *déjà
vu* of the forest-sorrel with its tiny leaves sun-folded
and bent like a head in uniqueness. Animal in look.
            to fold so. The moment I
        leave what I am in aelf-scin. Stand
        in wonder. Lose myself. Even to fear.
        A difference. Aelf-scin, Weir. But
        similar. Knowing its name the horror
        of void is gone. Knowing it almost
    with my ash spear over my arm in the black
    FOREST CLEAR WATER AND AIR SEA.
    The Anglo Saxons build huge boats, fight battles
            and rejoice in what they see,
                see beauty more clearly,
                    have words for what
                    I forget, Live in
                        liberty. For
                        ever. ! ! ! ! !

CALL IT FEAR NOW-GONE
the whole thing a star
breathing.

Philip Lamantia and I had spoken many times. He had mentioned his concept of Weir to me. Now I knew the phenomena I had seen with my still peyoted eyes—the chill luminescence—and the aelf-scin of the Anglo Saxons were the same radiance and halo. I saw that the aelf-scin was much the same light illumining what Philip called Weir. Weir is a solid spectral reality of light on particular objects in special moments of vision.

CALL IT FEAR NOW-GONE, the whole thing a star breathing. The scar was gone and healed!

In dictionaries of Anglo Saxon and Old English, and in dictionaries of forgotten languages of argot I found living and vital images and titles for forgotten sights. A man names what he sees and then puts away the fear of it.

In Old English I found a treasury of beauties that we still may see but are without words for. The names are lost and forgotten! The words make them more visible. I found black grottos and cliffs of unremembered meanings and beings. In my state I swallowed them whole and saw new beings and wonders with cleansed eyes. I saw the fields of tiny radiances and color on the bloodied body of a mackerel that I roasted whole and ate. I saw the dead body of the living that I consume—loving animals and beasts. I saw myself eating them. I felt my stride and chest as I walked. I sat silently in the *daegred-woma* and the *morgen-rot* and listened to a child sing wild wordless songs of her desires. I thrilled with the ecstasy of my spirit's physicality. I knew all of the subtle and gross variations of day and dark. The fear of aelf-scin flew from me in a clap of joy when I discovered that the Anglo Saxons, rich in forest and sea, had seen it.

Their words opened new forgotten beauties to me:

aedel-tungol . . . noble star.

an-sund . . . whole sound (meatspirit solid, vibrant, solid moving, free).

ae-man . . . depopulated (not de-populated but *ae-man*—manless).

ad-loma . . . fire lamed.

adl-bracu . . . force or virulence of disease (*adl* is disease).

ae-craftig . . . law crafty.

aedre . . . artery, vein (it is the sound of a vein).

aefen-glom . . . evening loom, twilight, gloaming.

aefen-leocht . . . evening light.

aefen scimmer . . . evening shimmer, evening splendor.

aefen steorra . . . evening star.

aefen-tid . . . eventide.

ael-cald . . . all cold.

aeled . . . fire, firebrand, conflagration.

aeled-fyr . . . flame.

ael-grene . . . all green, green on all sides.

aeppel-feau . . . apple fallow, apple yellow, red-yellow (Oh, joy to eat an apple!).

aerend-boc . . . message, letter.

aerend-gewrit . . . written message, letter epistle.

aer-mergen . . . daybreak.

aer-woruld . . . former world, old world, Ur Welt.

ae-sprynge . . . (1) waterspring, font; (2) what's to happen, fate, destiny.

aetran-mod . . . venom minded.

aedel cyning . . . noble king, Christ.

aedm . . . breathing (the sound of breathing?).

aewan . . . to despise, scorn, contemn.

an-floga . . . the alone, the lonely flyer.

agenslaga . . . ownslayer, self-slayer.

ar-craeftig . . . strong in honor.

ar-scamu . . . holy awe, respect.

bael-blaese . . . fire blaze.

bael egesa . . . flame fear, fire dread.

ban-hus . . . bonehouse, body.

ban-sele . . . bonehall.

becn . . . signal, beacon.

bell . . . forehead.

bellan . . . bellow, bark, grunt.

beag-gifer . . . ring giving.

bealu, bealo, balu . . . bale, evil, mischief, hurt, injury, affliction.

bealu-blonded . . . mixed with destruction.

bealo-hycgende . . . thinking of death.

bealu-inwit . . . deceit, cunning, treachery.

bealo-sorg . . . sorrow because of expected misfortune.

bearthm . . . splendor brightness (what it is that impresses the senses, makes a sound, comes out strong and bright. What comes straight through the nerves and synapses of the body without the recirculation and channelings of habit and custom—straight from the spirit and unbuffered. A bodyspirit movement of any size or quality).

beo-bread . . . bee bread, honeycomb.

breost cearu . . . breast care, sorrow.

brun . . . having a metallic color, dark, black.

brunwarm . . . dark brown, dusky.

bryne . . . tear, burning tear.

calic . . . chalice, cup.

ceoldheort . . . cold hearted.

ceor . . . anxious, careful, full of anxiety.

cleo . . . claw or hoof.

clingan . . . cling, shrink draw up, pine, wither, become weak.

I did not find *fuck* in Anglo Saxon dictionaries—but it is no matter whether the word was used then or if it was born in later days of Old English. In books of forgotten words and images from other times I found more words to give me new pictures and sensations. Part of a man is the words leaping from his lips. They are made by his real meat lips and throat and signalled by his real physical hands of spirit sending them on their way. They are groomed by the features of his face—lips, crinkle of eye, and swelling and collapse of cheek and chin. They free and liberate and lead to deeds and constructions and inventions of soul and spirit. Active living men had seen what I was seeing. They knew aelf-scin and did not fear it—they named it. They freed me of fear. I wanted to live in the sights named in Anglo Saxon and old shapes of language. I felt what men who knew the earth, the wind, and boiling-cold sea, drew from the air and light and beasts around them. I reached to feel things named in their languages; intensities of life that are wealthy living. I felt my heart, my real actual heart of blood and muscles in the ribcase of my chest fed by and feeding its arteries and veins. I saw my capillaries rise in heat. I dreamed in gloaming and heard the cries that fill the eventide and saw the beastwoman creatures and animal men that move around me (so many of them are not stirred to great and noble deeds but they are still such vital spirits!). Speeches and speech are part of living. Great plays of words can lead to high actions. Pleasures of words make voluptuous ease and needed rest and comfort and good sleeping for the mammal. Heavens of voluminous colors and stalwart actions are caused by sounds.

A man knows *what* he is by how he names his states. If I do not name my condition I am less defined and lack sureness. Speech cannot be censored without loss. Words are part of physiology. Lost parts of body are losses of spirit. There are men and women in honest suffering blaming themselves for misery when the name or word of their torment will assuage them. The mention of it is the first step to relief or cure—but it is denied them by their social company who are joined in a fear to use a word or hear it spoken.

One stanza of my poem "Dark Brown" begins:

OH EASE, OH BODY-STRAIN, OH LOVE, OH
                    EASE ME NOT! WOUND BORE
      be real, show organs, show blood. OH let me
      be as a flower. Let ugliness arise without care
      and grow side by side with beauty. . . .

In the first line I named the pain remaining from my dark night *Wound-Bore*. Previously I had no name for it. I christened it and gave myself that ease so I could know my state and therefore be more whole. Why do we refrain from naming our states?

Does lack of name and recognition of the spirit's true shape make us vague and pale? I believe it.

No actions or doings of the spirit should be called ugly. Or call some that, but remember they are living shapes and not to be denied. Beauty and bliss are other states and often they commingle. Ugliness, beauty and bliss if they are felt are to be named. For the sake of what is humane there should be no repression of statement. Suffering as well as joy should be titled. Good and evil must be put to words. Each genetic immeasurable titan manbeast must name his names and the shapes visible to his senses. If he does not he is incomplete and less manly. Silence is a grey cloud of denial of life.

Denied hungers of the physical-gene-body are contradictions of spirit. Hungers for sex, food, loveliness, and love are manifestations of the spirit who is a manbeast. What is the concern with measurement and denial? A real physical spirit is not in scale. There cannot be a proportion claiming a star is a size and man is another size. They both are alive! There is no living relativity of scale! Measurement and denial are destroyers of immortality. Words are the body as they float from tongue to air to other meatspirit or listener.

The only secret of speech is the way it is used. The good of words is not known enough. There are no mysteries of speech, there is no mystic language. (There are holy languages and ones that are kept secret.) Words are tools of men. All words are true when used with freedom, goodwill and honesty.

There are men who deal in false mysteries. They are frightened and hope to shake away their fears by rigid denial. They pretend that certain words and acts do not exist (and thereby make them mysteries). Men who condemn a word cannot use it to feel the shape of their spirit. They are cloudy and weakened and grasp for power to reassure themselves. They battle constantly to remove a word's meaning from reality. As they deny reality of their acts and feelings, a blankness, a destruction of human feelings, comes over them. It is amputation. They are amputated men and they desire like the fox without tail to make all fellows tailless in their image. They believe they have secluded themselves from their fears but they have *lost* reality instead. They believe all men have fears equivalent to theirs . . . or that they *should* have. They wish to protect the abridgement of their spirit. They are unaware that they are not whole. They make a mystery of words—*fuck* and many other straight words. They are fearful of sex and fearful of cleansing. All men who deny are destroying their spirits. Who can measure the desires or speech of a man?

Everyone must speak and act with pride of reality so that each can construct in full his unique spirit. First we must be whole and *then* condemn evil if we see it. We must be free in graceful liberty to see and *then* make denial.

Cynicism, denial, and censorship create corporeal bulkheads and walls that dam the human spirit. We live in a vision, but only experience is true life. For a man to make his spirit whole he must smash up the terms of his own vision before the edges of it freeze and become unshifting. What we say and do creates the real actuality of our bodies. Our meat calls for that! If we are hung up in our existent visions or confined by another's, we freeze to a solitary and unchanging idea of ourselves. Then our universe of possibilities, our human universe, is dead. We must make love. We must constantly move and seek without denials or censorship or rigid fantasies. We are creatures enchained if we freeze up our vision to inflexibility. Locked words make closed men.

The obscenity barrier is raised by censorships and fear. It is built by a fear of the natural and the idea that nature is obscene.

The fear ridden man and the politician believe the normal and the common are obscene and would have men erect a wall in their spirit. They are the few possessors of unnatural fears and they live their lives of terror in hypocritic self-brutality. They desire stability and a quiescence of their scare. They want to reduce the possibilities of life to a living death to calm themselves. Natural and normal men and women terrify them. Fear gives energy and persuasiveness, and they persuade men to build a wall (the fear of obscenity) across their feelings. The obscenity barrier freezes the spirit solid on the side that faces the outer world and shuts up the nascent infinitude of acts and loves on the other. "Obscene" is concerned with the cleaning of the body or its processes of love and birth. Discoverers of the obscene find death as unnatural as health and birth. They erect mortuaries and hospitals as masonry to protect themselves from death.

Behind the wall of censorship lie possibilities that cannot flow into the frozen and known and create new ideals. Mountain chains of loves and dim lovely valleys are walled away without a gate. They are the desires for creativity and the human divine. One stone of the barrier is the denial of true and wholesome words. The unused walls become a solid force within us and grow higher. The unchanging self is more cut off and takes on terrible smugness as other worlds become invisible. The smugness covers the pain of amputation. Any man retreats from his uncountable creative possibilities if he can be forced to fear acts of sexual beauty and to repress his natural desires. What is there to fear? The free man only desires to make himself whole. Fear of words is a symptom. What seraph cities and cherubic bridges are still unbuilt because of denial and censorship that hold back energy? Is man evil? Can spirit be evil? Is even ugliness to be as much feared as beauty? Because of love of stability and unchanging vision, what real dramas of love and kindness go unacted? How strange to see the pettiness of spirit cloistered up with the aid of unmade words. There are no mysteries of language or of meat. Those who deny reality make mystic languages and walls.

FUCK! The word fuck is a mantra. Sanskrit: *man* is the first syllable of *manana* or thinking. *Tra* is from *trana* or liberation from the *samsara* or phenomenal world. *Mantra calls thought-freedom forth!* The barrier against it makes a mantra of it. It will call forth. Shout FUCK and break your image up. Say all the words that are denied to you and make all deep desired acts that are mortal and have perfect meaning to your meat.

Mantra is a word to break the stable vision when it freezes solid.

After the escape from static representation of man in the arts came a period of great experimentation. The body was ignored, removed-from, twisted, distorted, and great spiritual beauties without human body have been laid down in paint, writing, and music. Now there is a new return to the body with all previously repressed virtues of human lovely beast spirit animal that were uncovered by the experiments incorporated into it. A new vivid completeness enters in the arts with all splashes, drips, and chance and abstract autobiographies of spiritmeat taken whole within a new portrait of man. Without change, that too will become a frozen imagevision of deadmeat.

Outside of our stable vision of ourselves and behind the walls in our spirits is *EVERYTHING!* All unmade acts and generosities and aspirations move there in a tangle, weaving one into the other like vines and briars. Among them are a few actions that would cause suffering but how much more good lies there!! What new virtues men could bring into being if there were no walls and inescapable visions!—What if each vision were stepped through and each image broken? No man can be denied a deep desire or kept from an honest word. Fuck!

Sing fuck. Shout FUCK. Say anything from deep within.

Say FUCK! Say I FUCK! Say FUCK because it is a spirit mantra as is any word that moves and vibrates the chest like a roar. Say any word that returns man to a meaning or names any noble act as vow. Any great swearing. All men are profane and rapturous, wrapped and coiled like one helix inseparable.

FUCK, say FUCK. Say FUCK GOD as a holy prayer. Those who accept a lifevision or a godvision will not *experience* life or God. And those who deny a word help to freeze up life into a denying form.

FUCK can be an exclamation that clears the senses: FUCK DEATH!!

My first conscious use of *Fuck* as a mantra to break a barrier that kept me from straight speech and act was in a poem. Wanting a woman I could not have, though she was willing, my repressed desire made my senses blur with smoke of anguish. I was too numb to speak. I wanted to tell her, but she was no longer there. I was smoke-blinded by myself. My desire was not obscene but the frustration of my impulse and my weakness put my want behind a barrier. I sat at a dark desk in unthinking state and stupefied. My urge to love her was lost inside myself. The need to speak to her was strong. Oh Christ oh God oh fucking shit oh shit-shaped pain of love, exploded through my lungs and head and I was released to speak of my state of being. The mantra was a part of me and a speech of my spirit. The line cleared me and gave vent to a whole statement. I was given ease by the mantra. It freed me to give name and words to my feelings.

Say FUCK, say FUCK, say FUCK, say anything that opens to acts.

Is there any more personal creative act than fucking? Fuck does not mean merely the act of copulation but all ramifications, doings, and movements that give sexual delight to the spiritbeast who is lonely and cold and in need of touch and warmth in his separateness. He joins with a woman to make a citadelheavenjungle of conjoined pleasure clearing the accumulated weight from senses. He gives ease and openness by aiding another. Is there a more *personal and creative* gesture? When copulation is unearthly it is fucking. Fuck is the old deep word. *Copulation* and *intercourse* are words made up from a dead language. To have intercourse or to copulate is not to fuck. To fuck is to give moments of ease and warmth to another and to accept the same from a loved one, and to join bodies and clear the spirit of its heaviness. After FUCKING we relax. The exalted pair are made more free by their generous act and are in a state of natural ease. They see freshness in one another and in the world.

Fucking is personal and should be spoken of. Men who say *copulate* or *intercourse* feel removed from their bodies. They use those words to create an illusion of objectivity—as if they look down on the doings of beasts. And don't they *fuck?* I would rather fuck with my meat body than have intercourse and watch it with my mind—or pretend that my mind-aloof looks down on a divisible body. I will not amputate myself into pieces that stare at one another and snicker. Fear of fuck is fright of men's desires and liberty.

Fuck is personal and athletic-physical. It is performed by the spiritbody. It is of most importance because it gives new vision and helps clear old visions so that men may pass from life into life. It is our contact with everything and with ourselves and other spirit-beastcreatures. Besides being an action and a mantra *fuck* is a vibrant adjective. It describes a state of matter or a creature that is otherwise without description.

Another stanza of my long poem "Dark Brown" ends with fuck as an adjective: "BREATHE BRIGHT FUCKING AIR!!!" Breathe bright fucking air. When the air is splashed with inspiration, when it is radiant and personal and it vibrates, what adjective could be used to describe the state of it? What word is descriptive of great personal act?

It was fucking quiet.

The fucking flower of silence breathes its fucking air.

I was so fucking high I trembled.

Oh fuck, fuck, fuck, shatter me and lift me free.

The night was fucking long.

Oh fuck, oh honest word oh.

FUCK YOU is a vow of anger and detestation. How the word is twisted! But in Dante's Hell the man who made fuck-signs at God—how deeply he felt to make *figs.*

"I will fuck you" is a vow of love and desire. I will *copulate* you? I will *intercourse* you? Or is the man who is a real man never to say *I will fuck you. . . ?* Is he to keep his desires secret and tamed and withering behind a wall of censorship and silence? Must he disrespect the desires that make his being? Does a man desire and dream of copulation and intercourse? Or doesn't our sleeping body dream of *Fuck?* Who is the waking man who thinks of *copulation?* Is that man whole—or does he deny himself? The word fuck is sizeless—it matches honest desire in simplicity of statement.

FUCK represents man beating upon what is not contained in humself. FUCK IT! I beat upon it! (It is a metaphor.) FUCK IT: As I beat myself upon another muscled body so I beat upon the world. I beat myself upon the body I love. I beat myself upon the inanimate (—but the inanimate is not lifeless—the metaphor of *fuck* reveals the truth) FUCK IT! FUCK IT! I acknowledge it is real! All FUCKING things are real. FUCK YOU! FUCK ME! I AM FUCKED! I AM FUCKED OUT! This FUCKING thing will never stop! There is no fucking end. *This is the fucking end.* The fucking earth and stars. Blue peaks that fuck the sky at twilight. The sights of solid and untrembling world that enter like a hammer on my clear spirit and fuck me like a solid fire! And how I move in these real things and fuck with them, and fuck them up, and build fine fucking things of them. How I love the fucking world, and long for fucking death to set me free of fucking pain. How I long to fuck all things, to hold all things of beauty and ugliness and make truth of them, and grip them in my fucking hands and brush them with my passing fucking shoulder.

How I long to be strong and FUCK. Fucking is the conscious or mindless beating of body on body, the touching of spirits in order to pass the gift of love from one to the other. All things are living and all things fuck. All men must know that all things fuck and that all men fuck. Oh, do not cast down the desire for FUCK or hide it in the veil and chain of lying censorship and thus dilute your spirit! Fucking is great sexual pleasure, is warm and soft and sleek and silent. Fucking is dear and sweet and nestling. Fucking is personal and silent. Fucking is a mighty roar. FUCK breaks down walls that hold men to a single vision. (Vision is the passage of vision into vision into vision into vision into vision with liberty.) Let no man name words mysteries or make comic laws.

FUCK is the agony of the statement of being fucked and should not be forgotten.

There is no secret language. Jacob Boehme used words to clear mysteries and in his agony yelled and muttered fuck. Aristophanes, before a black and smiling marble curtain, had servant and lord alike say fuck and shit their pants upon the stage. Brahms fucked. Beethoven shouted it in his bulging brows while angel wings of hair trembled on mute ears. Jesus blessed fucking. Buddha knew he was fucked by the world about him. All men who are fathers fuck. All women who are mothers fuck. We see young men think of fucking and old men look back on FUCK.

Billy the Kid bellows from eternity to show his pain: OH GOD, DEATH FUCKING ACHE!

After writing the opening stanzas of the poem I have quoted herein I believed I had inscribed a passing vision in poetry—but with the liberation of language and struggle to free desires I passed to statement of sexuality and wrote the next section and titled it "Fuck Ode." Then to be free again I wrote the last section titled "A Garland."

"Fuck Ode" begins:

THE HUGE FIGURES FUCKING, THE HUGE
   FIGURES FUCKING, THE HUGE FIGURES
FUCKING, ON THE CLIFFS, ON THE BANKS IN
      THE BLACK RIVER . .

[*1962*]

Revolt

Coming upon some words that begin a writing of mine I was moved by an impulse to write an essay on the meaning of *revolt* and to make an investigation and exploration. The lines that intrigue me are erotic and universal and I mean but to begin with them and to track down one physiological meaning.—The lines are the first stanza of a poem titled "Rant Block."

For a basic relevant meaning of revolt to us as many-celled meat creatures I seek in a lower phylum of the animal kingdom— the one first to have so many of the characteristics we have. This phylum has as I do 3 layers of flesh: ectoderm or outer skin; endoderm or inner stomach skin; and for the first time on the evolutionary ladder there is the third flesh layer—mesoderm or muscle and organ flesh. This phylum of beasts is the Platyhelminthes, or flat worms; they are at a main branching of many-celled beasts on the tree of evolution. In addition to being the most primitive animals having the 3 meat layers, they are first to be bilaterally symmetrical and to have head and tail at opposite ends of the body.

I pick up here, as an example of revolt, the planaria—an order of small flat black worms with triangular heads that live in icy streams. These tiny spirits move in cold water and seek out the tinier beasts they feed upon—to whom they are *raptors* or dragons of prey. They fall upon these desires of their hunger and swallow them whole, or fasten upon them with their bellymouths and shake them to pieces that they may be ingested in particles through their maw.

These are the first higher beasts. They have the first definite upper and lower surfaces to the body, and the first large eye organs, and complexities of nervous system, and digestion. They are our farthest close-cousins.

The planaria reproduce sexually (hermaphroditically by means of a penis and womb sac with a bisexual hermaphroditic partner) and asexually. I believe a qualitative point in evolution is reached. I say the asexual reproduction should be called revolt. Or, for the image of what I seek, I call the asexual division *revolt*.

The revolt is spectacular. Each sleek planaria creature is divided along its body into subindividuals joined together at the points of division, or revolt. BUT there is no morphological or physiological organic sign of these places of revolt—neither on the outside nor inside of the animal. They are physical spirit divisions of resentment and subindividuality. Simply, there are invisible lines where it is predictable that a revolt may take place and along which a planaria will divide into two. The individual to the rear grows a new head and organs after the division and swims away. The head end sprouts a new body.

The revolt takes place in this manner: the tail end of the beast tightens itself upon an object in the water, a stone or twig, and vigorously shakes from itself the head end . . . disavowing the domination of the old head that has made all decisions with its brain and eyes. The subindividual, become individual itself, is now headless and self-decisive. In turn the individuals of itself may revolt from the new growing head in their time. AHH!

I wish to make a fantasy as an image . . . the Head which is major receptacle of sensory impressions and sense organs in the higher beasts is most clear at birth or at its first growing, but gradually or quickly it fills with preconception and becomes locked in a vision of the outer world and of itself. The Head makes patterns and *phorms* of the environment and of the filling of its desires in regard to the flowing of circumstances surrounding it. By the nature of its meat these patterns or nervous synapses and chains of synapses become set and less at liberty to make swift change and new decision. The Head finally may act by self-image of itself, by a set and unchanging vision that ignores the demands of its body that follows with its load of less conscious desires and needs and protoplasmic instincts and intuitions. The Head is Chief and the Body follows.

With planaria the Comedy is that gut *and the mouth* belong to the Body—mouth is on the body and not the head. In evolution from this point on the mouth moves up into the Head and together they assert a more single spirit in control of all behind them. Head and Mouth control Gut in evolution after the planaria. But the old body spirits of revolt remain as tiny voices even in mammals.

My fantasy stops. No—here is a little more: the reward for eradication of subindividuals in higher creatures is coordination. (More basic beasts can live by randomness and hazard. In times of hunger they shrink, in times of plenty they swell. In dryness and heat they encyst and return to life when there is moisture.) Higher creatures must live with less *chance* in their lives. They must be totally co-ordinated to spring upon their desires that pass with speed *in* Space. They cannot encyst and have second chances. Except for the vertebrates, they have no concept of time. They do not plan. They cannot have argument from darkness within their meat. They must be co-ordinated to leap.

I I

At all times revolt is the search for health and naturality. Revolt is a desire to experience normal physiological processes that give pleasure of fullness and expansion. The problems of the earth, or the enactions of life itself, are desire and hunger. The basis of all revolt in one phase or another is sexuality. The Erotic impulse is the impulse to destroy walls and join units together into larger and larger structures. That is the heat of Romance!! To çreate love structures, the old visions, self-images, *phorms* and patterns must be disavowed or destroyed. Anything that chains life to preconceived goals and preconceived reality must go—they threaten the meat itself.

In society there is a revolt-of-revolt, a hysteria, often more visible (though perhaps not more present) than true revolt. It is nihilistic and dissipative. The man caught up by revolt-of-revolt is either weak in genetic spirit or dominated by circumstance. He makes a hysterical or passionate attempt to take any ANY other path than the one laid for him by society.

Hysteria is a real animal process—the trial of anything, any random activity, as a last meagre chance in the face of imminent death. (*Death* includes a death of the spirit's meaning!) Society has allowed for this random activity in its makeup and has proscribed activities for the revolter who is weak. He is channelled.

He is weakened further. He moves into, and fills out, another phorm of society and his fighting spirit dies in dissipation.

Freud, Jung and Reich assert the sexual beginnings of life and of neurosis. Freud is the dark poet of the real and conceptual real. Jung is an anagogic writer who leads out to flight of fantasy and imaginative cohesion of instincts and memories. Freud is like Shelley, Jung is like Keats who makes idylls. Wilhelm Reich is the creator of true romance and a golden medievalist and sexological pioneer of Freud's theories. The value of these men to the individual who is not a psychoanalyst is their greatness as sexologists. In sex lies the complexities of desire, satisfaction, and the meanings of revolt. Men should be freed, healed and cured, not adjusted. Revolt is a physiological process of seeking. It is an energy state and energy in any form—at rest or in use—is erotic. Without energy the body and soul are dead.

To the Elizabethans the body was the *Bulk*. To men who conceive of a Bulk there is no differentiation betweeen body and Spirit. Bulk performs the actions of the spirit no matter how fine or gross the nature of the gesture.

In the simple black spirits and fleshbulks of our lower cousins there are fewer complications of desire moving to fill need. Sub-Individual revolts from Chief-Head and divides to satisfy his desires. He tears away the head, becomes Chief himself, and grows a new one. It is an act and demonstration of physical-spirit as much as the violent capturing of a microscopic beast that satisfies his hunger. Size does not matter—and does matter! There is no proportion to gauge the intensity of desire.

For the swart flatworm as he moves on his thready cilia and glides on his strang of mucus there is no Time and no Society to act against. The background of his acts is the organization of his body and all the lesser individuals of it . . . It is a smaller universe of clearer beauty and simpler Good and Bad.

Light and seeing are themselves more evident. Degrees of radiance and dark combine with the tellings of fine senses on the eyes and cheeks of the beast. They turn him directly to his desires and flights.

Against the meaning the Head has accumulated and assumed in millions and millions of years are matched the needs of the sub-spirits darting behind.

III

Fish, Amphibians, Birds, Reptiles and Mammals operate freely in an invention. The invention is Time. Revolt in higher beasts necessitates coordination in Time. Backboned animals deal with time-factors and make intellective arrangements and memory constellations to achieve desires.

Liberty becomes complex. I see liberty as the possibility of constantly achieving new experience without hysteria or fear-caused chance taking. We are more free when love and not fright impells us to experiment. For backboned creatures, greatnesses and hugenesses of beauty and experience are available—newly possible lovelinesses. The Imagination makes us transcendant of Time and we see what is gorgeous. But physically in the hunger-world, as repayment for coordination, the subspirits of every beastcreature by necessity are sublimated. We must fill hungers within the passage of Time. OH!

The Subindividual in higher animals is not free to revolt. The *being* is Solo Chief—and must be to succeed in Chordate animals.

Revolt in animals living in Time no longer happens by a division of the flesh itself. For success I must remain one piece and whole by the nature of my evolved meat. My revolt must be of complete meat and spirit. I must fight the passing vision within myself that freezes into a cemented way of seeing. I must drive attitude and preconception from myself and remain as close as possible to the freshness of evolved and primal urges.

There is a single SELF now, I know it and feel it. The self is genetic and real. It is not an overlay of patterns of synapses and past actions layered on me by circumstance. The propensities for weakness and strength of action are inherited. They allow for the imprint of circumstance and environment—but they are a small part of the self. This needs must be and is truly beautiful—a creator of diversity.

Revolt is the striving for *success*. Revolt happens when the mind and body and almost voiceless tiny cries of the tissues rebel against an overlay of unnaturalities frozen into the nervous system.

As a Mammal I must deal with the layering of attitude in myself. There is an accumulation that tends to remain there by inertia. But my spirit calls for freshness of experience and chance to build love. THAT IS THE INTERIOR!

ON THE EXTERIOR—I stride in a Universe of greater choice than the planaria. Because of the complexities the Universe *seems* to impose on me, there is greater necessity for formulations—and they become Attitude. If the formulations remain when the reasons for them are gone I become burdened and live in a vision that has passed. If they heap up within me then there is no freshness of experience and I must revolt.

In addition: I live in Society that willfully and through previous agreement will force on me patterns of existence. Some of these patterns are dissipative and hysterical and are aimed toward the weakening of my spirit. Some are made with good intent. Some are to twine me in love-structures that I may or may not prefer to be joined to.

If my spirit is strong enough to revolt but still filled with fear, I revolt at random and move in panic. I become more weakened and exhausted. Another chainlink is made. Feedback adds to the original weakness till I become bound in an undesirable life . . . i.e. a new but *formalized* pattern of living.

I V

Revolt is a striving to a regimen that is conceived of as athletic and physical. Its function is to uncover and keep alive the natural physical urges of our meat. Some of these processes are sex, desire for awareness, and desire for pleasure. Perhaps they are not divisible but all erotic. There is no need to make instincts or godhoods of them except to divide them or place them together to speak of them. And there is no need for the godhood of the Erotic either, except to give it a passing name. We are free to divide, personify, invent and place all things together as we choose; that is a manifestation of liberty.

A classical division is INTELLECT and BODY! Intellect is a function of the body. But it gives us at moments the usable fantasy that it may stand separate from Body and judge or guide it.

EMOTIONS and DESIRES, like words, are physical parts of

the body composed of infinitudes of tissues and nerves and actions of the body-physical.

We are nothing if we are not the sum total of our physique and the history of the actions that we carry with us in body and memory.

FEEDBACK is energy that is not fulfilled and expended completely in a gesture of desire. It is left-over energy washing back in us like a broth that nourishes attitudes and strengthens patterns. The patterns become stronger and cause gestures to be half-hearted and conventional and make more feedback. The new feedback in turn makes the patterns and attitudes of action stronger and the desires are further weakened. They must struggle to show themselves: will-lessness, faintness and incapability grow in a cyclical process. It is a cycle and it must be broken for liberty.

The Intellect, used as an arbitrary division and joyful game in regimen *with* the body, can remind us to circumvent or ellipse patterns. In that way it stops the flow of feedback and breaks a cycle of outward actions composing an interior attitude. The use of the Intellect can be athletic and physical as it is a part of the athletic and physical Body. Regimen is a willful use of all forces to achieve an end with economy of exertion. The idea of intellect must be shifting and open to change, and must not itself become an attitude. Definition and personification must change constantly. INTELLECT MUST CHANGE CONSTANTLY AS BODY CHANGES CONSTANTLY, AND THE PICTURE OF BODY MUST CHANGE AS THE BODY CHANGES. Planaria changes as the physical spirit of its protoplasm changes. The intellect must be remembered to be a part of physique.

Body is the major force, and intellect is a contained auxiliary. The body-image is the picture we carry of our bodies; it is self knowledge. The body-picture ideally *is* the Body. But it is not if there are feedback, and images, and methods of action referring to past states that live and direct our gestures. These if they are too strong will stand as a barrier to new and incoming perception. If there are inert functions they must be ellipsed and broken. The breaking is revolt.

The physiological processes of the Body, and the emotions,

desires, hungers, organs, nerves, etc. are the Body. And the Body, as in the planaria, *is* SPIRIT.

V

There is no political revolt. All revolt is personal and is against interior attitudes and images or against exterior bindings of Society that constrict and cause pain.

(A "political" revolution is a revolt of men against a lovestructure that has gone bad. Men join in a common urge to free themselves.)

Memories are constructions of proteins and acids in the nerve cells. They are real particles and constellations of particles. They are not easily wiped from existence. But we are totally free. New experience creates new molecular deposits of memory and makes by abundance a greater "field" that we may act with. Traumatic memories are best healed by constant increase of experience and rest.

"Your hand by your side is never love" . . . means that if there is not strength enough of spirit in you to raise your hand to me, there is not strength enough of love. Love is noble—and acts! Sentiment, in its worst sense, is dissipation and does not move much.

The regimen and alignment of energy behind an act made to satisfy a desire is revolt when there is a blockade to its achievement.

The man in revolt is outside of everything he doesn't willfully place himself within. He makes a choice of his duration in a place—whether he chooses to be in Society or in a grotto.

Ideally Body-Spirit is in a regimen of revolt and constant creation of fresh vision and *reconstruction* of healthy processes. Men revolt outside in Universe World Air by acts of personal nobility; they refuse themselves as usable articles or objects. They revolt interiorly by destruction of matrixes—and hold with athletic regimen a changing and true-as-possible image of body and love.

BACK TO THE PLANARIA: The head of the planaria from which the subindividual revolts corresponds in higher animals to old images, and chains of synapses that cause attitudes, attitudes whose reasons are defunct. Life becomes inert through apathy—there is interference with the reality our sense organs report. There is an interjection of old knowledge before the body can react to new data of eyes, ears, nose . . . Head in the planaria is equivalent to the interfering processes in the being of the mammal. What Plato said was of great relevance in his day and is now historical and contains beauty and ideal wisdom—but those who apply him totally today are confused. Attitudes deal with the relevant problems of a year ago or two weeks ago or a moment ago—but not the vitalities of the instant. All things must be cherished and used while they are vital, and *remembered* for their loveliness and aid.

The body and outer circumstances change at all instants. We make a picture of the real physique and a *painting* of the real changing Universe is created and kept in constant flux of creation. As we grow, we see more and more what is unchanging. Each action fulfills a vital use or need—otherwise it is a Head or Attitude. The reaction of the Spirit Planaria is simple.

I must be aware of the immediacy of my physique, nerves, and emotions. I do not simply sweep on a tinier beast and go into retreat and safety until it is digested and I'm hungry again. My energy is gladly expended at all times—but I must revolt when energy passes into negations and half-loves that are not fulfillment of my wants. Pride and Nobility are the value of self and self's desires in the face of what would send them slanting.

VI

Aside from metaphysics and psychology there is a SELF and it is strong. I have seen it—it is a good thing to see. Self is the sure filler of needs and desires. Self is the organization of physiological needs that will revolt, the non-hysterical and cohesive force that moves straightly. The self does not acknowledge egocentricity, blind flights or narcissism. He is a solid fact underlying those diversions; they are useless to him and they gratify modified and near worthless desires. The self revolts from the old Head, i.e. the past that lives in us physically in nerves and habits of action and sight. The self resents being used as *object* by others or by circumstance. He is busy with needs, and he revolts. The self, if free, in constant revolt, can choose to be used, or not used, and to use or not use.

The mammal, in awe of Nature, sorts in life and invents anew constantly. Regimen must remind to listen for the tiniest voices of the body. (In moments of great spirit clarity, when I am without buffer, I can feel the ghostlike swift jettings of as-yet-unfelt ideas passing in me.) Listen to the heart, the lungs, the needs for fresh air and rest and the need for withdrawal . . . the need for withdrawal when habits assure that involvement is necessary! That is needed too.

Strength is needed for dis-involvement as well as for open gestures. Regimen and self-questioning are needed instead of self-punishment and dogged filling of unloved duties. Unloved duties turn a living being to an object. Honor of changing love is binding . . . but contracts are not.

Worldly revolt of the individual comes from interior revolts that seek out health and meanings both subtle and gross. There are physical processes so fine we have not yet conceived of them. Organs of sense line the walls of the mesentery-gut and they sing to us with voices we cannot hear without healthy knowing.

METAPHYSICS, in the bad sense, is the denial of what is told us by eyes, stomach, ears and nose. An idea related to metaphysics is this: I start with a truth . . . a beautiful truth of the real world and my seeing of reality. I toil with the truth to draw more beauty from it. I hang solely upon it thinking of nothing else. I push it out and out until it becomes attenuated and strung-out from reality. SUDDENLY the *truth* shatters, splits, divides, into stars and incoherent shapes . . . perhaps shapes of beauty. I am left obsessed with the pieces glimmering darkly at me. There is no way, no way, to put them together into reality again, or even to place them in a line that I may live or feel by. I am torn and disrupted. I have sent energy and feeling into nothingness. I was split from my sense organs.

VII

REVOLT is the constant reformation of the body image until it is exactly Spirit—with regimen and fluxing of intellect and emotions pushing the willful desires to success with sureness and energy.

Fresh physiology of the body is searched out with all intentness and awareness. Patterns of dissipation and hysteria are unlinked in the body. Getting rid of them we must know that the "unnaturalities" within us are not "bugs" to be ripped out . . . They are hamperings and blockings of success. They may be eased out and expelled by awareness of deep processes and growing truth of body-image till the picture is more solid and more fine and gross than we dreamed of. Coldly ripping ingrained parts of ourselves away is brutality.

Our senses and intuitions and the tools of science and art lengthening their scope, bring touch of the physical world. Only meeting life gives solidity to the body-image and causes it to conform to the exact shape and verity of the body. Each and every motion is a molding pleasure and a shaping test! Finally we are solidly what we are and we are beautiful.

Regimen is a vigilance and joy. It delivers new virtues; they are in constant state of appearance and disappearance. We are free to be aware of them and practice them by desire and choice. Each day a hundred Virtues are invented and come into being. A great love, or kiss—can become a virtue. There are natural warm acts heating the universe—those are virtues. There are sights and sounds and smells and acts that are virtues. They are emulated, or die, to be reborn perhaps in future.

There is a high state of being beyond temporal morals, and there is an honor that the free self sees. All of this is physical and of the spirit. Virtues do not serve and they are without reward except for the desire they calm or the successes wrought by them. They are without judgment and are unjudgeable save by the self who makes them. Revolt is without vanity and its pride is demonstrative and transcendental.

Denial of Self by the Universe must be battled both coolly and hotly, and as instantly as possible. It must be done heatedly with as much violence as is necessary, and coolly with a minimum of effort and maximum of direction. Revolt must be made as immediately as possible before the root of a "pattern" can take grip. It becomes more difficult to act when engaged in inactivities that do not bring rest or strength. The idea of Chivalry is the ability to raise one's hand to a Love and make offer and receipt. If there is no self there is no chivalry.

VIII

The Revolter *chooses* at all times. There is revolt in *apparition* (where a man chooses to be), and in acts, and in the denial of his person as an object for use. *Love* is not an abstraction but gross and fine desires and gifts. How much more it is I do not know yet. A man can be persuaded to true love by acts but he cannot be forced to love by coercion and misrepresentation. Neither coercer nor the *opponent-beloved* have true love. Both of them, like society, become dissipated. Each must raise arms of love. The revolter may withdraw willfully for fulfillment of his true desires or do battle if he choose. Battle is a health and comes from a regimen and investigation that spots *phorms* and listens for lovemeat's needs. Is not all meat Lovemeat?

Regimen of the planaria is direct and without qualm or consideration—like a flower its life IS its tissue and senses. There need be no thought—all voices of organs and desires are heard straightly. There is no moral issue or disruption—there is good, and bad, and need. If there is purpose then need is satisfied. There is strength in the healthy self and no desire for the bad.

We may hear and feel our needs with concentration and relaxation in moments of rest and bliss. The untrue ease of dissipation causes deafness. Metaphysics, denial of self, and attitudes are chimeras. The spirit may rest from its opponents but it cannot *relax away* from them . . . It is also possible to be free by search and discovery of happiness.

IX

A denial of Self may come through giving evil names to what is normal. A normal act named an evil is a depreciation. The self performs acts experimentally—and they are normal experiments for pleasure. Self can insult and bring flowers—both with perfect nobility—but not if either is done through habit or aggrandizement to fill out a role. Self is innocent—unless the *self* performs crimes. (Self does not often commit crimes, and they are the abominable crimes and memorable monstrosities lying on the bridge of civilization.) Most crimes are *enactments* of roles and are valueless to spirit and self. Planaria do not know of criminality. The free spirit knows crime only as acts of supreme despair. Theft and unnecessary murder are pitiful and poisonous and are crimes of circumstance.

There is no solution in a method of revolt. Revolt can't be practiced by method for it is ever changing. And revolt is no *answer* but a LIFE of the spirit and body.

Revolt necessitates destruction. Revolt must destroy the extraneous if we are to act in freedom. If the irrelevant had been managed and handled then the need for revolt would not accumulate. The self in the spirit becomes weighted with meaninglessness. The self must have a history and the history IS the body—the actions of the body made at all times. But a burdening, exterior burdening, or an interior stiffening of the mammal is confusion and a mire to self. On the inside of the body as at the outside, acts of revolt sort out and destroy when there is weighting and enchainment. The relevant must be kept and the irrelevant discarded. The process is intuitive, natural, and involves chance and randomness and boldness. Experiment must be made. Investment must be disregarded!—investment in acquired false histories of self and projected images that we twist to fill! Investments in histories, and speculations of self, must be destroyed by revolt. An examination of desires must be performed.

Poems, tales, ethics, governments, ghostly loves that are not relevant to the natural physique must be destroyed in extreme. Or they must be pushed beneath the level of relevance. This must be complete so the spirit's aspirations may return to the innocence of its meat-feelings.

Investments become contracts and contracts lead to Politics which is the protection of contracts. Revolt pushes aside politics of the world and the flesh. There can be no politics when revolt is a choice of the self. Those who call *politics* revolt are misguided. Revolt of a group is an agreement not a contract. There is no marriage but agreement—and no duty but love-duty. He who marries duty will deserve divorce—or if he does not deserve it he raises himself above his error with fineness of feeling.

Revolt does not fear to make errors. If it does have that fear it has become an investment in a projected image. The ideal of becoming a human of greatness involves pursuit of changing and flexible regimen—but not the rude battering of a preconceived ladder to power and glory. In all things is delicacy and fineness and beauty, and *with* energy they comprise revolt.

The natural processes only desire complete success . . . they do not ask for a permanent insurance which is false ease. Revolt establishes a way of life but does not take out revolt-insurance on the gain. The gain of life must pass and be changing or it is attitude. The planaria that revolts carries within itself its future revolutions.

My spirit does not invest in any thing, object, or idea, outside of me. There is nothing that I know will be forever of vital interest. All outward things change as all inward things. *It is not relative—* but it is the surge of life!

Revolt in its enactment passes through many frozen ways of seeing. Visions through which revolt passes are physical, erotic, and circumstantial. (My senses and intellect revolted violently in sheaths of horror and loveliness and desire for godhood; my body-spirit diverged from them in a chemical and physical way and remained inert and dissipative. To the outer world I was brunted and blurred.) There are many third states besides revolt and dissipation; they too must be recognized and named and understood and allowed to shift, change and live.

When the time for revolt comes, the states of inertia are studied and judged against. Other states are adjudged healths, or simple and innocent parts of the body and its history. How cold that sounds! . . . am I wrong? There is actually no blotting away of history or of act or action—but some things must be remembered and put from mind. Some must be held constantly in thought for the shape of what they represent. Health is not a constant state:

> In athletes a perfect condition at highest pitch is treacher-
> ous. Such conditions cannot remain the same or be at
> rest. Change for the better being impossible, the only
> possible change is for the worse. For this reason it is an
> advantage to reduce the peak condition quickly, in order
> that the body may make a fresh beginning of growth.

So Hippocrates, father of medicine, recommends the destruction even of health for the end of greater health. He recommends that investments be destroyed. He suggests that physical perfection is an aspiration that must be put aside before it freezes into debility.

X

It is raining and two lovely women come into the room with drops of water on their cheeks and hair. They are like flowers. Their faces are flushed. Through the walls I feel projections of rain tho I cannot hear it, it is too quiet for that. Perhaps I feel vibrations of moss upon the wall as it opens to life in the wetness. Perhaps the flat black worms, the dragons of sizeless tinyness, feel the growing of the great green plants about them as I faintly feel the rain and the lives that come with the rain.

(The sexual vision of my poem "Dark Brown" is a revolt I pass through. The last section of it is a revolt against a vision and a return to mimesis of the real.) Revolts do not freeze but continue as revolt. Revolt is easy—and not easy; it is not a gift but health that can be given by no one. It is the self's marshalling and division and concentration of forces seeking fresh reality. We live in the visions of men and pass through them as they passed. We live in the midst of spirit-inventions of men and women. The Inventions and Visions that they have created and torn open are signs to us of courage and desire. Lovers are highpoints of history. Desire is not mortal but moves on forever. The Universe is cold and warm with heats of energy in it. The heats are sizeless as the universe for there is no scale to apply. There is no Cynicism that may stand in judgement. Revolt pushes to life—it is the degree farthest from death. Stones do not revolt. There are no answers. Acts and violence with cause are sweet destruction. And the sadness that there must be any death. There is no plan to follow. All is liberty. There are physical voices and the Voice of Meatspirit speaking. There are physical voices of the dead and the inert speaking. The dead is the non-vital past that lives within us and about us. There is liberty of choice, and there is, or is not, a greater Liberty beyond this. But there is constantly revolt and regimen of freshness.

—for Keera and Susie
[1961]

LAWRENCE FERLINGHETTI

Genesis of
After the Cries of the Birds

Beginning in Rock & Roll folk-rock dances at Fillmore Auditorium
Fall 1965 . . . mixed with trips to my cabin Bixby Canyon Big
Sur and its wild beach of white sand rocks & kelp, far away below
the highway's great arched bridge . . . having withheld a "sym-
bolic portion" of my Federal Income taxes in unheard protest
against Vietrock War . . . lost in self and distracted age 45 body
passed somnambule through cauchemar Parises Lost Londons im-
perveable New York, to haven San Francisco 1951, family sprung
up with love . . . yet I still self-distracted & wandering after some
still voice of the fourth person singular mislaid in the function of
the orgasm . . . a poet against my will, no other life-alternative,
nothing else possible, poetry the only self-solution, the last and
only resort . . . finding my body then upon that beach in time
and broken consciousness, and finding no other mast & sail to set
up, no other oar at hand, took up Pentel pen then as now &
began . . . one more doomed attempt to ride out Doom over the
sea's breakers, time's waves, to write out the true poem of my life,
after the cries of the birds had stopped one strange evening on
Bixby Beach and later in redwood cabin by Bixby Creek rushing
with spring rains . . . Pen poised over Nothingness. Nothing to
say and not enough to say it with. Voice not as full as I had
wanted it, sounding on radio or tape recorder not as I heard it in
myself, yet no other self-voice available to turn on through, to
sound through, over & over, my own perceptions, world-view,
trauma & charisma, evidence of eye, heart (the heart some days a

bird turning about, about to fly, turning & turning upon itself, other days a stone imbedded in flesh, sinking, weighted), nothing to say which has been said before, since nothing at all has yet been said, all still to be perceived, all still to be articulated, all still darkness & ignorance even here on the West Coast of time . . . Nevertheless! the first trembling steps in the direction of the Dharma taken then in those woods, below those far hills & mountains, on that beach, as if dumb unborn poem were still to be discovered wherever I had not looked before on this Far Shore . . . mind's Guernicas left far behind, moon's Cuernevacas still possible, civilization & its crickets still up the coastal highway in Fort Ord & San Francisco rising white out of flat plains of its peninsula racked with freeways & defense plant suburbs, napalm made among the palms of Redwood City . . . Ahhhrrrr! Will we never learn! I turn South to Bixby, an imitation mad Zen Fool wandering out onto the night beach, sea lions bobbing among the bulbous floating kelp beyond the rocks & breakers . . . So the poem begins, sun down, birds gone, blown away, puerilely seeing "the future of the world in a new visionary society" . . . prophecy being the one great lost art of modern poets, none of them daring it, void of prophetic vision, except for Whitman-Ginsberg guru . . . Poem begun then in alienation by the Man Outside, as all tough poems must be, a poem of prophecy alienated from American Nation, for who wants Nation, and what good is Nation and Nationalism per se, a medieval form of vestigial barbarism to be cast off in all its forms in a new pastoral society after the cries of the birds have stopped, after the clouds clear at last beyond the final bomb, small scattered pockets of "civilization" survived only in handfuls of wandering, long-haired mystics chanting american mantras, the capital letter A having been finally abolished from american soil, american Sierra Maestra stretching from Aleutia to Tierra del Fuego . . . Pause & begin again. I began with the premise then that none of us are really a part of any nation, that I myself am not a part of America nor of any nation, that San Francisco itself is, at least in some sense, and in a sense not even possible for any other city in the United States today, not really a part of America. Its physical characteristics, its look, its location, perched high on the northern tip of its low peninsula, all contribute to San Francisco not feeling like the rest of America. Its political face may look the

same. The same Fuzz are present in its City Hall and in its Hall of
Justice built in the most advanced style of Mussolini Modern.
Servants of the People armed with real guns (in the best tradition
of the Wild West) still roam the streets. But its students in Black
Friday City Hall riots against Congressional Committees on Un-
American Activities, and its Berkeley Student Movement, and its
Free Speech Movement, and its Sexual Freedom Movement, and
its free bookstores, and its peace marches, and its Poets Peace
Fasts, and its Buddhist temples and its Zen Centers and its China-
town and its Japan-town and its psychedelic communities and its
Poets Outside still telling America to go fuck itself with its atom
bomb (which is something we don't hear those "revolutionary"
Russian poets telling their governments)—all these ephemeral
things creating a certain no doubt naive illusion of San Francisco
being not quite what the rest of America is, all these panic
ephemera creating some illusion of what San Francisco might pos-
sibly become apart from the rest of America, what San Francisco
might someday become as it finally becomes detached or detaches
its Self from what America still wants to be, from what the
dominant material mechanical militarist Mammon money America
will always still want to be. San Francisco someday perhaps pos-
sibly somehow beginning to be psychedelically what a growing
number of its youngest turned-on "Make Love Not War" citizens
conceive their own lives to be & thus their own city to be, the Man
Outside become the Man Within, and the latest Random House
dictionary defining "psychedelic" as "a mental state of great calm,
intensely pleasureful perception of the senses, esthetic entrance-
ment, and creative impetus." And the West Coast not only still the
Last Frontier but also where the Orient begins, where the Far East
begins again . . . Pause & begin again. The poem progressed as I
progressed, two steps forward, one step back, up and down the
coast of West several times last spring, Big Sur to San Francisco,
San Francisco to Bixby, into the summer, the poem still not
finished, begun & begun again. After a definite break, a break-
through, my first trip on LSD, one fine clear blue shining summer
morning on Bixby Beach . . . the light become an inutterable
brightness . . . Time is history . . . Like the sea, the level of
consciousness rises, lapping . . . Ah! Light out of light! I shield
my eyes from the pulsing blue & retreat to a cave at the far end of

the beach, alone, sit crouched there, looking out at the nude figures
gamboling through the surf . . . time before & time after; but no
time now; only light, time turned to light. Pulsing. Coming &
coming. Onto me. Washing over me. How clear everything! How
very clear & shining. The moon has risen in the day and cast its
shadow silver light against the sun. Far off the beautiful bodies
gambol, under that sun, running, hair streaming, blown, white
spume of waves blown back. There where the air is shaken with
light. Inutterable. Feeling of total loneliness, in the universe, a part
of it, yet apart, lonely in the cave with my body, after the cries of
the birds . . . Only silence remains. Voices blown off those far
bodies, reach me in tatters, distant echoes of themselves, echoes of
echoes torn, tattered sea voices far out among the drifting wreck-
age . . . Western civilization floats by, way out. It is a ship on
the horizon, a tanker in the sea lanes, hull-down now, disappear-
ing, it rocks to Vietrock music, Western folk-rock music, hull-
down into the Orient, ship's whistle sounding in Indian fog turns
into a tamboura. A Chinese scroll unrolls, ships threading far
islands in it. And are their hulls teak or steel? As far as the mind
can see. From Bixby. How far to that Mount Analogue rising out
of the sea not on any map whose heights we only know exist
because they exist in ourselves! . . . Horizon clear again now,
still pulsing with light. Pure Nothing. There is nothing but Noth-
ing. From our cave. Yet in that Nothing the door to the invisible
possibly visible. If America could see it! Pause & begin again . . .
I return up the coast again. San Francisco & my typewriter.
Putting the poem into our hieroglyph . . . Never finished, but
abandoned, done with anyway, yet still escaped, in the final clinch,
gone again. Where gone dumb poem, wrought from the dark in my
mother long ago . . . Made of paper now, it flies back to Europe.
And made of cellulose electronic tape it flies to Germany now in
translation, in the German voice of Heiner Bastian, born by the
Baltic long ago. Thus the theme of the poem exemplified, even in
this action. We have come about in the wind, on our most West-
ward tack. Our sails flap in the high wind, our hull without enough
momentum to come about completely, we still hang on the West-
ern horizon. And may raise Chinese junk sails to continue, which-
ever way. Who knows which, backward or forward? The compass
needle wavers on infinity, whirls about and stands finally on end.

In the end there is no way to go but In. Into ourselves . . . Pause & begin again. The poem wings Eastward, still looking Westward, itself an example of what it is saying. And I walk with the translator of it, high on pot, still on that Westernmost shore, Aquatic Park beach, sunset, black horizon, black water, sky still clear white, red at horizon, behind Golden Gate Bridge, the air glowing, pulsing up there, great gulls in it, sea-birds winging high over, sunlight under their wings, flying into the yellow sun they still see up there, we in darkness down here, on the still sand, looking up, at their sun-lit underwings . . . Mute white birds come about now, coasting inland Eastward, away from the Bridge & the set sun which still flames their underwings, high away, sailing silent, the air still light & pulsing up there, above us and above the Golden Gate and around the corner of the coast to Far Rockaway, Coney Island & Cliff House & the far Avenues wrapped in it, in the pulsing light holding us as in a great cupped hand, or a great still voice, somehow tender, embracing us, the hand curved over us, voice curved over us, from Aquatic Park to the far Beach avenues, embracing our bodies, our heads agape, in a great hush of pulsed light, lapped, for ever & ever, into eternity. . . .

[*Written New Year's Day 1967 and read by the author, together with the poem itself, at the Berlin Literarisches Colloquium, February 1967, on a program with Andrei Voznesenski. The poem is published in* The Secret Meaning of Things (*New Directions*).]

LENORE KANDEL

"Poetry Is Never Compromise"

Poetry is never compromise. It is the manifestation/translation of a vision, an illumination, an experience. If you compromise your vision you become a blind prophet.

There is no point today in that poetry which exists mainly as an exercise in dexterity. Craft is valuable insofar as it serves as a brilliant midwife for clarity, beauty, vision; when it becomes enamored of itself it produces word masturbation.

The poems I write are concerned with all aspects of the creature and of that total universe through which he moves. The aim is toward the increase of awareness. It may be awareness of the way a bird shatters the sky with his flight or awareness of the difficulty and necessity of trust or awareness of the desire for awareness and also the fear of awareness. This may work through beauty or shock or laughter but the direction is always toward clear sight, both interior and exterior.

This demands honesty wtihin the poet and the poem. An honesty sometimes joyful and sometimes painful, whether to the poet or the reader or both. Two poems of mine, published as a small book, deal with physical love and the invocation, recognition, and acceptance of the divinity in man through the medium of physical love. In other words, it feels good. It feels so good that you can step outside your private ego and share the grace of the universe. This simple and rather self-evident statement, enlarged and exampled poetically, raised a furor difficult to believe. A large part of the furor was caused by the poetic usage of certain four letter words of Anglo-Saxon origin instead of the substitution of gentle euphemisms.

This brings up the question of poetic language. Whatever is

language is poetic language and if the word required by the poet does not exist in his known language then it is up to him to discover it. The only proviso can be that the word be the correct word as demanded by the poem and only the poet can be the ultimate judge of that.

Euphemisms chosen by fear are a covenant with hypocrisy and will immediately destroy the poem and eventually destroy the poet.

Any form of censorship, whether mental, moral, emotional, or physical, whether from the inside out or the outside in, is a barrier against self-awareness.

Poetry is alive because it is a medium of vision and experience.

It is not necessarily comfortable.

It is not necessarily safe.

Poetry has moved out of the classroom and into the street and thus brought about a flow of cross-pollination, many of the fruits of which are viable in both mediums. Academia tended to breed the fear of offense, i.e. that which might offend someone. Visions and language both were often dwarfed and muted, the poem too often becoming a vehicle for literary gymnastics.

Street poetry avoids the fear-trap, but too often loses its visions through a lack of clarity, through sloppiness, through a lack of the art of the craft.

Poetry as poetry has no need to be classified in either of the above pigeon-holes nor in any other. It exists. It can not exist in the company of censorship.

When a poet censors his vision he no longer tells the truth as he sees it. When he censors the language of the poem he does not use those words which, to him, are the most perfect words to be used. This self-stunting results in an artificial limitation imposed on an art whose direction is beyond the limits of the conceivable. There are no barriers to poetry or prophecy; by their nature they are barrier-breakers, bursts of perception, lines into infinity. If a poet lies about his vision he lies about himself and in himself; this produces a true barrier. When a poet through fearful expediency uses language other than that which is perfect to the poem he becomes a person of fearful expediency.

When an outside agency takes it upon itself to attempt the censorship of poetry it is censoring the acceptance of truth and the leap toward revelation.

When a society becomes afraid of its poets, it is afraid of itself. A society afraid of itself stands as another definition of hell. A poem that is written and published becomes available to those who choose to read it. This seems to me to imply one primary responsibility on the part of the poet—that he tell the truth as he sees it. That he tell it as beautifully, as amazingly, as he can; that he ignite his own sense of wonder; that he work alchemy within the language—these are the form and existence of poetry itself.

A good part of the audience for modern poetry is young. We move in a world where the polarities and possibilities of life and death exist as a constant consciousness. Once the concept and availability of overkill was made public knowledge the aura of the possibility of cosmic death became visible. There have been eras when the young could slip softly into their elders' lives, when if they wanted to ignore the deeper issues of humanity, of man's relationship to man, it was made easy for them. This is not such a time and the choices of the young are deep and hard. At eighteen the young men must decide whether they will enter into the national pastime of death. A great many of the young are choosing to manifest a different way of life, one motivated toward pleasure, toward enlightenment, and toward mutual concern, instead of accepting the world of war and personal despair which has been offered them by the majority of their elders.

There are heavy choices to make and there is no avoidance possible.

Those who read modern poetry do so for pleasure, for insight, sometimes for counsel. The least they can expect is that the poet who shares his visions and experiences with them do so with no hypocrisy. To compromise poetry through fear is to atrophy the psyche. To compromise poetry through expediency is the soft, small murder of the soul.

[1967]

"Goldberry Is Waiting"; or, P.W., His Magic Education as a Poet

When I was in highschool I wrote for the fun and excitement of writing. Later on—after I learned that I couldn't go to college and learn medicine—I seriously tried to make myself into a writer, a professional novelist. I believed that I could write fairly correctly; I had learned a great deal about English grammar and composition by studying French and Latin and doing lots of translations, dramatic adaptations, parodies, poems, essays and stories. I supposed that the next thing I must do was to acquire a sparkling and witty style which the editors of magazines should find irresistible. I spent more time reading and working as an office boy than I did at writing, however.

Then I went into the Army Air Corps. While I sloppily soldiered along, I continued to write poems and stories. My comrades in arms (recruited from various colleges and universities) set me to reading Joyce, Faulkner, Proust, Huxley and Thomas Wolfe. Reading Wolfe encouraged me immensely. I, too, came from a poor family; we lived in a remote and beautiful section of the country, far from the intellectual life of New York and Paris. And my family and their friends had a fine salty way of speaking . . . I began writing page after page of romantic description and farm gossip and native folk speech. I discovered that I was a sensitive genius from the Oregon woods whose beautiful writings would bring immortal fame and lots of money.

I wrote lots of unfinished (and almost illegible) manuscript, hundreds of letters to my family and friends, long intellectually searching journals and worries and recollections, but no novels. I wrote poems from time to time, using every technique I had seen other poets use. I played with words and experimented with them, trying to find out what they would do and what they would let me say. At this time (1943), a friend of mine sent me a copy of Gertrude Stein's *Narration*. Reading the book gave me great encouragement and pleasure. I read as many of her books as I could find.

I wanted style, I wanted a theory of writing, I wanted to be able to explain, to whoever asked me, how come I should be a writer and why writing was so important to me. I also wanted a completely believable philosophy of life. I was having trouble interpreting my religious feelings—if that's what they were; perhaps they were only some kind of Druid backlash from all my antique Irish genes, I didn't know. I thought of myself as a "modern" agnostic rationalist: Were not all religions merely a confection of superstition and lies which were imposed upon the ignorant in order to make them obedient to authority? On the other hand, music and poetry and pictures and novels could move me profoundly. I would experience exaltations, "highs," and strange knowledges which seemed to correspond with what I had read about in the *Upanishads* and the *Bhagavad Gita*.

After the war I met a number of people at Reed College who were interested in writing and who were producing the school literary magazine. They persuaded me that it was no longer possible for anyone to seriously write poetry. Yeats and Eliot, Rilke and Pound had said all there was to say, quite perfectly. There was no more poetry to be had. There was no more in the well.

I was, as I say, persuaded—but from time to time I'd forget my despair and sophistication and write a poem. I found that I could at least finish poems, whether they were any good or not, whereas I seemed unable to invent a solid prose style. (I was continuing to work at making myself into a novelist.) Professor Lloyd Reynolds was most encouraging. I took his classes in creative writing. He taught us by using great examples: Joyce, Blake & Williams—and by his great enthusiasm for good writing in every genre. He succeeded in changing my mind about the hopelessness of writing poems or anything else in this late and decadent period of the world; his encouragement and advice and friendship cut through all the fogs and megrims which I had contracted from reading the "New Criticism" and *The Partisan Review*.

It was towards the end of this period that William Carlos Williams arrived—in person—to dispel what remained of those brumes and mists. He was interested in what we had to say. He made us feel like poets, not students any more; he talked to us as if we were his equals. It was at that point, I think, that I really could begin to take myself seriously as a writer.

Being an American, I imagined that life was a matter of owning things, having things. I wanted a family and a house and many books and musical instruments and cars and boats and a little place in the mountains and a small shack near the ocean. I suppose I was remembering all the *Esquire* magazines I had read back in 1937 and 1938. I thought that if I could just write a fine big novel and send it off to Harpers or Scribners in New York, they could not fail to accept it and print it and so my fortune (in the shape of this extravagant *Esquire* life) should be made.

Having all these illusions made it difficult for me to work at an ordinary job for any length of time. After working for a few months, I'd quit and spend perhaps a week buying books and squandering what money I had made, then I'd write for a few days but no novel came of it all. Soon I would be penniless and begging all my friends for help. I needed time to write. The time seemed only to be had for money. I had no money; therefore I couldn't write anything so I had better move out of my friend's attic (or basement or guest room or garage or backyard or living room) and get another job and make some money . . . there was usually someplace I wanted to go, someplace where I thought that I could live quietly alone and write . . . and there were usually some books I had to have very soon.

If my friends had not helped me, I should have starved or gone, at last, to the nuthouse. They fed and clothed and housed me, arranged poetry readings for me, got my work published and reviewed, made other people buy my books, and now they faithfully write letters to me, which I answer promptly. These experiences made me realize that I didn't need money in order to write: what I needed was love and poetry and pictures and music in order to live. This knowledge not only freed me from a lot of old hangups, it also changed my feeling towards poetry and all the other arts. I saw that poetry didn't belong to me, it wasn't my province; it was older and larger and more powerful than I, and it would exist beyond my life-span. And it was, in turn, only one of the means of communicating with those worlds of imagination and vision and magical and religious knowledge which all painters and musicians and inventors and saints and shamans and lunatics and yogis and dope fiends and novelists heard and saw and "tuned in" on. Poetry was not a communication from ME to ALL THOSE OTHERS, but from the invisible magical worlds to me . . . everybody else, ALL THOSE OTHERS, "my" audience, don't need what I say; they already know.

I had been very worried about theories and philosophies and orthodoxies; I now perceived that I had had far too many; so many, that I had been separated from my own senses, my own real experience of the natural world. (It took a great deal of experimentation and study and thought to find out the true nature and function of my various senses and faculties.) The impulse to write had overthrown all my theories as well as the question of "Where does it come from?"

People tell me that it must be very difficult to write, to be a writer. I no longer argue the point with them. I can only say here that I like doing it. I also enjoy cutting and revising what I've written, for in the midst of those processes I often discover images and visions and ideas which I hadn't been conscious of before, and these add thickness and depth and solidity to the final draft, not simply polish alone. In the act of revision and complication and turmoil, a funky nowhere piece of writing can suddenly pick up and become an extraordinary, independent creature. It escapes from my too certain, too expert control. It frees itself not only from my grasp but also from my ego, my ambition, my megalomania . . . simultaneously, the liberation of a piece of writing liberates myself from these delusionary systems. Ideally, the writing will give the reader that same feeling of release, freedom and exaltation: a leap, a laugh, a high.

"How long does it take you to write a poem," people often ask. "How much revising do you go through before you consider a poem finished? How many drafts?" No matter how I answer these questions, the inquirers always look disappointed afterwards. It is impossible to describe how poems begin. Some are simply imagined immediately, are "heard," quite as if I were hearing a real voice speaking the words. Sometimes I "hear" a poem in this way and it is a complete statement, a complete verbal or literary entity. Sometimes the same imagination provides me with single lines or with a cluster of lines which is obviously incomplete. I write them down and put them away. Maybe a few hours later I'll "receive" more lines. Perhaps they won't arrive until weeks or months go by. Some of my long poems took years to come, and then it took a few days or weeks in which to revise and fit all their pieces together.

Some poems arrive as dreams. Others begin from memories. Some start out of the middle of a conversation I'm involved in or words that I overhear other people speaking. An imagination of the life of some historical person may occur to me: I may suddenly suppose I understand what it felt like to be Johannes Brahms on a particular morning of his life. A landscape, a cat, a relative, a friend, a letter (or the act of answering a letter), walking, the unexpected receipt of a new poetry magazine full of work by new young writers, the arrival of a new book of poems by a friend or somebody I don't know personally; re-reading Shakespeare or reading Emily Dickinson on the streetcar and suddenly moved to tears; shopping for vegetables, making love, looking at pictures, taking dope, sitting still and looking at whatever is happening in front of me, getting a haircut, being afraid of everybody and everything, hating everybody, playing music, going to parties, visiting relatives, riding in trains, buses, taxis, steamboats, riding horses, getting drunk, dancing, praying, practicing meditation, singing, rolling on the floor, losing my temper, looking for agates, arguing, washing sox, teaching, sweeping the floor, operating this typewriter right now (bought in Berkeley 12 years ago and wrote ten books on it) while the cicadas and taxis all sing in ravening hot Japanese summer 1967 . . . all this is how to write, all this is where poems are to be found. Writing them is a delight.

People tell me, "Of course, writing prose is a great deal different, isn't it." I don't think so. I finally found the novel, *You Didn't Even Try,* while I was walking in the woods in Mill Valley. First I had a page of dialog between some man and his wife—they had no names then. For a number of weeks it went no further; I wasn't thinking of writing a novel; I was worried about too many other things. Then one day as I walked along through the woods I recalled that scrap of imaginary conversation. I began to see who the speakers were, where they were, and I could see or feel what they would do, and I suddenly knew that it could all be arranged in three sections, three blocks of prose. The "blocks of prose" would each have a specific weight and shape and color. I wrote many independent sections and paragraphs in the succeeding days. The book wasn't written in sequence: I didn't start with the first sentence and end with the final one. Instead I wrote a great deal of material and then fitted it together to form the first section of the book. The same technique was used to write the other two sections. The whole manuscript was typed and revised, then I could do no more with it until it had to be prepared for the press. At that time, my friend, Zoe Brown, went through the manuscript and pointed out places in which the language or the sense appeared to break down. I repaired them as best I could. The result is, I think, not a very good book, but sort of an interesting one.

At one point a friend of mind read the incomplete manuscript and asked me a question about how did one of the characters find the money to do something. The result of this question was my invention of a new character and a couple new scenes for the book, none of which I had planned on, and I was surprised to find the character already there in my mind, I had no trouble writing about her or the scenes in which she appears.

The novel which I completed earlier this year (1967), *Imaginary Speeches for a Brazen Head,* began to be written while I was sitting in a small bar in Kyoto. The place has a large and powerful stereophonic phonograph on which they play recordings of new American jazz. I sat listening and feeling homesick and so I began writing about an American couple in a hotel room in London. They weren't feeling homesick, but they were having lots of other feelings. Later I began trying to figure out how they got to London and where were they going next and what was their life like before and after, and who did they know and how. I had no architectural plan this time, I didn't know how long it would take—either in time of composition or in number of pages of writing—to tell all about these people. And did I want to tell all. And what, after all, did I really know. I had to invent London and Vienna and Katmandu and someplace in Ceylon and some places in Oregon and California and Massachusetts and Colorado, and that was difficult. But finally I wrote it all, then I typed and corrected it all, and then, to my horror, I found that I had to correct and retype it all again, although I very nearly couldn't, I hated typing and thinking and keeping the whole story in my head continuously. Maybe some day it will be printed. *

Writing this present essay or message or *cri de coeur* began several weeks ago. On July 9th I began writing what has become 48 pages of longhand notes, in reply to the request of Mr. Donald M. Allen that I write something about writing. I selected and condensed some of this material into three and a half typewritten pages on the 17th of July, but this typewritten version only suggested more ideas, recollections and fancies. This morning, 23 July, I wrote the final longhand notes and then began this typescript, adding and cutting as I went along. The idea of telling about the novels and the writing of this present essay occurred to me after I had typed five and a half pages. I must correct all of this and recopy it. Did I say that I did it by asking myself, "How do you do it?"

[*23:VII:67*]

* Published in 1972. Ed.

Chronology

A brief listing of significant books, periodicals, and presses of the period. We do not list all works by our authors. This is meant only as a guide for the reader.

1909   Pound, *Personae*; Stein, *Three Lives*; Williams, *Poems*
1910   Pound, *The Spirit of Romance*
1911   Stein, *Tender Buttons*
1914   *Des Imagistes,* ed. Pound
1920   Williams, *Kora in Hell*
1922   Joyce, *Ulysses*
1923   Lawrence, *Studies in Classical American Literature*; Williams, *Spring and All*
1925   H.D., *Collected Poems*; Pound, *A Draft of XVI Cantos*; Stein, *The Making of Americans*; Williams, *In the American Grain*
1926   Crane, *White Buildings*
1927   *transition,* eds. Eugene Jolas & Elliot Paul
1928   Lawrence, *Collected Poems*; Pound, *Selected Poems,* ed. T. S. Eliot
1930   Crane, *The Bridge*; García Lorca, *Poet in New York*
1931   Stein, *How to Write*
1932   An *"Objectivists" Anthology,* ed. Zukofsky
1933   Crane, *The Collected Poems*
1934   Pound, *ABC of Reading* & *Make It New*
1935   Stein, *Lectures in America*
1936   New Directions press, publisher James Laughlin
1939   Joyce, *Finnegans Wake*
1940   Zukofsky, *"A"*
1944–46 H.D., *The War Trilogy*

1965   Blaser, *Les Chimeres*; Dorn, *Geography*; O'Hara, *Love Poems*; Olson, *Human Universe & Proprioception*; Zukofsky, *All: The Collected Short Poems, 1923–1958*

1966   Ashbery, *Rivers & Mountains*; Jones (Baraka), *Home: Social Essays*; Kandel, *The Love Book*; Zukofsky, *All: The Collected Short Poems 1956–1964*

1967   Richard Brautigan, *Trout Fishing in America*; Kandel, *Word Alchemy*

1968   Blaser, *Cups*; Ginsberg, *Planet News*; Snyder, *The Back Country*

1969   Creeley, *Pieces*; Olson, *Letters for Origin*; James Schuyler, *Freely Espousing*; Snyder, *Six Sections from Mountains and Rivers without End & Earth House Hold*; Whalen, *On Bear's Head*

1970   Creeley, *A Quick Graph*; McClure, *Star*; Olson, *Archaeologist of Morning*; Snyder, *Regarding Wave*; Whalen, *Severance Pay*

1971   O'Hara, *Collected Poems*; Whalen, *Scenes of Life at the Capital*

1972   Schuyler, *The Crystal Lithium*

1973   Creeley, *Contexts of Poetry*; Welch, *Ring of Bone: Collected Poems 1950–1971*

Selected Grove Press Paperbacks

62480-7 ACKER, KATHY / Great Expectations: A Novel / $6.95
62433-5 BARASH, D. and LIPTON, J. / Stop Nuclear War! A Handbook / $7.95
17208-6 BECKETT, SAMUEL / Endgame / $3.95
17299-X BECKETT, SAMUEL / Three Novels: Molloy, Malone Dies, The Unnamable / $7.95
13034-8 BECKETT, SAMUEL / Waiting for Godot / $4.95
17106-3 BRECHT, BERTOLT / Mother Courage and Her Children / $3.95
17108-X BURROUGHS, WILLIAM S. / Naked Lunch / $6.95
17411-9 CLURMAN, HAROLD (Ed.) / Nine Plays of the Modern Theater (Waiting For Godot by Samuel Beckett, The Visit by Friedrich Durrenmatt, Tango by Slawomir Mrozek, The Caucasian Chalk Circle by Bertolt Brecht, The Balcony by Jean Genet, Rhinoceros by Eugene Ionesco, American Buffalo by David Mamet, The Birthday Party by Harold Pinter, Rosencrantz and Guildenstern Are Dead by Tom Stoppard) / $15.95
17327-9 FANON, FRANZ / The Wretched of the Earth / $6.95
62345-2 GETTLEMAN, MARVIN, et.al. eds. / El Salvador: Central America in the New Cold War / $9.95
62003-8 HITLER, ADOLF / Hitler's Secret Book / $7.95
17209-4 IONESCO, EUGENE / Four Plays (The Bald Soprano, The Lesson, The Chairs, and Jack, or The Submission) / $6.95
17226-4 IONESCO, EUGENE / Rhinoceros and Other Plays / $5.95
17016-4 MAMET, DAVID / American Buffalo / $5.95
62049-6 MAMET, DAVID / Glengarry Glen Ross / $6.95
62375-4 MILLER, HENRY / Tropic of Cancer / $7.95
17251-5 PINTER, HAROLD / The Homecoming / $5.95
17539-5 POMERANCE, BERNARD / The Elephant Man / $5.95
62498-X ROSSET, PETER and VANDERMEER, JOHN / The Nicaragua Reader / $9.95
62009-7 SEGALL, J. PETER / Deduct This Book: How Not to Pay Taxes While Ronald Reagan Is President / $6.95
62182-4 SELBY, HUBERT / Last Exit to Brooklyn / $3.95
17948-X SHAWN, WALLACE, and GREGORY, ANDRE / My Dinner with Andre / $6.95
17797-5 SNOW, EDGAR / Red Star Over China / $11.95
13033-X STOPPARD, TOM / Rosencrantz and Guildenstern Are Dead / $4.95
17474-7 SUZUKI, D.T. / Introduction to Zen Buddhism / $3.95
13020-8 TOOLE, JOHN KENNEDY / A Confederacy of Dunces / $6.95

GROVE PRESS, 841 Broadway, New York, N.Y. 10003